THE
SYMPHONY

THE
SYMPHONY

PRESTON STEDMAN

Professor of Music

California State University, Fullerton

PRENTICE-HALL, INC., *Englewood Cliffs, New Jersey* 07632

Library of Congress Cataloging in Publication Data

STEDMAN, PRESTON, (date)
  The symphony.

  "Selected list of study scores": p.
  Includes bibliographical references and index.
  1. Symphony.
ML1255.S83   785.1'1   78–10328.
ISBN 0–13–880062–6

Printed in the United States of America

10   9   8   7   6   5   4   3   2   1

Editorial/production supervision and interior design by Fred Bernardi
Page layout by Eloise Starkweather
Cover design by Wanda Lubelska
Manufacturing Buyer: Phil Galea

PRENTICE-HALL INTERNATIONAL, INC., *London*
PRENTICE-HALL OF AUSTRALIA PTY. LIMITED, *Sydney*
PRENTICE-HALL OF CANADA, LTD., *Toronto*
PRENTICE-HALL OF INDIA PRIVATE LIMITED, *New Delhi*
PRENTICE-HALL OF JAPAN, INC., *Tokyo*
PRENTICE-HALL OF SOUTHEAST ASIA PTE. LTD., *Singapore*
WHITEHALL BOOKS LIMITED, *Wellington, New Zealand*

Contents

PRELUDE 1

I ANTECEDENTS OF THE SYMPHONY 3

The Baroque 3
Baroque Instrumental Ensemble Music 3
The Symphony's Antecedent Musical Forms 5
Examples for Study 8

II THE PRECLASSICAL SYMPHONY 17

The Classical Period 17
The Preclassical Symphony 18
Examples for Study 26
Haydn as a Preclassicist 32
Examples for Study 34
Wolfgang Amadeus Mozart as a Preclassicist 37
Examples for Study 37

III THE CLASSICAL SYMPHONY 40

Haydn's Middle Period: Maturity of Style Established 40
Examples for Study 41
Mozart's Middle Period: Maturity through Absorption of Influences 44

v

Examples for Study 45
Late Mozart 48
Examples for Study 49
Haydn's London Symphonies 55
Examples for Study 56

IV THE SYMPHONIES OF BEETHOVEN 62

Examples for Study 78

V THE NINETEENTH-CENTURY SYMPHONY 92

The Romantic Period 92
The Symphony 93
Franz Schubert (1797–1828) 96
Examples for Study 102
Felix Mendelssohn (1809–1847) 105
Examples for Study 109
Robert Schumann (1810–1856) 114
Examples for Study 117
Program Music 123
Hector Berlioz (1803–1869) 123
Examples for Study 127
Franz Liszt (1811–1886) 135
Examples for Study 136
Johannes Brahms (1833–1897) 143
Examples for Study 158
Peter Ilyich Tchaikovsky (1840–1893) 166
Examples for Study 172
Anton Bruckner (1823–1896) 178
Examples for Study 186
Antonin Dvořák (1841–1904) 190
Examples for Study 197
French Orchestral Music of the Nineteenth Century 204
César Franck (1822–1890) 205
Examples for Study 206
Richard Strauss (1864–1949) 212
Examples for Study 218
Gustav Mahler (1860–1911) 224
Examples for Study 238

VI THE SYMPHONY IN THE TWENTIETH CENTURY 247

Introduction to Twentieth-Century Music 247
The Symphony 249
Jean Sibelius (1865–1957) 252
Examples for Study 259
Ralph Vaughan Williams (1872–1958) 269
Examples for Study 277
Music in Russia 283
Sergei Prokofiev (1891–1953) 284
Examples for Study 289
Dmitri Shostakovich (1906–1975) 298
Examples for Study 309
Igor Stravinsky (1882–1971) 317
Examples for Study 320
Paul Hindemith (1895–1963) 325
Examples for Study 333

VII THE TWENTIETH-CENTURY SYMPHONY IN AMERICA 338

Roy Harris (1898–   ) 340
Examples for Study 347
William Schuman (1910–   ) 353
Examples for Study 358
Aaron Copland (1900–   ) 367
Examples for Study 370
Wallingford Riegger (1885–1961): Serialism and the Symphony 377
Examples for Study 379

VIII OTHER TWENTIETH-CENTURY SYMPHONISTS 385

POSTLUDE 391

GLOSSARY OF TERMS 393

INDEX 417

THE
SYMPHONY

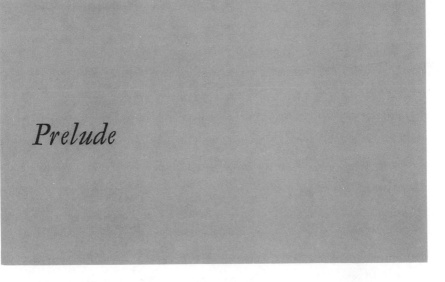

Prelude

The concert symphony, the musical form most often found on programs by symphony orchestras throughout the Western world, has had a fascinating history over the past 250 years. We will examine the forces that created the new art form around 1750 and that shaped it as it accommodated changing style norms and the individual biases of hundreds of composers during its meandering course of development.

Perhaps the most interesting developments have been those that resulted from the bias of individual composers acting upon the art form. A compositional bias of a single composer is itself subject to changes and influences throughout a creative life. Thus, what is valid Beethoven symphony style in 1800 may or may not be valid Beethoven symphony style in 1824. Within an individual work by a symphony composer it may also be possible to see a different series of values acting upon different movements. In other words, a slow movement in a Tchaikovsky symphony may sound quite different from a fast movement for reasons other than its different tempo. It is also possible to see conflicting values or influences within a single symphony movement. Through more detailed analysis, one may become aware of some of the many variables that constitute the style of an individual symphony, the style of works by a single symphonist, or the style of the symphonies written by a group of composers during a certain style period. Finally, viewing all of this in retrospect should be helpful in understanding the growth of the form.

The process required to understand music is a laborious one. Each work to be studied must be analyzed in some detail. This requires skills often not present in the artistic equipment of even the most sophisticated symphony-goer. These skills can be developed through deliberate and considered exercise. The ability to read music on a basic level is essential in such an undertaking. The field does have its own unique terminology. One cannot talk about the history of the symphony without delving deeply into musical style. Musical style is a very complex concept. One must cope with tonality, melody, counterpoint, orchestration, individual composer traits, and the like. There is just no other way to gain an intelligent grasp of the development of a musical form.

This book, then, becomes somewhat technical in approach, since it seeks to have the reader gain a thorough understanding of the growth of the symphony. For those who lack the technical background required, a glossary of terms is supplied. If this proves insufficient, two or three other sources can be employed.* The progress of the book, however, is slow and deliberate. The complexity of the materials also grows slowly as the symphony begins to reach maturity in the late eighteenth century. Skills in handling new concepts can be acquired as the history unfolds.

This volume is the result of many years of study, research, and teaching in the field of the symphony. During those years several persons have been influential in the book's development: Smith McCorkle, as a teacher in the author's undergraduate studies; Mike Winesanker, for encouraging a scholarly approach to a study of the eighteenth-century symphony; and A. I. McHose, for his infectious insight into the study of musical style. In recent years the patience and understanding, as well as the typing and editing skills, of my wife, Leslie, have been absolutely essential to the completion of the project. The seed, however, was planted in the winter of 1930, when the author as a first-grader settled into his seat high in the balcony of old Paschal High School in Fort Worth, Texas, to hear Maestro Brooks Morris conduct the Fort Worth Symphony in a stirring performance of Tchaikovsky's *Romeo and Juliet Overture* for the elementary school children of the city. It was a captivating event that led to the present effort some forty-five years later.

---

* Willi Apel, *Harvard Dictionary of Music*, 2nd ed. (Cambridge, Mass.: Harvard University Press, 1969); Robert A. Barnes, *Fundamentals of Music* (New York: McGraw-Hill Book Company, 1964); Bruce Benward and Barbara Garvey Jackson, *Practical Beginning Theory*, 3rd ed. (Dubuque, Iowa: Wm. C. Brown Company Publishers, 1975); Raymond Elliott, *Fundamentals of Music*, 2nd ed. (Englewood Cliffs, N.J.: Prentice-Hall, Inc., 1965); C. H. Kitson, *Rudiments of Music* (New York: Oxford University Press, 1957); Hugh Miller, *Introduction to Music* (New York: Barnes & Noble, Inc., 1963); Percy A. Scholes, *The Beginner's Guide to Harmony*, 2nd ed. (New York: Oxford University Press, 1950).

I

Antecedents of the Symphony

The Baroque

Between 1600 and 1750 most of the larger forms of music (opera, oratorio, overture, fugue, cantata, and suite) either had their beginnings or can be traced to precursors that flourished in the Baroque. This would be the case for the sonata and the symphony. In many ways it was a period of contradiction. On the one hand, much emphasis was placed on the large gesture and the spectacular such as opera and its magnificent staging. On the other hand, it was a period of some intimacy as shown in the thousands of trio and solo sonatas written. For the first time in history sacred music took a back seat to secular music. A true instrumental idiom was created, giving rise to thousands of concertos, sonatas, fugues, and suites. While the contrapuntal style of the Renaissance continued with a stronger harmonic basis, it was the new homophonic style which led to the great forms of the classical period. One of the prime features of the baroque style was the special bass line—*basso continuo,* or figured bass—a device which used certain shorthand numerical symbols to inform the harpsichord or organ player what chords to play above his bass part. Figured bass was a part of almost all baroque music. If the music had one other important quality it was the incessant drive of its rhythm. This quality often led to an unending, almost phrase-free melodic style in some instrumental works.

Baroque Instrumental Ensemble Music

Stimulated by the emergence of dramatic forms (opera, oratorio, cantata), instrumental resources in the early baroque period were rapidly expanded to include what would be accepted today as an orchestral concept. At the same time

3

there was a continued emphasis on writing for small ensembles (especially trio sonatas). The rapidly developing violin family soon replaced the subdued viols. Actual brass instruments (horn, trumpet, trombone) joined forces with woodwinds (flute, oboe, bassoon) to fill out the large ensemble complement. Early baroque writing also included lutes and other nonkeyboard chord instruments in addition to keyboard instruments (harpsichord and organ), for support of bass lines.

Emergence of new instrumental forms coincided with the availability of new instrumental resources. These forms, which led directly to the symphony, included the concerto grosso, the solo concerto, the solo sonata, the trio sonata, the suite, the French overture, and the Italian sinfonia. The general style of most of these new forms was still polyphonic—a polyphony, however, which was reacting both texturally and melodically to the virtuosic and technical possibilities of the new violin family. As violin technique became more involved, the ornateness of the soloistic writing was enhanced. Dance forms, while preserving their basic style, also responded to this more ornate style of instrumental writing.

The performance of baroque ensemble music was still what one would call today a chamber music experience. Ensembles were not usually large. A few isolated exceptions include Monteverdi's large opera orchestras, Handel's occasional mammoth presentations in London, and the resident orchestra at Bologna's San Petronio basilica.

There was generally no separation of the wind and string styles in baroque music. Winds usually doubled strings with virtuosic writing in evidence for flutes, oboes, and natural brass instruments. By 1700 texture had reduced itself from a five-voiced early baroque texture to a three-voiced sound in the works of most composers. Some exceptions can be noted in the works of J. S. Bach and in the opera scores of the period. This three-voiced sound consisted of two treble voices set with a bass voice on the underlying bass line and can be noted even in the music for larger ensembles. A tenor part was assigned usually to the viola when four-voice scoring was employed. In many instances this viola line doubled the bass line.

As a public performing body, the orchestra was still not an effective ensemble in modern terms. Concerts were still private, supported by royalty. Above all, these concerts featured performances by small ensembles when instrumental ensemble music was offered. Large orchestral resources were to be found only in opera house pits, by this time open to the public. If the public's taste for orchestral music was to be whetted, it would be done by the sounds from this pit orchestra. A few highly proficient "concert" orchestras, however, should be noted: the Twenty-four Violins of the King (Louis XIII [reigned 1610–1643] and Louis XIV [reigned 1643–1715]), Lully's Les Petits Violons, and Four and Twenty Fiddlers, the English version of Lully's group established by Charles II about 1660 after his return from exile. One of the final stimuli to the emergence of pure orchestral music was to take place in the early eighteenth century with the establishment of public concerts.

The Symphony's Antecedent Musical Forms

Five forms contributed in some way to the evolution of the concert symphony of the eighteenth century: trio sonata, suite, concerto and concerto grosso, French overture, and Italian sinfonia. Each was individual in style and form. With two possible exceptions (sinfonia and solo concerto), each would be unable to adapt its style to the demands of the classical period to ensure perpetuity beyond the baroque era.

The trio sonata was one of the textural parents of the early symphony. Its three-voice fabric dominated instrumental music of the baroque and in like manner subsequently influenced the basic texture of the early symphony. Two treble voices, quite often moving in parallel thirds or sixths, with a basso continuo played by the cello and some keyboard instrument filling in the harmony, constituted a characteristic sound which can be noted in many passages of the symphony well up to and including the mature works of Haydn. Its basically contrapuntal style, its four-movement church or chamber format, and its ornate and long-phrased melodic lines were not lasting influences in the growth of the symphony. The three-voice texture was.

The instrumental suite, similar in style and structure to the keyboard suite, contributed the concept of a binary instrumental form from its individual movement designs. It also presented a dance-style instrumental work as an alternative concert form, possibly promoting a dance movement (i.e., the minuet) as a part of the concert symphony. By the time the first true concert symphonies were written (c. 1740), the dance suite had long since been stabilized as a four-movement form (allemande, courante, sarabande, jig).

Dances added to the suite sometimes included the minuet. Most suite movements were basically homophonic. The individual dance movement form was divided into two sections, each generally repeated, with a modulation to the dominant key in evidence near the close of the first section. The second section would then begin in the dominant key and move back to the original tonic key as the movement concluded. This binary form can be outlined as follows:

Section:	A	:‖:	B	
Key:	I to V		V to I	

The binary concept became the primary skeleton for the gradual emergence of a fully developed sonata-allegro or first-movement form noted in all eighteenth-century instrumental music including the symphony.

The *concertato* principle of the baroque concerto, concerto grosso, and orchestral concerto permeated much of the instrumental ensemble music of the classical period. Contrast of materials via contrasting tone color led to a principle of orchestral development in the eighteenth century which was not limited in its use to the concerto. Development of materials through coloristic imitation can be found in some of the earliest concert symphonies. Even more specific was the frequent use of a concertino solo group (often three instruments) to define the secondary thematic group in a first movement of an early symphony. Some authorities also feel that the emergence of the second theme in sonata-allegro design was in some way related to the concept of duality of forces (small–large, loud–soft, etc.) in the concerto grosso. Many of the early symphonies of the classical period also included movements written in the style of the concerto with virtuosic solo writing as well as contrasting instrumental groupings. The attempt to carry forward soloistic virtuosic writing as a style mannerism of the concert symphony was not completely successful. The contrast of instrumental resources, however, utilizing blocks or groupings of instruments remains as an important compositional technique in the symphony.

The French overture dominated the operatic scene as the principal curtain-raiser to many musico-dramatic forms in the baroque. Handel and other German composers of the late baroque seemed to prefer the more intricate polyphonic style of the French overture for their Italian operas. Purcell used the form exclusively for his dramatic and large choral works. Building a form in two sections (slow, stately introduction with dotted rhythms followed by a fugal *Allegro*), composers tended to add optional movements when the form was used for nontheatrical purposes. One of the essential characteristics of the overture was the nonthematic style in its slow introduction. While overtures differ from composer to composer, most project poorly defined melodic structures in the slow introduction and seem to aspire more to harmonic goals with enriching suspensions and the like to create a degree of musical expression. Tunefulness was reserved for the subsequent *Allegro*. The form was popular. J. S. Bach's four orchestral suites (c. 1720) all begin with French overtures. His fourth partita for clavier used the form for its first movement. Early pre-classical symphonies were often French overtures when the Italian sinfonia model was not used.

The French overture was not, on the whole, an adaptable model for the classical symphony because of its essentially polyphonic style and its unified form which created a slow and rather nonthematic opening section that seemed to resist a more definitive formal structure. It did, however, represent another kind of model for the young symphony: a continuous two-section form whose first section was more transitional or introductory in character than was its second section. This concept of a slow section as an introduction to an *Allegro* or faster main section probably led to the appearance of slow introductions in many first movements of eighteenth-century symphonies. Further, some of the mature classical symphonies which used slow introductions retained some of the stateliness and poor thematic definition of the French overture. In addition, the dotted rhythms and quasi-contrapuntal nature of the French overture opening sections often surfaced in slow introductions to many eighteenth-century symphonies, including those of Haydn and Mozart. Little of the fugal nature of the second section was retained. This second section's strict polyphonic style made the form of the French overture even less adaptable to a homophonic form. Two concepts from the French overture, then, emerged as possibly related to the evolution of a mature classical symphony: first, a slow introduction to an Allegro first movement; second, an introduction whose basic style was primarily transitional, nonthematic, and lacking in musical self-sufficiency.

If the four previously mentioned forms were antecedents of the concert symphony, the Italian opera sinfonia was the true parent form. Designed as a quick curtain-raiser, the sinfonia was originally cast as a three-movement form (fast–slow–fast) in what could be termed a homophonic style. Since the level of involvement with the audience was hardly more than superficial, the musical complexity of the form was rarely stressed. Early examples by the great Neapolitan opera composer Alessandro Scarlatti (1660–1725) had very poor thematic delineation. Scarlatti's overtures were fairly standard in form and style: a first movement of a fast tempo generally in a homophonic style, the movement often opening with a flourish emphasizing fanfarelike materials; a transitional slow second movement, in many ways nonthematic in nature and stressing a chordal texture with the possible addition of a few suspensions; and a final section in triple meter which was almost invariably a dancelike movement. A few exceptions should be noted. In the first sections of some earlier sinfonias there might be vestiges of the older polyphonic or fugal style. A very small number of the opening movements also had a binary structure with double bars and repeat signs. Second movements of later sinfonias had better defined melodic content and therefore often achieved greater expressive results. The finales of sinfonias rarely departed from the original mold.*

Because of its popularity with opera audiences and its basically homophonic style, the sinfonia was quickly adapted to concert purposes by enterprising composers. Groups of sinfonias were issued between 1740 and 1750 as the first collections of concert symphonies. London publishers grouped assorted overtures and sinfonias into regularly-issued collections called "Periodical Overtures" for use in concerts during the latter half of the century. In many ways, those sinfonias by early eighteenth-century Italian opera composers who were active in the 1730s and 1740s were miniature concert symphonies. While recent studies are just now showing the relevance of this form to the early growth of the symphony, those examples by G. B. Pergolesi (1710–1736) show an amazing maturity of style.

---

* An exhaustive treatment of the opera sinfonia is available. See Helmut Hell, *Die neapolitanische Opernsinfonie in der ersten Hälfte des 18. Jahrhunderts* (Tutzing: Hans Schneider, 1971).

The basic styistic contributions of the sinfonia to the growth of the concert symphony were significant: a basic, three-movement (fast–slow–fast) plan; a homophonic texture for all of the three movements; and a concept of a light, dancelike final movement. While the three-movement concept was supplanted by a four-movement scheme, the overall homophonic style and the dancelike finale of the concert symphony remained as important traits well into the twentieth century. This relationship assumes even greater importance when the advanced style of sinfonias written around 1724 is compared with that of the early works of well-known preclassical symphonists such as Johann Stamitz (1717–1757) and George Matthias Monn (1717–1750), whose early works date from the 1740s and 1750s. The Italian sinfonias alluded to are more advanced in overall style and somewhat closer to the true classical spirit in their adherence to the *style galant* of the early eighteenth century. One cannot fail to be impressed by the maturity of the Pergolesi overture presented below.

EXAMPLES FOR STUDY

*Arcangelo Corelli (1653–1713): *Trio Sonata in f minor, Op. 3, No. 9 (1689)*

This work is an example of the church sonata (*sonata da chiesa*) and thus lacks the dance character of the chamber sonata (*sonata da camera*).

I: Grave (f minor). The movement lacks definition of themes with significant melodic interest. It stresses suspensions, harmonic materials, and contrapuntal flow in the voices.

II: Vivace (f minor). The second movement is fugal in style with a two-voice stretto near the end of the movement. The work abandons its fugal style in a middle section where suspensions are used to great expressive advantage. The pace of the work and constant rush of fast notes are typical of the baroque

---

and remain as continuing features in the *style galant* of the early eighteenth century.

III: Largo (f minor). This section's opening bars show the parallel thirds often associated with the scoring of the trio sonata. The movement soon loses its melodic interest in favor of suspensions and harmonic effect.

IV: Allegro (f minor). The movement is written in binary form but fails to define a secondary theme. The opening of the second section after the double bar states another version of the main tune. Parallel thirds are also abundant in the finale. The bass line is a typical baroque bass in its steady flow of eighth notes. Some imitation is noted in the first section.

SUMMARY

It is important to retain the sound of the basic texture of the trio sonata when listening to the sinfonias and concert symphonies of the mid-eighteenth century. A basic style premise of the baroque (counterpoint with an avoidance of clear phrase structure in favor of a continuous articulation of materials) is also evident in the first three movements more than in the finale, where a dancelike style is used. The legacy left by the trio sonata was difficult for the early classical symphonist to avoid. Even Haydn seemed to prefer three-part scoring for his strings in his early symphonies.*

J. S. Bach (1685–1750): *Orchestral Suite No. 3 in D Major, Gavotte (c. 1720)*

This movement is an excellent example of the binary form after which almost all movements of the baroque suite were patterned. The work has a very clear phrase structure, a second section which is based on another version (inverted) of the primary tune, and a trio whose form adheres to the same basic plan as used by the gavotte. The baroque orchestral style is also well illustrated, i.e., winds doubling strings, and in frequent sustained writing for brass. Trumpets, lacking valves, were frequently unable to follow the rest of the orchestra in passages which took them too far from the tonic key. In the second section of the trio more sustained materials were provided for the trumpets in addition to

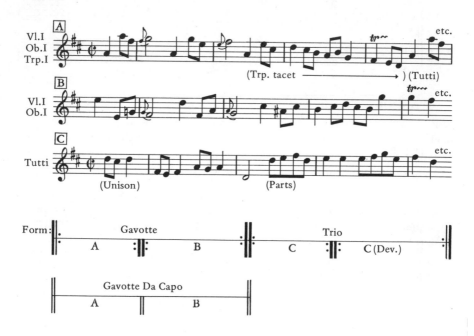

Form charts are provided to show the layout of each movement presented for study. Vertical lines generally represent divisions within the form. Double vertical lines denote sections. Dots before (or after) double lines indicate the repetition of the section bracketed by these marks. Letters below the form graph indicate theme designations. A Roman numeral below the graph indicates a tonal area (I–tonic, V–dominant, etc.). As the works grow longer, measure numbers are added to help locate materials in scores.

---

* Adam Carse, *The History of Orchestration* (New York: Dover Publications, Inc., 1964), p. 183.

a florid line at the beginning of the section. Much of the trio's second section can be called developmental, a late-eighteenth-century trend which Bach anticipated in this early-eighteenth-century work.

SUMMARY

Binary form was the primary movement form of the instrumental suite's dance movements. It appears to have been appropriated by the composers of early symphonies as those works' most frequently used form. This movement shows how the baroque composer handled a monothematic binary form.

Antonio Vivaldi (1678–1741): *Concerto Grosso in a minor, Op. 3, No. 8 ("Estro Armonico") (1715)*

While the earlier style of the baroque concerto grosso (as typified in the works of Corelli) best illustrated the concertato principle, the style of the hundreds of concertos written by the late baroque composer Vivaldi modified the original concerto concept by including greater amounts of virtuosic writing, another feature of the concerto which some of the early classical symphonies exhibited. The amount of literal imitation between *tutti* and *ripieno* is somewhat limited in this work, much more so than in similar movements by Corelli.

    I. Allegro. The composer worked three or four primary themes, or sections (handled by the tutti and solo groups), through various tonal areas. An implied middle section contains three of these themes in the subdominant key. One of these is restated in the tonic key as the movement concludes. Vivaldi seemed to think of blocks of material which might be considered thematic. He manipulated these blocks as integral sections within a very loose formal structure. The important concept of this concerto (as in all others of the period) was virtuosic display and contrast of groups. The composer seemed intent on presenting distinct soloists that used musical materials rarely played by the larger group.

II: Larghetto e spiritoso. The slow movement is scored with all of the primary melodic material in the solo violins with the tutti group playing a unison figure throughout as an accompaniment. The solo material is lyric and involves some degree of imitation which is usually sequential. At other times the solo violins play in parallel thirds. There is a continuo part for the first and last four bars only. The tutti violins and violas play the accompaniment figure unison in the remainder of the movement. The figure appears as a ground bass in the first twelve bars of the work.

III: Allegro. The finale is similar in structure to that of the opening movement, i.e., several blocks of material which are restated in no set order. There is, however, an extended soloistic section for the two violins which starts in measure 86 and continues through measure 113. Some of the solo passages are written in parallel thirds with the accompaniment dropping down to a single unison line in the tutti strings (measures 13–24, 118–28, etc.), thus carrying forward the original concept of a trio sonata concertino from the baroque.

SUMMARY

This work serves to illustrate those concepts of the concerto grosso which will carry forward into the early symphony: contrast of groups, a trio sonata concertino or solo group, and virtuosic writing for solo instruments which are accompanied by a tutti group. At the same time it also shows how little some late baroque composers grasped of new formal concepts which were being projected in the new harmonic style of the rococo period.

George Friedrich Handel (1685–1759): *Overture to the* Messiah *(1741)*

This is an excellent example of the mature French overture style. The work has the traditional two large sections (slow introduction and fugal *Allegro*). The introduction has all the trappings it should: dotted rhythms, a continuous stream of melodic thought not punctuated with obvious cadences, some counterpoint but not as much as in earlier overtures by other composers, and a closing half-cadence. The work has a clearer definition of melodic thought than did many other French overtures. Handel indicated a repeat for the first section. The fugue is a three-voice fugue scored for four voices. In the opening exposition of the fugue the fourth voice (viola) fills in missing harmony pitches and then later figures into the imitative writing. This fugal section retains its fugal style fairly consistently throughout the movement.

SUMMARY

Although endowed by Handel with a clearer melodic style in the first section and with a more consistent fugal treatment in the *Allegro*, the work is still very much a baroque work. The concept which seems to have carried over into the classical symphony, however, was that of a slow introduction preceding the main *Allegro* section of a first movement of an orchestral work.

G. B. Pergolesi (1710–1736): *Sinfonia to* L'Olimpiade *(1735)*

Pergolesi's work was written for his opera seria, *L'Olimpiade,** a work which enjoyed modest success in Naples. The sinfonia is an excellent example of the type of curtain-raiser associated with early-eighteenth-century Italian opera. It was scored for oboes, horns, trumpets (finale only), strings, and continuo.

---

* The work was originally conceived as the overture to Pergolesi's *S. Guglielmo Duca D'Aquitania* (1731), but this first setting was not preserved. A second version was used as the sinfonia to *L'Olimpiade* in 1735. See Hell, *Die neapolitanische Opernsinfonie,* pp. 548–49, 552.

I: Allegro. More typical of the sinfonia than the symphony, the first movement rushes quickly through three identifiable motives which, if treated as such, could have been material for a miniature sonata-allegro movement. The movement, however, lacks both the tripartite division of sonata-allegro into exposition-development-recapitulation and the binary structure (with repeats, etc.) of many first movements of preclassical symphonies. The movement modulates to the dominant in its second half to begin a restatement of the opening material in that key. This is quite short-lived, since the material, after only a few bars, returns to the tonic key for the balance of the movement. The theme identified as the secondary (B) theme reappears in the tonic key in this second half, giving the movement an appearance of sonatina form to some extent. The *style galant* pace of the sinfonia is completely compatible with this same kind of style seen in early classical symphonies. A half-cadence connects the first movement with the second.

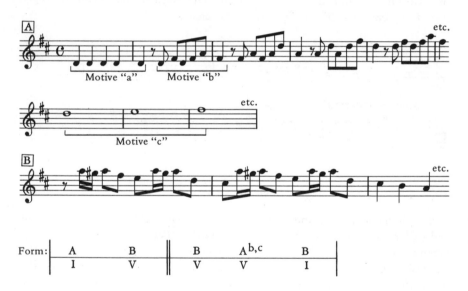

II: Largo. A slow movement for strings alone in miniature sonata-allegro design, this *Largo* is hardly the transitional style one would expect in a brief sinfonia. Using the Scotch snap as a unifying device for his principal material, Pergolesi made a fairly successful attempt at delineating a second theme in the relative major key (F). Once in that key, he restated the main tune, briefly employing the same tonal manipulations of the theme he had used in the opening bars. This led him quickly back to the tonic key, where he restated all of the materials, including the B theme.

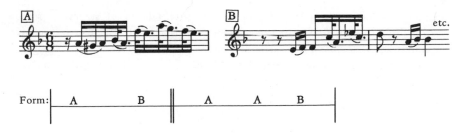

Form: A   B   ‖   A   A   B

III: Allegro. This movement shows how far advanced the style of the sinfonia became in the early eighteenth century. Complete with repeats of both sections, two themes, and a miniature (four bars!) development section, the work also shows how the early-eighteenth-century composer employed the dancelike nature of the finale to justify a fairly strict formal manipulation of his materials. The movement sounds like a minuet even with its lack of a trio.* Pergolesi respected all of the tonal requirements of sonata-allegro form in this movement also. Again, the rushing sixteenth notes or measured tremolo moves the work well into the rococo style period. The composer added trumpets to the finale.

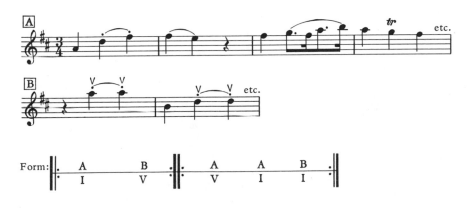

Form: ‖   A   B   ‖   A   A   B   ‖
          I   V   V   I   I

SUMMARY

The work is a veritable treasure trove of style mannerisms which foreshadow the eighteenth-century concert symphony. While the first movement fits more into the frivolous concept of a quick and rousing curtain-raiser, the two re-

---

* The minuet had a three-part overall form, minuet–trio–minuet, in which the final minuet was a repeat of the first minuet. Both the minuet and the trio were also divided into sections, usually into a rounded binary based on two themes: A:‖:BA.

maining sections contain several progressive traits. Clarity of structure, some
well-defined themes, abbreviated development sections, absence of counterpoint
or imitation, and a complete surrender to the *style galant* show the extent to
which the Italian sinfonia provided the basic raw materials for the concert
symphony.

II

The Preclassical Symphony

The Classical Period

The classical period in music can be seen as a blend of several sub-periods or general style manifestations such as rococo, *style galant*, Viennese classical period, high classical, *Empfindsamer Stil*, and *Sturm und Drang*. The overall period extends from approximately 1750 to 1825. The rococo period (1725–1775) serves as a bridge between the baroque and classical periods. *Style galant* is a particular kind of musical manifestation of the rococo period and is characterized by an elegance, a lightness, and a rapidity of pace. The Viennese classical period extends from 1770 to 1830 and embraces the music of Haydn, Mozart, Beethoven, and some of Schubert's music. *Empfindsamer Stil*, a style of the second half of the eighteenth century (1750–1780), is associated with composers such as W. F. Bach, C. P. E. Bach, Georg Benda, and other North German composers. It was an attempt to project "natural feelings" into music and to stress a change of affections in a given movement or work. *Sturm und Drang* came from a movement in German literature and manifested itself in music of the late eighteenth century as an element of forced expressiveness.

Musically, the classical period was a time of growth for all developmental forms, such as the sonata, symphony, string quartet, and concerto. Anticipated by the Age of Reason (early 1700s) in philosophy, classicism stressed balance and design in music. Melody became clearly defined with regular phrase structure. The short melodic motive characterized all instrumental music. Homophonic style permeated all music with counterpoint usually reserved for brief episodes in development sections. Tonality was strengthened through a simple and direct harmonic style. While it was a great period for the flowering of instrumental music, it also saw the culmination of a particular style of Italian

17

opera and the beginning of German opera. The classical style had tremendous impact on the history of music in that it perfected forms and crystallized a tonal style, both of which became points of reference for all music since that time.

Formal matters were dominated by the sonata concept, i.e., a multi-movement (usually four) plan of contrasting tempos (fast, slow, fast, faster) and forms which expressed itself in all instrumental music. A sonata for orchestra was called a symphony; for four strings, a string quartet; for a single instrument, a sonata.

The Preclassical Symphony

Symphonies written between about 1740 and 1770 have been referred to as preclassical in style. The period, which begins with the publication of the first set of symphonies (T. A. Arne's *Eight Overtures*) in 1740 and ends with the emergence of the mature classical symphony around 1770, shows an amazingly consistent use of common style traits and treatments in most works of the period regardless of the geographical location of the composers involved.

Several factors were beneficial to the growth of the symphony during the early and mid-eighteenth century. A new homophonic style had developed in instrumental music after having surfaced in vocal music about one hundred years earlier, and it required new forms. Existing dance forms continued to meet this need to a limited extent. The sonata concept was the primary organizing element in the development of new instrumental forms. Public concerts also created a demand for more music written especially for the orchestras presented in these concerts. By the end of the eighteenth century noted composers (J. C. Bach, C. F. Abel, Haydn, and others) were being sought out to write and conduct symphonies for special subscription concerts. Technical improvements in orchestral instruments made available a richer orchestral palette for composers. In some cases the continued patronage of royal families made possible the establishment of a few excellent orchestras. Music printers also helped by publishing, on a regular basis, works which would be suitable for orchestral performance. Many of the mid-eighteenth-century symphonies were frequently distributed as these publishers' "Periodical Overtures."

The growth of the symphony was also encouraged by the activities of certain schools of composers in Mannheim, Italy, and Vienna. The primary Italian symphony composer who overshadowed all others was Giovanni Battista Sammartini (1701–1775), the leader of a school of the symphony in Milan. Current research supports the probability that Sammartini was the first significant composer of the concert symphony and establishes that he may have written about seventy-five of these preclassical works. As research produces

RACCOLTA
DELLE MEGLIORE
SINFONIE
DI PIU CELEBRI COMPOSITORI
DI NOSTRO TEMPO,
ACCOMODATE
ALL' CLAVICEMBALO

Raccolta I.

No. I - VI.

LIPSIA

Preſſo *GIOV. GOTTL. IMMAN. BREITKOPF.*

1761

The public's appetite for symphonies became so great that the German publisher Johann Gottlob Immanuel Breitkopf issued four volumes of symphonies arranged for harpsichord ("clavicembalo" above), the first in 1761. The above set contained works by K. H. Graun, Hasse, Frederick the Great, and his sister, Anna Amalia. Copies of the complete set exist in Sibley Library of the Eastman School of Music. Courtesy Sibley Library.

additional edited examples of his works, a better view of his place in the development of the eighteenth-century symphony will be possible.*

The court at Mannheim, Germany, well known as one of the cradles of the symphony, supported the services of no less than eight active symphonists: Johann Stamitz (1717–1757), Ignaz Holzbauer (1711–1783), Franz Xavier Richter (1709–1789), Anton Filtz (c. 1730–1760), Franz Beck (1730–1809), Christian Cannabich (1731–1798), Karl Stamitz (1745–1801), and Anton Stamitz (1754–1809). Most were members of the orchestra maintained by the court. All were productive symphonists who made a major contribution to the development of the symphony. The works produced by this school showed certain mannerisms. First, there was a preference for homophony with much of the melodic interest relegated to the violins. Second, there was a continuation of the fast tempos associated with first and last movements of the sinfonia. Third, there was frequent use of a crescendo device usually intensified by the use of measured tremolo in the upper strings, often referred to as the "Mannheim roll." Fourth, orchestral effects such as measured tremolo or arpeggiated chords, in sixteenth notes, many of which originated in seventeenth-century opera scores, were used. Fifth, an opening flourish was used in many first movements which was similar to the attention-getting trumpet-call materials of the opening section of the sinfonia and the *premier coup d'archet* of the Paris orchestra. Many times (as in the sinfonia) this opening flourish did not reappear in the recapitulation of the first movement. Sixth, a unique kind of theme that quickly ascended a simple chord outline, called a "rocket" theme, was used. Seventh, there was frequent use of an expressive device called the "sigh," this involving an accented dissonance in the melodic line which usually resolved upward by step.

In North Germany, another group of composers was active: Johann Adolph Hasse (1699–1783), J. C. Bach (1735–1782), C. P. E. Bach (1714–1788), Johann Gottlieb Graun (1703–1771), and Karl Heinrich Graun (1704–1759). Hasse, primarily an opera composer, edited a number of his sinfonias to Italian-style operas and issued them as concertos in 1741. Almost all of J. C. Bach's symphonies were either opera sinfonias or three-movement sinfonia-style works. The symphonies of C. P. E. Bach generally follow the Italian model but are much more expressive because of the composer's involvement in both the *Sturm und Drang* movement and the *Empfindsamer Stil*. Karl Heinrich Graun also followed the sinfonia model in his symphonies. J. G. Graun reportedly wrote over one hundred symphonies. Only a handful exist in available sources and indicate his preference for the three-movement Italian model.

In Vienna, another group of symphonists were active, including George Christoph Wagenseil (1715–1777), Franz Aspelmayr (c. 1721–1786), Josef

---

* B. Churgin, ed., *The Symphonies of G. B. Sammartini* (Cambridge: Harvard University Press, 1968), p. 4.

EIGHT OVERTURES
in 8 Parts,
Four for Violins, Hoboys, or German Flutes
AND
Four for Violins, French Horns, &c.
with a Bass
FOR THE
VIOLONCELLO & HARPSICORD.

COMPOS'D BY
THOMAS AUGUSTINE ARNE.

London. *Printed for* I. Walsh *in Catharine Street, in the Strand.*

Of whom may be had Just Publifh'd
For CONCERTS

Handel's 60 Overtures. 8 Parts	Handel's 12 Grand Concertos	Caftrucci's Concertos
Haffe and Vinci's Overtures	Handel's Concertos for Hoboys. Op. 3.	Stanley's Concertos
Dr. Greene's Overtures	Geminiani's 12 Concertos	Weideman's Concertos G.F.
Handel's 80 Selected Songs. 6 Parts.	Corelli's 12 Solos made Concer-	Haffe's Concertos G.F.
Handel's 2d Set of 80 Selected Songs	tos by Geminiani	Alberti's Concertos
from his lateft Oratorios. 6 Parts.	Corelli's 12 Concertos	Vivaldi's Concertos
Mudge's Concertos	Defefch's Concertos	Teffarini's Concertos
St. Martini's Concertos	Locatelli's Concertos	Albinoni's Concertos

The earliest set of published symphonies was issued by I. Walsh in London and contained "concert" versions of eight overtures by the English composer Thomas Augustine Arne. Published in 1741, three are known to be overtures to stage works (#3: "Henry and Emma," #7: "Comus," and #8: "The Judgement of Paris."). Four of the works were French overtures; four were *sinfonia* examples. Above set of parts is located in Sibley Library of the Eastman School of Music. Courtesy Sibley Library.

Starzer (1726–1787), Leopold Hoffman (1730–1793), Georg Matthias Monn (1717–1750), Johann Baptist Vanhall (1739–1813), and Karl von Dittersdorf (1739–1799). The works of Monn and Wagenseil, while probable offshoots of the patterns contributed by the Italian sinfonia, were more formally sophisticated than many of the preclassical symphonies of other composers. Monn's D major symphony (1740) is a four-movement symphony of admirable maturity.

It is possible to divide the thirty-year period of preclassical growth into three decades. During the years 1740–1750, composers and publishers frequently "borrowed" French overtures or sinfonias for use as concert symphonies. Most of the works were in three movements. Some French overtures had additional movements, usually of a dancelike nature. Concert symphonies were quite rare, with Sammartini being the primary contributor. Four-movement symphonies were even more rare, with Monn being one of the few composers to use the form. Between 1750 and 1760, borrowing techniques continued. Increasingly true concert symphonies (still primarily in three movements) were written. Composers in Vienna and Mannheim were quite active. Haydn began his symphonic composition during this period. In the final decade (1760–1770), the sinfonia and the French overture as concert symphony surrogates almost disappeared. Four-movement form became standard. Mozart's first symphonies, mostly three-movement examples, were composed starting in 1764.

The gradual change from a style characterized by borrowed forms in the late baroque to a style which represented some degree of maturity can be described fairly well. Changes in the overall formal design of the young symphony, in its basic style (baroque versus classical), and in its orchestral technique are quite steady or continuous throughout the preclassical period. What often is confusing are the apparent and frequent shifts in style from a baroque to a classical emphasis (and vice versa) in works by a single composer within a limited time span of one year or less. Since works were as often as not undated, one must rearrange the accepted chronology on an evolutionary stylistic basis or assume that individual composers in the preclassical era switched styles frequently in these early symphonies. The problem remains one of music history's most frustrating perplexities.

The overall form of the symphony began as a three-movement scheme, patterned either as a French overture or as an Italian sinfonia. By 1770, the dimensions had expanded to include a fourth movement. A few composers (e.g., Monn) had preferred the four-movement form from the beginning. This four-movement plan was somewhat characteristic of the German symphony in the mid-eighteenth century, especially as written by composers in and around Vienna. The four-movement plan involved the insertion of the minuet into the symphony as the third movement. This expansion of the outer design may be attributable to the existence of several kinds of three-movement symphonies, two types in particular: three-movement symphonies with minuets as finales and three-movement models with dancelike finales whose movement forms resembled sonata-allegro or rondo. It is plausible that the four-movement symphony with a third-movement minuet resulted from combining into a four-movement outline the best elements of the two types of three-movement symphonies mentioned above. Thus, the appearance of the minuet as the third movement of a four-movement symphony results from preserving both kinds of three-movement finales: the minuet relocated as the third movement, and the dancelike movement retained as the actual finale. Although a rare species, the three-movement form with a minuet finale was used by both Haydn and Mozart in a few of their early symphonies.

Individual movement forms within the symphony also underwent evolutionary changes in the preclassical period. First movements can be found in a variety of designs. French overture first movements were subjected to a minimal amount of experimentation with some rare attempts to superimpose a binary or miniature sonata-allegro design on the slow first section. Sinfonia movements were generally written in a through-composed fashion in a form approximating binary. Many lacked a clear thematic delineation. Some of the fast first movements were binary in design with repeat signs for the first section. Many also repeated the second half. The gradual change from a binary form to a miniature sonata-allegro form can be seen in a variety of stages in hundreds of works written during the period. Some of the versions noted in this gradual change included forms with the following outlines and key schemes:

Section:	‖: A :‖: A :‖	‖: A B :‖: A B A :‖
Key Scheme:	I to V V to I	I V V I I

‖: A B :‖: A B :‖	‖: A B :‖: A A B :‖
I V V I	I V V I I

*‖: A   B :‖: A dev.   B :‖
I   V   V   I

By far the most used first-movement form in the first decade of the preclassical period was the form noted with an asterisk (*). It was in these "irregular" sonata-allegro movements that one finds the length of the second section (after the double bar) expanded to include repetitions, sequences, and (rarely) motivic development of the principal materials from the movement's first section.

Second movements at the beginning of the period were for the most part in the transitional style of the early opera sinfonia with poorly defined melodic materials. Most were scored for strings, sometimes muted. The gradual evolution of second-movement form was from this nondescript beginning toward either a binary form (with repeats) or a simple sonatina. On rare occasions some were in a miniature sonata-allegro. The melodic style, once the composers had begun to come to grips with the basic melodic nature of the second movement, tended to be ornate with both pitch and rhythmic coloration.

Third (and final) movements were very much influenced by the dance concept of the sinfonia final movement. Most had well-defined forms, clear-cut binary, from the outset. These finales, although less complex and developmentally involved, experienced the same gradual evolution from a simple formal organization to a more complex developmental style. It would be in error, however, to assume that the final movement of the symphony lost its basic dance-like nature during this process. The dance character of the finale continued as a style principle in most symphonies through most of the nineteenth century.

The overall musical style of the preclassical symphony evolved in the same manner as other instrumental music of the eighteenth century. Starting with the fading of the contrapuntal idiom as early as the works of Vivaldi, those forms which were essentially polyphonic, notably the French overture, disappeared from the life line of the eighteenth century. For a number of years imitative techniques and contrapuntal treatment in general receded as a style device in instrumental music, being revived to some extent in the more mature works of Haydn and Mozart. The sequence became a staple for extending the length of all sections in the first-movement form. Even in the mature works of Mozart, the sequence organized that composer's most innovative harmonic meanderings. The driving rhythm of the baroque was replaced with the ultra-rapid tempos of the rococo, expressed quite often through measured tremolo in the upper strings and an almost baroque-like stream of eighth notes in the bass line. The bass line activity gradually disappeared as the mature classical symphony arrived. Repeated sixteenth notes receded at a slower rate. The concepts of dualism and thematic development were important style trends in the preclassical works and tended to indicate the degree of stylistic maturity achieved by individual works. Thematic treatment other than fugal began slowly, with early works being limited to the repetition of material at related key levels, to sequences, and to an occasional extracting of motives. Long, contourless, and spun-out baroque tunes lost favor (except in slow movements), while short, motivic, and well-punctuated tunes gradually appeared, especially in the finales. In the early works finales often had well-defined sections rather than tunes, possibly an influence of the sinfonia. Texturally the preclassical symphony moved from the French overture and Italian sinfonia textural styles to an almost simplistic homophonic fabric which gradually became developmental and, at the end of the period, reasserted counterpoint as an effective developmental device.

Orchestration also evolved during the preclassical period. The instrumentation principles inherited from the baroque had considerable impact on orchestral treatment in the first decade of the preclassical period. Scoring of overtures and sinfonias showed an essential band of strings with one or two pairs of

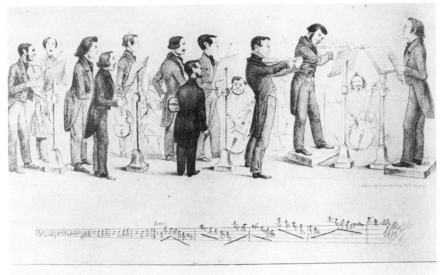

An early print of the orchestral ensemble used in the 18th century Gewendhaus Concerts in Leipzig shows the limited instrumental resources of the early orchestra that appeared there starting in 1781 in an annual subscription series of twenty-four concerts led by J. A. Hiller. Later, in 1835, Mendelssohn became the group's conductor and was primarily responsible for the ensemble's most fruitful period. Courtesy Bettmann Archive.

winds (oboes or flutes and horns, sometimes trumpets). The continuo harpsichord remained as both a harmonic and an instrumental resource well into the early Haydn and Mozart symphonies. The attempt to define a true wind idiom in the symphony took almost fifty years of trial and error. The shift to a more classical instrumentation style was characterized by several refinements.

First, the maturation of a wind style decreased the amount of simple doubling of string parts by the winds. Winds played more sustained harmonic materials and helped reinforce cadence points, both more appropriate functions for winds. They were also used to add volume to the overall sound of the orchestra, reinforcing accents, enunciate more idiomatic melodic materials to string accompaniment, and play matter essential but secondary to string scorings (countersubjects, simplified string parts, underlying harmonies, and essential rhythmic figures).

Second, a more idiomatic string style also gradually evolved. Ways were designed for strings to sustain harmonic materials with measured tremolo and arpeggiation, and in harmonic part-writing. Much of this had been used earlier in opera scores.

Third, the viola and the cello developed some degree of independence. While four- and five-voice scoring for the string section in a symphony is often thought of now as a standard procedure, viola lines many times merely doubled the bass line. The cello line rarely departed from its basic role. In the early eighteenth century orchestration in opera scores was often reduced so that both violin parts were grouped on the top line and the viola, cello, and bass covered the bass line. The harpsichord filled in the remaining inner parts needed to complete the chords being used. Haydn, in his early symphonies, often resorted to three-voice scoring for his strings (two treble and one bass line).

The orchestra grew in size to as many as fourteen separate parts (instruments) in the latter part of the century, including pairs of flutes, oboes, horns, trumpets, timpani, and strings. Clarinets did not become regular members of the symphony orchestra until the late part of the century.

EXAMPLES FOR STUDY

*G. B. Sammartini (1701–1775): *Symphony No. 1 in C Major (JC 7) (c. 1720–40)*

Probably the first significant composer of concert symphonies, Sammartini reacted to developments in the solo sonata and the concerto possibly more than to the opera sinfonia. A collection of his early works has been edited which establishes certain periods in his output, placing this work in the first period.†
The overall style is a mixture of baroque and rococo. While the scoring is for strings only, there is evidence of preclassical tendencies (measured tremolo and repeated-note scoring of harmony) that place the composer in the mainstream of symphonic development quite early in the eighteenth century.

I: Allegro. Using a very loose binary design, the work appears fugal on paper but sounds homophonic because of the lack of melodic motion in the opening measures of the first tune. The composer created six sub-sections within the principal section, the last three being a restatement of the first three in the dominant key. The subsequent second theme follows in e minor. Portions of the first section are restated followed by a restatement of the second theme in the tonic major. The basic rhythm of the movement has the rococo hustle, sustaining this style for the entire movement. Measured tremolo and arpeggiation in sixteenth notes are another indication of a more progressive orchestral style. The overall style is similar to that of the sinfonia: it fails to define its themes clearly; there are no sectional repeats; the busy rhythmic style is practically identical with that of the early sinfonia; it lacks only the dramatic flourish at the beginning to be a convincing sinfonia.

---

† Churgin, *G. B. Sammartini,* p. 10.

II: **Andante piano.** This movement has the same sectional thematic organization as does the first movement, presenting at least three different groups of ideas which reappear at least one other time as the movement progresses. The movement is not amelodic as many of the transitional sinfonia second movements had been. Like the first movements, it did not settle into any clear-cut form. The final nine bars contain material not significantly related to any previous section. Harmonically, the work makes use of various tonal inflections in the minor mode, thereby adhering to the older concept of a slow movement's having harmonic rather than melodic interest.

III: Presto. The finale uses a form found in many preclassical symphonies in the first half of the eighteenth century:

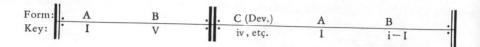

In many instances the C theme involved a simple restatement of the first tune but in a related key or as a simple extension or working out of a portion of the tune. In more instances, however, composers favored the insertion of new material. As in other finales of a dance character, themes are in clearly defined phrases of multiples of two measures each in length. The texture of early finales also had simpler parameters as noted by the frequent three-voice writing in this particular finale.

* From *The Symphonies of G. B. Sammartini,* ed. by B. Churgin. Copyright 1968 by the President and Fellows of Harvard College.

SUMMARY

This work is an example of the early concert symphony by the one major composer in that media in the early eighteenth century. Written prior to 1740, it illustrates a transitional syle leading from baroque to rococo. Whereas early sinfonias were scored for strings, winds, and continuo, this composer scored most of his early works for strings alone with continuo. Texture at times is reduced to the three-voiced format of the trio sonata. Form is embryonic to say the least. Tunes are not well defined except those in the finale. In general the concepts of the early sinfonia apply: rapid tempos, poorly defined tunes, dancelike character to the finale, and, for the greater part of the work, simple contruction and overall style.

This work is in four movements and, though it approaches a mature classical style in some respects, it uses many of what have been called typical preclassical style devices. It is scored for horns and oboes in pairs, strings, and continuo.

I: Presto. Stamitz opened the work with a typical Italian sinfonia flourish, followed by the Mannheim crescendo mannerism called the "roll." Two melodic parts of the theme then follow, the second in the dominant key. The subordinate theme (B) is quite typical of the sinfonia style: oboes in parallel thirds over a tonic pedal played by the violins on repeated eighth notes. The twenty-four measure development section (without repeats, another sinfonia trait) starts with a repetition of the roll and contains a sequence on the A^3 tune as the high point of the section. The recapitulation omits a portion of the flourish and the entire opening roll and reverses the order of reappearance of the A^2 and A^3 themes. The movement concludes with a return to the roll. The movement does have fairly well-defined themes, all of the Mannheim mannerisms except the rocket theme, a more advanced handling of the winds (less doubling of the strings, more sustained playing, reinforcement of accents, solos with horns joining with oboes in restating the B theme), and rhythmic energizing of the harmonic lines in the strings through measured tremolo and repeated notes. The bass line does maintain considerable rhythmic activity in the tradition of the *style galant*.

The form of the first movement very clearly subdivides into the three major divisions of sonata-allegro form: exposition, development, and recapitulation.

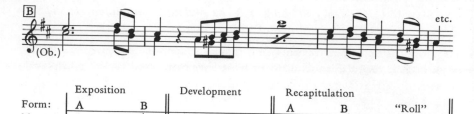

Form:	Exposition		Development	Recapitulation		
	A	B		A	B	"Roll"
Measures		↓	↓	↓	↓	↓
		38	58	82	104	115

II: Andante non Adagio. Scored for strings alone, the movement is written in the simple binary form used so frequently in second movements of preclassical works. The movement has no fewer than three thematic groups which somehow fail to separate themselves into independent themes. The material is repeated after the double bar, starting in the dominant key and gradually returning to the tonic. Stamitz resorted to three-voice writing for a significant portion of this movement.

Form:	A		A	
Key:	I	V	V	I

III: Minuet. This is a standard minuet written in song form with a trio. The winds are prominent in the trio. In the minuet proper Stamitz had his winds double string parts in most of the measures. In the hands of Haydn and Mozart the minuet made further progress in the area of thematic development. Stamitz, however, in this example merely states material and refrains from any tendency to develop.

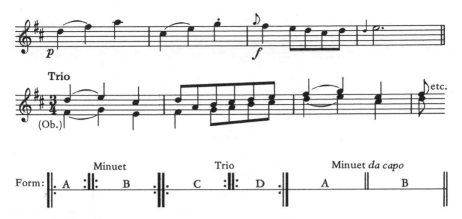

IV: Prestissimo. In general Stamitz used the same formal scheme that Sammartini (and a great many other composers) had used in the Symphony No. 1 previously discussed, avoiding any lengthy development and substituting new material for most of the middle section:

	Expos.					Dev.			Recap.			
Form:	A^1	A^2	B^1	B^2	C	D	A^1	E	A^2	B^1	B^2	C
Keys:	I	I	V	V	V	V–I	I	(Various)	I	I	I	I

Most of the themes are simple in design and usually have some motivic unity. As in this kind of simple finale, there is quite a bit of repetition of tunes as they are presented. The orchestral style of the work is also somewhat regressive, with winds generally doubling strings except where they are used for emphasis in solo passages.

* Used by permission of Broude Brothers Limited.

SUMMARY

As mentioned above, Stamitz's *Sinfonia a 8* resembles many of the preclassical symphonies of the period 1750–1760, with some exceptions. First, three of the movements (I, II, and IV) are longer than most preclassical symphonic movements. Second, the style mannerisms of the Mannheim school provide a unique flavor. Third, the orchestral technique is more advanced. Fourth, there are beginnings of skillful development in the first movement. Finally, there is more emphasis on the motivic structure of themes in general.

Stamitz merits the esteem he is accorded as one of the symphony's eighteenth century pioneers. His mature works, as illustrated by the above example, are excellent examples of the early classical symphony.

Haydn as a Preclassicist

Franz Joseph Haydn (1732–1809) had a major impact on the development of the symphony. Few men in music history have worked with a single musical form over a period as long as that in which Haydn worked with the symphony (1757–1795). In this span of almost forty years Haydn's 106 symphonies embraced a full spectrum of styles, influences, biases, and results. The very early works are truly preclassical in style. By 1770, he had settled into a full-fledged classical version of the symphony. His final works show a degree of formal experimentation that enriches the mature classical symphonic output of the late eighteenth century with works of ingenuity and charm. While a systematic study of all 106 symphonies does not tell the full story of the development of the classical symphony, it does provide an insight into the symphony's history that is not available in the work of any other composer.

Haydn's early symphonic output began in the preclassical period and extended in ten years to include almost thirty symphonies. The exact chronology of many of these works must be inferred since few carry a date of composition. Haydn's early self-cataloging efforts also failed to identify accurately the dates of most of the early symphonies. Thus the first critical edition of the Haydn works, begun in 1907 (Breitkopf and Härtel), assigned numbers to the symphonies which do not conform to their exact order of composition in light of later research. The numbers have endured despite the exhaustive treatment of the subject by Haydn scholar H. C. Robbins Landon as noted in his edition of the symphonies issued beginning in the mid-1960s. One manuscript located by Robbins Landon contained fourteen symphonies which were written prior to

Haydn's move to Eisenstadt in 1761. This "Fürnberg" manuscript collection had ostensibly been ordered by a young officer ("Obrist. Lieut. Fürnberg") who was attached to the court located at Weinzierl Castle near Melk in Lower Austria, where Haydn was active just prior to his joining forces with the Eisenstadt court. The fourteen works (symphonies 1–5, 10, 11, 15, 18, 25, 32, 33, 37, and Symphony "A") were probably written over a five-year period (1757–1761).

The preclassical nature of these early works is unique. Haydn had not evolved a symphonic style that began with his adapting dramatic overtures for concert performance. His very first efforts were concert symphonies. In spite of this "fresh start" approach, he did use estabished patterns in many of these preclassical works. The most telling indication is the use of the "irregular" sonata-allegro form in two of the first movements (symphonies 15 and 37), a movement-form which completely permeates most of the symphony scores prior to 1765. Haydn also used the three-movement sinfonia outline for six of the fourteen works. He also employed the French overture outer design for the first movements of two symphonies (symphonies 15 and 25). In scoring secondary themes in opening fast movements the composer frequently resorted to the sinfonia device of employing two woodwinds in parallel thirds or sixths above a simple bass line. In other ways this early collection anticipates a more mature classical style. For the period in which the fourteen were written the incidence of Haydn's four-movement symphonies is much higher (50 percent) than the norm (16 percent) for the other preclassical symphonies written during the same time span. Haydn also used irregular sonata-allegro as a first-movement form much less often than did other preclassical composers. He also used fewer triple-metered finales and avoided employing rondo as the primary form for his finales. Thus Haydn's earliest symphonies are unique because in them he gradually abandoned the precepts of preclassicism.

When Haydn arrived at Esterhazy in 1761 he proceeded to write three symphonies of a programmatic nature (*Le Matin, Le Midi, Le Soir*). While the works are in many ways an immediate contrast to the "Fürnberg" collection in their exclusive employment of a four-movement scheme and their greater overall length, they still contain many of the preclassical traits noted in the earliest collection. Each also shows some influence of another budding classical form: the divertimento. Primarily written for small chamber groups, the form had from three to ten short movements. Some movements were in dance forms; others were more akin to the movements in a sonata. It is Robbins Landon's belief that the divertimento was responsible for much of the chamber-like writing in these early symphonies, especially the reduction of orchestral forces to small groups of instruments. Haydn did write over 160 compositions which he entitled divertimento. Of these at least fifty are quite properly in a chamber form which was designed primarily for incidental entertaining at social events. This small ensemble writing trait in the Haydn symphonies can also be viewed as an influence of the concerto grosso.

EXAMPLES FOR STUDY

*Haydn: *Symphony No. 6 (Le Matin) (1761)*

I: Adagio, Allegro. Starting with a brief, slow introduction which uses the dotted rhythmic style of the French overture, the movement shows a variety of cross-influences: concerto, sinfonia, rococo rhythmic style, divertimento, trio sonata, and others. Because of the assignment of most of the principal material to solo winds, the work sounds more like a concerto or a divertimento. The violins have no important thematic materials until the entrance of the B theme, itself for some reason not restated in the recapitulation. While some of the material of the development section (measures 58–72) does not appear very closely related to the exposition, the section has elements of thematic development and is certainly more than just a statement of the main tune in the dominant key. Far more important was Haydn's attempt to begin his development of the principal theme in the exposition (see measures 14–20). The form is fairly clear. Tunes are constructed with a strong motivic unity. Orchestration, under the influence of the concerto (and possibly the divertimento), is unique, with considerable emphasis on solo winds, and small chamber groups. Violins, when not playing primary material, play accompaniment figures using measured tremolo and repeated note figures, both typical devices of the mature preclassical symphony.

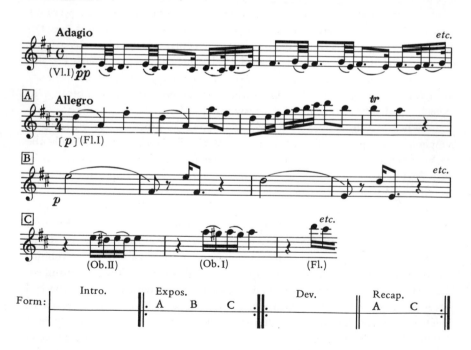

II: Adagio, Andante, Adagio. With the *Adagio* sections serving both as introduction and coda, the *Andante* section is primarily a concerto movement for solo violin and solo cello, the inner movement itself being patterned after the form of a melodic variation. This *Andante* section is scored for strings alone, with the tutti group generally playing a simplified version of the cantus while the solo instruments embroider the tune in ensuing interludes. Haydn wrote a number of slow movements in his early symphonies which are concerto-like in style. He retained an affection for the use of solo instruments in symphony movements throughout his entire output but with a marked decrease in emphasis in the mature works.

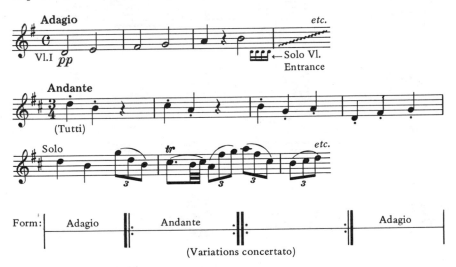

III: Minuet. This movement continues the concertolike concept of the first two movements, relying upon woodwind solos and adding the viòla and the cello to that grouping in the trio. In the opening strain of the trio, the solo violone supplies an ornamentation of the bass line.

IV: Finale (Allegro). In addition to solo woodwinds, Haydn used a solo violin and a solo cello in this movement. The development section has the appearance of a passage from a violin concerto. Orchestrally the movement offers quite a bit of unison writing for the strings both in thematic and accompaniment roles. Other than this, the work has no great forward thrust orchestrally because of the reliance on the concerto style, which separated winds from strings, with the winds frequently supplying tunes.

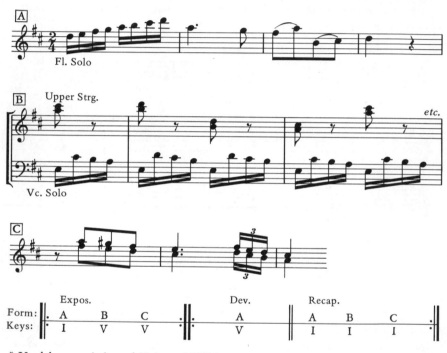

Fl. Solo

Upper Strg.

etc.

Vc. Solo

		Expos.				Dev.		Recap.		
Form:		A	B	C		A		A	B	C
Keys:		I	V	V		V		I	I	I

* Used by permission of Universal Editions.

SUMMARY

An interesting example of Haydn's absorbing the concerto and possibly the divertimento into his symphonic style, *Le Matin* fits well into preclassical history. No work could better illustrate the basic condition of the symphonic milieu with its hybrid sinfonia-concerto-divertimento nature. The slow introduction even has some of the traits of the French overture. The concertato style dominates all of the movements. Readers should keep in mind Haydn's use of a woodwind concertino in passages in this work. It is a personal trademark that did not desert him.

Wolfgang Amadeus Mozart (1756–1791) as a Preclassicist

While the exact chronology of the early Haydn symphonies has been subject to considerable speculation and scholarly revision, the early works of Mozart have been dated with some degree of assurance. This particular work, composed during a childhood visit to London, is one of the better examples of the use of the sinfonia style in an early concert symphony. The greatest influence on Mozart at this time of his life as far as the symphony was concerned was J. C. Bach, whose concerts the child attended in London in 1764. Bach, thoroughly schooled and productive in Italian opera, wrote sinfonias of great charm and pace that were very much in the rococo style. Thus Mozart's line of development as a composer of symphonies began with a work in the style of an Italian sinfonia. Of the first fourteen symphonies written in London, The Hague, Vienna, and Italy, half are in three movements and closely approximate the style of the Italian sinfonia.

EXAMPLES FOR STUDY

Mozart: *Symphony No. 1 in E-flat Major, K 16 (1764)*

I: Allegro molto. In many of his early works Mozart adhered to the section concept of thematic construction rather than to the concept of writing definitive tunes. The opening theme was cast in an unusual formal structure: a three-bar opening "motto" theme followed by an eight-bar harmonic passage in whole notes. The second portion of the subordinate theme (B^2) has a characteristic melodic structure which lends it some degree of formal integrity. There is still another thematic "group" that the young child used for a closing section which consists of scale passages in the bass under measured tremolo accompaniment in the upper strings. The development consists of repetitions of the first themes until the subordinate themes return in the tonic key, thus making the movement an irregular sonata-allegro example. The formal style, however, is not as advanced as is the work's orchestral style. Though winds double the strings for about 50 percent of the measures, they were used idiomatically for the balance of the work, generally for reinforcing harmonies or accents. The work was scored for two oboes, two horns, strings,* and continuo.

---

* The string section was normally comprised of five parts: violin I, violin II, viola, cello, and bass. The scoring was done on four staves, the cello and bass sharing the same written part. In early symphonies this bass line also served as the continuo part, with the continuo player (usually a harpsichord player) filling in the harmony with his right hand while playing the bass line with his left. The use of a single staff for both cello and bass parts continued into the early nineteenth century. Beethoven and Schubert at times split the parts into two staves. After Schubert, composers gradually adopted the use of five staves for the five parts. The separation of the two parts was closely related to the increasing solo role of the cellos rather than to any calligraphic progress.

II: Andante.

II: Andante. While the form of this movement is binary, it lacks any real subordinate material. Some would say that it also lacks a good principal tune since the opening section is primarily a harmonic pattern with a melodic motive in the bass line. This prominent motivic structure is a formal step toward a sinfonia-style second movement. It shows its strongest linkage with the sinfonia in its failure to define a secondary tune and in its reliance on harmonic effect for its overall style. Orchestrally the second movement is similar in style to the first movement: the winds reinforce the harmony in sustained notes while the strings play these same pitches in a repeated note chordal texture.

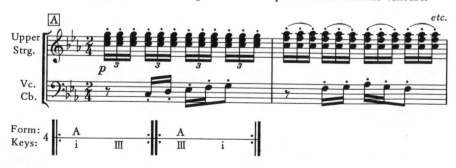

Capital Roman numerals indicate major keys. Lower-case numerals represent minor keys.

III: Presto. Again, Mozart stuck very close to the sinfonia model. The work is in 3/8 meter; the form is nondevelopmental; the phrase structure is simple and well defined in dance-movement tradition. The strict rondo shape of the form can be modified somewhat if one considers the new materials offered after the double bar as being related to the descending scale passages in measures 5–8 of the first tune. This is a rather obscure inference since Mozart brought back two of the three segments of the second thematic group as the movement moved toward conclusion. The form then became:

Form:	A		B	C	D	A	B	C	A	
Keys:	I		V	V	V	I	V	V	I	

At least two of the secondary tunes have a contrapuntal texture created by the countermelodies in the second violin part. The winds generally double the strings except in the thirty-seven measures where the winds are silent.

SUMMARY

As stated, Mozart's first symphony was written in the style of the sinfonia. The work does show certain progressive traits: a growing awareness of the importance of melodic motives and symmetrical phrase lengths in defining formal shape of a movement, the recognition that development requires that tunes be moved about tonally, and a sensitivity to tone color through careful use of wind doubling in the first and second movements. Whereas Haydn, as a mature artist, tended to experiment in his earlier symphonies, Mozart, as a child genius, tended to follow established models, in this instance, the J. C. Bach sinfonias the young child heard in London. The form of the first movement is particularly characteristic of the preclassical period.

III

The Classical Symphony

Haydn's Middle Period: Maturity of Style Established

Many Haydn authorities regard the symphonies written in the years 1771–1774 as the composer's greatest orchestral achievements until he wrote the twelve London symphonies. The works included in this three-year output are symphonies 42, 43, 44, 45, 46, 47, 48, 50, 52, 54, 56, 64, and 65. After having come to grips with *Sturm und Drang* in some of the symphonies in the previous period (1766–1770) and after infusing a more expressive nature especially into the slow movements, Haydn had a wide variety of styles from which to choose in writing additional symphonies. For this reason it is hard to see clearly any trends which encompass all thirteen symphonies: each is a work of its own with characteristics the others may not have. Generally, in those years Haydn was writing mature classical symphonies. Some features may be considered stabilizing in these works: greater harmonic richness than in his earlier symphonies, more emphasis on dynamics, more use of counterpoint, especially in development sections, greater use of syncopation, and the removal of the harpsichord continuo from the orchestra. First movements seem to contain unison principal subjects with a loud opening bar and frequent dynamic changes, double statements of the principal theme, some slow introductions, and an occasional false start in the recapitulation. All of the slow movements use muted strings, are longer, and have a form that seems to be a hybrid between binary and sonata-allegro. Finales are either a brisk variation-rondo or a sonata-allegro.

EXAMPLES FOR STUDY

*Haydn: *Symphony No. 44 in e minor, Trauer (Mourning)† (1771)*

    I: Allegro con brio. A monothematic sonata-allegro movement, it has one of the tightest motivic structures of all first movements in Haydn's symphonies up to 1771. As soon as the composer introduced the two versions of the principal theme, he began a development of the A theme in measure 20 which continues until the closing section starts; this development also lasts over twenty bars. One would assume that Haydn was substituting the treatment of the main theme for a secondary theme. Haydn's use of sixteenth-note countermelodies above the principal theme gives the section a contrapuntal flavor. The development section dwells on the first two parts of the main theme and then launches into an extended contrapuntal development using imitation of short motives of the A[3] tune, essentially the sixteenth-note countermelody. A recapitulation which omits this A[3] section leads via a fermata to a short coda on the principal tune. The first few bars of the coda are fugal.

    Orchestrally the movement seems to have arrived at a mature style which Haydn would then maintain throughout his remaining symphonic output. Soprano woodwinds double strings for both emphasis and color. No longer is there evidence of the baroque practice of continuous doubling of winds and strings. There are excellent passages where the oboes sustain long harmony lines to support some of the more demanding passage work in the strings. One particularly expressive color device appears: violins doubled at the octave on primary thematic material of a lyric nature (measures 47–51, 133–39).

---

    † Names for symphonies have obscure origins. In many cases publishers inserted nicknames to improve the marketability of a symphony. Other names originated from a particular audience reaction to an initial performance. Thus the sudden timpani stroke in the second movement of the ninety-fourth symphony was such a surprise that the work was immediately termed the "Surprise" symphony by London audiences in 1792. See Robbins Landon, *The Symphonies of Joseph Haydn* (London: Universal Edition and Rockliff, 1955), pp. 489–90.

II: Menuetto (Allegretto—Canone in Diapason).*

Remaining in a two-voice canon for the balance of the minuet, the work adds the winds to fill in harmonies where needed without disturbing the plan of the canon. The trio continues a minimal degree of counterpoint but does not offer further canonic treatment.

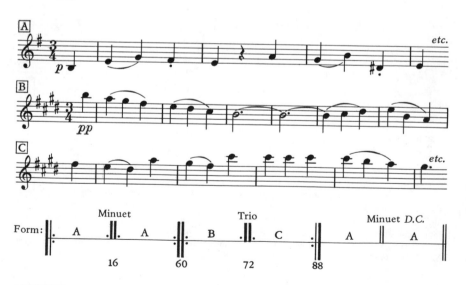

---

* Canon at the interval of the octave.

III: Adagio. This movement strongly resembles the parent binary form of the suite. Built on long and expressive lines of melody, the work sounds somewhat like one of the variation movements of some later symphonies. Haydn scored it for muted strings and occasional wind parts. A large portion of the movement depends on three-voice scoring with violins doubling the tune at the unison.

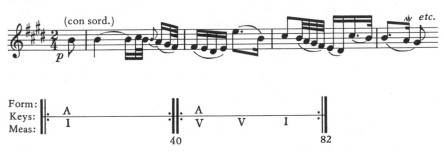

IV: Finale (Presto). In some ways the form of the finale is similar to that of the first and third movements. It is monothematic, has a strong motivic organization, and fails to present a complete recapitulation. It resembles the earlier binary structure since materials in the second half very closely approximate those of the first half. It retains the simplicity and simple phrase organization of the sinfonia but resorts to extended developmental techniques once materials have been presented. The exposition tends to divide itself into sections which could approximate subordinate and closing sections. Haydn by this time had mastered motivic development and used it to great effect in this finale.

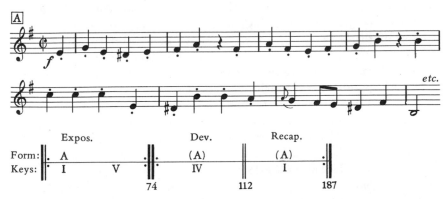

* Used by permission of Universal Editions.

SUMMARY

This symphony illustrates Haydn's concept of the mature classical symphony, a concept which included the expressive element, motivically unified forms, use of counterpoint as a developmental tool, some flexibility in the use of forms, and a rapid pace closely associated with the *style galant* and rococo period. Haydn's use of monothematic developmental forms was an indication of the level of experimentation he was employing to give some degree of diversity to forms which became quite rigid in the hands of less adventuresome composers. This was to remain a key feature in his use of the sonata-allegro form. The mood of the work undoubtedly springs from the *Sturm und Drang* thrust noted in some of the symphonies Haydn wrote in his late thirties.

Mozart's Middle Period: Maturity through Absorption of Influences

Mozart's development as a symphonist was conditioned by two strong and conflicting influences: the Italian style of the lyric symphony with a strong *style galant* flavor and the German style of greater emphasis on development, fugal or imitative usage, and formal complexity. As he moved from locale to locale, his style also seemed to mirror the country in which he worked. During his stay in Vienna in 1767–1768, he shifted the style emphasis in his symphonies to the four-movement form favored by the Viennese composers.

The style reached a plateau of maturity in a group of works written in Salzburg in 1773–1774 after his contact with Haydn had begun to be expressed in his music. Before the beginning of this long friendship with the older Haydn, Mozart had either met, studied, or worked with many of the major musical personalities of his time, all of these contacts coming during the formative years. The group included J. C. Bach (1735–1782), an excellent representative of the Italian style of the symphony; K. F. Abel (1723–1787), a joint promoter with J. C. Bach of a series of symphony concerts in London when the child Mozart was visiting the city and a composer whose style represented the German approach to the symphony; G. B. Sammartini (1701–1775), Italian symphonist; Padre Martini (1706–1784), Italian composer and teacher of Mozart; Pietro Nardini (1722–1793), great Italian violinist and composer of lesser gifts whom Mozart's father greatly admired; Muzio Clementi (1752–1832), famed Italian pianist and composer not particularly respected by Mozart; Niccolo Piccini (1728–1800), Italian opera composer whose 139 operas gave him considerable prominence; Niccolo Jommelli (1714–1774), Italian opera composer of the Neapolitan tradition whose broad European travels resulted in a more serious and involved personal operatic style; Farinelli (1705–1782), famed *castrato* soprano who dominated much of operatic Europe during the first half of the eighteenth century; F. J. Gossec (1734–1829), leading French composer of operas and symphonies whose works Mozart heard during his Paris visits; C. W. Gluck (1714–1787), greatest opera composer of the time, next to Mozart, with a style which evolved from Italian to French with more emphasis on drama; J. A. Hasse (1699–1783), North German composer; Johann Stamitz (1717–1757), leader of the Mannheim school; and F. J. Haydn (1732–1809), one of Mozart's closest friends.

The strongest national influence throughout his entire creative life was Italian. Under Haydn's influence he gained both a greater respect for craft and a depth of feeling. The line of Mozart's development as a symphonist was, then, from an extremely secure Italian *style galant* to a brilliant classical style of unequaled craft and expressiveness. His symphonies, while not heralded by some as his greatest works, were indeed typical of his creative development.

EXAMPLES FOR STUDY

Mozart: *Symphony No. 29 in A Major, K 201 (1774)*

The work is scored for oboes, horns, and strings.

I: Allegro moderato. The principal theme, while tightly motivic, lacks a degree of thematic identity since it sounds almost introductory in its slowly ascending contour. A subsequent canonic passage (measure 13) gives more significance to the tune. Two or three other motives close out the primary section as the secondary theme is presented, a more typically cantabile tune in an allegro tempo. A third theme, also presented in an imitative texture, closes the exposition. Mozart inserts a scalar filling in of the octave motive (theme A) as the material for the opening half of the development section and builds an eight-measure passage on an imitative treatment of this scale motive and its inversion (measures 80–87). For some reason he reverted to older models and inserted a fourth theme as the second half of the development section. The recapitulation is an almost exact repetition of the exposition. The movement's coda gave Mozart a final opportunity to work out the main tune in imitative style, this time in a three-voice texture. The movement has the traditional repeats of the two main sections with the coda added after the final repeat. The use of winds is almost completely for harmonic support with doubling of strings almost nonexistent. The movement makes extensive use of measured tremolo. Mozart had moved quite a distance from the *style galant*, as also noted by the infrequent motor activity in the bass line.

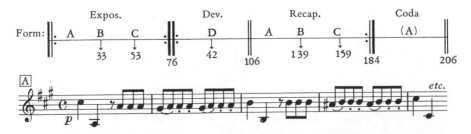

II: Andante. As in other second movements of Mozart symphonies of this period, this movement was cast in the outline of a sonata-allegro which lacked only a real development section. What substituted for actual motivic or thematic development were harmonic excursions that continued some of the triplet activity found at the close of the exposition. The melodic materials (D) have a vague relationship with the B theme, parts which may have been both augmented and diminished in rhythmic values. The coda ensues after the repetition of the second half of the movement and restates portions of the first theme. The orchestral technique is characterized by a four-voice scoring for strings with winds either doubling the first and second violins an octave higher or reinforcing harmonies in a more sustained style. There is a brief wind concertino statement of the first theme in the coda. The overall effect is of considerable refinement and delicacy, a position quite close to that of the *style galant*. The ornateness of the melodic writing continues a tradition for slow movements which all classical slow movements tend to embrace. The noteworthy feature of the work is the basic handling of the principal theme in a polyphonic texture with a two-voice effect lasting for more than eight measures (measures 5–13) of the first section and the recapitulation. The gradual reappearance of a contrapuntal style has been noted as evidence of the maturing styles of both Haydn and Mozart. Counterpoint as a developmental device became one of the important aspects of the sonata concept in the late eighteenth century. It was this absorption and redirection of old principles in the evolution of a new form such as the symphony (and other sonatalike forms) which enhanced the "learnedness" (or German style) in the overall style of the symphony.

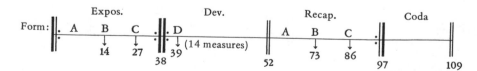

III: Menuetto. The minuet section has a very concise and unified organization through the employment of a rhythmic motive throughout the section. The motive shifts from tune to accompaniment and back. The trio infuses the customary degree of lyricism.

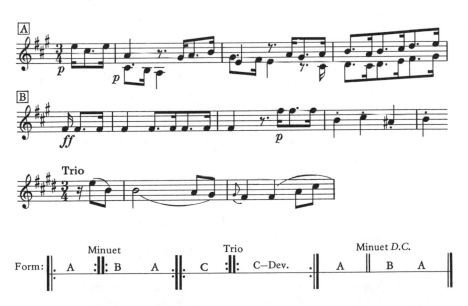

IV: Allegro con spirito. The exposition presents two main themes with a motive from the first being developed antiphonally before the second tune appears. This latter tune uses a treatment similar to that of the first tune in the *Andante:* two-voice writing based on an ostinatolike line in one voice and a fully shaped melody in the other. The development section is probably one of Mozart's most ingenious up until that time. Starting with a sequential treatment of the first theme which passes through several keys, an imitative section continues the tonal wandering in the same sequential style. Winds are used as before with greater emphasis on support roles. There is one wind section solo in the coda (measures 172–74).

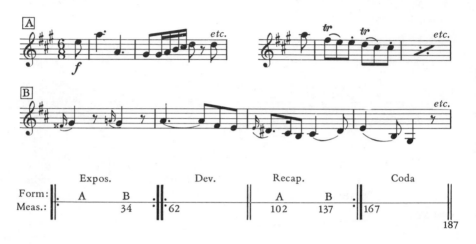

SUMMARY

Mozart's twenty-ninth symphony shows that growing balance between the learned style of the German symphonists and the lyric *style galant* of the Italian tradition, a balance which typified the mature symphonies of the composer. The symphony also shows greater skills in development and instrumentation. The formal maturity of the composer's craft is apparent not only in the advancing developmental techniques but also in the use of unifying motives in two of the movements.

Late Mozart

The various influences that had probably contributed to Mozart's overall style seem to coalesce in his final three symphonies. Mannheim had produced for Mozart a greater sensitivity in orchestral writing; Haydn's continued influence probably was responsible for Mozart's use of more extended forms, more involved development sections that avoided a mere tonal contrast of leading themes, greater use of counterpoint, and a greater use of unifying motives in all movements; and the ever-present Italian core of the young composer's style remained a tradition that Mozart could not renounce. The most individual of the three symphonies is undoubtedly the middle work of the trilogy: Symphony No. 40 in g minor.

EXAMPLES FOR STUDY

Mozart: *Symphony No. 40 in g minor, K. 550 (1788)*

I: Allegro molto. From the outset, the materials identify one of the basic devices used to organize this work: dissonance. The main theme, starting on an appoggiatura, was created from one basic motive. The six-measure (measure 14–20) cadence passage which closes the main theme also emphasizes accented dissonance. The other feature which the work stresses is chromaticism, not only inflections of the melody but also chromatic chord progressions. Mozart, in contrast to Haydn, moved much further into the future by frequent use of such chromatic chord progressions. Many were organized in sequences; a few were not. Some were held together by the traditional circle of fifths relationship of chord roots or tonal areas, this latter usage being typical of the barbershop harmonies of the late nineteenth and early twentieth centuries:

The materials of the exposition contain two primary thematic groups. The closing theme (measure 72) is derived from the first tune and again stresses dissonance by use of long suspensions in the violin and bass lines. The overall aural impression of both melodic and harmonic chromaticism is that of the dissonant half step. This fairly well pervades the entire symphony. Free tones (or unprepared appoggiaturas) which enter without preparation are often resolved by half step to an important chord member. The first pitch of the first theme illustrates this principle. The development section is one of Mozart's most complex and exciting. Again, a chromatic chord progression (g minor chord to g-sharp diminished seventh) sets up a development in f-sharp minor, from whence it moves through the keys e, d, C, B-flat, A and then back through B-flat, c, and g via another sequence. By measure 115 Mozart has added a brilliant contrapuntal line in eighth notes in the violins. This section (115–33) has the basic appearance of a two-voice fugal development as the sequential treatment of the theme and the counterpoint move toward the tonic key. Once reached, the section continues an antiphonal treatment of the main theme. A final chromatic sequence (160–64) leads back to the recapitulation. A brief coda, also fugal (measure 285), concludes the movement. The movement, like the remaining movements, is scored for flute, oboes, clarinets, bassoons, horns, and strings. Winds (except flute) are in pairs. The usage is completely in the mature classical tradition: limited doubling of strings by winds, idiomatic solos for the winds, sustained harmonies by winds and some individual doubling at the octave of string lines for color effect. There are a few instances of sensitive and colorful writing for the winds, for example, measures 168–72, where the bassoon solo enters on the sustained submediant pitch (E-flat), holds it for two full measures above the returning principal theme, and then descends by outlining the dominant seventh chord in half notes. The passage exploits the lovely tenor register of the bassoon, creating the effect of a counter-melody below the violins playing the main tune, and shows how far orchestral technique had come from its modest beginnings in the early eighteenth century, when the bassoon only doubled the bass line.

II: Andante. This movement reaffirms the contrapuntal nature of the first movement by introducing a first theme in an imitative style. In fact, most of the materials of the principal section have this contrapuntal tendency. As the work continues through the secondary theme, it is subjected to another chromatic chord progression which, like others, was constructed to emphasize half-step chromatic melodic motion.

measures 43–47

The appearance of the E-flat minor seventh chord at the beginning of this progression (when Mozart had been reaffirming the dominant key, B-flat major) was an aural shock that Mozart must have enjoyed slipping in (note the *f* dynamic marking, tutti scoring) at this quiet moment. The bass line was part-written to emphasize (again) the half-step motion in the chromatic progression. It's one of the more expressive moments in the symphony. After a false start at measure 69, Mozart extracted a motive from the bass line of the first tune and continued the development briefly, this motive emphasizing an accented upper neighbor tone (also only a half step from its consonant neighbors) as a dissonance. Orchestrally, the movement continues the mature style of the first movement with some increase of woodwind solos and sectional playing. Note in the development section (measures 54–63) an example of winds supplying the entire harmonic support for the violins (with the exception of the bass line in the lower strings). This passage also involves winds and strings developing materials antiphonally *as sections,* an idea related to the baroque in principle but more closely allied with the nineteenth-century practice of giving equal status to strings and winds.

III: Menuetto (Allegretto). What to do with a minuet in the symphony was always a problem for late-eighteenth-century composers. As a dance form with rigid style requirements (form, meter, texture), it did not lend itself well to extended developmental techniques. Mozart's solution in this instance was to make the second strain of the minuet a miniature development of the first theme, turning this second strain into a display of his contrapuntal skills. First he added a countermelody above the first subject. Then he started a fugal development of the main subject, never going beyond a basic texture of two voices. The trio is a more relaxed section, using reduced orchestral forces and less complex treatments as well as a reduction of contrapuntal devices. From an orchestral standpoint the minuet is a more conservative setting than the other three movements due to the greater frequency of the doubling of string parts by the winds in the minuet.

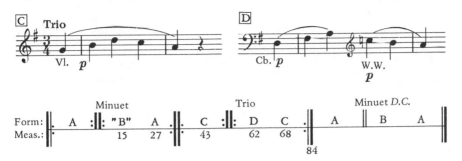

IV: Allegro assai. As an example of the use of dissonance to unify this work, the opening Mannheim rocket theme is an effective transporter of an appoggiatura that appears at the very top of the rocket's ascent. Like many previous melodic dissonances in this symphony, this pitch (and most which follow in the same contour and thematic location) resolves by half step. By measure 49 Mozart started a motivic development of the quarter-note pattern from the third measure of the first tune. This development is characterized by a swiftly running countermelody based on the eighth-note passages from the third measure. The rhythmic activity of this line continues through measure 68, making this development section of greater length than the expository section which presented the main theme. The next thirty measures present the subordinate material. The closing section is a return to the development idea of the first tune. The main development section is just as obscure tonally as was that of the first movement. Using a series of melodic intervals of diminished sevenths Mozart moved in a circle of fifths, implying the keys of C, G, D, and A without resolving any of the melodic sevenths (measures 125–34). This introductory passage leads to the development proper, where Mozart treated the first theme in another imitative sequential passage. The passage (measures 135–87) reversed the tonal order to A, D, G, C, and F, pausing to some extent in E-flat and c before retracing its steps through g, d, a, e, b, f-sharp, and c-sharp in an imitative and sequential fashion. Another sequence based on the same contrapuntal device and motive leads the work back via c-sharp, f-sharp, e, a, d, and g (measures 187–205). The recapitulation is orderly, covering all of the themes and materials from the first section. Orchestrally, this movement is similar to the first movement. Mozart relied on octave doubling in the violin section more in this work than in his earlier works. With winds assuming more of the harmonic support function, second violins have been assigned some of the main melodic thought with the first violins. At other times, especially in the velocity passages, both violins double at the unison; the violas and cellos do so less frequently.

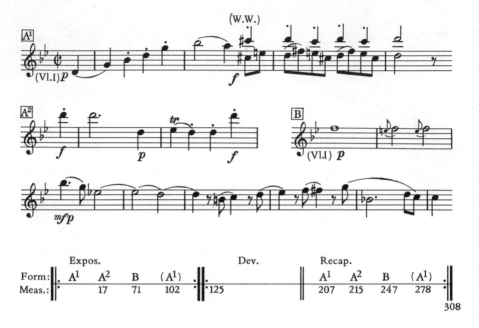

SUMMARY

Mozart's fortieth moves the classical symphony closer to the general musical frontier than do the Haydn London symphonies. Tonally, it presents chromatic and dissonant material that anticipates the nineteenth century. Always consistent in organizing his wandering tonal effects, Mozart generally sticks with fifth relationships for most of his tonal experimentation. In this particular work, dissonance is almost always handled with some kind of half-step resolution, keeping the basic sound of the work uniform throughout all four movements. This use of the minor second as the organizing sound for an entire work goes beyond the principles used by most nineteenth-century composers and anticipates twentieth-century musical principles. The process of immediate development of materials in an exposition section anticipates the nineteenth century and in particular the mature works of Beethoven. Unifying each movement with one or two motives is a refinement of the motive concept not seen until the late works of Beethoven. Orchestrally the works are quite mature, with winds on an almost equal footing with the strings. There is expressive scoring for strings. Some attempts at instrumental color are seen in doubling between individual wind and string lines. While the work has retained a great deal of the hustle and rush of the *style galant,* it is an excellent mixture of the Italian and German symphonic style, with the German learned style predominating.

Haydn's London Symphonies

In 1761 Haydn was employed as assistant Kapellmeister at the court of Prince Nikolaus Esterhazy at Eisenstadt. In 1766 he succeeded to the top position with the death of Gregorius Werner, the Kapellmeister. That same year the prince moved the court to a large castle being erected at Esterhaza (Estoras) near Oedenburg, Hungary. Though the prince had originally conceived of the Hungarian castle as a summer retreat, he soon began spending more and more time there each season and, at the same time, greatly expanded the musical activities and resources of the court. After Prince Nikolaus's death on September 28, 1790, his successor, Prince Anton, greatly reduced these activities and resources. Since Haydn's constant services were no longer needed, his position became nominal. The London impresario Johann Peter Salomon, traveling in Europe, heard the news and quickly persuaded Haydn to come to London to produce a series of new symphonies and symphony concerts. Haydn left Vienna on December 15, 1790, saying goodbye to his friend Mozart for the last time, and arrived at Dover on January 1, 1790. Mozart died on December 5, 1791, before Haydn could complete his work in London. In June, 1792, Haydn returned to Vienna. Between that time and the time of his next visit to London, he accepted Beethoven as his pupil, composed the six quartets of Opus 71 and Opus 74, completed Symphony No. 99, wrote portions of symphonies 100 and 101, and incurred the displeasure of Prince Anton for wanting to return to London. He left Vienna on January 19, 1794, arriving in London on February 4.

The twelve London symphonies were, in many respects, a summation of Haydn's entire symphonic output and style. Knowing that he had to respect the English taste, Haydn used a larger orchestra and employed more virtuosic writing. His fondness of folk tunes as themes was reflected in the English folk songs and street cries he included in some of these works. The symphonies are generally longer than his previous works. The formal patterns established by the composer for the external dimensions of the works remained fairly constant. First movements usually employ a slow introduction leading to a fast sonata-allegro main section. Nine are in duple meter and three in triple. Most second movements are cast in some type of variation form in either duple or triple meter; all are slow in tempo. Third movements are fast minuets. Second strains of both minuets and trios tend to be developmental. Most finales are a very brisk sonata-allegro or sonata-rondo; all are in duple meter. In the handling of movement forms and tonal relations within those movements Haydn, in many instances, avoids traditional patterns, especially in first movements. Some opening movements employ a dominant statement of the first theme as a substitute secondary theme (99, 100, 103, 104) with a clearly-defined closing theme following soon thereafter. Key choices for starting development sections emphasize mediant (97, 99, 100) or submediant (95, 96, 98, 104) keys. Four (93,

94, 102, 103) use plagal keys (ii or IV). Only one development (101) starts in the dominant key. Conversely, in the choice of an opening tune for each development section, Haydn is more tradition-bound; eight start with the principal theme.

Haydn's orchestra for the first set of six included: flute(s), oboes, bassoons, horns, trumpets, timpani, and strings. Numbers 95 and 98 used only one flute; otherwise, winds were in pairs. For the second set he used flutes, oboes, clarinets, bassoons, horns, trumpets, timpani, and strings. He omitted the clarinets in No. 102. In No. 100 (*Military*) he added triangle, cymbal, and bass drum to the second and fourth movements.

EXAMPLES FOR STUDY

*Haydn: Symphony No. 104 in D Major ("London") (1795)

The final symphony of Haydn's illustrious career is rather simple in style and structure. It also has a number of the style features that tend to distinguish Haydn from other eighteenth-century symphonists: a principal theme in the dominant key rather than a subordinate theme, variation-form second movement, slow introduction to the first movement, simple folklike melodies as primary tunes, and at least one appearance per symphony of a small woodwind concertino, usually in the recapitulation of a fast movement.

I:Adagio, Allegro.†   The slow introduction (in d minor) is organized completely around the basic dotted motive stated in the first measure. Haydn introduced an expressive nonchord tone in the third bar by having the melody enter using an appoggiatura figure, a device strikingly similar to the first motive in the opening of the Mozart Symphony No. 40 (g minor). The introduction develops this tune for the entirety of the section. The exposition presents in four bars a main theme with two motives which Haydn used extensively as the movement progressed. Two more parts of the theme follow, leading to a brief extension based on motives from the main tune. After a modulation to the dominant, Haydn restated the main theme as his subordinate tune. A closing tune which spins forward into a new setting of the first melody ends the exposition. The development from the outset uses the repeated quarter-note motive from measures 3 and 4 of the first theme, combining it with the theme's first two measures in two-voice counterpoint. As the section moved toward conclusion, Haydn added an eighth-note countermelody in the violins in opposition to the repeated-note motive. In the recapitulation Haydn restated the repetition of

---

† Double tempo markings indicate two divisions of the movement. In this case, the first indication, *adagio,* applies to the introduction of the movement. The *allegro* applies to the main body of the movement, which follows the introduction.

Information on Individual Symphonies

Number	Date	Intro.	I	II	III	IV
93	1791	yes	SA (Sonata-allegro)	Variation-rondo	Minuet	Sonata-allegro
94 (Surprise)	1791	yes	SA	Variation	Minuet	Sonata-rondo
95	1791	no	SA	Variation	Minuet	Sonata-rondo
96 (Miracle)	1791	yes	SA	Sonatina-variations	Minuet	Sonata-rondo
97	1792	yes	SA	Variation	Minuet	Sonata-rondo
98	1792	yes	SA	Sonatina	Minuet	Sonata-allegro
99	1793	yes	SA	SA-variation	Minuet	Sonata-rondo
100 (Military)	1794	yes	SA	Variation-rondo	Minuet	Sonata-allegro
101 (Clock)	1794	yes	SA	Variation	Minuet	Sonata-rondo
102	1794	yes	SA	A–A dev–A	Minuet	Sonata-rondo
103 (Drum Roll)	1795	yes	SA	Double variations	Minuet	Sonata-rondo
104 (London)	1795	yes	SA	Variation	Minuet	Sonata-allegro

the main theme in a small woodwind group, as was often his practice. He shortened the regrouping by moving quickly to a climax on the repeated-note motive in measure 228. His restatement of the main theme (in the subordinate theme's position) was also shortened and again used the woodwind concertino. A short coda substitutes for the closing section again using the repeated-note theme at the outset of the coda and then finishing with an extended cadence passage. Haydn's orchestral style is slightly more conservative than Mozart's. Using the winds for support and emphasis, Haydn tended to rely on more doubling at the unison on soprano lines, especially the flute and first violins. There are a number of passages where the woodwinds assume complete responsibility for thematic material.

Form:	Intro.	Expos.			Dev.	Recap.			Coda	
		A	A	B		A	A	B		
Meas.:		17	65	100	124	193	250	267	284	

294

II: Andante. The form of the slow movement is that of a series of three free variations. As the movement unfolds, elements of a rondo design are implied by the presence of new materials in some of the variations. The theme is in three parts, or, according to some authorities, rounded binary. The first variation, opening with a woodwind concertino stating the theme's first phrase in g minor, moves very quickly into materials which lack any obvious thematic connection with the theme except for the interval of the falling fifth. The second variation (in B-flat major) begins in the same way, presenting the first section of the theme and then starting a new variation. The third variation follows the same procedure but extends to include all parts of the theme. The form, unlike that of some variation movements, is not periodic.

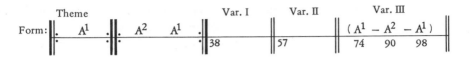

III: Menuetto (Allegro). Haydn, like Mozart, attempted to make the minuet stylistically compatible with development by changing the second section of both the minuet and the trio into developments of each section's main theme. In the minuet this development first uses superimposition of duple upon triple meter to intensify the contrapuntal effect and then employs melodic variation when the A theme returns at the end of the minuet. The second strain of the trio uses an eighth-note countermelody to vary the trio tune. As in other trios, instrumental forces are reduced, with the oboe and then the bassoon doubling the tune in the first violins for color. Other strings are pizzicato for the trio's first strain.

IV: Allegro spiritoso. This movement follows fairly closely the scheme of the first movement by withholding a subordinate theme at the proper instant and inserting a statement of the first theme in its place. Note that the version of the tune *with* its countermelody was used here. Haydn then developed a short scale motive from the main theme as he prepared for the real second theme ("B" in chart), presented in a quasi-imitative section based on motives from the main tune. In the development motives are combined in a freer contrapuntal texture. A little more extended statement of the second theme closes the section. The recapitulation is more brief than the opening section, with an extended coda added. This coda is more in the nature of a second development section, since it reworks the first motive from the first theme for about twenty measures. A final statement of A closes the movement.

* Used by permission of Universal Editions.

SUMMARY

This symphony provides an excellent example of the flexibility that Haydn employed in most of his symphonic movement forms. While the orchestral technique lacks some of the progressive features noted in the Mozart symphonies, it does represent a mature classical orchestral style. Haydn had somewhat simplified his overall symphonic style for the London visit while at the same time extending the length of each work and expanding the orchestra to include clarinets. Because of his accountability to his London public, Haydn avoided some of the expressive chromaticism and dissonance that attracted Mozart and worked in a fairly conservative style in all twelve symphonies. The relaxation of certain formal expectations for sonata-allegro and variation movements does show Haydn as a composer who tried to avoid the obvious and the stereotyped. The urge to develop material in places usually reserved for expository elements is also apparent in some of the movements. Like Mozart, Haydn attempted to make the minuet more developmental in style. Haydn's contribution to the history of the symphony is immense because he, almost alone, helped establish the mature classical symphony. His effort not only produced the end product, but also a large body of literature characterized by variety, experimentation, and musical excellence.

Comparing Haydn's earliest symphonies with his last twelve, composed some thirty-five years later, one notices not only a formal and orchestral maturation but also some indications of what lies ahead for the symphony in the ninteenth century. Haydn sums up much of his own symphonic style in the London symphonies by drawing upon a variety of formal treatments for individual movements, by establishing some balance between contrapuntal and homophonic treatments in development sections, and by including just about every instrumental device noted in previous symphonies.

IV

The Symphonies of Beethoven

Ludwig van Beethoven's (1770–1827) position in the history of the symphony is unique. Since his life span more or less bridged the classical and romantic periods, we might assume that his musical output was similarly transitional. However, it was much more than this. The conflicting influences of the two periods resulted in what could be considered the perfect symphony, a mark of the composer's character. As a classicist he handled musical forms with perfection while at the same time expanding and experimenting with these forms. As one of the first romanticists he infused many of his works with a depth of personal expression that rivals the expressive quality of the music of the nineteenth century. The architectural grandeur of the third, fifth, seventh, and ninth symphonies is equalled only by the expressive impact of each work. On the other hand, a true classical symphonic style can be clearly seen in the movements of the first, second, fourth, and eighth symphonies.

There is no argument as to how Beethoven contributed to the growth of the symphony. His expansionist tendencies created longer introductions, development sections, and codas. The coda itself became in some instances a second development section. He substituted the more easily developed scherzo for the less easily developed minuet. While the frequency of his use of variation form did not increase in his symphonies, the scope of the form broadened considerably in some of the symphony movements. Orchestral resources were also expanded with the addition of the trombone, piccolo, contrabassoon, and vocal-choral resources. Most important, however, was the highly articulated sense of formal structure that permeates many of the works. This one feature, more than anything else, points the way for subsequent symphony composers.

In what ways do the symphonies of Beethoven differ from the classical symphonies of Haydn and Mozart? From the standpoint of texture, the works have a heavier and denser sound brought about by the increased number of parts and a greater use of wind instruments. There is a compelling logic in the composer's progression of musical thought, created for the most part by the superb articulation of much of the thematic material and by the emphasis on repetition of materials at important breaks in the form. The range of the sound is wider because of the addition of such instruments as the piccolo and the contrabassoon and, more importantly, the expanding of the tessituras of the instruments already in use (e.g., lower bass instrument parts and higher soprano instrument parts). The flow of musical materials is often expanded by the composer's use of long and sustained passages where he has dwelt on one idea (either a theme, a chord, or a cadence progression) primarily. Contrapuntal passages are more extended than those by Haydn or Mozart. The handling of dynamics and tempos seems impulsive at times in comparison to that of the classicists.

Beethoven's melodic style encompasses two distinctively different melodic concepts: the broad and flowing tune (e.g., the main tune of the fifth symphony's second movement) and the motivic theme (that same symphony's main first-movement theme).

The composer's handling of rhythm and tempo is also imaginative. Rhythm is quite regular with an emphasis on syncopation or offbeat rhythmic devices. Beethoven apparently liked the offbeat echo effect achieved by having one orchestral choir answer another. There are fermatas that interrupt the rhythmic flow of some movements and tempo changes within movements. Rhythmic motives were an important part of the motive concept of the composer.

Beethoven's harmonic style represents a regression from the chromaticism of Mozart. Traditional chord progressions are simple and direct. One style feature persists: an overemphasis of harmonic materials at important breaks in the form; this can take the shape of a repeated cadence progression or a repeated chord. In this manner harmonic thought is used to emphasize formal outlines. In a similar way Beethoven liked to build a long and gradual crescendo over a single harmonic bass, usually a dominant pedal. His use of altered subdominant and supertonic harmonies has provided textbook examples of secondary dominant harmonies. His favored sonority, however, is the triad. His use of counterpoint is also broader than Mozart's. The thematic dimension is expanded by his two-dimensional tunes: a rhythmic tune with a lyric countermelody. Fugal imitation is a regular developmental device.

His formal contributions are immense. He practically invented the coda as a second development section. He sought to integrate entire movements and works with a single musical idea. His fondness for variation form has been mentioned, as has his substitution of the scherzo for the minuet. Beethoven immediately began to develop material as soon as it was introduced. His use of dynamics is much more significant in symphonic style than ever before. He favored not only abrupt changes in dynamics but also long and gradual crescendos. Beethoven seemed to consider the orchestra as having two choirs: string and wind. He scored frequent solos for clarinet, oboe, and bassoon (in the tenor register). He liked to use the horns for exposing new tunes. His octave doublings in the strings continued this preromantic trend, which had previously been used by both Mozart and Haydn.

In the nine symphonies there is a division of style into two different categories. Symphonies 1, 2, 4, and 8 closely adhere to the style norms of the classical symphony as represented by the mature works of Haydn and Mozart. These works are more concise, of smaller dimensions, and less expansive in the use of developmental principles. Symphonies 3, 5, 7, and 9 are of greater length, expressive import, and developmental complexity. The sixth symphony, the composer's sole program symphony, has the same extended dimensions of the more complex works but in its depiction of mood avoids the developmental and formal intricacies of that group.

During the twenty-five-year period in which the symphonies were written there are indications of a style maturation in both categories of works. While some elements of the mature Beethoven symphonic style are evident early in the period, the flow of musical ideas undergoes some changes, especially in developmental movements. A comparison of the first movements of the first and eighth symphonies shows two markedly different methods of moving from one major thematic group to another. In the earlier work the composer uses unrelated cadence and "filler" passages as a transition to the subordinate theme. The later work employs a primary motive from the principal thematic group in a similar transition; this motive subsequently continues as an undergirding for much of the subordinate section. The earlier work depends more on a steady rush of *style galant* rhythm to unify dissimilar thematic groups and transitions, while the eighth symphony uses actual thematic material for this synthesis. The same disparity exists between the first movements of the fifth and seventh symphonies but is expressed in an entirely different way. Both movements employ one primary unifying motive. The motive in the fifth symphony, however, is used as an "overlay" in some sections while other thematic matters are being pressed forward. The unifying motive in the seventh symphony, conversely, is used as the generating motive from which all materials are extracted. The contrast is more evident when the total effect of each movement is examined. The fifth symphony breaks down quite succinctly into the normal divisions of sections, contrasting themes, etc. The seventh is a work of much greater continuity, articulation, and synthesis because of its reliance on an ever-present generating motive.

If one were to isolate the single factor that probably contributed more than any other to the greatness of Beethoven's symphonies, he would have to select the composer's architectural-expressive line. By Beethoven's time it was no longer enough to construct a work so that it met certain formal expectations; the manner of composition must also unfold continuously, almost imperceptibly, and have an overpowering logic and expressive impact. In the more expansive symphonies Beethoven was able to accomplish this. By so doing he left a challenge to all composers who followed him. Few, as will be seen, had the ability to equal or surpass him.

Information on Individual Symphonies

No.	Date	Intro.	I	II	III	IV	V
1	1800	yes	SA	SA	Minuet	SA	
2	1802	yes	SA	SA	Scherzo	SA	
3	1804	no	SA	Song form w/trio	Scherzo	Variations	
4	1806	yes	SA	SA	Scherzo	SA	
5	1807	no	SA	Variations	Scherzo	SA	
6	1808	no	SA	SA	Scherzo	Free form	SA
7	1812	yes	SA	Variations w/trio	Scherzo	SA	
8	1812	no	SA	Sonatina	Minuet	SA	
9	1824	no	SA	Scherzo	Rondo w/variations	Sectional w/variations	

SYMPHONY NO. 1

The composer's first symphony is one of his more classically oriented symphonies. Scored for the classical orchestra of winds in pairs (including clarinets), the work conforms to the classical symphonic outline with the exception of its use of sonata-allegro form in its second movement, the appearance of a scherzolike minuet third movement, and the addition of a lengthy coda to the finale. The first movement also contains the first example of the composer's concept of a lyric slow introduction to a symphony's first movement. The exposition of the opening movement goes through the same multiple sectioning in each of its three thematic groups as would be seen in some of the mature Haydn and Mozart symphonies. Only the more clearly defined motivic structure of each subgroup immediately differentiates this new style from that of the other two composers. The conclusion of the development section also shows the composer's forceful manner of moving from one tonal era to another. Completing a half cadence in a minor (measure 171) on the unison pitch E, he quickly outlines the pitches of the dominant triad in C major in descending order and again in unison scoring and moves into the recapitulation (measure 178). The coda continues the development of the first theme for some dozen measures before launching into one of the composer's rhythmically offbeat orchestral passages (measures 271–77). The second movement, an *Andante*, exposes its first theme in a quasi-fugal exposition of four entrances. The return of this subject in the recapitulation is varied by the use of a countermelody to accompany each entrance of the tune (measures 100–116).

The third movement, labeled a minuet by Beethoven, is probably unique among the four movements. Its adjusting of the minuet style to that which more closely approximates a scherzo style is an early indication of the composer's plans for the symphony's third movement. The internal dimensions of the song form itself (A:‖:B A:‖) are distorted. Its first section (A) is only eight bars long; the second section (B) expands to thirty-six bars as a result of the motivic and tonal development of the B theme. The final statement of A is also expanded to thirty-five measures by the addition of a syncopated closing tune (measures 66–79). The trio also tends to develop its first tune in its second half rather than present a contrasting theme.

The finale generally reverts to an earlier and more conservative style. This is recalled by the horn fifths in measures 30–32 and the *style galant* similarity of the materials in the first thematic group. Only the contrapuntal development section clearly distinguishes the movement from most classical symphonies (measures 116–55). A coda works briefly on a scale motive drawn from the introduction of the finale before returning to the principal theme. A new tune in the coda (measure 266) begins in the horns and oboes to the accompaniment of this scale motive.

SYMPHONY NO. 2

This work uses the same instrumentation as that found in the first symphony. It emphasizes some sections of the wind instruments, an orchestral treatment that differs markedly from the wind color employed by both Haydn and Mozart. Much of the past melodic emphasis in wind sections had been assigned to flutes and oboes, with the oboe becoming the soprano member of the wind section. In the second symphony it is the clarinet that becomes an increasingly important solo woodwind instrument, at times more important and useful than the oboe. Frequent use of pairs of clarinets, doubled at the lower octave by a pair of bassoons, is characteristic of this symphony (first movement, measures 73–76; second movement, measures 25–32, 181–89). In another scoring, the bassoon and the clarinets provide a complete four-voice setting of an important phrase (second movement, measures 9–16). Solo writing for the bassoon and clarinet, doubled at the octave, is also noted (second movement, measures 87–89, 248–56; fourth movement, measures 32–37, 52–58, 216–19, and 340–42).

The symphony itself is a continuation of the Haydn-Mozart approach with very obvious Beethovian departures. Three of the movements are in sonata-allegro form (I, II, and IV). Finally, Beethoven added a scherzo and advertised it truthfully as that. The codas of the first and final movements are both longer than those corresponding movements in the first symphony.

The extensive coda for the finale is the beginning of a trend toward codas in many symphonies as the largest single sections in individual movements.

The first movement has a long introduction (thirty-three measures, *Adagio molto*) which calligraphically resembles the French overture (dotted rhythms, rapid scalelike embellishments, and trills and melodic ornaments), but which projects a much more mature and lyric style. Much of the treatment of the introduction is developmental in nature; imitation and counterpoint are quite important. The *Allegro* movement proper has the same sectioning of its principal materials into several parts as found in the expository style of Haydn and Mozart but with an increased emphasis on the motivic structure of each section or theme. As was the custom in the early classical symphony, the subordinate theme is presented by the clarinets and bassoons in a doubled-thirds passage. The exposition is also an interesting display of dynamic exploitation, with sforzando markings characterizing at least one primary thematic group (measures 86–95). Much of the subsequent development is contrapuntal, many of these passages having the same sequential organization as those designed by Mozart for his development sections. The concluding measures of the development (measures 196–205) have a rush of eighth notes in the bass line reminiscent of the *style galant*. This passage moves the tonal center of the section to f-sharp minor with its final cadence resting for three measures (212–14) on the dominant pitch C-sharp, which the composer then treats as the leading tone to the home key of D major. The recapitulation is orderly, leading to a sizable coda that further deals with the primary theme. This is speeding to its conclusion in another passage of almost Mozartian flavor (rushing eighth-note bass line, measured tremolo and repeated cadence figures, and harmonic formulas) when suddenly an abrupt change of style occurs (measure 354) as an extended passage of cadence repetition concludes the movement. This latter passage involves the echoing of materials between two orchestral choirs. Both the repetition device and the offbeat echo device become two of the most obvious style features in subsequent orchestral works. Such traces of the *style galant* noted in the coda are hard to come by in many of the works which follow.

The *Larghetto* second movement is another mixture of classical and Beethoven styles, with the latter's lyric and expressive elements getting the upper hand. While the first theme does not quite reach the broadness of later Beethoven melodies, it gives ample indications of an emerging melodic style quite different from that of Haydn and Mozart (see measures 1–30). The lyric emphasis of the movement also places the cello in a melodic-doubling role on the concluding theme, a tune which is more appropriately characterized as a mixture of both rococo and classic elements (with a nineteenth-century orchestral melodic doubling). A repetition of this particular doubling occurs in the recapitulation (measures 246–48).

After a concise statement of the first strain of the third movement Beethoven expands the second half of the scherzo proper beyond the dimensions associated with similarly expanded minuets of both Haydn and Mozart. Beethoven's expansion of the materials in this case is in the nature of both extension and development. The melodic materials he employs are almost monothematic, with the secondary scherzo melody being extracted from its first tune. The scherzo still retains the basic formal outline of the minuet (song form with trio), observing all of the structural repeats and da capos. With the absence of any thematic contrast in the scherzo, dynamic contrast becomes an important ingredient in the design of the primary materials of the movement.

The finale (*Allegro molto*) is a reaffirmation of the quickness and lightness of a typical classical finale. Formal sectioning of the first theme also occurs. Only the subordinate theme (measure 52) strives for a more lyric effect in its simple line and even simpler chordal accompaniment in the strings. The development section provides a rondo affectation by starting in the tonic key of D major, then moving very quickly to distant keys as the movement rushes onward. The same manner of modulation (from f-sharp minor to D major this time) occurs at the conclusion of the development section (measures 180–84), as was noted in the first movement (measures 171–78). The extended coda divides into three sections separated by fermatas that allow some regrouping of forces. The final section also uses a "vamp" (measures 338–57), probably derived from an earlier accompaniment figure associated with the subordinate theme. As before, the coda develops and extends materials from the exposition.

SYMPHONY NO. 3

The *Eroica* represents a change in the basic nature of the concert symphony, a change that markedly affected the history of the symphony perhaps more than any other single work. While Beethoven's two earlier works gave some indication of the nature of this change, it was the *Eroica* which established a style norm for his more expansive works. Whether or not Beethoven actually perfected the form of the symphony in the *Eroica* is not pertinent. What is important is that the *Eroica* and the fifth, seventh, and ninth symphonies crystallized a concept which has remained more or less intact to this date and thus became the single most influential group of symphonies in the history of the genre.

Several concepts seem to permeate the *Eroica* to a much greater extent than they did the first two symphonies. Thematic material has a greater motivic unity within movements and within groups of themes in a movement. This creates a more highly articulated and continuous style than was apparent in the first two symphonies. Motives are easily extracted for further unification of the work in developmental passages. There is also a greater emphasis on counterpoint and imitation to extend and to develop. This contrapuntal development becomes quite complicated, as the double fugue in the second movement exemplifies. All movements are much longer, largely because of extended development, even in codas. The adoption of a much more complex variation style as a movement form occurs in the third symphony. While Haydn used variation form for slow movements, Beethoven deemed the form appropriate for either slow or fast movements. The composer also was able to emphasize musical line in his works through the use of unifying motives, continuous development, and a sure and inevitable sense of harmonic progression.

The orchestral resources somehow sound larger in the *Eroica*. The actual expansion was quite modest: three French horns rather than two. Other factors probably cause this bigger sound: there is a frequent separation of the cello from the bass line, a use of double stops in accompaniment passages by the strings, and a doubling of wind parts at the octave. All of this thickens the orchestral effect and creates the impression of a larger orchestra.

The first movement is tightly constructed around several concise motives which lend themselves to frequent development even in the exposition. Counterpoint again becomes the primary treatment in the formal development section. In the heat of this development, a new theme is inserted (measure 284) in a distant key (e minor; original key, E-flat major). The recapitulation progresses through the required material, cadences in the tonic key, and then moves abruptly into D-flat major for the start of the coda (measure 557). This immense appendage (134 measures long) almost equals the length of the exposition (147 measures). Much of the coda is developmental; it even includes the new tune from the development section (measure 581).

The second movement, a funeral march (*Adagio assai*), is a song form with trio. It departs from this basic form in its return of an expanded song (normally a da capo in classical-style minuets); an elaborate fugal treatment occupies over a third of this returning section. A coda which starts with a deceptive resolution to A-flat major (tonic, c minor), actually starts in D-flat major, the Neapolitan key. This tonal area maintains considerable dominance throughout the coda.

The third movement, a true scherzo (*Allegro vivace*), is monothematic in the scherzo section, with the second portion of the scherzo being primarily developmental. The trio features three horns in an ensemble display which has forever endeared the work to brass aficionados. The written-out da capo of the scherzo is an exact repetition except for a single metric digression in which four measures of duple meter substitute for a syncopated passage in the original setting (measures 381–84).

The finale is a theme with ten variations. The theme itself adheres to the two-dimensional style noted also in the second movement of the Symphony No. 7. In both movements a rhythmic theme is established as the basic theme for the set of variations. In an early variation (third in the *Eroica,* first in the Seventh) a more lyric second theme appeared very much in the style of a countermelody. This lyric theme is then employed in each subsequent variation with some exceptions. The contrast between the rhythmic theme and its more lyric countermelody is marked. The rhythmic theme of the *Eroica* resembles a ground and is introduced as a single-line, unison theme (doubled at the octave) in the strings pizzicato. The variations differ in length; some of the earlier ones are only a single statement of the theme without an extension. In the sixth variation, a new theme overlays the basic theme (measures 211–55). Variations 4 and 8 are both fugal. The ninth variation (*Poco andante*, measure 348) is built primarily on the lyric countermelody introduced in the third variation. The tenth variation grows out of the ninth and very closely resembles it in style. It also uses the same lyric countermelody from variation three. As the ninth variation unfolds, some lovely new melodic lines in the solo woodwinds arise from the spinning out of this new lyric theme. The writing for woodwind ensemble is particularly expressive and effective in this variation and stresses the composer's excellent appraisal of the technical possibilities of the clarinet. An extended coda, involving an increase in tempo and some thematic relationship with the lyric theme, closes the movement.

SYMPHONY NO. 4

The fourth symphony returns to the more classical style of the first and second symphonies. Though it is much shorter than the *Eroica*, the fourth symphony still continues some of the expansive tendencies of the longer works. The symphony has the composer's first five-part scherzo:

SCHERZO — TRIO — SCHERZO — TRIO — SCHERZO

In addition, the first and fourth movements both have codas. The coda of the first movement, however, fails to develop or expand previous materials but merely emphasizes the harmonic basis of the final cadence, unifying itself with the movement proper by using a short figure taken from the transition to the recapitulation (see measures 337–39).

The opening movement has a slow introduction which sustains the tonic (b-flat minor) tonality and routes itself through B major before finally regaining its tonal bearings near the introduction's final half-cadence. The thematic materials of the introduction are related to the materials in the exposition through the motives based on chord outlines which appear in both sections. The exposition moves quite briskly through the first group of themes until it finds itself in d minor while working with the second group of themes. At this point a typical Beethoven device begins: a unison passage for purposes of modulation (see measures 121–32). This is further enhanced by a steady crescendo from pianissimo to forte.

The beginning of the development section is intriguing as it winds down the frenzy of the closing measures of the exposition by having the first tune restated on successively lower pitches (diatonic) until the tonal level of the development has been reached (see measures 189–200). A quick modulation from F major to D major leads to a working out of the first tune in D major with a new countermelody above it (measure 217). The development section continues to work with the first theme in a flexible tonal environment until the section begins to migrate homeward tonally via a grace-note-studded passage previously alluded to in measures 305–32.

The *Adagio* second movement is broader and more lyric than are the slow movements of the first and second symphonies, apparently reaching for the more noble cantabile style of the composer's later works. The emphasis on the woodwinds to carry much of the melodic material of the movement shows advances in orchestral writing beyond that in the scores of Haydn and Mozart. The woodwinds are used in over half of the exposition alone to state thematic materials. The development section, starting in the tonic key, embellishes the principal theme in the ornamental style associated with the early classical period. A great deal of emphasis is placed on short rhythmic motives associated with the accompaniment patterns of the first and second themes.

The scherzo continues the developmental concepts Beethoven adopted for many of his symphonies' third movements. The midsection of the scherzo proper moves into D-flat major (from the movement's tonic of B-flat major) for a tonal development of the main scherzo material. Both the trio and the scherzo are repeated in the da capo, with an abbreviated scherzo added to complete a five-part form. The woodwind section supplies most of the thematic materials of the trio.

The finale (*Allegro ma non troppo*) is closely aligned with the early classical style in its multisectioned thematic groupings. The movement also is reminiscent of the *style galant* with its incessant rush of sixteenth notes. The closing section (measures 70–100) is especially rococo. In the middle of this section (measure 88) a Beethovian countermelody spins out over the principal theme. The development section keeps the sixteenth-note motion fairly intact in a short expansion of previous material that takes on a certain pseudocontrapuntal aura, promising more than it delivers. Beethoven was very faithful to the air of informality and near frivolity that infects many finales in symphonies between 1750 and 1850. In the fourth symphony's finale, this off-the-cuff attitude is further compounded by starting the recapitulation with the solo bassoon playing the demanding principal theme with only a soft pizzicato accompaniment in the strings (measures 184–87). The work closes with the coda mentioned earlier. The symphony preserves the best of the Haydn and Mozart conceptions of the symphony and yet infuses just enough of the expansive style of Beethoven to maintain both stylistic integrity and individuality.

SYMPHONY NO. 5

This work is probably the best known of all symphonies. Its expressive nature, its formal conciseness, and its stirring finale have firmly established it as a favorite on American symphony programs.

Three concise themes, each developed immediately after presentation, comprise the essential materials of the exposition. The development section is probably one of the best examples of motivic development to be found in Beethoven's symphonies. Short motives are extracted and manipulated with a directness and a sense of formal line that literally propel the listener forward. So concise is the technique that the listener soon finds himself hearing single pitches echoed between contrasting sections as a part of the general thematic development (measures 210–27). A long coda completes the movement; it contains not only additional development of previous material but also the introduction and development of a new theme (measures 423–68).

The second movement (*Andante con moto*) is organized as a theme with a series of extended variations. The coda could be considered a final variation since it continues additional variation treatment while restating segments of previous variations. The true final variation that precedes this coda contains a marvelous, soaring passage with a canonic structure (measures 184–95), with the strings leading the woodwinds in an imitative format.

The scherzo section is in a modified five-part form which uses two contrasting themes very much as in the exposition of a first movement. Both themes are introduced separately, repeated or developed separately in the same order, and then grouped together for further development in the fifth section of the scherzo. The trio is divided roughly into three sections, all based on one single theme which is developed rigorously in all three sections. The scherzo returns in a varied instrumental setting (pizzicato strings). It is shortened considerably from its original length of 140 measures to an abbreviated 87 measures. A long transition (measures 324–73) uses the secondary motive from the scherzo to connect the third movement to the finale. This motive uses the same rhythmic pattern as that of the unifying motive from the first movement. The transition is also built over a sustained tonic pedal point in quarter notes in the timpani. The transition gradually increases in strength from triple piano (ppp) to fortissimo (ff) at the opening of the finale.

The finale (*Allegro*) has three main themes, the first or principal dividing itself into a number of subsections. The exposition of the finale, like that of the first movement, is repeated. As the development begins to work with the closing theme, a countermelody appears in the second violin and viola parts (measure 92). This countermelody becomes increasingly more important as the development progresses, reaching a striking climax at measure 142. At this point a quotation from the third movement is injected (measures 153–206) in order to return to the transition that opened the finale. Although shortened considerably, this transition serves as a bridge to the recapitulation. The coda (measure 295), using essentially the same passage as that which opened the development section, starts with more working out of the subordinate theme. This is followed (at measure 317) by a treatment of the second part of the principal theme (from measure 26, exposition). The coda accelerates its tempo to presto at measure 362, using the faster version of the opening two measures of the subordinate theme extracted from measure 64 of the exposition. At the height of the coda's frenzy the main tune returns (measure 390) and leads to the final cadence. This cadence is repeated and extended almost interminably (thirty-nine measures) before the movement concludes.

The orchestral resources in the work are expanded in the finale to include piccolo, three trombones, and contrabassoon. The trombones generally double the tenor wind and string parts. The contrabassoon plays along with the bass line. The piccolo, however, has several important sololike passages where its color and brilliance are an enhancement to the ensemble. Otherwise, the piccolo usually doubles the first flute in most tutti passages.

In its expressiveness, combined with the results of the composer's almost perfect grasp of formal matters, this symphony unites the best and most important features of both classic and romantic periods in a single work.

SYMPHONY NO. 6

This was Beethoven's best-known attempt at program music and his only program symphony which has survived in modern repertory. A *Battle Symphony*, arranged from an earlier work for the Panharmonicon, never drew any measurable audience support in spite of its liberal quotation of fanfares, battle sounds, and patriotic tunes.* The sixth symphony was a less depictive attempt to describe moods and surroundings of a country or pastoral scene. Each movement was subtitled by the composer:

    I   Cheerful Impressions on Arriving in the Country
    II   By the Brook
    III   Peasants' Merrymaking
    IV   The Storm
    V   The Shepherd's Hymn

Each of the movements is in a traditional form except for the fourth and is of extended length. The orchestration retains the use of two trombones and a single piccolo, which appear first in the fifth symphony. The work has a simplicity created by the extended repetition of many of its primary sections and by the conservative tonal plan in each movement.

The first movement is unified by a short melodic motive taken from the second measure of the first theme. The developmental section continues the emphasis on this motive but moves quite slowly through extended tonal blocks, some of which seem more Schubertian than Beethovian, particularly the key

---

* The Panharmonicon, invented by Johannes Maelzel of metronome fame, was a mechanical instrument designed to re-create or imitate the entire spectrum of orchestral sounds.

relations used in measures 150–210 (e.g., B-flat to D to G to E). The coda of the movement is as extended as other sections. Texturally, the work does not offer much in the way of counterpoint and, conversely, seems to emphasize parallel thirds when harmonizing the primary melodic line.

The second movement (*Andante molto mosso*) depicts its subject through a murmuring accompaniment in the strings which starts early in the movement (measure 5) and continues for much of the *Andante*. Orchestrally the work has some interest. Two solo cellos (muted) are used in addition to a regular section which usually doubles the bass line. Most of the time these two solo instruments noodle along with the murmuring. More interesting is the emphasis on the woodwinds, which carry much of the thematic material of the movement. The clarinet in particular has an extended passage quite idiomatic for the instrument (measures 69–83). The movement closes with a coda that contains solo passages for the flute, oboe, and clarinet, which imitate, respectively, the nightingale, the quail, and the cuckoo (measures 129–36), identified as such in the score by the composer.

The scherzo is devoid of the older repetition signs. The trio uses duple meter in contrast to the scherzo's triple. Though the score calls only for a simple da capo of the opening scherzo, most conductors insert both scherzo and trio repeats before an abbreviated scherzo concludes the movement. The work moves without pause into the storm movement, which itself shifts without delay into the finale.

Entitled "Happy, thankful feelings after the storm," the finale is the most pastoral of the symphony's movements; its primary theme is reminiscent of a shepherd's horn call. The principal materials dominate the movement to such an extent that, when brought back in the recapitulation, the primary theme is cast in the form of a melodic variation (measure 117). The coda continues the emphasis on the first theme.

SYMPHONY NO. 7

This work is discussed beginning on page 78.

SYMPHONY NO. 8

This work is discussed beginning on page 85.

SYMPHONY NO. 9

Beethoven's final symphony was his largest orchestral work. It required his largest orchestra plus four vocal soloists and a mixed chorus for the finale. Starting with a typical classical orchestra of winds in pairs and strings, he added piccolo, contrabassoon, two extra horns (four total), three trombones, triangle, cymbals, and bass drum. The four horns are used in all four movements, while the trombones appear only in the first, second, and fourth movements. The additional percussion instruments are used only in the fourth movement's coda. The scoring for the four horns generally involves two pitches with each pitch doubled at the octave. In many passages only two horns are active (either first and third or second and fourth). Where full scoring occurs, voicing is a traditional four-part setting with one horn doubling another at the octave. This octave, rather than unison, doubling makes for a fuller sound from the section. Only in rare instances does a four-voice chord settle into the horns (first movement, measures 435–52). The presence of two trumpets, four horns, and three trombones does much to increase the mass of orchestral sound. This particular distribution of brass instruments was to become the standard brass section for many nineteenth-century symphonies.

This symphony is also longer than any that precede it. Using the metronome markings indicated by the composer, the work would take over an hour in performance. Modern performances may exceed that by another ten minutes.

The work has some new or expansive features. Most obvious is its choral finale employing sections of a poem by Friedrich von Schiller (1759–1805), "Ode to Joy." The translated text used in the finale is available in several sources.* The finale is a large set of variations in which several stanzas of the Schiller ode are employed, each stanza generally coordinated with an individual variation. The scherzo section of the second movement is expanded to such an extent that it very closely approximates sonata-allegro form. The ensuing trio shifts into a duple meter from the scherzo's triple. The interesting overall effect is the composer's expansion not only of the symphonic form to include noninstrumental resources and vocal and choral forms but also of the individual movements of the symphony to a much larger size and scope than seen previously. Though public and professional opinion of the work was somewhat mixed,† history has shown it to be one of the strongest catalysts in the growth of the concert symphony from a purely instrumental experience to one which embraced a variety of noninstrumental resources.

The first movement (*Allegro, ma non troppo, un poco maestoso*), though tightly organized around a single theme (and its unifying motive) announced early in the work, still presents a large number of themes for the various sections of the three main thematic groups. Several rhythmic motives (including the previously mentioned unifying motive) help to bind the work together. The development section opens in a manner similar to that of the exposition

---

* See Robert Bagar and Louis Biancolli, *The Complete Guide to Orchestral Music* (New York: Grosset & Dunlap, 1947), pp. 51–52; and Earl V. Moore and Theodore E. Heger, *The Symphony and the Symphonic Poem* (Ann Arbor: Ulrich's Books, Inc., 1974), pp. 46–47.

† For a glimpse of the reaction to early performance of the ninth symphony, see Nicholas Slonimsky, *Lexicon of Musical Invective* (New York: Coleman-Ross, 1953), pp. 44–52.

with an introductory passage to be discussed below. A new theme intrudes in the early part of the development (measures 192–95), probably derived from a scale fragment in the principal theme (see measure 19). Contrapuntal textures are typical of the development and generally embrace both fugal and counter-melody textures. The recapitulation is also prefaced by the same introductory passage, which opens each main section of the movement. It is a type of intro-ductory passage quite unlike others in previous symphony history. First, a tempo or key change does not occur between introduction and exposition. Second, the introduction is related motivically to the main theme of the move-ment. Third, it seems to be inseparable from the first statement of the main theme. An extended coda (120 measures long) continues the development of several of the movement's themes. It is difficult to compare this movement with other first movements, since in its multiplicity of themes and motives it differs markedly from many of them. The treatment of these themes, however, is indeed similar to that of the other movements. In this abundancy of materials it anticipates some of the Mahler first movements.

The second movement, a scherzo, was Beethoven's final symphonic solu-tion to the problem of a workable developmental form for a traditional minuet-style movement. In the works of Haydn and Mozart, development gradually intruded, displacing the contrasting theme often found after the first double bar in the minuet. Beethoven, by his second symphony, had discarded the rigid style of the minuet for the nonprecedential form of the scherzo. Gradually each scherzo became more and more developmental, especially the scherzo move-ments in the third, fifth, seventh, and ninth symphonies. Often single themes or motives unify each scherzo, with any contrast left to the trio to inject. Only the scherzo of the fifth gives an inkling of what the possibilities might be if development were to become the basic thrust of the scherzo. Finally, in the ninth symphony the composer expands the scherzo to embrace the outer shape of sonata-allegro form and introduces two contrasting themes (second theme, measure 93), as would be required in that developmental form. After the double bar of the ninth's scherzo, a true development of the first tune occurs. The return of the first section (as in the old rounded binary of the minuet) then takes the shape of a recapitulation with both themes present. The sub-ordinate theme returns in the tonic key (d minor) in contrast to its original setting in C major in the exposition. The trio changes to duple meter and works primarily with two themes of scalar dimensions. A short coda, added after the da capo of the scherzo, regroups the main themes of both scherzo and trio. One additional interesting twist can be noted in the use of the timpani as a motivic soloist in the development of the scherzo (measures 195–204 and other subse-quent measures in this section).

The third movement, a slow *Adagio*, is in a modified rondo (A–B–A–B–A–A–coda), with each return of the first section modified in the style of a variation. As in some other slow movements, the woodwind section is employed extensively in the playing of primary melodic materials. The first tune is a broad, singing tune which has its expressive quality enhanced by judicious use of dissonance. The B theme is constructed over a dominant pedal, this enhancing considerably its musical line. At each return of the main theme, a variation of the melody begins. A coda concludes the movement. It also continues the variation of the first tune. The movement is probably the composer's noblest slow movement. It is difficult to identify a more impressive series of melodic ornamentations.

The finale is also unified by the variation principle. A long introduction which contains, among other things, an instrumental recitative for the bass strings, regroups segments of main themes from previous movements. The main theme eventually begins in the lower strings, unaccompanied. The movement progresses through a tutti statement and returns to the introductory materials, at which time solo vocal and choral resources are introduced. This introduction starts with a dissonant sonority that increases in complexity with each repetition, starting with a d minor triad with an added sixth (D-F-A+B-flat) in the first measure and concluding with a seven-pitch chord that contains all of the pitches of the minor scale (D, E, F, G, A, B-flat, C-sharp) in measure 208.

The structure of the vocal sections of the movement correlates with the individual stanzas or parts of stanzas of the poem. The opening section (measures 1–207) introduces the main theme of the movement and the recitative materials, both later used with text. The composer used only about one-third of the poem's original ninety-six lines; they do not necessarily follow the original order of the poem.

The ode gives an almost religious connotation to joy, a joy that can be found in all of nature, unifies the universe, and binds all mankind together, a joy that is part of the behavior of all living creatures and can make men almost Godlike in its emphasis on generosity and charity, producing noble and lofty actions. The stanza that dwells on the power of joy to unite mankind and the stanza that elevates joy to a Godlike virtue dominate much of the latter part of the movement.

The variations begin in the instrumental version of the main theme and continue throughout the movement. Larger divisions of the form can be noted. Variations 7 and 8 (measures 331–594) are in the style of a march. An instrumental interlude, quite a bit of it in fugal style, separates the two variations. A new theme creates another broad section (measures 595–654) and relates to the style of the opening recitative. What would be the ninth variation (measures 655–762) is a double fugue that uses the text of two stanzas simultaneously. A long coda (measures 763–940) contains a vocal quartet section dealing with one of the opening stanzas and a choral section in another setting of an earlier stanza.

As a final work in a series of nine symphonies which bridge the gap between the classical and romantic periods in music history, the ninth symphony remains a remarkable departure from the almost simple beginnings of the first symphony by Beethoven. As in other works from the last creative period in the composer's output, there is a concept of stylistic expansion which means more than just creating bigger and longer works. In the case of the ninth symphony, inner dimensions of the form of the symphony are expanded to include what could be called the process of continuous development, wherein the returning segment of a rondo form undergoes constant variation in each successive appearance. A scherzo expands in its search for an ultimate developmental form to become, in truth, a mini-sonata-allegro form. The materials of a very traditional first-movement form are expanded to include a multitude of short motives, each well articulated in a fairly continuous sonata-allegro first movement. Finally, a concluding movement returns to one of the favorite forms of the composer (variation) in a very free application of the principle using an expanded conception of symphonic resources: orchestra, chorus, mixed vocal quartet, and vocal soloists. The work is an eloquent contribution to the history of the symphony.

EXAMPLES FOR STUDY

Beethoven: *Symphony No. 7 in A Major, Op. 92 (1812)*

The work is scored for flutes, oboes, clarinets, bassoons, horn and trumpets in pairs, timpani, and strings. Cello and contrabass have separate staves in the score.

     I: Poco sostenuto, Vivace.   In an introduction of sixty-one measures the work exhibits how far the composer's style had progressed since the writing of the first symphony's introduction in 1800. The preface has been expanded not only to include two main themes but also to contain a development of each group. The first theme has two components: a slowly moving main theme based on an arpeggiation of the A-major chord and a faster moving ascending scale passage in sixteenth notes. The second theme is formed with concise motivic unity. After both themes are presented, brief developments follow. The introduction ends on the dominant scale degree, E. At this point (measure 57), Beethoven extracts the unifying motive of the main *Vivace* section in an eight-measure passage which connects the introduction to the exposition without pause. As mentioned earlier, the exposition is a display of synthesis and formal unity achieved through the use of a single generating (and unifying) motive which has just been evolved in the introduction. Two themes constitute the primary group, both exposed by the woodwinds and then developed by a long orchestral tutti. The bipartite secondary section moves through an impressive array of tonal areas (c-sharp minor, a-flat minor, and E major) before being displaced by the closing section. After the latter section closes on a unison cadence in C major (measure 141), a lengthy development of the opening tune ensues. Mention should be made of internal matters in the exposition: the composer's imitative and contrary-motion techniques in the tutti development of the first tune (measures 97–109), the sixteenth-note scalar countermelody which accompanies the B^2 theme (measures 120–23), the short bass motive which enhances the contrapuntal effect of the concluding development passage (measures 142–51), and the final contrapuntal section of the exposition (measures 164–70).

The development has a complex contrapuntal structure throughout the section. *Forte* or *fortissimo* interjections of the unifying rhythmic motive (harmonized usually in full orchestra or winds) provide an element of contrast to the involved contrapuntal procedures. The development never states the main theme in its entirety, quite a contrast to many development sections of other classical symphonies. Fugal entries which start in measure 185 and 222 use only the first four pitches of the unifying motive. Beethoven reversed the sequence of events in the recapitulation section by having the principal theme return in the full orchestra *fortissimo* (rather than *piano* in the woodwinds as in the exposition) and then turned to the woodwinds in measure 300 for a further development of the materials. This then leads to the subordinate section, which returns in a minor to remain consistent with its minor mode in the exposition.

The coda moves quickly from A to A-flat in a unison modulation and then (measure 401) starts another long crescendo pedal passage like that which connects the final two movements of the fifth symphony. The twenty-one-bar passage has a two-measure ground bass in the lower strings, a pedal E in the winds, and an embellishment of the pedal in the violins. Two different rhythmic lines are superimposed; both are from the unifying theme. The harmony is a simple, two-measure, tonic-dominant progression. The movement ends with a section based on the climactic materials which ended the exposition. Two developmental devices emerge in addition to those which create a contrapuntal texture: Beethoven energized a long harmonic passage with the rhythm of the unifying motive in order to enhance the building of a climax; he also extracted short excerpts from the motive to use as melodic unifying devices in the development. This was consistent with his concept of a melodic section's having not only a melodic (or lyric) dimension but also a rhythmic dimension and it seems to have carried over into his developmental style.

Form: ‖ ① ②–Dev.—③–Dev. ‖: A^1 A^2 Dev. B^1 B^2 C A^1 Dev. :‖ Dev.

Intro.
10   23   63 75   110 119 130 142   177

Recap.
‖ A^1 A^2–Dev. B^1 B^2 C A^1 Dev. ‖ Coda A^1 Dev. ‖
278 309   324 331 342 354   391
450

II: Allegretto. This movement is a hybrid blending of variation form and song form with trio. The overall effect is of a five-part form with two appearances of the trio interjected among the variations of the main theme. Vari-

ation 1 (measure 27) introduces a lyric countermelody aspect of the theme
which then becomes part of variations that follow. Each subsequent variation
generally brings both tunes (i.e., the rhythmic counterpart and the lyric aspect)
into play, with one exception (variation 5). The fifth variation is a fughetta on
the rhythmic theme. The final coda is based on the rhythmic theme alone. As
in the first movement, Beethoven depended a great deal on contrapuntal devices
to sustain interest in the movement. The one variation which omits the lyric
tune inserts a counterpoint that functions as a countermelody in some respects.
The trio keeps the basic rhythm of the rhythmic theme alive by repeating it in
the bass line as a rhythmic ostinato.

III: Presto. This is a scherzo in five-part form. Each statement of the
scherzo theme is followed by a lengthy development of the theme. Even what
appears to be a return of the scherzo tune after some development (as would be
expected in song form) turns out to be another extended development of the

theme. The trio does introduce two themes rather than one, as in the scherzo, but is unified by the use of a dominant pedal beneath the entire section. The scherzo returns as stated in the first part of the movement. The return of the trio is also identical with its first appearance. The final scherzo is as before.

IV: Allegro con brio. Beethoven was faced with the problem of designing a finale which could approximate the typical dance character of a fourth movement in spite of the existence of two earlier movements with overall dance styles (movements 1 and 3). His solution was similar to that achieved by composers before him: make the movement less learned (in this case, less contrapuntal) so that it could contrast specifically with the complex first movement. He also relaxed the rigid single-motive style of the opening movement by employing no less than eight motives in the themes of the finale. The resulting melodic material has a highly motivic structure within each small section but departs from the concept of an all-embracing unifying motive by moving from one section to another without carrying forward any common motivic materials. The A[4] motive also presents a section in which free imitation of its theme occurs (measures 36–51). Again Beethoven wrote a transition to a secondary group which anticipated the motive of this new section (measures 52–62). The closing section reverts to the style of the middle-period Haydn symphonies, in which closing sections were based on harmonic progressions rather than on pertinent melodic materials. There is an accompanying sixteenth-note scale motive in the second violins and violas (measure 114) which has a remote connection with the principal theme, A[2].

The beginning of the development section is reminiscent of older preclassical practices in its almost verbatim restating of the principal theme in a series of tonal areas (F major, C major, etc.). Repeat signs for the exposition are also used. A two-note bass motive which accents the second half of each measure has been an important aspect of this part of the principal theme and becomes more important in the development section. At measure 162 a long winding down of the intensity of the movement begins using this bass motive and the A[1] motive. The recapitulation starts exactly as did the exposition. The materials reappear in their original order and context except for tonal considerations. A coda starts a second development which is more contrapuntal than the original development section and which involves the use of several ground motives in the bass line. This section builds toward a climax for another tutti statement of the A[3] theme, the material of which sustains much of the final section of the movement. The final fifteen bars return to a portion of the first tune; the last two bars are a slight modification of the first two bars of the finale, giving the work a slightly arched form.

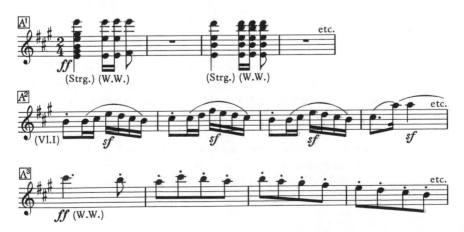

The orchestral style of the seventh symphony shows that Beethoven thought very clearly in terms of two orchestral choirs: strings and winds. From the wind choir he extracted a unified woodwind group which he used as a separate choir in many sections of the symphony. Brass writing is not as unified, probably because of the limited number of brass parts (only four). The horns quite frequently join the woodwinds to create a third wind choir. This latter wind choir distinction is noted especially in the first, third, and fourth movements. The woodwinds comprise the basic wind choir in the second movement. The trumpet is used primarily for rhythmic emphasis especially in the first movement, where the exactness of brass tonguing can emphasize the essentially rhythmic nature of the unifying motive.

The string writing shows an independent viola part (independent of the bass line, that is); separate lines for the cello and bass in some instances; not too much octave doubling of parts (note viola doubling second violin, measures 189–94, first movement; and viola doubling first violin, measures 201–216, first movement), except for passages requiring a crescendo to a climax (return to recapitulation, first movement, measures 262–77); and a decrease in the amount of measured tremolo assigned to strings to fill in harmony parts.

Timpani are used to assume some of the role which brass instruments had assumed in the classical symphony: to reinforce accents, emphasize cadences, and supply roots in cadence progressions. Beethoven also used rolls on the timpani to help build crescendo passages and to sustain *fortissimo* effects. In the first and last movements Beethoven also found the timpani useful in emphasizing basic rhythmic motives in *forte* and *fortissimo* passages. There is one subtle timpani solo (first movement, measures 315–19) in which the timpani plays *pianissimo*, supplying the only version of the unifying motive in the orchestra as the woodwinds continue the development of the principal material early in the recapitulation section.

SUMMARY

Conceived within classical dimensions, the symphony under Beethoven expanded in scope and expression. His seventh symphony represents a considerable advancement in those two directions. His emphasis in this symphony on the learned aspect of classicism as well as on enlarging the formal dimensions while deepening the affective sector is a refreshing combination of the old and the new. The first movement in particular shows a work almost continuous in nature, a feature of style which is more appropriately a late-nineteenth-century feature. The variation-oriented second movement shows the two-dimensional thematic skills that pervade many of Beethoven's works. Under Beethoven, the scherzo is basically a developmental form, as the scherzo of the seventh symphony demonstrates. The finale, supposedly another dancelike movement in the scheme of the classical symphony, shows how Beethoven respected this convention and yet still expanded the treatment of the finale with an extended coda that continued the development of the materials of the exposition. Overall, the symphony is a testament to the composer's contrapuntal skills, coming at a time when counterpoint was diminishing as an integral part of musical style.

Beethoven: *Symphony No. 8 in F Major, Op. 93 (1812)*

This symphony and symphonies 1, 2, and 4 comprise a grouping of symphonies that are individually shorter in length, less expansive and overly expressive, and more closely allied with the style expectations of the traditional eighteenth-century symphony. As noted above, symphonies in this grouping do show a maturing of the composer's symphonic style, especially in the articulation of formal elements within a single movement. The eighth symphony is Beethoven's final contribution in this style grouping and should represent a unique tempering of the composer's expansionist tendencies.

I: Allegro vivace e con brio.   The opening section of this movement has been briefly discussed earlier. The movement opens with an extended tutti statement and development of the principal theme's two sections. The first two pitches of the A^1 theme tend to dominate much of the thematic material of the movement, with the interval of a third and its inversion (sixth) cropping up in a variety of places. As in the seventh symphony's opening movement, that of the eighth also employs two keys (consecutive) for the exposition of the secondary theme (D major, C major). The second portion of the secondary material (B^2) is a vague and contrapuntal manipulation of diminished sonorities. As the exposition moves through the closing section, a motive is extracted from a woodwind passage (measures 93–95) which becomes the final cadence figure and the unifying motive for the first half of the development section. Most of this first half is an antiphonal treatment of the first tune. The second half (measures 144–89) is a fugal development of this first tune which includes a strettolike section (measures 167–79) between first violins and basses. This moves the work back to the recapitulation, where the bass part carries the main tune. The final section shortens some of the earlier development of the first theme but otherwise presents most of the themes as before. The coda (seventy-two measures long) continues more development of the first themes, starting in D-flat major and in its opening section working imitatively with the first theme. The final cadence is prolonged for sixteen bars as the wind and string choirs echo the final chord and then close very quietly with a statement of the first measure of the first tune.

II: Allegretto scherzando. Again reverting to one of the favored second-movement forms of the early classical symphonists, Beethoven creates a sonatina outline by adjusting the tonal scheme of the older binary form. The movement is organized around three groups of themes with an exposition and a recapitulation, the latter involving some melodic variation of the first section's themes. A motive from the first theme (first three pitches of A, below) is used as a unifying device in accompaniments, counterpoints, or rhythmic figures. This is similar to the use of the unifying motive in the first movement of the fifth symphony. The scoring is interesting: the winds provide a repeated-note harmonic accompaniment for the first and second themes, a reversal of the orchestral roles observed in some classical symphonies. There is some variation of these tunes in the second half of the movement. A coda briefly treats a part of the first theme in diminution as the movement closes on a *fortissimo* B-flat unison in sixty-fourth-note measured tremolo.

Form:	A	B	C	A (Dev.)	B	C	Coda
Keys:	I	V	V	I	I	I	
Meas.:		20	30	41	50	63	73

III: Tempo di Menuetto. Rather than use the freer form of the scherzo for the third movement, Beethoven returned to the older minuet but did not abandon his concept of the third movement's having a developmental dimension. The theme of the minuet seems to be more lyric in style, lacking some of the strong rhythmic organization of scherzo tunes. The second section of the minuet develops the opening theme both imitatively and antiphonally, returning to a full statement of the theme in the solo bassoon (measure 24). A concluding theme which sounds like a fanfare is extracted from the minuet theme (measure 36). The trio's scoring stresses solo clarinet and horns. The cellos have a constant acompaniment figure of arpeggiated chords in triplets throughout the entire trio. The second section of the trio is also developmental, taking the section to A-flat major (tonic = F major) for a brief instant.

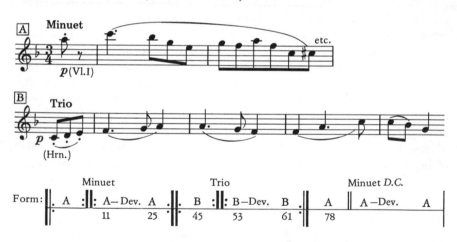

Form:		Minuet			Trio			Minuet *D.C.*	
	A	A—Dev.	A	B	B—Dev.	B	A	A—Dev.	A
		11	25	45	53	61	78		

IV: Allegro vivace. Beethoven organized a rather complex finale in a hybrid sonata-rondo with the usual motivic unity, contrapuntal development, and extended coda. As the exposition presents the first two portions of the principal theme (A^1, A^2) a real note of mystery is sounded. In measure 17 the orchestra suddenly pounces on the pitch C-sharp, holding it for the value of a full measure, and then quickly jumps back into a second statement of the first tune, again in F major, the movement's tonic key. The pitch is neither prepared for nor resolved when first heard. One must wait until the coda for the puzzle to be explained. Beethoven introduces the third part of the principal theme (A³) in measure 28 and then proceeds to develop it using inverted stretto imitation. The subordinate tune is stated first in A-flat major and then in C major. The work returns to F major in preparation for the return of the first tune at the beginning of the development section. By measure 110 the composer has started a fugato on the A² tune. The subject is then inverted in what becomes one of the better fugal developments in Beethoven's symphonies.

By measure 150 the movement is nearing the recapitulation section, which will be stated as presented in the exposition, complete with the mysterious C-sharp. Just before the recapitulation begins, the movement moves into A major, where the melodic pitch C-sharp is emphasized in a statement of the first theme (measures 151–55). A quick (and blunt) modulation, consisting of two measures of octave leaps on E followed by four measures of the same leap on F, ushers in the recapitulation. The brief episode in A major conditions the ear for what will happen with relation to the C-sharp in the coda.

The long coda starts at measure 267 and leads to a fugue on a new theme (theme D), which gradually returns to a statement of the main theme in D major (measure 345). Continued development of the theme in other keys leads to a reappearance of the C-sharp, this time qualified fully as the dominant of the f-sharp minor tonality in which Beethoven developed the theme. As previously mentioned, the work quickly returns to the tonic key and works with other main themes before coming to a final close. The coda in some ways combines the features of a development and a recapitulation. It covers all of the themes except the closing melody. It also introduces a new theme (D) as the subject of an extensive development (measures 282–329), using some of the motivic interplay found in the development section. It also clarifies the mysterious C-sharp by using the pitch as the dominant preface (measures 376–78) for a statement of the opening theme in F-sharp minor (measures 380–90). After this lengthy second working out of the first theme, the subordinate theme reappears as if a part of a recapitulation. Starting with measure 438, the coda begins one of the composer's most long-winded closing formulas: sixty-four measures of finality. From measure 450 to the last, a pedal F is always being sounded. There are six consecutive authentic cadences (measures 483–90) plus fourteen repetitions of the final tonic chord (measures 492–502). It is either the best or the worst example of this device in the symphonies.

The orchestral style is similar to that used in the seventh symphony, with the woodwinds and horns frequently being grouped as the main wind choir. The scoring of the subordinate section in the first movement (measures 234–48) is an interesting study in doubling. The violin I and the viola carry the tune an octave apart. Cello, bass, and second violins sustain a harmonic background with pizzicato. Clarinet and bassoon (at the octave) supply a countermelody in quarter notes. This system of doubling is then reversed for the repetition of the section (woodwinds on the tune, an octave apart, etc.). In general there is more use of measured tremolo in the violins in the first movement, a reversion to classical devices which originated in the rococo.

SUMMARY

This work was the last of the more conservative, classically oriented group of symphonies by Beethoven. Despite the composer's effort to write a work with smaller external dimensions, the eighth symphony has many of the traits of the more expansive symphonies. Both first and last movements have codas, the finale's being much longer than that of either the exposition or development sections. The second movement economizes with the symphony's length by using a faster tempo and employing an abbreviated sonatina form. The minuet is in three-part form rather than five-part. Repeats are omitted in the last movement. As in the seventh symphony, Beethoven made good use of contrapuntal textures in both development sections and codas. Some imitation was also used in the second movement. The only compromises with general symphonic style, then, seem to have been the overall shortening of some of the movements, the use of a faster tempo in the second movement, and a return to the three-part minuet in the third movement.

V

The Nineteenth-Century Symphony

The Romantic Period

The nineteenth century has been called the Age of the Romantic. Romanticism emphasized the dignity of the individual and the freedom of the emotions, and minimized formal considerations for a more subjective approach to all art. It was this last aspect which in some ways threatened the growth of the symphony, though at the same time it was also responsible for some of the most appealing orchestral music of the century. The genre as an orchestral expression of a reasoned and logical unfolding of a complex music form seemed somewhat inappropriate for a broad expressive manifestation of the romantic spirit.

Musically, romanticism deeply affected composers who sought to give personal expression to their own art. In melody there was new interest in lyricism and expression, the latter often obtained by an increased use of melodic dissonance. Expressiveness also led to greater harmonic and tonal freedom. Tonal chromaticism reached a high point in the works of Wagner. All composers in one way or another began to express themselves more freely in the handling of tonality: they began to write works that modulated not only to related keys such as the dominant but to any key and/or mode of the composer's choice. Rigid and stylized contrapuntal procedures almost disappeared. Counterpoint, however, continued to thrive in a freer style, since through it the lyric dimension was often emphasized even more, as seen in Berlioz's and Tchaikovsky's combining of tunes in countermelody style.

Romanticism gave rise to more musical forms, especially small forms for solo piano and for the voice or new forms like the symphonic poem or music drama. At the same time there was less emphasis on the intricate inner organization of works and more emphasis on the freely spun-out quality of an unfettered lyricism. The great geniuses of the period could achieve this marvelous unrestrained quality while at the same time employing highly subtle motivic organization more complex than that found in the most involved scores by Beethoven.

Above all it was a period of colorful writing for the orchestra, which became the most expressive musical force of the century next to the human voice. It was also a great period for the community of the arts. Musicians, poets, painters, and dramatists shared experiences through a kind of cross-fertilization that encouraged the creation of literary-dramatic forms such as the *lied* and the symphonic poem and carried the development of opera to its most expressive and dramatic heights. Sometimes this trend bordered on the ridiculous, as when a composer provided as many different stories for his symphony as the public required or even created the story of his work long after the work had been completed.

The Symphony

After the death of Beethoven, the development of the symphony took two courses. In one, composers attempted to sustain the more traditional concept of the symphony, continuing the line of development which led from Haydn and Mozart through the less expansive works of Beethoven. The other route, which seemed to have been based on the more expressive and expansive of the Beethoven works (especially the sixth and ninth symphonies), led from Beethoven to Berlioz, Liszt, Smetana, Strauss, Mahler, and other composers who sought to expand both the scope and the expressive qualities of the symphony. From this second line of development came program music, the symphonic poem, the program symphony, and a group of massive works which employed choral and vocal resources in an attempt to bridge the gap between large orchestral forms and large choral and dramatic forms.

The symphony after 1840 did not appear to enjoy the same popularity it had in the eighteenth and early nineteenth centuries. Major composers wrote increasingly fewer symphonies. Some of the most gifted never approached the form after their student days. Chamber music suffered a much greater decline, possibly because of its essentially absolute nature. The orchestra, however, prospered in other ways. Alfred Einstein, in his writings on the period,* described instrumental music as a powerful force capable of expressing what words could not, a conception which most romantic composers held. Thus one finds that the most expressive forms of the period (lieder, opera, and program music) all required the thoughtful and imaginative undergirding by an instrumental sound to accomplish their individual purpose. There can be no doubt of the

---

* Alfred Einstein, *Music in the Romantic Era* (New York: W. W. Norton & Company, Inc., 1947), pp. 32–33, 140. Used by permission of W. W. Norton & Co., Inc.

Am Sonntag den 27. November 1842

Mittags um halb 1 Uhr präcis

wird das sammtliche

Orchester-Personal

des k. k. Hof-Operntheaters,

unter Leitung des Herrn Kapellmeisters

Otto Nicolai,

im k. k. großen Redouten-Saale

das zweite

Philharmonische
CONCERT

folgenden Inhalts zu geben die Ehre haben.

Erste Abtheilung.

1. **Symphonie** in G-moll, von **W. A. Mozart.**

2. **Arie** „Du schöner Stern," aus der Cantate: Das befreite Deutschland, von **L. Spohr,** gesungen von Herrn **J. Staudigl.**

3. **Arie** „Fest wie Felsen ꝛc." aus der Oper: Cosi fan tutte, von **B. A. Mozart,** gesungen von Frau van **Hasselt-Barth.**

Zweite Abtheilung.

4. **Concert-Arie** „Non temer, amato bene," von **B. A. Mozart,** gesungen von Fräulein **Jenny Lutzer,** mit Orchester, und obligater Clavier-Begleitung, vorgetragen von Herrn **Theodor Kullak.**

5. **Die grosse 5te Symphonie** (in C-moll), von **L. v. Beethoven.**

Sämmtliche genannte Künstler haben ihre Leistungen aus besonderer Gefälligkeit übernommen.

Sperrsitze auf der Gallerie zu 3 fl., Sperrsitze im Parterre zu 2 fl.; Eintrittskarten in die Gallerie zu 1 fl. 30 kr. und Eintrittskarten in das Parterre zu 1 fl. C. M. sind im Billet-Verkaufsbureau des k. k. Hof-Operntheaters, in der k. k. Hof-Musikalienhandlung des Hrn. P. Mechetti, und in der Musikalienhandlung des Hrn. A. Diabelli & Comp. zu haben.

A copy of the second program from the Vienna Philharmonic's first season in 1842. The orchestra, formed by the opera director Otto Nicolai as the Philharmonic Society, was responsible for symphonic and orchestral leadership almost unequaled by any other orchestra. The November 27, 1842 program shows a concert that included Mozart's fortieth (g minor), Beethoven's fifth, two Mozart arias, and one Spohr aria. The program identifies the orchestra as being that from the Vienna Opera. Courtesy the Vienna Philharmonic.

effect of this concept on the orchestra as a solo instrument. Those composers who were the most experimental (or revolutionary?) in their handling of the orchestra (Berlioz, Liszt, Strauss, and Rimsky-Korsakov, for example) all attempted to use it as an expressive device rather than solely as a purveyor of musical ideas in the abstract. As opera neared its zenith of development in the late nineteenth century in the works of Verdi and Wagner, the orchestra became as important as, if not more important than, the voice in providing expressive support for the word, for action on the stage, or for feelings of characters on stage.

In spite of a decreased interest in the concert symphony, the list of composers writing symphonies was impressive:

Composer	Dates	No. of Symphonies
Ludwig Spohr	(1784–1859)	9
Carl Maria von Weber	(1786–1826)	2
Franz Berwald	(1796–1868)	3
Franz Schubert	(1797–1828)	9 or 10 (tenth has not been found to date)
Hector Berlioz	(1803–1869)	4 (symphonylike works)
Felix Mendelssohn	(1809–1847)	5
Robert Schumann	(1810–1856)	4
Franz Liszt	(1811–1886)	2 (also numerous symphonic poems)
Niels Gade	(1817–1890)	8
William Sterndale Bennett	(1816–1875)	1
César Franck	(1822–1890)	1 (also several symphonic poems)
Joachim Raff	(1822–1882)	9 (program symphonies)
Anton Bruckner	(1824–1896)	11
Anton Rubinstein	(1829–1894)	6
Alexander Borodin	(1833–1887)	3 (last two finished by Rimsky-Korsakov and Glazunov)
Johannes Brahms	(1833–1897)	4
Camille Saint-Saëns	(1835–1921)	3
Georges Bizet	(1838–1875)	1
Peter Tchaikovsky	(1840–1893)	6
Antonin Dvořák	(1841–1904)	9
Nicholas Rimsky-Korsakov	(1844–1908)	3
Hubert Parry	(1848–1918)	5
Vincent D'Indy	(1851–1931)	3
Charles Villiers Stanford	(1852–1924)	7
Ernest Chausson	(1855–1899)	1
Edward Elgar	(1857–1934)	2
Gustav Mahler	(1860–1911)	10 (tenth was incomplete)
Richard Strauss	(1864–1949)	3 (symphonylike works; also 7 symphonic poems)
Paul Dukas	(1865–1935)	1
Alexander Glazunov	(1865–1936)	8 (between 1884 and 1905)

This list of thirty composers represents all geographical locations and omits a few whose works were more properly a part of the twentieth century (Sibelius, Debussy) or whose symphonic careers did not start until the early twentieth century. The number of the above composers whose works have survived to appear on concert programs presented by major orchestras in the mid- and late twentieth century is significantly smaller: it would probably include only Schubert, Berlioz, Mendelssohn, Schumann, Liszt, Franck, Bruckner, Brahms, Tchaikovsky, Dvořák, Mahler, Strauss, and Elgar. From the collective output of this last group one could extract around forty works which have continued to be performed with some degree of regularity. Works to be discussed in this text will be drawn from these forty.

Franz Schubert (1797–1828)

Many of Schubert's symphonies, especially numbers 1 through 6, were written under the influence of Haydn and Mozart. There are certain rhythmic and textural similarities between Schubert's style and that of the other two composers. First, the pace and constant eighth-note motion relate many of the fast movements to the *style galant*. Second, the orchestral setting has much in common with earlier, more classic works: the size of Schubert's orchestra is almost identical with Haydn's; the constant reliance on the violins for carrying much of the *Vivace* subjects also recalls Haydn. The overall style of the orchestration, however, is peculiarly Schubertian. Almost all of the early movements in sonata-allegro form observe the traditional repeats of the exposition, even some of the finales. Five of the first six symphonies, especially the first, second, and third, have slow introductions which still show minute traces (primarily dotted rhythms) of the French overture. The first five also have third movements entitled "Minuet." In tempos and overall style most of these are closer to the scherzo than to the minuet. The final two symphonies are much more expressive and expansive, thus more typical of the century. There are in many of the symphonies a few unique style features which should be mentioned. Almost all trios of third movements are based on a tune which is very folklike in style. Scoring in all movements often places the violins an octave apart on passage after passage, fast or slow tempo, tune or filler passage. Schubert's lyric bent would have it no other way.

Schubert's music style was dominated by lyricism, even in his earlier works. His themes are lyric, vocal, conjunct, and frequently folklike in character. His choice of keys stressed third relationships and showed him to be more adventuresome than Beethoven in this respect. Tonal relations in development sections are daring. Repetition was his primary developmental device; repetition using striking contrasts of tonal areas is quite characteristic. Some of the earlier works seem to have endless passages of nonthematic (or filler) writing where the composer seems more bent on harmonic and tonal effect than on formal and thematic relevance. Schubert also showed an interest in the brass section, scoring for trombones quite sensitively in the last two symphonies. Woodwinds receive greater emphasis from Schubert than from any previous composer, including Beethoven. Many themes are introduced by the woodwind choir alone with a subdued (if any) string accompaniment.

Information on Individual Symphonies

No.	Key	Date	Intro.	I	II	III	IV
1	D	1813	yes	SA	ABA	Minuet	Rondo
2	B-flat	1814–1815	yes	SA	Variations	Minuet	SA
3	D	1815	yes	SA	ABA	Minuet	SA
4 (*Tragic*)	c	1816	yes	SA	ABABA	Minuet	SA
5	B-flat	1816	no	SA	ABABA	Minuet	SA
6	C	1817–1818	yes	SA	ABABA	Scherzo	Sonatina
6a (?)	D	1818	Only a sketchy piano score of this work remains.				
7 *	e/E	1821	Only sketches of this work remain.				
8 (*Unfinished*)	b	1822	no	SA	Sonatina	—	—
9	C	1828	yes	SA	ABAB	Scherzo	SA

* The manuscript of this work was given by Schubert's brother Ferdinand to Mendelssohn's brother Paul, who then gave it to Sir George Grove. The latter left it with the Royal College of Music in London, describing it as having four movements (*Adagio-Allegro; Andante; scherzo; Allegro giusto*). Only the *Adagio* and a short portion of the *Allegro* first movement were scored by Schubert, although the instrumentation is indicated at the beginning of each movement. Attempts have been made to score it; none has been satisfactory. See Arthur Hutchings, *Schubert* (London: J. M. Dent and Sons, Ltd., 1945), p. 96.

SYMPHONY NO. 1

A slow introduction opens the first movement and returns at the conclusion of the development to usher in the recapitulation. The second theme of the movement sounds like a typical Viennese tune: simple, lyric, and of balanced phrase structure. Only this tune is treated in the development. The second movement relies generally on the woodwinds for thematic support. The minuet is traditional in form if not in orchestration. Violins, spaced an octave apart, carry the first tune. The trio's tune could be a folk tune, because of its simple charm. The finale's principal theme is supported by an Alberti bass figure in the accompaniment which initiates a rush of eighth notes that lasts throughout the movement.

SYMPHONY NO. 2

A slow introduction starts the first movement but mixes French-overture dotted rhythms with double octave scoring for the strings on a secondary figure in which every other pitch is an appoggiatura. The *Allegro's* first theme is another theme of rushing eighth notes, keeping this symphony also closely tied to at least one aspect of the *style galant*. The tune is soon carried by the violins doubled at the octave, again an exhibition of the composer's desire to score expressively and of his affection for early classical materials. This movement contains one of the best examples of this doubling in string passages; it abounds, either in the violins or in the violas and cellos. Double-octave scoring involves the violins and violas (measures 245–55). The second movement is a set of classical-style variations, the theme of which is in rounded binary form, complete with repeats of both sections. Each variation preserves this strict form (two sections, eight and nine bars in length). Solo woodwinds are used prominently in several of the variations. The minuet is another near scherzo. While preserving the large outline of a minuet song form, it does show an expansion of the second section. The extra length is primarily used for repetition of thematic scale passages extracted from the main theme. The trio's tune is another charming dance tune, played on the solo oboe with help from the flute and the clarinet. The trio's form is more traditional: a first section of eight bars followed by a second of sixteen. The finale has a rondolike progression of themes in its exposition (which is repeated) and an extended development of the opening motive of the first theme.

SYMPHONY NO. 3

The introduction is similar in style and format to that of the second symphony, although traces of the French overture are minimal (fast, anticipatory scale patterns). These scale patterns reappear in the movement's coda, continuing a trend for the composer to integrate introductory materials into subsequent sections of a movement. They also are used as part of the materials of the exposition. The second movement is simple in structure and in melodic style. The middle section is in the subdominant key (C major) and relies on woodwinds for carrying most of the tune. The minuet repeats the approach of the previous symphony: the style of a scherzo, an expanded second portion (of minuet), and a folksy tune for the trio. The finale has a Haydn sound, attributable to its 6/8 meter and presto vivace tempo. The development moves through typical Schubert key choices (b minor, C major, G major) before settling into A major (the dominant) for a statement of the main tune (measure 196) as the beginning of the recapitulation. This gives the finale a form which relates to preclassical models:

Intro ‖:	A	B	:‖	A	B		Coda
(Key)	I	V		V	I		

SYMPHONY NO. 4

There is very little in the introduction that smacks of the French overture except a few rapid scale passages as melodic embellishments. More interesting is the canonic relationship between the soprano and bass line statements of the introduction's tune. The *Allegro* continues the *galant* rush of eighth notes used in the earlier symphonies. Although in c minor, the movement moves to A-flat major for a lyric second theme. This exposition is also repeated. Development starts in b-flat minor. Later the first theme is restated in g minor in the recapitulation (measure 177). After all of this tonal obfuscation, the coda supplies the clarity of C major. The *Andante* is another slow movement of simple structure and appealing lyricism. The middle section is based on the passing around of a short motive, sometimes only two pitches, among various woodwinds while the strings supply a measured tremolo chordal accompaniment. A unison theme opens the minuet and stresses the interval of the diminished third and accented dissonance on first beats of the tune. The scherzo influence has by now become quite strong; hardly a trace of the old minuet style remains. Only the folk dance tune of the trio continues Schubert's original concept of a third movement. The finale (*Allegro*) is a study in repetition of thematic materials in orderly packages of short phrases, much of which hinders any concept of melodic line. To offset this choppiness, the movement resorts to the *style galant* device of providing continuity through a steady undercurrent of accompaniment rhythm. After a repeated exposition, the development moves through about thirty bars of tonal meandering before establishing A major as the home key for the section's first complete statement of the theme. The keys quickly flow by: D-flat major, f minor, c minor. The recapitulation is entirely in C major.

SYMPHONY NO. 5

The opening movement has no introduction and follows the same plan as used by the finale of the third symphony (no principal theme in the recapitulation). It also continues the *galant* accompaniment rush of eighth notes. The orchestra is quite small: flute; pairs of oboes, bassoons, and horns; strings. The *Andante* is a continuation of the simple lyricism of Schubert second movements. The theme is in rounded binary form with repeats of both sections; the key is E-flat major. The key of the second section is C-flat major. The rococo-style measured tremolo accompaniment is also used for this section. The third movement is another scherzo entitled "Menuetto." The second strain of the movement expands to thirty bars before returning to a final statement of the tune. The opening strain is almost as long. Even the second strain of the folksy trio has been expanded. The finale (*Allegro vivace*) holds to the Haydn model again. The tune is placed in a rounded binary outline with both sections repeated. The entire exposition is repeated. For some reason the opening of the principal theme is always harmonized with the first inversion of the tonic chord.

SYMPHONY NO. 6

The slow introduction reverts to some of the French overture mannerisms but offsets these with a tighter motivic structure and a more dramatic use of dynamics. The work quickly shows traces of a Rossini influence (grace notes embroidering triplet figures in the woodwinds and strings, and parallel thirds in voicing some of the woodwind thematic segments). These suspected influences continue in the *Allegro,* especially in the ostinatolike accompaniment to the second tune (measures 79–94). A *piu moto* rushes the movement to conclusion. The second movement (*Andante*) continues this strange Italian-style invasion through a tune which could have been lifted from any Rossini opera, especially its course in measures 5–8 (accented dissonance, triplet embellishments, and the raised fifth scale degree, C-sharp, in the cadence segment of the tune). A middle section further stresses the grace-note proclivity of the adopted style. The return of the first section is shaded by the triplet action from the middle section, in the nature of a variation. Both sections reappear in shortened versions before the movement concludes. A scherzo (so named by the composer) is a movement of considerably greater length and development than previous third movements. Its C major is followed by the trio's A major, the latter section at a much slower tempo. This trio also attempts to carry off an Italian effect (parallel thirds and an "um-pah-pah" accompaniment in the oboes for the second strain). The finale moves a step lower in its inspiration, presenting a succession of tunes which continue the Rossini imitation. Its form consists of three thematic groups in one large section which are then reworked and restated in the second half of the movement. Certain tonal adjustments imply a sonata-allegro outline.

SYMPHONY NO. 8

This work is discussed beginning on page 102.

SYMPHONY NO. 9

At one time this work was numbered as the composer's seventh symphony. Later research has established the existence of another two symphonies in fragmentary condition, the first a D major work in piano score dating from 1818 (O. E. Deutsch's thematic index number 615)* and the second a very

---

* O. E. Deutsch, *Schubert: Thematic Catalog of All His Works in Chronological Order* (New York: W. W. Norton & Company, Inc., 1951).

sketchy score in E major dating from 1821 (Deutsch No. 729). Two attempts have been made to reconstruct the E major work, and it has even been performed.* All of this reshuffling has caused the works to be renumbered as indicated above. The numbering is still not correct. There are actually only eight completed symphonies; the *Unfinished* is the seventh in order; the C major is the eighth. The C major is still alternately called the seventh or ninth.

The orchestration for the last two symphonies is identical: pairs of flutes, oboes, clarinets, bassoons, horns, and trumpets; three trombones; timpani, strings. The work is written in a much broader scale; the movements are longer and more complex; the folk flavor is minimized; more emphasis is placed on motivic unity than in the first six symphonies. The first movement has an extended slow introduction in a five-part rondolike structure (ABACA). The first theme is based on two rhythmic motives. Each is developed as presented. Development for Schubert often meant repetition. The secondary theme also has a motivic structure which is immediately developed. A somber trombone theme leads to a closing section. The exposition is repeated. The development works on all of the primary motives, at times simultaneously. It is the composer's most involved development section. The recapitulation is followed by an accelerated coda whose thrust seems more harmonic and tonal than thematic. It rushes to a final statement of the main tune in its last fourteen bars. The second movement (*Andante con moto*) returns to the binary form of the early classical period but adjusts the tonality so that a sonatina emerges: A B A B, with the first B section's F major contrasting with the movement's overall a minor. There is an almost martial drive to the materials of the first section. A long coda is based primarily on the first tune.

The scherzo expands to embrace a complete sonata-allegro outline. Its subordinate theme has an almost waltzlike quality (measure 31). The development transforms the first tune into a more folklike woodwind dance tune (measure 66). The rounded binary concept (and its repeats) causes Schubert to indicate not only repeats for the exposition but a repeat from the final section which includes the development and recapitulation. The trio does not reduce its forces or resort to a characteristic folk dance but focuses on a broad and appealing lyric tune in the woodwinds which floats through a minor and C major before returning to its home key of A major. There is a da capo of the scherzo.

The finale presents three groups of themes, each with its own motivic unity. Much of the material is subjected to development (repetition with tonal contrast at times) and considerable extension, producing an exposition of some length (380 bars) which is then repeated. The choice of keys for the develop-

---

* Maurice Brown, *Schubert Symphonies* (Seattle: University of Washington Press, 1971), pp. 32–39.

ment is typical: E-flat major, A-flat major, c-sharp minor, E major, e minor, G major, g minor, and C major. The closing theme dominates the section. The recapitulation begins in E-flat major and moves to g minor, the second theme returning in the tonic C major. The coda (measure 973) is another long development section which touches upon many of the themes, routes itself through a variety of "Schubert" keys, and finally concludes in bar 1,154.

EXAMPLES FOR STUDY

Schubert: *Symphony No. 8 in b minor (Unfinished)* *

I: Allegro moderato. Schubert's version of sonata-allegro form was original, to say the least. First, he designed a principal theme which was basically lyric and divided into two segments. The first segment, announced as almost an introductory theme, is heard only once at the beginning of the exposition. The balance of the exposition Schubert dedicated to exposing and developing the second segment of the principal theme and the subordinate theme. Second, the development section is completely involved with a working out of this introductory part of the principal theme. The recapitulation section does not return this first portion of the principal theme, but rather starts with the A^2 theme. Third, after an orderly recapitulation, a coda follows which is based entirely on the first segment of the principal theme.

The principal material involves about forty measures of the exposition. In that span of time Schubert spent about thirty measures stating and restating the second portion of the principal materials and another ten measures developing the material, in this instance repeating a portion of the tune in sequential fashion. It should be noted that Schubert relied on the winds to play most of the thematic material once the first segment of the theme had been announced. The subordinate theme is carried by the strings—cellos first, then violins. Schubert's closing section starts with an antiphonal setting of the last two bars of the subordinate tune and concludes with an imitative segment based on the first two bars of the subordinate theme. The development section is in four large sections with a fifth section serving as a transition to the recapitulation.

Section 1: Canonic treatment of A^1 theme (measures 122–45)

Section 2: Section based on harmonic vamp to subordinate theme (measures 146–74)

Section 3: Section based on sixteenth-note countermelody over A^1 in lower brass and strings (measures 175–83)

---

* A superior analysis and history of the work can be found in an edition of the score by Martin Chusid. See Franz Schubert, *Symphony in B Minor,* ed. Martin Chusid (New York: W. W. Norton & Company, Inc., 1971).

Section 4: Varied version of A^1 in strings with rhythmic accompaniment in winds (measures 184–94)

Section 5: Transition to recapitulation; source of material somewhat vague (measures 195–217)

    The development section is very expressive. Each part manages to achieve either a standard *fortissimo* marking or to build to or retreat from that marking. This is in contrast to both exposition and recapitulation, where much of the material is of a subdued nature with an occasional crescendo to a *fortissimo*. Schubert's conception of sonata-allegro, if this movement is any indication, was a lyric one. The exposition section not only contains three primary tunes, all lyric in nature, but also has a development of some of this material which extends the lyric impact of two themes. The development section, in general, is a lyric experience with the exception of the transition to the recapitulation. The coda returns to the first section of the principal theme and thus extends the lyric thrust into the final portion of the movement.

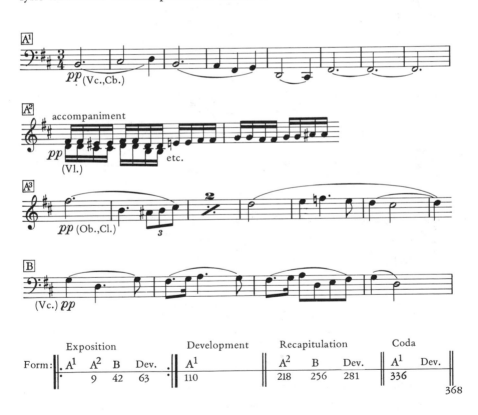

	Exposition				Development	Recapitulation			Coda		
Form:	A^1	A^2	B	Dev.	A^1	A^2	B	Dev.	A^1	Dev.	
		9	42	63	110	218	256	281	336		

368

II: Andante con moto. The form of the second movement, sonatina, tends to stress development in its latter portion. The first theme is stated in E major, repeated in G major. A second portion of the first tune with a dramatic countermelody in the strings starts in measure 33. The work then returns to the first part of the theme and cadences in the tonic key (measure 60). A secondary theme in c-sharp minor follows in the solo clarinet accompanied by a syncopated chordal figure in the strings. The tune is repeated in D-flat major starting in measure 84. A second portion of the subordinate material continues with a sixteenth-note countermelody in the middle strings at measure 96. A final section, using a canonic treatment of the B¹ tune, closes the first half of the movement. The restatement begins at measure 142 and retraces much of the same exposition's journey in appropriate order. The canonic closing material is not restated. In its place Schubert fashioned a coda based on the first tune.

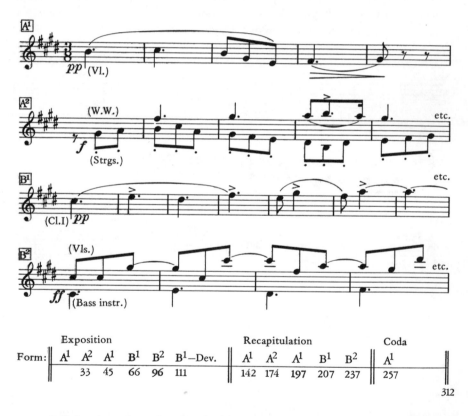

Form:	Exposition						Recapitulation					Coda
	A¹	A²	A¹	B¹	B²	B¹–Dev.	A¹	A²	A¹	B¹	B²	A¹
		33	45	66	96	111	142	174	197	207	237	257

312

Schubert's orchestral style relied heavily on woodwinds as a solo group to present important themes. The brasses generally sustain harmonies or supply accents and cadence materials. The horn often joins the woodwinds in playing themes. Trombones carry thematic materials in *forte* passages (first movement, measure 176; second movement, measure 33). Schubert showed a real sensitivity to the sustaining quality of the winds by having the wind section play much of the lyric material in both movements, something very few composers up until that time had done. The same could be said of the thirty measures in the slow movement in which the solo clarinet and solo oboe play the secondary tune. The fuller wind resource may have allowed Schubert to use more octave doubling in the string parts. In the first movement quite a large portion of the main melodic material played by the strings is doubled in this fashion, enhancing the expressive quality of the lyricism in the movement. The writing for cello and bass is also differentiated for a portion of each movement. Schubert was one of the earlier group of composers who wrote for bass and cello in an independent fashion.

SUMMARY

Schubert's eighth symphony represents a high point in symphonic history: a work conceived entirely as a lyric experience, which may account for its universal acceptance as one of history's four or five most played symphonies. The level of craft exhibited by Schubert is sufficient to support an admirable working out of both movements' materials. The work is a major step forward orchestrally. Woodwinds become the primary medium for essential thematic material. Expressive scoring for all instruments firmly places Schubert in the romantic period on the basis of his orchestral technique alone.

Felix Mendelssohn (1809–1847)

Felix Mendelssohn's position in the history of the symphony was that of a classicist who attempted to respect the conventions and expectations of the classical style and yet expand some of the musical resources which went into the writing of the large orchestral form. Of his five works in that form, four are four-movement symphonies. The *Lobgesang* represents a combining of the cantata form with that of the symphony. Within the four remaining works, Mendelssohn did alter some of the internal dimensions of the four-movement plan. His first symphony (1824) was a product of his youth and more or less adhered to the general form of a classical symphony with the exception of the third movement. The latter was a minuet more in the style of a scherzo in duple (6/4) meter. The *Scotch* Symphony reverses the internal order of the slow-fast movements with a scherzolike second movement in a form which closely approximates sonata-allegro. The third movement of the *Italian* Symphony, in song form with trio and triple meter, is, according to Ulrich,* in

---

* Homer Ulrich, *Symphonic Music* (New York: Columbia University Press, 1952), p. 168.

An 1860 Vienna Philharmonic subscription series poster advertises, among other items, performances of Beethoven's seventh symphony, Schumann's fourth, and Mendelssohn's "Italian" symphony. Courtesy Vienna Philharmonic Orchestra.

the style of a German *ländler*. The finale is a saltarello in rondo form. The *Reformation* Symphony also places the scherzo as the second movement. Its finale is a chorale with variations.

Mendelssohn's overall musical style shows a strong classical influence, especially in matters of form. Romantic innovations are limited to melodic expressiveness through accented dissonances and to some harmonic experimentation (parallel similar sonorities, more emphasis on functional second-inversion triads, and use of the added sixth above the dominant seventh in a cadence passage). He was an extremely skillful contrapuntist and used polyphony frequently as a developmental device. His baroque forms included preludes and fugues for piano and chorale prelude movements for organ and for symphony. His melodic style, however, was characteristic of the early romantic period in its use of dissonance for melodic expression. His preferences in tonal usages were conservative and often provide examples of the eighteenth-century tonal practice as carried forward into the nineteenth century. He cannot be classified as a chromatic composer.

His orchestra is basically an eighteenth-century ensemble, expanded to include a slightly larger brass section. His scoring can be brilliant, especially his handling of the violin and the woodwinds. One orchestral device above all others typifies the orchestral style: a scherzo scoring for woodwinds in rapid tempo with staccato tonguing, rushing sixteenth notes, and closely spaced voicing of parts. The scherzo of his *Midsummer Night's Dream* incidental music is an excellent example of the device. His symphonies show a varying wind requirement:

Symphony No. 1: Flute, oboe, clarinet, bassoon, horn and trumpet (all in pairs); timpani and strings.

Symphony No. 2: Same as 1 except that four horns and three trombones are used.

Symphony No. 3: Same as 1 except for four horns.

Symphony No. 4: Same as 1.

Symphony No. 5: Same as 1 but adds three trombones and contrabassoon.

Information on Individual Symphonies

No.	Key	Date	Intro.	I	II	III	IV
1	c	1824	no	SA	ABACBAC Coda	Minuet	SA
2 (*Lobgesang*)	B-flat	1840	yes	SA	ABA	ABA	Cantata in 10 mvts.
3 (*Scotch*)	a	1842	no	SA	SA (fast)	ABABA (slow)	SA
4 (*Italian*)	A	1833	no	SA	Sonatina	Scherzo	Saltarello
5 (*Reformation*)	d	1830	yes	SA	Scherzo	ABA (slow)	Chorale and variations

SYMPHONY NO. 1

This work was written when Mendelssohn was fifteen years old. The second movement could be considered in a modified sonata-allegro form since the key scheme for the movement is as follows:

Section	A	B	A	C	B	A	C	Coda
Key	E-flat	C-flat	B-flat	B-flat	B	E-flat	E-flat	E-flat

The three middle segments do have the appearance of development if only by tonal contrast. The minuet is in 6/4 meter, making the basic metrical structure duple; the movement is developmental in both minuet and trio and is more a scherzo than a minuet. The finale has a fugal development section. The subordinate tune is accompanied by pizzicato strings, an instrumental device which occurs frequently in the symphonies. The coda continues contrapuntal procedures, another illustration of Mendelssohn's affection for counterpoint.

SYMPHONY NO. 2

The *Lobgesang* is actually a ten-movement cantata on scriptural texts with a three-movement sinfonia as an introduction. The work, written for the unveiling of a statue of Gutenberg in 1840, commemorated the four hundredth anniversary of the invention of printing. The first movement continues the use of contrapuntal textures. The cantata ends with a chorale, "Now thank we all our God."

SYMPHONY NO. 3

In performance all movements of this symphony are connected ("attaca") without pause. The introduction to the first movement is sixty-four measures long and has a ternary design with a developmental middle section. An eight-bar section of the introduction returns as part of the coda. The development section of the *Allegro* makes extensive use of counterpoint. The second movement is in the mood of a scherzo and uses a tune which may have come from the folk tune "Charlie Is My Darling." The finale adds a coda whose tune may have been derived from the tune of the first movement. The finale also has considerable contrapuntal development.

SYMPHONY NO. 4

This work is discussed beginning on page 109.

SYMPHONY NO. 5

This work commemorates Martin Luther's Augsburg Confession of 1530. The *Reformation* Symphony uses musical motives from the Protestant tradition and relies on the chorale prelude as the form for its finale. The introduction of the first movement employs the Dresden Amen (later a *Parsifal* theme), which then reappears in the subsequent *Allegro*. The chorale, "Ein' feste Burg ist unser Gott," is the subject for the finale.

EXAMPLES FOR STUDY

Mendelssohn: *Symphony No. 4 in A Major, Op. 90 (Italan)*

I: Allegro vivace. The first hundred measures of the exposition set forth the principal theme in a treatment that is largely developmental. Starting with a repeated-note harmonic background in the winds, the movement presents the main tune in the violins doubled at the octave. This wind accompaniment affects the scherzo scoring previously mentioned. Some relief from the unison and octave scoring for tunes is provided with the use of parallel thirds for the introduction of the subordinate theme. A closing section is based on the first theme. In the sixteenth measure of the development a new tune becomes the subject of a fugal treatment. The contrapuntal accompaniment to the new theme is based on the eighth-note motive from the materials of the transition to the subordinate theme (measure 90). By measure 218 the fugue has encompassed all four voices. After forty-two bars of fugal activity, the first two measures of the principal theme are superimposed above the fugal lines somewhat in the style of a choral prelude (measures 245–60). By measure 262 the principal theme has gained the upper hand, the fugue more or less evaporating. From measure 274 to measure 295 the fugue theme is carried by the entire orchestra. A ground-like bass passage starting at measure 332 leads back to the recapitulation. This section is somewhat abbreviated even though the fugue theme takes its turn at measure 433, immediately after the completion of the subordinate theme. A coda which uses both the fugue theme and the principal tune begins at measure 475. A steady progression of triplet eighth notes helps unite this final section.

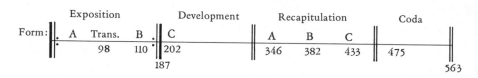

Form:	Exposition				Development		Recapitulation			Coda	
	A	Trans.	B	.	C		A	B	C		
		98	110		202		346	382	433	475	
				187							563

II: Andante con moto. The slow movement, placed in a sonatina form, has a first tune which includes a baroque "walking bass" as its countermelody, a reminder of the composer's affection for the baroque style. The orchestral setting of the tune for the first eight bars is in two voices: melody with bass. The melody is doubled at the octave, the upper line played by oboe and viola, the lower by both bassoons. Alternate phrases are then played by the flutes and violins above the same bass but in a full four-voice setting in which the added voices are "figured" into a more contrapuntal flow (measures 11–19). A second theme in the solo clarinet concludes the first half of the movement. In the final half of the movement the first tune is developed briefly, followed by a brief return of the second tune. A coda based on parts of the first theme concludes the movement. An example of the composer's use of parallel chord motion can be seen in measures 92–93.

Form:	A¹	A²	B		A—Dev.	B		(A¹	A²)	
	4	45			57	75		86		

III: Con moto moderato. Designed in triple meter with a gentler folk influence than noted in the Schubert minuets, Mendelssohn's version of the symphonic scherzo sounds more like a subdued waltz. The form (below) implies a strict adherence to the classical shape of the minuet but in actuality is a more continuously developed form. The second strain of the "minuet" portion develops two-measure motives from the theme and then returns the full tune (measure 41) in a broadly extended version. What had taken only sixteen bars to accomplish in the initial statement now occupies thirty-five measures. The trio resembles that of the classical minuet only in its reduced orchestral setting and contrasting theme. The four-voice scoring for two bassoons and two horns in the fanfarelike tune matches the effective registers of these two instruments in a well-blended ensemble. The da capo is written out, although it only duplicates the original "minuet." A twenty-measure coda is based on both minuet and trio tunes.

IV: Saltarello.   The finale is in a unique binary form with identical principal material in both sections but different contrasting tunes. Each section starts in a similar way, thus creating the impression that the second section is to be a restatement or development of the first. Such is not the case. The opening bars of the first section articulate a triplet motive which unifies the whole movement. The real first theme starts at measure 6 in a scherzo scoring for the woodwinds (A¹ below). Two additional sections pass by before a transition to the B theme begins. The basic rhythmic figures of the A section are interspersed through the new B section. The C theme, again supported by the movement's basic rhythmic motive, concludes the first section. The second large section does resemble a development of previous material if one could overlook the new D theme, which tends to unify this section as did the first rhythmic motive in the first section. This new tune is handed about in a quasi-fugal style at first. Later, it does get more involved in imitation (measures 189–210). A second portion of the section (measures 156–88) intersperses both A and D material in a conversation between winds and strings. A coda based on the A materials closes the movement. It is an original interpretation of the lighter, dancelike character which had become the stylistic norm for final movements. It combines many of the composer's gifts into a single movement: rapid, staccato scoring for woodwinds; counterpoint; clarity in formal structure. The overall form is interesting for its underlying plan of continuous development.

SUMMARY

The Mendelssohn *Italian* Symphony is an example of a conservative nineteenth-century composer's contribution to symphonic literature. Based on traditional forms and outlines, this work is primarily in the line of development of the Viennese symphonic school. What efforts Mendelssohn made to expand the style of the symphony are to be found in the waltzlike style of the third movement and the unusual dance style and form of the finale. There is a certain amount of unifying of both the first and final movements with one or two rhythmic motives, a process similar to that used by Beethoven in the seventh symphony. Mendelssohn was one of the few skillful contrapuntists of the early nineteenth century. Counterpoint as a developmental tool is found in all of his symphonies. It allowed Mendelssohn to inject his own brand of learnedness into the mainstream of symphonic thought at a time when intellectual manipulation of the symphony was giving way to more sensuous and colorful procedures.

His orchestral technique centered around the manipulation of woodwinds and strings. Horns were used for some solo passages and as part of the various wind choirs. In the *Italian* Symphony the woodwinds effectively enhance the dancelike quality of the first and last movements.

Mendelssohn's craft as a composer is unequalled by many of his contemporaries. Only his failure to recognize either the dramatic possibilities or the broad expressive implications of his times prevented him from moving his symphonies more toward the frontier of nineteenth-century symphonic writing. Parts of his symphonies do have an elegance and a momentary brilliance which will probably endear them to many audiences.

Robert Schumann (1810–1856)

Although a contemporary of Mendelssohn, Schumann was much more a musician of the romantic period than was Mendelssohn. Schumann's symphonies, while adhering to some of the principles of the Viennese classical symphony, give evidence of the composer's attempt to experiment and to expand the orchestral form. From the standpoint of sheer sound, the works make use of a consistently larger brass section. The availability of nine brass instruments in eight of the seventeen separate symphony movements gave the composer ample opportunity to exploit this "heavier" sound. Though counterpoint continued to be a useful developmental device, it was not used in an imitative fashion by Schumann as much as by Mendelssohn. Schumann generally preferred to combine two different tunes as countermelodies. The level of chromaticism is higher in his works than in those of Mendelssohn, and there is greater tonal freedom, a quality evident also in the works of Schubert. Schumann's use of melodic dissonance for expressive purposes is similar to that of Mendelssohn. The tunes from his slow movements are, like those of Mendelssohn in similar movements, excellent examples of such devices as appoggiaturas at high points of phrases, elongated or accented passing tones, and suspensions.

Schumann's most individual mannerism was his experimentation with the form of the symphony, as shown in the subsequent chart of the various movements. His formal innovations are noteworthy. First, he often caused themes from one movement to reappear in later movements, a cyclic device that became accepted in the nineteenth century. Second, six of the seventeen movements are connected in performance either by a slight pause or by a direct move into the later movement (Symphony 1, movements II and III; Symphony 4, all movements). Third, themes of one movement are sometimes derived from material of an earlier movement, a concept different from the cyclic idea. All of the fourth symphony's four movements use this device. Fourth, Schumann also adjusted the primary form of a movement (usually sonata-allegro) so that either it lacks a development or a recapitulation or these two functions are combined in a single section. Fifth, new material is introduced in development sections and codas. Sixth, there is some experimentation with both style and form in the scherzo. Duple meter is used for both scherzo and trio in one work (Symphony 2) and for one trio in another (Symphony 1). The theme of a trio is sometimes evolved from the material of a scherzo.

Schumann, in spite of this tendency to experiment with the form of the symphony, still followed the basic line of development begun by more conservative classical composers. The symphonies, written in a twelve-year period of growing maturity, became less directly expressive and representational as their number increased. Schumann's first symphony originally had a program based on a poem by Adolf Bottger. In the end the composer minimized any direct references to the source of his inspiration and deleted subtitles to the four movements ("The Beginning of Spring," "Evening," "Merry Play," and "Spring In Bloom"). Most of his instrumental ensemble music is nonprogrammatic but projects the same expressive ingredient noted in all of his works, especially smaller works for piano.

Schumann's contribution as a symphonist was not monumental either in quantity or quality. What he did give was an interesting combination of the traditional and the experimental. His attempts at expanding the symphony and changing its inner relationships may not have achieved significance in music history but were symptomatic of the crosscurrents of style which affected the development of the symphony in the nineteenth century.

Information on Individual Symphonies

No.	Key	Date	Intro.	I	II	III	IV	V
1 (*Spring*)	B-flat	1841	yes	SA	ABA	Scherzo	SA	—
2	C	1846	yes	SA	Scherzo (fast)	ABA (slow)	SA	—
3 (*Rhenish*)	E-flat	1850	no	SA	Scherzo (fast)	ABA (slow)	Prelude	SA
4	d	1853	yes	SA	ABA	Scherzo	SA	—

Orchestration:

> No. 1: Two flutes, two oboes, two clarinets, two bassoons, four horns, two trumpets, three trombones, three timpani, triangle, strings
>
> No. 2: Same as No. 1, except that there are two horns, two timpani, and no triangle
>
> No. 3: Same as No. 1, except that there are two timpani and no triangle; trombones only in fourth and fifth movements.
>
> No. 4: Same as No. 1, except that there are two timpani and no triangle.

SYMPHONY NO. 1

This work is discussed in full beginning on page 117.

SYMPHONY NO. 2

Some of the first-movement themes are derived from material in the movement's introduction. A new theme is introduced in the coda. The scherzo (second movement) is in 2/4 meter and has two trios, both also in 2/4 meter.

The development and recapitulation sections of the finale are combined. The finale's subordinate theme is derived from a third-movement tune; the movement has an extended coda (309 measures) which has three new melodies and a restatement of the introductory theme of the first movement. The coda seems to serve both as a second development section and as a regrouping of themes from the entire symphony.

SYMPHONY NO. 3

The scherzo (second movement) has a modified trio that contains not only new material but also a reworking of some of the themes of the scherzo. The middle section of the third movement is based on new material and on themes from the first part of the movement. The fourth movement has a sectional design with two main themes; it is only sixty-seven measures long and in a slow tempo. Two of the themes of the finale are from the fourth movement. A middle section of the finale develops the subordinate theme along with a theme from the fourth movement. One new theme is introduced for the first time in the final part of this development.

SYMPHONY NO. 4

This work was first performed in 1841 as the *Symphony Fantasy* but was reorchestrated in 1853 and renamed the fourth symphony. The symphony is in four movements, bound together by common thematic material. The main tune of the first movement gradually evolves in the last seven bars of the introduction. The subordinate theme (measure 59) is the same material as the principal theme. The first movement has no recapitulation; two new themes (measures 121, 147) are used in the development section; a new theme is also inserted in the coda (measure 337) and will be used again in the fourth movement's coda. The middle section of the *Romanza* (second movement) has a theme based on the introductory themes of the first movement. The subordinate song uses a solo violin for an obbligato figuration. The second theme of the scherzo is also related to the introductory theme of the first movement. The first theme of the trio (measure 65) is derived from the solo violin figuration (measure 26) of the second movement. The trio has two statements (scherzo–trio–scherzo–trio). A transition in 4/4 meter is added and connects the third to the fourth movement; the section is also thematically related to the introduction of the first movement. The finale's main theme is derived from the theme in the development section (measure 121) of the first movement. The finale's coda also contains a new theme (measure 172), which also is derived from the material in the first movement's coda.

EXAMPLES FOR STUDY

Schumann: *Symphony No. 1 in B-flat major, Op. 38 (Spring)*

As previously mentioned, Schumann's first symphony originally had a program that linked its four movements to various aspects of spring. Later the composer removed the descriptive subtitles from each movement. To this day the work still retains a subtitle linking it to the original poem. Though not as representative of the composer's efforts to change the internal organization of the form of the symphony, the *Spring* Symphony remains one of Schumann's most popular orchestra works. It, like the fourth symphony (also written originally in 1841 and later reorchestrated), uses Schumann's largest orchestra (nine brass instruments) in three of its four movements.

I: Andante un poco maestoso, Allegro molto vivace. The introduction that opens the movement presents a "motto" theme in the horns (theme ①) which will serve to unify much of the first movement. The balance of the introduction attempts to develop the motives from the introductory theme. The final fourteen measures are used to filter out the tonality of g minor and establish the tonic key, B-flat major. The materials of this modulatory section are not related to primary themes of the movement. The *Allegro* section quickly covers the two parts of theme A and moves into the subordinate theme in measure 81. The forty-two measures associated with the first theme are unified almost completely by the two parts of this first theme in a manner which is developmental in essence. The subordinate tune's second part is accompanied by a sixteenth-note countermelody in the viola line. Schumann extended this subordinate section for about forty-two bars and then closed the exposition with a brief scalar theme. The development section is limited to the "motto" portion of the first theme with a brief mention of the A^2 theme. Schumann added a sustained countermelody in this section (theme D) at measure 150 and achieved an element of contrast with the crisp rhythm of the "motto" theme. The final section of the development sequences the closing theme in an imitative fashion. The basic nature of the development is tonal; the repetition of the "motto" theme is used to unify the section. The recapitulation section shortens the principal material from its original eighty measures (including the slow *Andante*) to twenty-six measures by omitting both the A^2 theme and the extended development of the A^1 tune which occurs in the exposition. The recapitulation concludes without a return of the closing section. The coda, marked *animato,* continues the motivic development of the primary motive, introducing a more lyric theme (E) in measure 438. Its descending contour resembles the second portion of the introductory "motto" theme. After an augmented statement of the "motto" theme, an extended cadence passage closes the movement.

II: Larghetto. Schumann's form for the second movement was drawn from a basic ternary plan. The first part exposes a melody which clearly illustrates the use of nonchord tones on accented beats. The middle section of the movement consists of a restatement of the lyric melody in the dominant key with a transitionlike B theme opening and closing the section. A third theme (C), motivic in structure, becomes the second half of the middle section and is approximately equal in length to the statement of the lyric theme in the dominant key. The final part of the movement restates the lyric tune in the tonic key with a change of orchestration. A transition which anticipates the next movement's principal tune closes the second movement on a half-cadence.

Form:	Section 1		Section 2					Section 3			
	A¹	A²	B	A¹	A²	C	B	A¹	Coda	Transition
		9	25	41	49	55	70	78	101	113

III: Molto vivace. The scherzo third movement is written in five-part form with two different trios; the da capo of the scherzo is written out with slight changes in orchestration. The second trio, in 3/4 meter, is built upon an ascending scale passage which is reversed in the second strain of this trio. The second da capo of the scherzo is abbreviated to include only the first section. A coda is added which contains the second strain of the scherzo and a short excerpt from the trio I. Of the five parts of the form, the trio I is the most developmental in style, with trio II having a somewhat similar thrust.

	Scherzo			Trio I				Scherzo			Trio II		
Form:	A :	B	A .	C	C	Dev.		A	B	A .	D :	Dev.	D .
Meas:		17	33	49	81			233	249	265	281	289	

		Scherzo		Coda		
	Trans.	A		B	C	D
	329	345		361	376	390
						408

IV: Allegro animato e grazioso. The exposition of the finale contains four basic themes: a principal tune in three segments and a secondary theme. The development section uses the subordinate theme and the first portion of the principal theme in what becomes a somewhat contrapuntal and sequential section beginning at measure 117. The varied version of the first tune closes the development section. A cadenza for horns and then flute leads to the recapitulation, where the first tune has been omitted. This regrouping of themes is quite similar to the exposition. The coda of the finale is based on a variation of the opening theme.

Schumann's orchestral technique has often been impugned as less than skillful. In the first movement Schumann makes a distinction between wind and string technique, allowing for the difference in flexibility (i.e., strings, especially violins, can play faster than winds). Idiomatic writing for strings in the first movement, other than the passage built around the A^2 theme, is restricted to measured bow and finger tremolo in sixteenth notes. In the coda this creates an effective crescendo when the entire string section uses this same technique. At other times Schumann appears just to be filling in harmony notes in the middle strings. The second movement, a more sustained setting, does allow more opportunity for orchestral color. These melodic doublings can be found:

Violins doubled at the octave (measures 1–24)

Flute doubled by oboe with violins (measures 17–24)

One violin line doubled octave higher in flute and another imitating violin line doubled at the octave in the oboe (measures 55–66)

Horn doubled octave higher by oboe (measures 78–91); this same section has the violins doubled an octave apart on an accompaniment figure.

A considerable number of measures of harmonic support have been assigned to the violas, playing either double stops or divisi. Frequent accompaniment figures in the strings resemble piano figures, especially those which provide
a rhythmic offbeat figure, as in the passage beginning at measure 25. The woodwinds do not use similar figures when participating in harmonic support. The
scherzo makes little distinction among various instrumental idioms. There is,
however, one interesting orchestral effect in the finale. In placing the A^3 theme
in a four-voice setting in the woodwinds, the composer also has the violins and
violas pluck the essential melodic pitches on all strong beats (measures 43–45).
Schumann also uses measured tremolo in an extended passage in the same movement (measures 117 onward) to both increase and decrease dynamic requirements as the development section reaches its conclusion. The trombones are
employed sparingly as an individual wind resource and generally double either
the bass line or the tenor part in the violas. The one solo section for the trombones is in the transition to the scherzo. There are very, very few instances
where brass instruments are doing anything other than reinforcing the basic
volume of sound by doubling the inner parts. It would appear that Schumann
had difficulty thinking orchestrally in this first symphony.

SUMMARY

Schumann's first symphony must be considered the product of a composer who
did not excel in the handling of an orchestra. Had he reacted more favorably
to the coloristic developments being sustained by Berlioz and Liszt, he might
have contributed orchestral works of greater interest. This kind of reaction was
probably not possible in view of his philosophical opposition to the superficial
and dazzling in music. The musical materials employed in the *Spring* Symphony
are typical of the transitional style in which Schumann wrote, a style which
showed both conservative and progressive sides. The first movement is an
example of the composer's attempt to employ Beethoven's motivic concept to
unify a movement. The second movement offers an example of a nineteenth-
century melody which uses dissonance as an expressive device. The third movement is a scherzo with two trios, one in triple meter, the other in duple. The
scherzo is probably the most effective developmental movement in this particular symphony. In view of the success of Schumann's smaller piano pieces (or
larger works comprised of smaller pieces), one cannot help wondering whether
his orchestral efforts might have enjoyed the same success if they had been
directed toward the suite, incidental music to plays, or other miniature settings.
These smaller forms might have stimulated his orchestral imagination more than
did the abstract symphony.

Program Music

The expressive nature of romanticism, and the belief that the sounds created by an orchestra could describe what words could not, gave rise to orchestral story-telling, or program music. Equally as important in the early growth of the new genre was the brotherhood, or community, or artists which brought artists, writers, and composers together to share their aspirations and outpourings. Poets were one source of inspiration for orchestral composers. Liszt used Lamartine's *Poetic Meditations* to explain his symphonic poem *Les Preludes*. Goethe's works served Liszt and others as well. Strauss used a broader inspirational base: Shakespeare, Nietzsche, Ritter, and a folk tale. Composers, particularly Liszt, were also influenced by paintings. The orchestra, then, in the hands of a composer bent on depiction of a mood, a story, a geographical feature, or a picture, became the ultimate expressive vehicle of the nineteenth century. This expressive urge often produced a wide variety of results, from the bleating of sheep (Strauss, *Don Quixote*) to conjugal love (Strauss, *Domestic* Symphony).

In addition, the rigid, formal treatment of the symphony was being relaxed, even by those composers whose works could be classed as conservative. Mention has already been made of the broadening of the scope of the symphony by Beethoven and the less significant adjustments made by Schubert, Mendelssohn, and Schumann. Thus the nineteenth century set the stage for an assault on the symphony that was to have lasting effect. How this passion for description, along with a distaste for formal complexity, modified the course of orchestral music can be explained by studying the orchestral efforts of three composers: Berlioz, Liszt, and Strauss.

Hector Berlioz (1803–1869)

Berlioz, a true musical revolutionary, was attracted to the descriptive possibilities of the orchestra, quickly studied the technical skills required, and then sought to create a new and more dramatic approach to orchestral depiction. He soon became the champion of orchestral depiction, an intriguing exercise that many of his fellow composers found difficult to resist. Berlioz's freewheeling life-style, his hunger for the new and different, and his desire to create a new genre combined with an impressive musical talent to produce works and sounds that became the points of departure for others seeking to expand the mission of the orchestra.

Berlioz's orchestral music includes something for everybody: symphony, concerto, opera, oratorio, incidental music, dramatic overtures, and opera overtures. Those works which he identified as symphonies are a radical departure from the kinds of works written in the early nineteenth century by Beethoven, Schubert, Mendelssohn, or Schumann. His first symphony, *Symphonie Fantas-*

Berlioz's orchestral works soon became the target for frequent caricatures in nineteenth-century Paris. Courtesy Bettmann Archive.

tique (1830), is a five-movement work using traditional forms in all movements except the finale, which has a sectional layout. All of the company's movements are unified by a single motive (*idée fixe*), which changes shape (generally only rhythm, tempo, or harmony) to fit the mood of the moment. His second symphony, *Harold in Italy* (1834), is a four-movement descriptive work inspired by Lord Byron's *Childe Harold* which features a solo viola; it was supposedly written in response to Paganini's request for such a work. An *idée fixe* also unifies *Harold*. Berlioz called his *Romeo and Juliet* a dramatic symphony. Its resources are described below. The "band" symphony, transcribed later for orchestra, is in three movements. Of these works, only *Harold* and the *Symphonie Fantastique* employ the idée fixe.

Berlioz pushed the orchestral frontier back still further with the *Damnation of Faust* (1846), a work he called a "dramatic legend." Its final version had twenty scenes calling for three vocal soloists, a chorus, and the orchestra. It was not intended to be performed on the stage. Berlioz must have sensed that the concert symphony as a descriptive work was not a suitable or lasting cornerstone upon which to erect a nineteenth-century symphony tradition. After *Harold* (1834), Berlioz's works shifted to the more dramatic and operatic, with the expansion to the dramatic symphony and the dramatic legend representing his point of departure from the purely instrumental symphony.

His style is basically descriptive. His study of instrumentation during his student days in the Paris Conservatory gave him a command of orchestral resources which could produce effects unequaled in novelty, clarity, or color. Musical effect became a formal device wherein the color of a section was just as important as its pitch or rhythm structure. Melody and rhythm were almost as important as color in the style. On one hand he tended to avoid overly square tunes, preferring long and uneven phrase structure. On the other, his rhythmic symmetry (varied by frequent syncopation) is extremely strong in sections which seem to spring from the dance.

Berlioz was also a skilled contrapuntist. His imitative sections, his canons, and his combination of two melodies (often in a coda or a final section of a work) show a craft of admirable quality. The harmonic style is not complex, although frequent progressions of a retrogressive nature startle some listeners. There seems to be a fondness for parallel chords of the sixth in some of the more exciting passages. In general, tonality is conservatively organized. His choice of forms (when used) is traditional. Dynamics and tempo change rather impulsively at times.

The most characteristic style features are orchestration and tone color. His constant searching for the most apt setting often caused frequent changes of orchestral scoring. For instance, in the first movement of the *Symphonie Fantastique* at least sixteen different orchestral combinations are used in the seventy-one measures of the introduction. In the *Roman Carnival* Overture he used at least thirty-five different instrumental combinations and effects. In the slower first section, no setting lasts longer than ten measures. When the tempo accelerates, the most enduring setting is forty measures in length; most average around fourteen measures. Very few composers seem to have sought such variety in the use of orchestral color.*

---

* For an exhaustive treatment of the Berlioz style, see Brian Primmer, *The Berlioz Style* (London: Oxford University Press, 1973).

Information on Individual Symphonies

Name	Date	I	II	III	IV	V
Symphonie Fantastique	1830, rev. 1846	SA	ABA	ABA	SF w/trio	Sectional (ABCD)
Harold in Italy	1834	SA	SF (song form) w/trio	SF w/trio	Sonatina	—

Description

Romeo and Juliet 1839

Called a Dramatic Symphony by the composer, the work is a setting of the Shakespearean tragedy that uses an accompanied vocal setting of a French translation of certain portions of the text or an orchestral depiction of the events or emotions of that part of the story not accorded this vocal setting. The work is in three large parts as follows:

Part I
1. Introduction (all orchestral)
   Combat (fugue)
   Tumult
   Intervention of the Prince (fugal)
2. Prologue (all vocal)
   Choral recitative
   Song (alto solo)
   Recitative (tenor) and scherzo

Part II
1. Romeo Alone (orchestral)
   Sadness (orchestral)
   Festive Spirits at the Ball (orchestral)
   Coda: Themes of Sadness and Ball Combined (orchestral)
2. Goodnight Chorus (double male chorus, offstage)
   Capulet's Garden (orchestral)
   Love Scene (orchestral)
3. Queen Mab Scherzo (orchestral)

Part III
1. Juliet's Funeral (choral)
2. Romeo at Capulet's Burial Vault (all orchestral)
   Invocation
   Juliet's Awakening
   Delirious Joy
   Death of Both Lovers

Information on Individual Symphonies (cont.)

		3.	Finale (choral with vocal solo)

                    3.   Finale (choral with vocal solo)
                         Choral recitative of Friar Laurence (double chorus w/solo)
                         Aria (double chorus w/solo)
                         Sermon (triple chorus w/solo)

Funeral and Triumphant Symphony   1840   A three-movement work scored first for band, it was later augmented by string parts to become the composer's fourth symphony. The work is not known in this country.

EXAMPLES FOR STUDY

Berlioz: *Symphonie Fantastique, Op. 14a* *

Program synopsis: A young musician, lovesick and in fear of losing his loved one, ingests opium and experiences a series of visions which involve his lady. Each movement of the symphony is one of these visions. "Reveries and Passions" allows him to reflect on the dimensions of his love. In "A Ball" he sees her in the midst of the dance. By this time the audience is associating Berlioz's unifying theme (*idée fixe*) with the young lady, an association which Berlioz has explained in his program preface in the score. "In the Country" shows the young man retreating to the country for self-renewal only to see his lover again. He dreams in the "March to the Scaffold" that he has killed his loved one and dies on the gallows for his crime. She appears to him just as death strikes. In the final movement he dreams of being at a Witches' Sabbath commemorating his own death. Even his beloved is in attendance, her theme turned into a grotesque dance. Another tune, the *Dies Irae* ("Day of Wrath," from the Catholic mass for the dead), assumes equal importance in the eerie celebration.

    The work is scored for piccolo, two flutes, two oboes, English horn, two clarinets, four bassoons, four horns, two cornets, two trumpets, three trombones, two tubas, four timpani, a variety of percussion, bells, two harps, and strings. Each of the five movements has a different orchestral requirement.

    I: Reveries and Passions: Largo, Allegro agitato e appassionato assai. A slow introduction starting with muted strings leads to a tune (introduction no. 3) in the winds which is extended for about twenty-four bars with a return

---

* For an in-depth discussion of this work, or for an edition of the score which has been based on detailed research the reader should refer to Hector Berlioz, *Fantastic Symphony*, ed. Edward T. Cone (New York: W. W. Norton & Company, Inc., 1971). It covers the historical background and includes analyses by Fetis, Schumann, and Cone, and comments on the work by Mendelssohn, Liszt, Wagner, Gounod, Wolf, Saint-Saëns, Virgil Thomson, and Aaron Copland.

to the introduction no. 2 theme near the close of that passage. Relying on the strings and woodwinds, Berlioz moves from the introduction to the exposition, using those two basic choirs for the balance of the first movement and changing combinations frequently. The principal theme, based on the *idée fixe*, has a rhythmic accompaniment (accompaniment figure no. 1) in the strings which projects the same rhythmic vitality as had the *style galant* rush of sixteenth notes one hundred years earlier. Whereas the eighteenth-century application related more to formal continuity and musical line, Berlioz's usage sought to establish a mood. The two techniques are quite similar; the intent is quite different. The accompaniment figure no. 2 represents the setting in the recapitulation. The secondary theme of the first movement is also a version of the idée fixe, with a two-bar extension of a contrasting contour. The development works with the secondary theme, using both motivic and orchestral techniques to extend the work. A passage of parallel chords of the sixth (all major triads) leads to a three-bar general pause and the recapitulation. The sixth chords progress in half steps, with dynamics rising and falling. The effect is arresting if not musically pertinent. The recapitulation returns the first theme in the dominant key, omits the first part of the subordinate theme, and moves into an extended coda which continues the development of the main material. Berlioz has fashioned a new tune to use as a countermelody above his first theme at measure 358. After a final restatement of the idée fixe, the movement concludes with a subdued plagal cadence.

II: A Ball: Allegro non troppo (Waltz). Berlioz added two harps to the second movement to better project the spirit of the waltz and to brighten up his orchestral palette. Most of the waltz material is carried by the string section, with the harps and woodwinds providing rhythmic and harmonic support. Woodwinds from time to time take over the waltz tune. The instrumentation of the waltz rhythm departs from the usual um-pah-pah style; a notable example is the repetition of chordal material in equal eighth notes distributed as follows:

First beat	Second beat	Third beat
strings	harps	woodwinds

See the passage beginning at measure 94. Berlioz used a number of other eighth-note and sixteenth-note accompaniment patterns with the waltz tune as it is shifted from strings to woodwinds. One of the more expressive settings occurs with the return of the first section at measure 176. Doubling the waltz melody in a two-octave voicing (violin II, viola, and cello), Berlioz assigned the accompaniment to woodwinds, violin I, and harp.

Form:	Intro.		A¹	A²	A³	A¹		B		A¹	A²	A³	A¹	
Meas:			39	56	68	94		121		176	193	206	233	

Coda

	C¹	C²	B	
	257	265	302	

368

III: In the Country: Adagio. Berlioz scored the movement for wood-winds, horns, strings, and four timpani. An imitative passage between oboe and English horn opens the movement, the oboe placed offstage as an echo instrument. As the oboist returns to his stage chair, the first tune begins. A middle section uses the *idée fixe* as a cantus to the counterpoint being played by the bassoon and lower strings (theme B¹). A second portion of the middle section (B³) uses a sixteenth-note pizzicato countermelody in the middle strings. The style of the setting is carried forward into the return of A but with faster notes in the countermelody, this time arco in first violins. Near the midpoint of the third section, both the A¹ theme and the B² (idée fixe) are combined in a similar polyphonic texture. The coda contains a chordal passage in the timpani which has been identified at measures 189 and 196 in the ensuing examples. The twenty-measure passage is, according to Berlioz, representative of distant thunder. Four-note chords are used in two of the measures, three-note in nine, and two-note in three. In the coda, Berlioz has used these drums to provide a minor triad for the tonic chord while the other members of the orchestra support a major sound. The dual modality is never concurrent but shifts back and forth (measures 175–99).

IV: March to the Gallows: Allegretto non troppo. Timpani, after having closed the third movement with a three-voice minor chord, open this movement with the tonic minor third as an accompaniment to an ascending motive which will generate the subordinate theme. Pizzicato chords (four voices, divisi) in the contrabass part support the strong beats in each measure of this passage. The passage is completely lacking in upper partials because of the composer's choice of instruments. The effect is both drab and stark. Again, without the descriptive potential of Berlioz's large orchestra, this effect would not have been possible. The first tune of the march is a descending scale passage in the bass strings, with a striking counterpoint in the tenor register of the bassoon played by all four bassoons. A second counterpoint then follows, with the tune shifted to the soprano strings (see counterpoint 1 and 2 in examples). The tune is then inverted and played against the original version with an eighth-note countermelody in the four bassoons, all of this leading to the middle section played by all of the winds. This section offers a short second motive (B^2) noteworthy for Berlioz's use of pedal tones in the bass trombone, in one instance written *fortissimo* in all three trombones (measure 108). After a short development of the middle section, the first tune returns with a much louder and more active accompaniment in the strings and woodwinds. A coda contains a new theme which uses the dotted rhythmic motive of the midsection. A *fortissimo* tutti chord closes the movement, with timpani again playing a three-note chord. The *idée fixe* makes a final appearance in the movement just prior to the last chord.

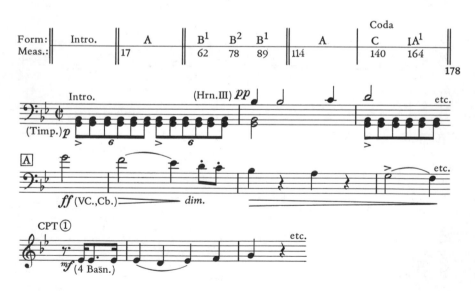

V: Witches' Sabbath: Larghetto, Allegro. A subdued passage opens the movement, with another one-measure section of parallel chords injected, this time diminished seventh chords. Materials of the introduction are not musically or thematically significant but do establish a mood for the diabolic section which concludes the symphony. The *Allegro* opens with a parody of the *idée fixe,* again accompanied by four bassoons in a striking arpeggiated figure. As the orchestra builds up its forces to a *fortissimo* tutti passage, two bells playing the first and fifth scale degrees as a melodic interval start the second section. Finally, four bassoons and two tubas, unison, introduce the *Dies Irae* as the theme of the second section of the movement. The bells continue to toll the tonic and dominant pitches as a ground motive under the primary tune. Other brass instruments punctuate the ends of each phrase of the main tune with a diminution of each preceding phrase. At measure 187 a restatement of the *Dies Irae* begins in the tubas and bassoons with an offbeat solo accompaniment in the bass drum. This passage has a bass line in the cellos and basses which is also syncopated. The second section ends by building a climax toward the "Witches' Dance," the composer's third section. This dance is organized at the outset in fugal style in the string section. The winds double as the texture gets thicker. Strangely enough, though the balance of the movement has been in c minor, the dance sustains C major for most of its duration. After a full orchestral setting of the fugue, Berlioz combines both the *Dies Irae* and the dance tune in the final section. One of the final color devices used occurs in measure 444, where the violins and violas play a *col legno* rhythmic accompaniment to the dance

tune. This combined with the embellishment of the tune with trills in the woodwinds gives the music a most unusual effect. After an extended tutti final cadence passage, the movement concludes with every instrument playing except the large bells.*

SUMMARY

Though the forms and treatments employed deserve comment, it is orchestral manipulation that becomes the substance of this symphony. Effect must succeed for the work to have credibility. Thus the major thrust of the program became to suggest, to describe, or to chronicle, where in previous styles the major goal was to present a series of musical ideas connected in some logical fashion: this logic was itself the principal effect. In the overpowering onslaught of Berlioz's orchestral skills, one can overlook some of the musical devices he used in extending and developing each movement. His use of counterpoint is skillful,

---

* Berlioz did not require the use of modern tubular bells (chimes), since they had not yet been invented. His directions imply regular "church" bells: "If it is not possible to *find* [author's emphasis] two bells low enough to sound one of the three C's and one of the three G's which are written . . ." (Author's translation of French text from Cone edition of score, p. 212).

revealing a craft equal to that of any other composer of Berlioz's time. On more than one occasion he resorted to the setting of one tune against the other in the latter portion of a movement, probably one of his most effective ways of working toward a musical climax. *Symphonie Fantastique* holds a unique position in the history of music as one of the few surviving program symphonies. It well documents Berlioz's position as one of the orchestral pioneers of the early nineteenth century.

Franz Liszt (1811–1886)

The influence of Berlioz was felt by most nineteenth-century composers who either knew him or followed him in symphonic history. Liszt, who was present at the first successful performance of the *Symphonie Fantastique,* realized that his main thrust in symphonic composition would be expressive. There is a point of departure, however, which distinguishes his approach from that of Berlioz. While Berlioz attempted to adjust the dimensions of the symphony in his two major orchestral works (excluding his dramatic orchestral efforts), Liszt generally abandoned the four-movement form and created other ways of accomplishing his purposes. From this departure came the one-movement symphonic poem and Liszt's two program symphonies, neither in four movements. Liszt did profit from Berlioz's *idée fixe,* using this concept to organize each of his works with one or two major motives, or themes. Adjusting the unifying theme to fit the mood and purpose of the moment, Liszt developed a principle which has become known as *theme transformation.* In the one-movement symphonic poems, form was quite loose, the unifying theme providing a germ from which much of the melodic material was drawn. Liszt's musical style is distinguished by theme transformation in most of his orchestral works.

Like Berlioz, he sought orchestral effect to depict or describe feelings associated with his programs. Since his conception of program music was quite different from that of Strauss or the more descriptive composers, Liszt never completely explained the exact meaning he was assigning to various orchestral effects. A typical Liszt program was more philosophical in nature, dealing with the source of his inspiration or with the overall effect or thoughts the music might suggest.

The overall aural impression one receives from Liszt's orchestral works is similar to that obtained from Berlioz. The works are colorful, expressive in orchestral resources, ever-changing in tempos and dynamics, somewhat chromatic in both melody and harmony, and not seeking an inner musical logic such as that exhibited in the works of the more conservative composers. The works' rhapsodic style places what formal implications Liszt used in a subservient position; most of the works employ forms that are less constraining in design or are relaxed versions of some larger forms. The harmonic style was one of the most innovative of the mid-nineteenth century, employing a type of chromaticism that at times avoided traditional root relationships such as up a second or down a fifth. Liszt never really systematized his harmonic resources with the types of sequential procedures that helped stabilize Wagner's chromaticism. Melodic development in the larger works does use sequence and repetition abundantly. Dynamic contrasts and changes of tempos appear impulsive as Liszt adjusts his resources to his program. In the first movement of the *Faust* Symphony there are eleven tempo changes in the exposition section alone. Liszt also adhered to the use of accented dissonance in his more expressive melodies. Like Berlioz, Liszt relied on effect (orchestral, harmonic, dynamic, tempo, etc.) as the primary expressive device. His orchestra was a typical "large" orchestra of the nineteenth century, the enlargement being primarily in the brass section, where he often used four horns, three trumpets, three trombones, tuba, and a large percussion section. Woodwinds were generally in pairs.

Information on Individual Symphonies

Name	*Date*	*I*		*III*	*IV*
Faust	1854 (revised, 1861; revised, 1880)	SA	ABA	SA	Choral ending added to III in 1857
Dante	1856	"Inferno"	"Purgatorio"		Magnificat for women's voices added to second movement in place of the planned third movement, "Paradiso."

EXAMPLES FOR STUDY

Liszt: *Faust Symphony, completed in 1854; finale chorus added in 1857*

The legend of Faust was based on the real life of Magister Georgius Sagellicus Faustus, Junior (first mentioned in a letter of August 20, 1507, from the abbot of Spanheim, a Benedictine monk). Successive writers gradually evolved a story of Faust, an elderly man who trades his soul to the Devil (Mephistopheles) for the possession of supernatural powers. During succeeding eras, the story was changed. Goethe made Faust capable of being saved through repentance. Operas have avoided a higher plane of intellectual thought, stressing Faust's yearning for power and youth rather than his desire for understanding and eternal life. Thus the seduction of Gretchen (or Margaret), while a typical operatic scene maker, served to represent Faust's futile grasping for the essence of life.

I: Faust: Lento assai, Allegro impetuoso, etc. Liszt selected the three main characters of the Faust story (Faust, Gretchen, and Mephistopheles), as subjects for each of the three movements, adding a final male chorus with tenor soloist as a sectional fourth movement which he attached to the third movement in the manner of a coda. The form of the first movement was designed as a fairly free sonata-allegro. The orchestra required for the first movement consists of: piccolo, two flutes, two oboes, two clarinets, two bassoons, four horns, three trumpets, two tenor trombones, bass trombone, tuba, three timpani, cymbals, and strings. The five main themes have been identified as suggesting the following aspects of Faust's personality:*

Theme A: Mystical, magical nature of Faust
Theme B: Faust's emotional character, his longing for a life he has not been able to attain
Theme C: Faust's urge for life, his restlessness
Theme D: Faust's longing for that most painful joy
Theme E: Faust's heroic aspirations

The movement opens with a slow section in which the first two themes (A, B) are presented. The construction of the first theme is from augmented triads; it also contains all of the twelve tones. An *Allegro* section with little thematic significance leads to a short development of the A theme. A fermata separates this portion of the movement from the third theme (C), a more agitated section with an extended development. This section climaxes just as the D theme enters. This new theme is also subjected to a brief development, with fragments of other themes in the background. At measure 147 Liszt starts a passage which has as its basis a series of chords in third relation with one another:

Above this harmonic background Liszt states short motives from the first theme. A continued development of the C theme leads to the heroic E theme, aptly scored for brass. The development concerns itself primarily with the C theme and the A theme. A recapitulation adjusts the order of events slightly by omitting the D theme and by ending with a contrapuntal combination of the A and C themes, a technique similar to that used by Berlioz. The work soon has adjusted its materials so that the E theme (heroic) becomes the climactic material. There is a brief return to the combined A and C themes just prior to the start of the coda. The final section of the movement dwells on the E, A, and B themes, in that order. The B theme is stated only once, in the bass strings, as the movement concludes.

---

* Humphrey Searle, "Franz Liszt" in *The Symphony*, ed. Robert Simpson, 2 vols. (Baltimore: Penguin Books, 1966–67), 1, 265–68.

II: **Gretchen: Andante soave.** This three-part (ABA) movement is scored for three flutes, two oboes, two clarinets, two bassoons, four horns, two trumpets, three trombones, tuba, timpani, cymbals, harp, and strings. The work assumes a more intimate mood through the extensive use of solo instruments and chamber music effects. The introductory section is for a woodwind quartet

(two oboes, two clarinets). The Gretchen theme is played by the solo oboe
with an arpeggiated accompaniment by a solo viola, which is then handed to
a solo second violin at measure 26. Gradually more woodwinds and strings appear in the fabric (two strings on a part and finally the entire section). A brief
appearance of one of the Faust themes (ID—i.e., first movement, theme D) at
measure 45 supposedly signals Faust's appearance on the scene. After a brief
development of the Gretchen theme, the middle section begins, marked *dolce
amoroso*. This middle part soon becomes a delicate intermingling of the themes
representing both Faust and Gretchen. Muted strings, reduced forces (at times
only two strings per part), flute arpeggios in three parts as harmonic support,
quiet harp accompaniments, and even an emphasis on piano dynamic markings
for the few tutti passages (which represent some of the Faust motives) are
indicative of the intimate atmosphere Liszt attempted to convey to the listener.
A quartet of first violins restates the Gretchen tune as the return of the first
section occurs at measure 208. By the time another Faust theme reappears,
Liszt has added the full string section. The coda dwells quietly on the Gretchen
theme from the middle section. There is a quiet mention of the Faust heroic
theme as the movement comes to a close.

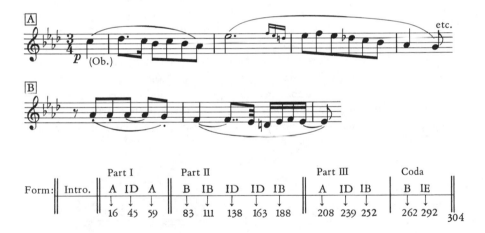

III: Mephistopheles; Allegro vivace, ironico. The finale, while fitting into
the overall outline of sonata-allegro form, is a study in theme transformation
which transcends traditional formal considerations. Attempting to project the
corruption of Faust by Mephistopheles and the eventual salvation of his soul
through the love of Gretchen, Liszt created extended musical parodies of three
of the basic Faust themes from the first movement. There is no thematic repre-
sentation for Mephistopheles. The only theme which resists transformation is
the Gretchen theme, appearing near the conclusion of the instrumental section
of the movement. The third movement then becomes a study in Liszt's tech-

nique of theme variation. Practically every melodic thought (with a few exceptions) can be related to basic themes presented in the first movement. Only the initial Faust theme from the first movement (the mystical Faust) is not changed.

The movement opens with a quiet introduction in which three basic motives are announced. The second introductory theme (I^2) was supposedly borrowed from an earlier piano concerto and could be interpreted as the ridiculing laugh of Mephistopheles. The exposition opens with a new version of the IC theme, which had served as one of the principal themes of the first movement. After a short development the A^2 theme (from IB) enters, also in parody style. Liszt then launches into an extended development of this theme, with some references to the IB theme interspersed. Finally, the A^3 theme begins at measure 153. After a brief reflection on the IA theme (measure 173), Liszt inserts a fugue on a subject derived from the IB theme. This treatment and further working out of a motive from the A^3 theme lead to subordinate theme B (derived from the Faust heroic theme IE) at measure 301. This is the ultimate of parodies, resembling the treatment Berlioz accorded the theme of the "Witches' Dance" in the finale of the *Symphonie Fantastique*. Several of the other Faust themes interrupt, the IE theme reenters with tremendous energy at measure 362. As the sound subsides, the Gretchen theme makes a subdued appearance (measure 421), followed by an equally subdued Faust theme (IA) and a very quiet "laugh" theme (I^2). A quick crescendo into a recapitulation follows; this section treats only the A^1 and B themes. A coda contains a number of the previous themes, including the Gretchen tune at the very end of the coda. At this point Liszt wrote two endings; the second connects to the choral finale. This transition is built entirely on a German sixth chord which filters out on a tonic pedal in the timpani. The analysis of the choral section follows as the fourth movement.

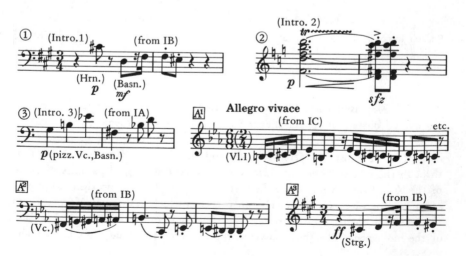

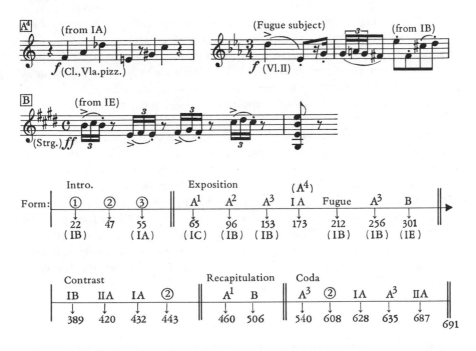

Choral finale or coda. Liszt selected the "Chorus Mysticus" from the final section of the second part of Goethe's *Faust* as the text for the choral finale. It translates as:

All that is past of us	All indescribables
Was but reflected,	Here we descry;
All that was lost in us	The eternal feminine
Here is corrected;	Leads us on high.

The orchestration of the final section includes piccolo, flute, two clarinets, two oboes, two bassoons, four horns, three trumpets, three trombones, tuba, two timpani, cymbal, organ, harp, tenor solo, four-part male chorus, and strings. Liszt changed musical styles for the choral finale, resorting to a more placid and musically simple setting. The harmonic materials tend to remain in a free style; a firm C major is established for most of the movement, with a sequential motion through A-flat and B major, then back to C. This tonal plan is repeated as the text is sung for a second time. The composer has used a large number of dominant harmonies which resolve irregularly in embellishing the simple setting being sung by the male chorus. The final cadence returns to the same German sixth chord which closed the transition at the end of the third movement. This time, however, Liszt had the tenor soloist resolve the chord while singing the words "Leads us . . ." by taking its third (A-flat) to the tonic (C). The final eight bars contain only the tonic chord.

The setting of the text could be considered symbolic in the composer's use of the Gretchen theme to support the words "Eternal feminine." The first six lines of the poem are sung in unison by the male chorus on a single pitch for each couplet (or complete thought in the translation). Starting on the tonic center (C), Liszt moved each couplet up the tonic chord outline to the next chord member. The choral melody remains on a single pitch for each setting of the words. The passage is sequenced twice, the third setting taking the work back to C major. At this point the soloist sings the entire final couplet, with the chorus injecting a slight punctuation in the background. The whole setting is repeated with much stronger support from the orchestra and a fuller dynamic level from the male voices. The chorus finally departs from its single-pitch tunes by ascending the E-flat major triad, *forte,* on the same words, "Leads us on high." After a slowly descending tenor solo, the men break into four parts to set up the German sixth. Their final voicing is in three parts on the final tonic chord. The setting is very effective since it does stress an extremely reflective male chorus contrasting with a lyric and soaring tenor line on the Gretchen motive.

SUMMARY

Considered by many Liszt's greatest masterpiece, the *Faust* Symphony carried forward the expressive aspect of nineteenth-century music in a type of program symphony that did not sustain itself as a viable form for the remainder of the nineteenth century. The work, especially in the third movement, is truly a brilliant illustration of theme transformation. There can be no doubt what the implications are when the primary Faust themes are corrupted to the extent seen in the third movement. The tonal and orchestral characterization reflects the same exceptional usage. Liszt's harmonic style tends to delay or ornament the normal resolution of dominant harmonies in the emphasis on stressing chromatic motion in individual lines. A semblance of traditional harmonic usage scattered along the way lends a certain amount of familiarity to the tonal materials. The consistent half-step motion in the parts, the reiteration of motives, and the single orchestral effect maintained throughout the passages in question help unify what the relaxed tonal structure seems to have abandoned. His concern for depiction not only enlarged both the scope and function of the symphony but also resulted in an expressive and experimental dimension in his handling of tonality and harmony. The *Faust* Symphony can be accepted, then, not only as a prime example of the program symphony under the influence of Liszt's concept of theme transformation but also as a progressive work exclusive of its programmatic import. The third movement should be studied extensively in order to understand the nature of Liszt's transformation of themes and other supporting materials. Liszt's harmonic vocabulary, while not yet as well-ordered as that of the more conservative composers (Brahms, etc.), still shows a freedom of usage which supports his position as one of the progressive composers of the nineteenth century.

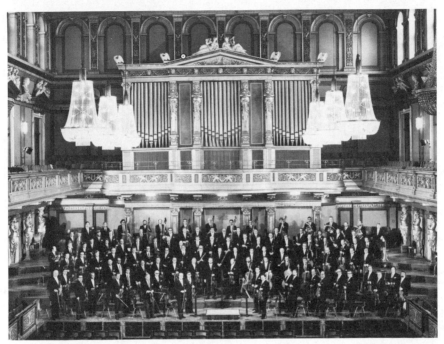

The present home of the Vienna Philharmonic was opened on January 5, 1870, and subsequently has become known as the finest concert hall available, according to most conductors. The above picture is of the orchestra during the 1976–77 season. Courtesy Vienna Philharmonic and Siegfried Lauterwasser.

Johannes Brahms (1833–1897)

> In this age of turmoil and iconoclasm Brahms' symphonies still stand four-square to the world: pillars of classical architecture on whose firm, consonant foundation nineteenth-century romantic sounds soar upward in a pre-conceived plan mindful of every detail however small. Nothing is left to chance; each movement has its course determined from the very first note.*

After the ascendency of Berlioz and Liszt into positions of leadership among the more progressive nineteenth-century composers, a new champion appeared in the person of Richard Wagner (1813–1883). Having met Liszt in 1840, Wagner made such a positive impression on the virtuoso that Liszt produced *Lohengrin* for him in 1850 in Weimar. By 1854, Wagner had completed the

---

* Julius Harrison, "Johannes Brahms," in *The Symphony*, 1, 316. Quoted with permission of publisher.

Philharmonische Concerte.

Sonntag den 2. November 1873,

Mittags halb 1 Uhr, im

großen Saale der Gesellschaft der Musikfreunde:

1ˢᵗᵉˢ Abonnement-Concert

veranstaltet von den

Mitgliedern des k. k. Hof-Opern-Orchesters

unter der Leitung des k. k. Hof-Opern-Kapellmeisters Herrn

Otto Dessoff.

PROGRAMM:

Mozart . . . . . Sinfonie *Nr. 5, D-dur.*

Brahms . . . . Variationen *über ein Thema von Jos. Haydn (NEU)*

unter Leitung des Componisten.

Schubert . . . . Ouverture *zu „Alfonso und Estrella".*

Beethoven . . . Sinfonie *Nr. 7, A-dur.*

Streichinstrumente: Lemböck.

Das 2. Philharmonische Concert findet am 16. November 1873 statt.

Programme unentgeltlich.

Sunday, November 2, 1873: An 1873 subscription concert by the Vienna Philharmonic that featured the premiere of the Brahms *Haydn Variations,* a Schubert overture, the Beethoven seventh, and a Mozart *Sinfonie Nr. 5, D-dur (major)*, which was either Mozart's Haffner (No. 35, K. 385) or Prague symphony (No. 38, K. 504). Note the appearance of Brahms as a conductor of the variations. Courtesy the Vienna Philharmonic.

Philharmonische Concerte.

Sonntag den 30. Dezember 1877.

Mittags präcise halb 1 Uhr.

im grossen Saale der Gesellschaft der Musikfreunde:

4ten Abonnement-Concert

veranstaltet von den

Mitgliedern des k. k. Hofopern-Orchesters

unter der Leitung des k. k. Hofopern Kapellmeisters Herrn

HANS RICHTER.

PROGRAMM:

Mendelssohn . . Ouverture zu „Ruy Blas."

Mozart . . . . Drei Sätze aus der Serenade für Blasinstrumente.

Brahms . . . Zweite Symphonie (Erste Aufführung).

J. S. Bach . . Präludium und Fuga mit Choral. orchestrirt von Abert.

Streichinstrumente: Lemböck.

Das 5. Philharmonische Concert findet am 13 Jänner 1878 statt.

Programme unentgeltlich.

Wallishausser's Druckerei, Dorotheagass 7

Sunday, December 30, 1877: The premiere of Brahms's second symphony is noted in this program.

145

CONCERT

des

Anton Bruckner,

k. k. Hoforganist und Professor am Conservatorium,

Sonntag den 26. Oktober 1873,

Mittags halb 1 Uhr.

im großen Musikvereinssaale.

PROGRAMM:

1. **Toccata** *in C, für Orgel* . . . . **S. Bach.**

2. **Improvisation** *für Orgel.*

3. **Symfonie** *in C-moll* . . . . **A. Bruckner**

unter gütiger Mitwirkung der **philharmonischen Gesellschaft.**
dirigirt vom Componisten.

Preise der Plätze:

Sitzplätze im Parterre, in den Logen und der I. Gallerie, 1. Reihe	à fl. 3.—
Sitzplätze in den Logen, der I. Gallerie, 2. und folgende Reihen	à fl. 2.—
Sitzplätze der II. Gallerie · · · · · ·	à fl. 1.50
Eintrittskarten · · · · · · · ·	à fl. 1. –

Billetenverkauf in den Musikalienhandlungen **Haslinger, Spina's Nachfolger, Lewy, Wessely, Buchholz & Diebel** und am Concerttage an der Cassa.

Sunday, October 26, 1873: A Bruckner concert with the composer performing as organist, and later, conductor. While not indicated, this was the premiere of the composer's second symphony.

first of the *Ring* cycle operas and was fast becoming the leader of a new German musical style, a style which had its roots in the expressive nature of the music of Berlioz and Liszt. The expressive role of the orchestra, the programmatic intent of much of the mid-nineteenth-century music, and the new principles of unifying musical forms (idée fixe, theme transformation, etc.) all created a fertile soil for the growth of the expressive Wagnerian musical style. It was during this expressive onslaught best personified by the Wagnerian style that Brahms appears as the major orchestral composer of his day.

Brahms often considered himself a man who lived after his times, a classicist adrift in the torrents of romanticism. Brahms chose to follow the concepts of the classicist, imbuing his own brilliant formal craft with a lyricism and an expression most appropriate to the essential nature of nineteenth-century music as an art of personal expression. Completely rejecting both the ultraemotional and the programmatic, Brahms found himself elevated to a position as the champion of absolute music, a role which implied active opposition to the works of Wagner. From this position Brahms began writing symphonies in 1876 and thus established himself as the greatest symphonist of the nineteenth century, possibly the greatest of all since Beethoven.

Brahms's style is one of great complexity and intricacy. His textures are often muddy and thick because of the great amount of contrapuntal figuration used in almost all his works. The general level of continuity is high; works are constructed out of highly integrated materials; a constant flow and line are always evident in all of his works. Cadences are elided or avoided by the frequent overlapping of phrases. The music also has a richness of sonority since Brahms often avoided the fifth in triadic structures.

A Brahms melody can be folklike, triadic, or motivic. Above all, it is lyric. Slow movements often have long, spun-out tunes. Some themes which outline triads (a favorite Brahms usage) will omit the fifth. His skill in the use of melodic motives to unify or articulate a work is unequaled by any composer of symphonies after Beethoven. Brahms was also able to project a sense of line in his melodies through the avoidance of cadences, the overlapping of phrases, and rhythmic independence.

Rhythm is a unique style feature. Brahms was one of the greatest rhythmic innovators of the nineteenth century. His use of syncopation and superimposed rhythmic backgrounds (triplets against duplets) is a prime feature. His shifting metric accents (heavy beat on fourth beat of a four-beat meter, for example) sometimes permeate an entire section of a work.* Rhythm becomes a formal device in its delineation of a basic texture, its disrupted flow

---

* Brahms's ability to diversify the rhythmic aspect of his music has been referred to as "softening the hard edges of the bar-line." See Julius Harrison, *Brahms and His Four Symphonies* (London: Chaplam & Hall, Ltd., 1939), p. 53.

at breaks in the form, and its motivic application to give a section some degree of unity. Brahms also used rhythmic devices to establish melodic independence in texture that tended toward the polyphonic. Thus one part in duple background (♩ = ♫) might contrast with an accompanying part in triple background (♩ = ♪♪♪).

Brahms's harmonic technique is characterized by a chromaticism organized to some extent like that of Mozart: traditional root relationships, sequential writing, emphasized linear chromaticism, and accented dissonance. The sequence also is crucial to the organization of chromatic materials. Many times a nontonal device will be employed to organize a section which has some degree of tonal instability. This can be a textural device (two voices in canon), a rhythmic device (frequently a rhythmic ostinato or pedal), or a more characteristic device of a complex nature. Plagal cadences and progressions occur more frequently than in the works of Brahms's peers. The basic vertical unit is still the triad.

Tonality is treated with greater freedom than is harmony. A key center in a Brahms work may appear to be a single pitch rather than a single modality (e.g., the key of E rather than the key of E major). This apparent freedom from major-minor bias in tonality allows him to use either or both plus all of the harmonic materials which the broadened pitch spectrum of the major-minor mix makes available. Brahms's concept of a related key encompasses practically any tonal area that might exist in the pitch spectrum, with a definite preference for third-related keys. Tonality is constantly shifting to related and unrelated areas.

Form is an absolutely essential element of the style. Carrying on the intellectual tradition established by Beethoven, Brahms sought an even tighter and more subtle formal integration of his own works. The dovetailing of phrases and the emphasis on articulation of materials gives his music a somewhat rhapsodic, nonpunctuated effect. There is also a renewal of interest in contrapuntal procedures and forms. The symphonies adhere to standard forms with the exception of the finale of the fourth symphony, a chaconne. Of the sixteen symphony movements, only seven (44 percent) are full-blown sonata-allegro movements. Six are part forms or modified rondo forms. Two are sonatina form. The declining usage of sonata-allegro form in the Brahms style shows a contrast with Beethoven's twenty out of thirty-seven movements (54 percent) in the form. It does compare with other nineteenth-century composers such as Schubert (43 percent), Mendelssohn (40 percent), and Schumann (47 percent). Exactly 50 percent of the Haydn London symphonies have sonata-allegro related movements. The apparent lack of sonata-allegro form might be deceptive in the case of Brahms, since most of the individual symphony movements are preponderantly developmental in style. Brahms's ability to construct a work of considerable internal formal complexity and yet to imbue it with an almost total lyric aura testifies not only to his affection for two often conflicting style values but also to the genius of his talent in being able to blend both styles so subtly. While every pitch and rhythmic value appear to be part of a deliberately premeditated plan, each work sounds as if it were the gradual unfolding of a free and unending lyric line.

As a contrapuntal composer, Brahms had an unchallenged position in the nineteenth century. The extensive use of imitation, canon, and fugue is much more important to his overall style than it is to the style of other nineteenth-century composers. He worked for a contrapuntal effect in other ways also: through contrary motion between primary lines in a work (i.e., a descending melody pitted against an ascending arpeggiated accompaniment), two lines in free counterpoint supported by a pedal (as in the introduction of the first symphony's opening movement), contrary motion between two arpeggiated lines used as an accompaniment texture (Symphony No. 2, second movement, measures 74–75), two lines in contrary motion over a pedal (Symphony No. 2, second movement, measures 1–2), antiphonal imitation between two choirs of the orchestra (Symphony No. 1, second movement, measures 63–66), and many other similar devices. Brahms many times used one of these contrapuntal textures in his most expressive passages (Symphony No. 1, second movement, measures 34–47, and Symphony No. 2, first movement, measures 134–51: a modified canonic passage over a pedal; or Symphony No. 2, second movement, measures 73–75: the use of contrary motion between two groups of arpeggiating instruments which are providing the accompaniment to a lyric line). A particularly ingenious passage, where Brahms placed an ostinato figure in the upper strings and a pedal in the bass line (root and fifth of the chord primarily) to accompany the tune harmonized in parallel thirds and sixths, is located in measures 62–65 of the second movement of Symphony No. 3.

Brahms's orchestration tends toward somber combinations, since no effort seems to have been made to employ striking orchestral effects. Expressive lines are treated in a typical nineteenth-century fashion: octave doublings within a given choir, particularly in the violins. Arpeggiation is a typical device in all instruments except some of the brass instruments. This textural device is used in all of his music, regardless of medium (piano music, chamber music, etc.). Parallel thirds abound in all of his music and tend to support a sonority concept which neglects the fifth of a triad. Other composers have used the same device but not to the extent employed by Brahms. Pizzicato is also an effective device when used by the entire string section (Symphony No. 1, fourth movement, measures 6–12), by a single string part (Symphony No. 1, second movement, measures 66–70), or by the bass strings as the only instruments on the bass line (Symphony No. 4, fourth movement, measures 41–48).

Information on Individual Symphonies

No.	Key	Date	Intro.	I	II	III	IV
1	c	1876	yes	SA	ABA	ABACA	SA
2	D	1877	no	SA	SA	ABACA	SA
3	F	1883	no	SA	ABA	ABA	Sonatina
4	e	1885	no	SA	Sonatina	ABA DEV. ABA Scherzo Trio Scherzo	Chaconne

SYMPHONY NO. 1

This work is discussed fully beginning on page 158.

SYMPHONY NO. 2

After the complexity of the first movement of the first symphony, the simpler lyricism of the second symphony represents a stronger affirmation of the lyric nature of the nineteenth-century symphony. The second symphony is traditional in many ways: it has an emphasis on development in the three sonata-allegro movements; simple, clear-cut, lyric tunes in all four movements; tight motivic organization in all four movements; and the use of the classical repeat of the exposition of the first movement. Its departure from tradition results more from the application of the overall Brahms style than from a radical infusion of any new element in the treatment of the symphony.

In the opening nine measures of the first movement the lyric principal theme presents three germinal motives upon which the first movement is based. The horns, aided at times by the woodwinds, carry the triadic first tune for almost twenty-four measures, an indication again of the increasing importance of the winds in the expression of the lyric aspect of the nineteenth-century symphony. Two additional segments complete the principal thematic material. A short transition passage (measure 78–81) follows, illustrating Brahms's use of meter as a formal device. In this case, meter is contracted from the movement's basic three-beat scheme to two beats to help delineate more clearly the end of the principal and the beginning of the subordinate sections. The new theme (measure 82) is a simple lyric tune harmonized in parallel thirds in the violas and cellos, the latter scored as the upper voice. Bass pizzicato on the first two beats of each measure provides delicate support while the violins echo motivic triad outlines for the remaining harmonic materials. The passage contains three characteristic Brahms devices: parallel thirds, arpeggiation, and pizzicato. Two themes plus a return to the lyric second theme comprise the closing section. One theme (measures 134–51) is constructed upon a pedal with two voices in canon. The passage is in three sections, the first energizing the dominant pitch level of A major by placing the root and seventh of the dominant chord (E, D) in the pedal. This tonal thrust changes at measure 144 as the pedal focuses on some of the pitches of the D major dominant chord (A, E, G). Measure 149 shows a similar change to E major. This entire passage also shows how Brahms could retard the harmonic rhythm to the repetition of a single chord for nine measures, five measures, or three measures and yet maintain the line in the music by use of an extended canon in two opposing orchestral forces. This emphasis on the achievement of line and lyricism through nonmelodic means (texture, harmony, etc.) illustrates that Brahms was more innovative than might be discerned by the casual listener.

The development section works with a variety of themes and emphasizes contrapuntal procedures in some sections. An extended and climactic section using the three parts of the first theme (measures 224–301) leads to a greatly abbreviated restatement of the first materials (forty-seven measures versus eighty-one measures in the exposition). The subordinate theme returns with a slightly modified orchestral setting. The coda, after disposing of the first tune, launches into a long and impassioned horn solo based on the simple motive (E, F-sharp, E) from the third measure of the first theme.

The *Adagio* movement is one of Brahms's most expressive slow movements. Its sonata-allegro form lacks only the restatement of the subordinate theme. The first theme's opening sixteen bars are in a vague ternary structure, the middle phrases providing some of the composer's most inspired lyric writing (measures 6–12). Measures 6–8 are particularly attractive and yet constitute one of the simplest textural, melodic, and harmonic contributions in the movement. The harmony is quite normal: iii–vi–ii–V–I. The melody is phrased in groups of eight pitches, not unusual in a four-beat meter. The texture is simple homophony, melody with accompaniment. Only the rhythm serves to inject just enough instability to increase whatever tension is created by the sequence-like melody. The accompaniment is placed entirely on the second and fourth beats. The tune is shifted one eighth note off the beat so that the meter of the tune seems to lag perceptively behind the meter of the accompaniment. It is a masterful example of the composer's ability to fine-tune simple materials to achieve a more expressive result. These opening bars reveal another Brahms tonal trait: starting a work with indefinite tonality by implying the use of a diminished triad for the tonic chord. A second portion of the opening section (measures 17–28) moves into a fugal treatment of some complexity. The secondary theme, in 12/8 meter, is syncopated against a pizzicato cello bass line. The developmental section works with the closing theme but under greater contrapuntal stress. Near this section's conclusion (measures 57–58) the principal theme appears as a countermelody above the closing materials. This texture continues as the recapitulation begins. This continuation of a procedure begun in the development section accomplishes two goals: the blurring of a major break in the form and the sustaining of a fairly continuous development over the last half of the movement. Those uncomfortable with the broad outline of the above analysis might find a ternary assessment an attractive option (A = 1–32, B = 33–61, A = 62–96, plus coda).

The third movement, a strikingly original scherzo, achieves rondo form using thematic, metric, and temporal contrasts:

Section	A	B	A	C	A
Meter	3/4	2/4	3/4	3/8	3/4
Tempo	*Allegretto*	*Presto*	*Allegretto*	*Presto*	*Allegretto*

Continuity among the five large sections is achieved by a subtle interrelationship among many themes. The B theme is actually a faster version of the A theme. The B section's contrasting theme (measure 51) is extracted from the contrasting tune of the A section (measure 11). The C theme (measure 132) bears a strong resemblance to the contrasting theme of the B section (measure 51). A fascinating tonal diversion occurs as the movement opens. The first theme implies a strong modal (Aeolian, e) organization in its first five measures while the accompaniment is firmly placed in G major. In the return of the A section (measures 107–25) the B pitch level (measures 114–25) is emphasized while the tonality moves through e minor and C major, cadencing finally in E major (final beat, measure 125). In the final A section (measures 194–240), the e minor implication is weakened considerably by the use of g minor as a base for the tune.

The finale returns to some of the thematic complexity of the first symphony by using a germinal motive extracted from the opening theme of the symphony (D, C-sharp, D, F-sharp) to unify many of the finale's themes. Further, another portion of the finale's main theme (measure 9) is based on a motive from the fifth measure of the first movement's opening tune. While dominating the first 150 measures of the exposition, the germinal motive moves into the background as a part of the accompaniment figuration of the second theme (measure 78). Considerable motivic fragmentation occurs in the development section, especially in measures 188–94. The development ends quietly, using the theme from measure 9 of the exposition. The recapitulation is orderly but deals rather irregularly with the principal theme: the second portion of the theme is inverted; a development of four pitches (F-sharp, A, G, F-sharp) from the theme involves a long, ostinato passage and an inversion of the germinal motive (measures 267–73); the principal section is shortened from its original seventy-seven-measure length to only thirty-six measures by removing most of the developmental materials used in the exposition. A dramatic coda brings the movement to a close. Much of the conclusive impetus of the coda can be attributed to an emphasis on brass instruments, particularly the tenor and lower brasses. This emphasis is seen in a section (measures 386–405) where the lower brasses double the bass line (measures 397–402) at the unison. The coda closes with the three trombones sustaining the final tonic chord while the rest of the orchestra punctuate the first beat of each measure with single-beat chords.

SYMPHONY NO. 3

This work shows a more highly integrated conception of the symphony through its use of a germinal motive for many of the themes of all four movements. This "motto" theme is stated in the first two measures: an ascending minor third (F, A-flat) which alternates between major and minor in subsequent themes. The interval is also inverted in some themes. A secondary germinating motive has a neighbor-tone pattern: F–G–F or F–E–F. The opening motive appears in its original form in the finale. Its basic contour is also a part of many of the symphony's themes.

The opening of the first movement exhibits both major and minor modes in the setting of the germinal motive (measures 3–4). Each measure also exhibits a metric duality wherein a 6/4 measure alternately (and simultaneously) phrases in two three-beat or three two-beat patterns. The subordinate theme opens with a static harmonic setting (measures 36–43). A countermelody in another wind part completes a typical Brahms texture: ostinato support for two contrapuntal lines with the tonic chord serving as the ostinato. A similar setting of the theme occurs near the beginning of the development section (measures 77–87) but has an implication of tonic and dominant chord changes in the chord-bearing members of the accompaniment forces. These chordal inferences are almost contrapuntal in conception. A coda closes with a cadence based on the movement's opening chord progression: B diminished seventh chord resolving to an F major (tonic) triad. The progression is plagal in origin and is a refinement of the composer's plagal tendencies. The progression, because of the tritone root relationship between both chords (B–F), is also somewhat ambiguous. This is not altogether inappropriate, considering its original use in accompanying a motto theme based on the ambiguous concept of dual modality.

The second movement is in ternary form that also includes features of sonata-allegro. The middle section, in particular, is in part developmental. This middle section at one point moves quietly to a series of seemingly disjointed chords (measures 56–62) which are echoed in groups contrasting in register and color (low strings versus high woodwinds, for example). This widely-separated scoring conceals a progression of conservative origin: IV–II–V–I. Each basic function, however, undergoes some kind of transformation. The IV chord starts as a minor seventh chord and becomes a dominant seventh; the II chord begins as an augmented sixth chord and also becomes a dominant seventh; the third experiences a similar change. As did Mozart in similar passages,

Brahms conceals the basis of the progression by emphasizing the chromatic potential of the passage by creating a prominent melodic line containing the pitch changes for the clarinet and bassoon at the octave. Then follows the developmental part of the middle section, a part which portrays considerably rhythmic instability (measures 62–70). The passage has a quasi-ostinato definition in the uppermost voices and a progression of parallel thirds for some of the melody-carrying voices. Later the passage begins to merge both ostinato and melody voices into a strange line which seems to lurch either ahead of or behind itself. In this instance the conflicting rhythmic background of each line (two versus three) helps establish a degree of independence for each line. The composer's intent may have been expressive, since parts are doubled at the triple octave in the strings. Just prior to the coda, the horns convert a motive from the third measure of the movement's first theme into a version of the symphony's motto theme (measures 106–7). The final cadence is plagal.

The third movement is in a moderately paced ternary form, almost a waltz in its opening and closing sections. The first theme is scored at the outset for the upper register of the cello and stresses dissonance at the high point of each segment of its phrases. A second portion of the first section has an imitative segment which gradually evolves into an extended passage in parallel tenths (measures 32–37). The first of two themes in the large middle section is subjected to rhythmic displacement in its bass line.

The finale opens with a first theme of four parts, the third of which (measures 19–28) seems to have been extracted from the first theme of the second movement's middle section (measures 40–43). The exposition progresses through the three main thematic groups, each containing at least two subthemes. In some respects the second half of the sonatina form of this movement can be considered a blending of the elements of both development and recapitulation. This is implied in the handling of the principal materials in measures 134–48 and 149–71. In the former section a scale motive is extracted from the theme and is used as a countermelody in a contrapuntal working out of the opening motive. In the second section the quiet triple theme is transformed into a more expansive and powerful statement. The remaining themes return in the same broad manner, finally subsiding for a coda which starts with a triplet version of the movement's principal theme (measures 252–60, muted violas, etc.) and moves to an augmented statement of the same theme (measures 267–71). The motto theme from the first movement quietly closes the movement (measures 301–9). This has been prefaced by a double statement of the F, A-flat motive in the woodwinds and horns.

SYMPHONY NO. 4

The first movement (*Allegro non troppo*) starts with an eighteen-bar statement of the first theme, a long, somewhat lyric expression of three primary ideas (measures 1–2, 9–10, and 13–14). The first segment converts the princi-

pal chords of the tonic key (e minor) into a sequential passage of ascending
and descending pairs of notes. The arpeggiated accompaniment in the cellos and
violas and the quasi-canonic chords (actually parallel thirds) in the woodwinds
combine to create the impression of a mildly contrapuntal texture when, in
essence, a simple homophony underlies it all. Contrary motion typifies the two
remaining segments of the principal theme (measures 9–12, 13–16). For the
next thirty-four measures a mini-development of the three basic ideas of the
first theme occurs. The contrapuntal style of previous materials is continued.
A fanfarelike passage introduces the subordinate theme (measure 53), an extended lyric tune which is doubled in the beginning in the cellos and horns
(first and second). The fanfare tune shifts into the background as an accompaniment figure but becomes more assertive as the closing section nears. An
antiphonal treatment of the opening theme of the movement (pizzicato strings
versus staccato woodwinds) is followed by two lyric segments of the closing
section, the second (measures 95–106) getting more emphasis. A second portion
of the closing section uses a motive from the subordinate fanfare theme to
work up an impressive climax (measures 110–36). Offbeat accents in both
triplets and duplets (measures 127–29) displace the meter by one-half beat.
The transition to the development is very subtle: a quiet extension using the
opening motive (falling third) which implies a shift to the dominant major key
(B major), only to become quickly the dominant seventh of the true tonic for
the beginning of the development (measures 137–44). After an almost exact
restatement of the movement's opening eight bars, a new figure occurs in the
woodwinds (measures 157–64). The new figure becomes increasingly more important as the development progresses. Its origin is probably from the lyric tune
of the subordinate section. As the imitative interplay of short motives continues, this new figure becomes the subject of a terse contrapuntal development
which contains canonic and mirror features (measures 168–83).

Soon the fanfare theme becomes the center of developmental efforts and
carries the movement into a section wherein the opening tune is accompanied by
a new theme spun from the ongoing line of the fanfare theme (measures 219–
26). The recapitulation has the same quiet beginnings as did the development in
that the opening tune of the movement very slowly enters in augmentation in
the woodwinds, which play the first eight pitches of the rising-falling interval
series (measures 246–58) in four-note segments. The last of these segments is
sustained while an arpeggio figure from the initial fanfare section helps to extend the harmonic materials. Before one knows it, the recapitulation is under-
way, with the interval direction of the tune inverted. The restatement fairly
closely approximates the exposition. A coda starts with a marvelous canonic
passage between the lower strings (plus a horn or two at times) and the rest
of the orchestra. The passage quickly narrows its imitative gap from a full beat
to a half beat by measure 397. The movement closes with a short lyric motive
from the closing section (measures 430–31).

The second movement (*Andante moderato*) begins as a unison statement of a Phrygian melody on E. In the fifth measure, however, a change of mode to E major occurs in a fully harmonized version of the tune placed a third higher. The scoring is subdued: a four-voice setting in pizzicato strings, doubled in the upper three voices by the clarinets and bassoons. In the process some of the Phrygian modality is retained by lowering the sixth and seventh scale degrees in the melody. The theme is briefly reworked orchestrally before a more lyric transformation occurs at measure 30. At this point a typical Brahms treatment begins: tonic pedal, pizzicato arpeggios on the tonic chord as accompaniment, and a primary melody in parallel sixths. A second set of voices enters intermittently with a passage of descending parallel thirds. The setting is further enhanced by the superimposition of triplets in the accompaniment against duplets in the violin line. The second theme, a quietly moving lyric tune played by the cellos, is scored so that the cello line weaves gracefully among the three alto string voices providing the slowly moving harmonic support. The first violin line is a most delicate obbligato of ascending (and occasionally descending) arpeggios. This obbligato line begins to figure into a more specific imitative style in measure 48, the interplay of lines implying a sequence of ninth chords to enhance further the expressive nature of the entire passage. After an extension based on short motives from the final measures of this section, a first theme reappears (measure 64), carried primarily by the string section. Descending arpeggios (parallel thirds mostly) in the woodwinds flow gradually from upper flute range to lower horn range during each two-bar phrase statement of the tune by the strings (measures 64–71). The secondary theme reappears, scored this time in the first violins. The voicing of the parts is just as tight as that used in the original setting and is further congested by the subdivision of the string section into as many as nine parts, all in close harmony. A four-bar syncopated version of the theme, orchestral tutti, brings the section to a climax (measures 98–101). The movement then quietly slides into its coda, which begins with a very quiet version of the first theme set above a diminished chord on G-sharp. A final restatement of the first tune as a Phrygian melody closes the movement. The movement ends on the tonic major (E major).

The third movement has a faster tempo than the third movements of the other three symphonies and thus more closely approximates the spirit of the scherzo. The overall form, however, is developmental; in place of a trio the opening scherzo is contrasted with a development of its materials. The da capo of the scherzo is subverted to the extent that the three parts of the primary theme are regrouped in reverse order. The scherzo section of the movement is in ternary design, with the opening theme made up of three basic motives (measures 1–2, 6–8, and 10–12). The first motive is one of the thematic oddities of the symphonies: its bass line is almost a true mirror of the theme itself. The development undergoes a thematic transformation in measures 182–98. Brahms has converted the lively triplet third motive of the opening theme in this passage to a more lyric theme by radically adjusting its rhythmic and dynamic structure and by phrasing the entire segment to emphasize its singing quality. The movement is well known for its prominent triangle part, the only use of the instrument in all of the symphonies.

The finale, as mentioned before, is a chaconne with thirty variations. The chaconne subject is exactly eight bars in length and at times involves both a harmonic pattern and a melodic pattern. The variations total thirty in number plus two or three extended variations in the coda. Each of the thirty variations is exactly eight measures in length. Each variation retains either a harmonic or a melodic connection with the theme. Variations tend to gather themselves into groupings of twos and threes:

Theme + Variation 1	Variations 17 and 18
Variations 4, 5, and 6	Variations 19 and 20
Variations 8 and 9	Variations 22 and 23
Variations 12 and 13	Variations 24 and 25
Variations 14 and 15	Variations 26, 27 and 28
	Variations 29 and 30

Factors which tend to encourage this grouping are orchestration, melody, texture, or a specific treatment being used in a group of variations. For instance, variations 4, 5, and 6 all use a lyric version of a countermelody in the upper strings, which places its metric accent on the second beat of each measure. Variations 12 and 13 share a similar accompaniment pattern in the strings. In addition, the movement has a large ternary design with a slow middle section of four variations (12, 13, 14, and 15). In those variations where the melody is the constant, the movement resembles a passacaglia (variations 1, 2, 3, 4, 5, 8, 9, 16, and 24). Variations which retain the harmonic pattern (1, 2, 16, and 24) are even fewer in number.

Brahms's strong developmental tendencies probably did not allow him to retain the restrictions of a repetitive harmonic pattern and thus subjected the "inviolate" pattern to many transformations. The same could be said of the "fixed" melody, although it seemed to offer a lesser threat to the ongoing work of the movement. His adaptation of the baroque form into a developmental form was consistent with similar adaptations made in eighteenth-century movement forms by nineteenth-century composers, especially the third movement form (first, minuet; later, scherzo; still later, scherzolike; etc.). Space does not permit a detailed analysis of each variation.* What can be surmised is that an emphasis on lyricism in the composer's symphonies continues in this movement. The intricate and involved nature of the developmental treatment used in the set in no way diminishes the lyric appeal of the movement. This added to the

---

* A brief description of each variation is available in at least one other source. See Harrison, *Brahms and His Four Symphonies*, pp. 297–306.

dramatic use of the orchestra in many of the variations and an emphasis on expression through both melody and dynamics makes the movement one of the composer's most significant symphony movements.

EXAMPLES FOR STUDY

Brahms: *Symphony No. 1 in c minor, Op. 68*

I: **Un poco sostenuto, Allegro.** The first movement is a fairly straightforward sonata-allegro movement with introduction. The introduction is an organic part of the main body of the movement, presenting four basic motives upon which the themes of the *Allegro* section are based. The opening seven bars of the movement contain one of Brahms's unique textures: a sustained pedal (tonic) with a rising melody in the violins and a descending tune in parallel thirds in the woodwinds. The violin tune is displaced metrically to enhance the contrapuntal effect. The *Allegro* opens with a quick statement of the four motives (now the main theme) previously quoted in the introduction. The chromatic motive (A^1) is used as a counterpoint either above or below the upward rising motive based on the interval of a major third (theme A^2). After a thirty-measure presentation of this first section, Brahms moves into an extended development of some of the principal material. As this development subsides, four motives of the subordinate section are presented, two of which (B^2 and B^3) are related to the principal material. The closing section, based on a descending minor third, is a study in contrary motion as upper and lower strings are pitted against each other (measures 157–83). The exposition closes in e-flat minor. A common-tone enharmonic modulation (C-flat = B) in the second ending places the development in B major with a short treatment of the A^2 theme. An extended development of the closing theme follows, emphasizing G-flat major for the most part. What appears to be a new theme beginning in measure 232 is actually an inversion of the A^4 motive. In measure 273, Brahms repeats the same textural device used in the introduction: an extended pedal point with the A^1 motive ascending in the violins and another tune in parallel thirds descending in the woodwinds and violas. This starts a long transition back to the recapitulation, most of which is based on the A^1 motive. With so much emphasis on the A^1 generating motive in the transition, Brahms starts the recapitulation with the A^2 motive. He then omits the development of the principal material that had ensued after the presentation of the opening material in the exposition.

The closing material is generally similar to its first presentation. A coda which starts with a development of the closing theme and moves to a slower final section concludes the movement. This slower section is a minature replica of the introduction complete with tonic pedal point, ascending A^1 motive, and descending counterpoint in parallel thirds. The movement ends in C major.

Primarily an exercise in motivic integration, the first movement has extended sections of polyphonic texture, including the opening eight bars of the introduction, the first measures of the exposition (measures 38–51, where two of the motives are used as organizing motives for two lines of free counterpoint), an extended contrary motion section in the closing part (measures 161–76), an antiphonal section in the development section (measures 240–71), a ground-like section involving a quasi-canonic effect between upper and lower strings (measures 293–320), and a repetition of some of these treatments in the recapitulation.

The articulation of the three main sections of the work through use of unifying motives creates the effect of a continuous unfolding of musical thought with somewhat obscure sectioning (cadencing) into major subdivisions. Whereas the classicist normally sought to create a very clear-cut formal outline of individual movements, Brahms used the classical motivic structure to integrate all of his material into a unified whole.

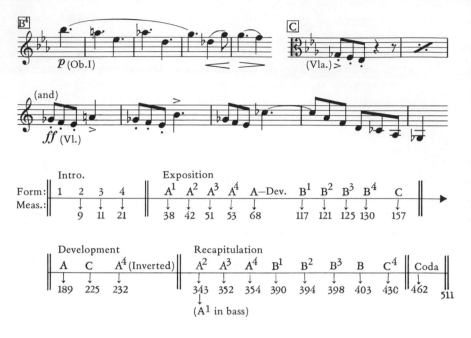

II: **Andante sostenuto.** This second movement is another example of the composer's ability to project a sense of line and continuity into a slow movement and yet construct this movement from themes made up of many short, two-measure phrase segments. The opening theme has four different short segments, two of which are shown below in the theme sheet. In the sixth measure of the theme a triplet accompaniment figure begins in the lower strings and later occurs in several subsequent sections in a similar role. A second part of the principal theme (A² below) is stated in a full scoring of the entire woodwind section, the oboe carrying the tune. The third part of the section (A³ below) achieves considerable expressive impact through a syncopated melody and a soaring canonic passage constructed over a pedal point (measures 34–37). The subordinate theme (B below) which permeates much of the middle section (measures 38–62) is a long and ornate tune that moves from oboe to clarinet, bass strings, and flutes as an offbeat accompaniment in the strings supports it. The third section, supposedly a return of the first section, actually continues a development of the materials of the first section. The return of the A² theme is provided by a solo violin with full orchestral accompaniment, a scoring which continues until the conclusion of the movement. The concluding coda is based on statements of the A² and A³ themes.

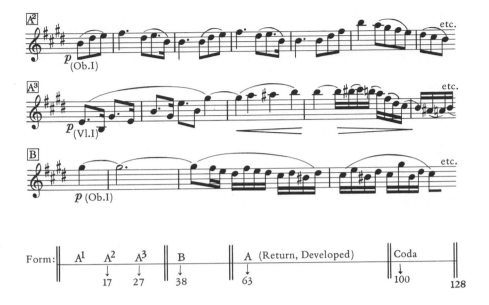

III: **Un poco Allegretto e grazioso.** Conforming to the outer structure of the traditional scherzo, the third movement establishes marked contrast between the scherzo and the trio:

	Scherzo	Trio
Key	A-flat major	B major
Meter	2/4	6/8

The scherzo affects the traditional rounded binary form of the older minuet but without the strict structuring of the form with repeat signs and balanced phrase lengths. All of the themes of the scherzo are introduced by the wood-winds. In many cases the scoring is for the entire woodwind section. The wind emphasis is more than obvious: woodwinds carry essential thematic materials *alone* in fifty-four of the scherzo's seventy measures. There are many examples in these fifty-four measures where the composer has scored three pairs of wood-winds in parallel thirds, each pair an octave distant from an adjacent pair.

The trio places emphasis on the woodwinds again, much of this scoring also in parallel thirds in three pairs of instruments (measures 72–75), doubled over the same two-octave span. The second strain of the trio, a development of the trio materials, is repeated. The return of the scherzo is abbreviated to include only the first section of the scherzo. The coda is based on materials from the trio.

IV: **Adagio; Piu Andante; Allegro non troppo, ma con brio.** Like the
first movement, the finale's introduction contains motives upon which the main
tunes of the *Allegro* are based. A slow tune in c minor opens the introduction
followed by a mysterious pizzicato passage, both ideas reappearing later in the
main body of the movement. After a change to the tonic major key, a broader
theme is heard in the first horn and is repeated by the first flute. A choralelike
section in the trombones and bassoons interrupts this broad tune. A return to
the introductory (1) tune closes the introduction. The *Allegro* is placed in the
tonic major (C), starting with another broadly flowing tune which is related to
the first motive of the introduction. A short quotation from the introductory
(3) theme (horn solo) leads to the subordinate theme, the first ten bars of
which are set above a one-bar ground in the bass. Two themes constitute the
closing section, the second theme being combined with the first in a rhythmic
counterpoint on two different tonal levels (C and e).

The recapitulation, also serving as development, restates the material in
the same order but with considerable variation. The pizzicato introductory

passage is injected at measure 208 and is used in alternation with a tonal development of the first theme. A scale passage from measure 106 is extended through canonic devices into a major portion of this development (measures 234–73), with several other motives being inserted in the progress of the section. A coda starts with references to the first theme and then accelerates for a final faster section (measure 391), which uses a theme somewhat related to the first tune. A climax is reached on the chorale tune from the introduction. This leads to a very freely modified tune from the first theme (measure 417). Brahms emphasizes the final cadence in unison passages which stress the melodic pitches C, A, A-flat, F-sharp, and G, a linear spelling out of the augmented sixth chord on the raised subdominant scale degree. Finally, the II^7 is spelled out in a descending line (C, A, F, D), leading to an imperfect authentic cadence (measures 446–47). The closing cadence is plagal and involves the final eleven bars of the work. While the harmonic formula is unfolding for this IV–I close, the violins and violas are playing six measures of a motive which starts the fast section of the coda (C–B–C, etc.). It is derived from the second, third, and fourth pitches of the principal tune. In this case one could say that melodically Brahms presents a leading tone to tonic cadence while undergirding this with a plagal cadence harmonically. Like much of what he wrote, the concept is contrapuntal in origin.

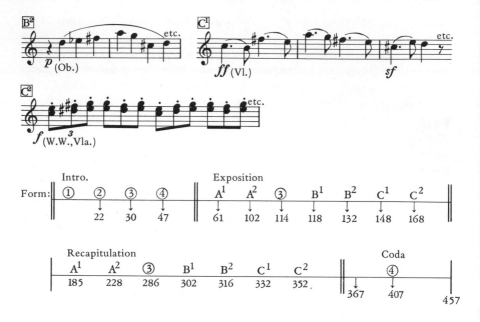

Orchestrally the symphony does not stress effect and tone color for mere expression as much as it does orchestral effect as a device of development in the tradition of the classical composers. Brahms generally respected the individual characteristics of the three choirs but tended to mix choirs to achieve emphasis on important lines. Frequently the violas join the entire woodwind section (see introduction, first movement; see also measures 273–81, same movement, for a similar passage; and the introduction to the finale for the doubling of bassoons and violas in measures 4–5). In general, when not supplying needed inner parts, the violas double either the violins an octave lower or the bass and cello an octave higher. Sometimes, in the heat of a congested passage where every instrument seems busy, the violas are grinding away harmonic support divisi and in double stops (measures 228–31, finale). This may be attributable to the frequent use of both violin parts on either unison or octave scoring of important thematic lines. Many passages of climactic import are doubled in this manner, sometimes at the double octave with three voices involved. Note the subdued use of the same device in the woodwinds in measures 11–14 in the third movement, this time a passage in parallel thirds doubled in two-octave spacing. This same woodwind color opens the finale.

SUMMARY

Brahms's contribution to the history of the symphony was to reestablish the abstract manipulation of musical materials as the basic concept of the symphony, rejecting effect and expression for extramusical purposes. The first movement of the first symphony is perhaps the best available summary of the Brahms style. Using short, concise motives, the composer created a continuous movement which was stylistically every bit as contemporary in its day as was the element of continuity being used in Wagner's music dramas. Brahms used the forms of the classic and baroque periods, manipulating these forms with an articulated and continuous unfolding of musical materials made more unified by the use of motives and through the deemphasis on strong cadences and sectioning. Continuous development and some avoidance of exact restatement also contributed to the unendingly spun-out quality of much of Brahms's music. Rhythmic devices that promoted irregularity of beat, meter, and points of repose also helped propel the music forward.

Brahms's use of counterpoint in the first symphony differs from that usage noted in the works of Mendelssohn, Mozart, and Haydn. Classical composers and those composers in the nineteenth century who seemed to adhere to classical values used counterpoint much as it had been used during the baroque period: imitative textures, fugal development, and little else. In the nineteenth century the restrictive requirements of fugal writing apparently did not appeal to the more expansive composers. Beethoven was probably the last major nineteenth-century composer to absorb fugal writing into the writing of major instrumental works for small and large ensembles. In his symphonies fugal passages, though representative of the best of contrapuntal skills, rarely last more than fifteen to twenty bars. Mendelssohn continued to transplant baroque fugal techniques to the development passages of the concert symphony. With Berlioz, contrapuntal writing began to change. Imitative writing became less involved, more antiphonal in nature, and more canonic in treatment. Berlioz's real forte was in the combination of two different melodies, not a particularly classical technique. This corruption of a baroque principle (counterpoint) to preserve the lyric status of two tunes sounded simultaneously again demonstrates one of the basic principles of music composition: use of old concepts to achieve new results. Thus Brahms' avoidance of long imitative passages seems appropriate in the nineteenth century. His complex contrapuntal textures result from a part-writing technique which stresses contrary motion between two primary melodic parts in what would probably be termed a basically homophonic texture. Using constrasting rhythmic lines (two versus three) in two simultaneous melodies also enhances the contrapuntal effect. Sometimes just a simple arpeggiated accompaniment in triplets to support a melody in duplets creates the degree of melodic independence Brahms required.

While Brahms would certainly be considered the most learned of the nineteenth-century composers, his version of the learned style contrasts greatly with other versions in its emphasis on lyricism and its apparent rejection of the complexities of imitative counterpoint. The learnedness of his style is reflected in the use of integrative techniques (in rhythm, melody, and harmony) to achieve great continuity and articulation of musical thought. Brahms's genius lay in his ability to achieve these results without the appearance of learnedness.

Peter Ilyich Tchaikovsky (1840–1893)

Tchaikovsky occupies a unique position in symphonic history. He was unashamedly nationalistic in most of his works. Folk music abounds in many of his serious compositions. The finales of most of his symphonies fit into the style of what has been called the Russian festive finale. Yet, his overall style is western European. His command of form, especially the smaller forms, reflects European traditions. His choice of larger forms and media is also similar to that of composers from Germany and Austria. Rather than restrict himself to Russian elements as the dominant aspects of his style, he used them as a part of a late-nineteenth-century stylistic mixture. While other nineteenth-century Russian composers may have shown individual skills superior to those of Tchaikovsky (i.e., Rimsky-Korsakov's orchestral depiction or Mussorgsky's harmonic and tonal experiments and musico-dramatic skills), Tchaikovsky's eclecticism seems to have carried him forward to twentieth-century audiences as the major Russian composer of that period.

The musical style in the symphonies reflects his general stylistic tendencies. It is characterized by the prominence of melody, by the repetition and sequencing of materials, and by a masterful orchestral sensitivity. His great stylistic shortcoming was the inability to sustain a convincing development passage.

Tchaikovsky's melodies fall into several categories. First, he wrote many attractive lyric tunes very typical of the nineteenth century. These lyric melodies can be found quite abundantly in the final three symphonies: Symphony No. 4, first movement, measure 121; No. 5, II, 8; No. 6, I, 90; No. 6, IV, 38. A second classification of tunes consists of marchlike melodies: No. 4, II, 126; No. 5, I, 41; No. 6, III, 9. A third group of tunes is primarily waltz-style; No. 5, I, 170; No. 5, III, 1; No. 6, II, 1. A fourth consists of folk tunes or folklike melodies: No. 4, II, 1 (minor key, quite wistful, a favorite of the composer); No. 4, IV, 10 (has march imprint also); No. 5, I, 41 (also marchlike). Expressive melodies make frequent use of accented dissonance. This is particularly true of the main theme of the second movement of the fifth symphony.

Tchaikovsky was more successful at manipulating smaller forms, variation forms, and dance forms (waltz, scherzo, etc.) than at handling developmental forms. Only four of the twelve movements of the last three symphonies have extended development sections. His handling of the internal aspects of form (phrase structure, etc.) is of the highest order. Repetition is a primary formal device in extending sections of a form. Sequence is also present abundantly for either spinning out a melody or working toward a climax. In a few of his works he makes use of cyclic principles, especially in the use of motto themes in the fourth and fifth symphonies. His symphonies (all six) generally adhere to an external tempo scheme which has formal implications:

I	*II*	*III*	*IV*
Fast	Slow	Dancelike	Fast

The quality of his counterpoint may have been underrated. He shows great skill in combining two melodies, one as a countermelody above or below another. He does not use extended imitative passages, with the exception of the fugato in the development section of the fifth symphony's first movement. He does make use of "short" canon in many of his works wherein one voice sustains while the other imitates. There is some short antiphonal imitation in some of the fast movements.

Tchaikovsky's skill as an orchestrator is well known. His scores remain textbooks for young composers today. He seems to respect several principles:

1 *Separation of orchestral choirs.* He generally does not mix unlike instruments.
2 *Octave doubling in strings.* He seems to use this device more than any other nineteenth-century orchestral composer. It is almost always associated with an expressive tune. It can be found in woodwinds also.
3 *Rhythmic materials primarily in winds.* This is especially true of fanfares, motto themes, and underlying rhythmic motives. It is effective in working toward climaxes.
4 *Use of scale passages for filler material.* Many times a contrapuntal effect can be created by superimposing random scale passages in instrumental voices not involved in the primary melodic or harmonic materials; there are many examples in all symphonies.
5 *String pizzicato.* Tchaikovsky seems to like this either as a device where the entire harmonic support is being played by the string section or as a means of carrying a single line.
6 *Lower register of woodwinds.* This seems to be a favorite orchestral color of the composer.
7 *Equal prominence of all instruments.* He does not favor any single instrument or group of instruments, except that he does seem to neglect the lower brass.

His typical orchestra includes piccolo, two flutes, two oboes, two clarinets, two bassoons, four horns, two trumpets, three trombones, tuba, three timpani, bass drum, cymbal, and strings.

Tchaikovsky's tonal and harmonic language is conservative, much more so than that of Liszt, Brahms, Strauss, and Mahler. His choice of keys within a movement is quite free. There is no overall pattern in the keys of symphony movements. Five of the six symphonies are in a minor key. He appears more interested in creating expression in his music by the melodic tension caused by stressed dissonance in melodies than by the use of chromatic harmonies. The use of sequence does involve somewhat random choice of keys at times. Chromaticism often appears primarily as melodic chromaticism in unison passages or in inflections of inner parts. Tchaikovsky does use pedal points to emphasize tonal stability in some of his passages.

Information on Individual Symphonies

No.	Key	Date	Intro.	I	II	III	IV	V
1	g	1866	no	SA	ABABA	Scherzo	Rondo	
2	c	1872	yes	SA	ABA	Scherzo	SA	
3	D	1875	yes	SA	Scherzo	ABA	Scherzo	SA
4	f	1877	yes	SA	ABA	SF w/trio	Sonatina	
5	e	1888	yes	SA	ABA	SF w/trio	SA	
6	b	1893	yes	SA	SF w/trio	Sonatina	Sonatina	

SYMPHONY NO. 1

This symphony was revised and finally issued as the third and final version in 1875. The work has programmatic origins. The first two movements, however, are the only ones with subtitles: "Reveries of a Winter Journey" and "Land of Desolation, Land of Mists." The first movement opens with a tune which supposedly had folk origins. The finale uses a folk melody ("The Gardens Bloomed") in its introduction and as the second theme. The first movement lacks any extended contrapuntal passages except for the slower-moving countermelody which accompanies the secondary tune (measures 137–90). The initial movement contains endless measures of unison writing for the strings, usually in some kind of sequential treatment. Much of the development consists of sequential treatment of the principal theme. The movement also contains many passages of unison scales. The climax of the development section is reached in a long fanfare passage, with trumpets and horns playing a unison call on a pedal F-sharp (twenty-one bars) and a pedal G (fifteen bars). The fanfare rhythm then serves as a transition to the recapitulation and subsequently adapts itself to serve as the rhythmic design of the accompaniment for the primary theme. The opening measures of the second movement have a two-voice contrapuntal texture (measures 1–8) of a nonimitative nature. Strings are muted from the outset. The second appearance of theme B (measure 103) is scored for first violins and clarinet (unison) with a divisi pizzicato accompaniment in the strings. There is frequent tremolo scoring for the string section, sometimes divisi and doubling woodwinds.

The scherzo begins a new tradition for symphony third movements: a somewhat whimsical and dancelike nature which may have been an offshoot of the Mendelssohn scherzo. The scherzos of the third, fourth, and sixth symphonies all seem to follow this same model. The trio of this particular scherzo was Tchaikovsky's first symphonic waltz, a form which he would use in much of his orchestral music. One primary motive dominates the scherzo section of the first symphony. The final cadence is somewhat original: VI–I, thus covering the two main tonalities of the movement (A-flat major–VI and c minor–I). The finale uses the introductory theme for its subordinate tune.

This is one of the first samples of the Russian festive finale which can be traced back to Glinka (primarily his overtures to *Russlan and Ludmilla* and *The Kamarinskaya*). Tchaikovsky consistently returns to this type of finale in all his symphonies except the sixth.*

SYMPHONY NO. 2

This work was called the "Little Russian" by a contemporary critic in 1896, alluding to its use of Ukrainian folk songs. In Tsarist Russia the Ukraine was referred to as "little" Russia. The introduction to the first movement is a variation on a Ukrainian version of the Russian "Song of the Volga Boatmen." The theme for the second movement was taken from the composer's opera *Undine,* whose manuscript he later destroyed. The theme of the middle section is another folk tune ("My Spinning Wheel"). The scherzo is in 3/8 meter, the trio in 2/8. The finale, as mentioned before, continues the festive-type final movement. The principal theme is another Ukrainian folk tune, "The Crane." The tune appears frequently in the music of several nineteenth-century Russian composers. The development section is a series of variations on this tune.

SYMPHONY NO. 3

This five-movement work opens with a slow introduction in the style of a funeral march. Its theme then becomes the first tune of the ensuing *Allegro.* The closing tune is another folklike creation, this time in dance style. The development section of the first movement is more complex (motivic development, counterpoint, etc.) than previous examples. The second movement is a waltz. Strings are used extensively in a pizzicato accompaniment texture. The trio remains in waltz style but employs a triplet figure in the rhythmic background. Woodwinds are featured and again are reminiscent of the Mendelssohn

---

* Daniel Zhitomirsky, "Symphonies," in *Russian Symphony* (Freeport: Books for Libraries Press, 1969), p. 91.

woodwinds in his scherzo style. The two styles, however, are different. Mendelssohn voiced full chords for the woodwind section in the scherzo scoring, while Tchaikovsky usually assigned only a single line to the woodwinds, doubling it at the octave or double octave. Mendelssohn's scoring, because of its close harmony, also placed the instruments in close proximity to one another; Tchaikovsky's octave doubling spreads the woodwinds more. The trio of the second scherzo states its tune in seven different keys above a pedal D in the horns. The composer has affected the style of a polonaise in the finale.

SYMPHONY NO. 4

This work is discussed fully beginning on page 172.

SYMPHONY NO. 5

The work opens with a motto theme which unifies the entire symphony, particularly the first and fourth movements. The *Allegro* has a marchlike theme whose rhythm recurs throughout the principal sections of the movement. One of the subordinate tunes (measure 170) is cast in complete rhythmic displacement for the entire twenty-eight bars of that section of the exposition. The movement makes extensive use of solo woodwinds. The second movement starts in b minor and slowly modulates to the tonic (D major) for the expressive horn principal theme. The entire second movement is filled with expressive countermelodies, perhaps the composer's best contrapuntal writing in his symphonies. The motto theme from the first movement precedes the return of the first section. The movement lacks a harmonic cadence, employing in its stead a 9–8 accented (and sustained) passing tone, which, as a melodic figure, has been extracted from one of the countermelodies to a part of the principal theme.

The third movement, again a waltz (scherzo), has a trio with a more scherzolike melodic construction. The motto theme opens the finale in the introduction and is developed during the entire introduction (fifty-seven measures). The finale has a marchlike rhythmic and melodic construction and fits into the festive finale concept. The composer adds a countermelody to the principal theme in its restatement in the recapitulation. The motto theme closes the exposition and the recapitulation and dominates the coda. The final section of the coda shifts to the tonic major (E) and assumes a more stately march style. The tempo accelerates as the movement concludes with a quotation of the main theme of the first movement, again in the tonic major key.

SYMPHONY NO. 6

The *Pathetique* starts its first movement with an *Adagio* introduction which dwells exclusively on the main theme of the movement. The ensuing *Allegro* version of the tune uses a sixteenth-note, ostinatolike figure in the woodwinds and strings to accompany it. This rhythmic figure aids in unifying the first section. The subordinate section (measure 89) is an extended sixty-measure section which is inserted into the movement much like the middle section of a part form. It is developed extensively and closes the exposition, giving the *Allegro* a basic binary design. The development starts with an extended fugal development of the main tune. A new theme appears in the coda. The second movement continues the waltz style of some of the Tchaikovsky symphony movements but is in 5/4 meter. The third movement, a scherzo in march style, departs from the scherzo outline by not having a contrasting trio section. The finale, one of symphonic history's oddities, sustains a slow or moderately slow tempo for its entirety. The opening theme has an interesting *stimmtausch* scoring in which the first and second violins alternate on a descending melody (measures 1–4). The finale is primarily a lyric movement using two themes. The development, such as it is, depends on repetition and sequence. Many sections are unified by extended pedal points in the lower strings and winds, the horns, or the timpani. A rare divisi contrabass passage is included in the closing section (measures 157–71).

Note: Tchaikovsky wrote two other symphonies, including a programmatic work entitled *Manfred,* based on Byron's poem. The work is in four movements. An extensive program was attached to the score by the composer. Using the Berlioz concept of the *idée fixe,* Tchaikovsky employs a Manfred theme in all movements. For two reasons the work is not often performed today: it is long (one hour and five minutes); it is exceedingly difficult to perform, making extreme demands on all instruments. Thus the time required for rehearsal may not justify the results in many conductors' views. An eighth symphony, discovered in the recent past and reconstructed by Semyon Bogatreiv, was performed in the early 1960s. The work (Symphony in E-flat Major) dates from about 1892. It has not yet been accepted by most conductors as part of the composer's usable output.

Tchaikovsky's symphonic style, then, is a curious mixture of the programmatic and the absolute. His symphonic poems and overtures all have descriptive titles and are generally supported by significant extramusical details in spite of their overall formal cohesiveness. Several of the works are standard symphonic fare today (among them, *Romeo and Juliet, Francesca da Rimini, 1812 Overture,* and *Italian Caprice*). His last three symphonies are among the most popular performed in America. Tchaikovsky's first piano concerto, the violin concerto, and the *Rococo Variations* for cello are enjoying similar popularity with orchestral audiences.

This style is based primarily on an orchestral skill almost unequaled in the nineteenth century, which, when combined with the composer's impressive melodic gift, produced credible works of extended proportions. His symphonic style is a continuation of the lyric style of the more conservative composers represented best in the early nineteenth century by Schubert. While probably more skilled at nondevelopmental forms, Tchaikovsky was still somehow able to project his attractive tunes into an effective symphonic format. Several of his treatments are standard: the waltz or waltzlike movements, the use of the march or marchlike sections, the use of secondary themes which offer such great contrast that their entire sections appear as a part of a part-form exposition, a strong rhythmic unity in many of the movements or sections of movements (which probably substitutes for the more complex motivic continuity noted in the more classically oriented works of composers like Brahms), and a generally expressive mood in all of the movements. The symphonies do not present a complex series of musical ideas unified in a subtle and highly intellectual fashion, as in works by Brahms and Beethoven. The works may have survived primarily because of the excellence of the tunes and the clearly defined orchestral style. The basically expressive quality of the works, with little emphasis on a complex presentation of musical thought, may also endear the works to the average concert-goer.

EXAMPLES FOR STUDY

Tchaikovsky: *Symphony No. 4 in f minor, Op. 36 (1877)*

I: **Andante sostenuto, Moderato con anima (In movimento di Valse).** The first movement opens with an extended statement of the motto theme (called the "Fate" motive by the composer in a letter written after the work's composition). The section is a brilliant scoring of the theme for winds, especially brass instruments. As the introduction closes, the composer begins evolving the tune of the fast section, stressing the added sixth (or sixth scale degree). The exposition then begins with this added sixth (D-flat) as the first pitch of the main tune. The tune is phrased rhythmically in an irregular grouping of eighth notes, i.e., 2+2+2+3 in each measure of 9/8 meter. The accompaniment is structured in a similar fashion. The passage is one of Tchaikovsky's most interesting rhythmic experiments and to some extent parallels the rhythmic innovations accomplished by Brahms. The work intensifies this rhythmic instability by mixing it with a more straightforward 9/8 structure in some of the phrases. By measure 70 the composer has worked himself up into quite a state and begins to intensify the expressive impact of the moment by adding chromatic scale lines as countermelodies (woodwinds, measures 70–72, and 74–76) and as filler passages connecting the repetition of phrases in the strings (measures 72–73). This application in the strings is typical of his use of scale passages, usually in fast notes like this passage, to provide a little more excitement or orchestral interest in a passage.

After a short transition (measure 104), a very quiet section begins (measure 115), introducing the first part of the second theme in a-flat minor. In measure 121 one of the composer's lyric gems begins to weave around the tune; this new countermelody (B^2) has equal importance with the subordinate tune B^1. This is followed by the closing section with its simple waltz tune stated in parallel thirds in the violins above a simple tonic-dominant-tonic bass line in the timpani. Interpolated between phrases of this theme are very soft woodwind statements of the opening part of the main tune (A^1). The scoring shows an amazing sense of balance. Six woodwinds are divided into two groups of three instruments each, with the music scored in three parts or voices. The upper group (two flutes, one oboe) is doubled an octave lower by two clarinets and one bassoon. The blend between clarinets and flutes is extremely smooth, as is that of the oboe and bassoon playing the third part. The bass line, as mentioned, is reduced to chord roots and played by the timpani. Tchaikovsky quickly begins working toward another climax, doubling the quotation from A^1 at the double octave in the strings and adding winds for harmonic support (measures 147–60) as the work builds for the final theme of the exposition (C^2), a superheated (fff) tune based on a descending arpeggiation of the tonic triad. All of this is accompanied by other lines carrying the rhythmic motive from the A theme. The passage works out to be one of the composer's more memorable climaxes in this symphony.

As the strings carry the A^1 motivic line downward, the motto theme signals the beginning of the development section. Most of the material in the development section is drawn from the A^1 theme or from an associated motive. There is an attempt at sustained contrapuntal writing. By measure 237 the composer has generated another tune which will be suitable for one of his climax-directed sequences. This does crest quite effectively in measure 253, where the composer has added the motto theme to help intensify the expressive import of the moment. At the same instant other parts are playing either scales or lines embossed with the primary A^1 motive, all at the fff dynamic level. The combination is repeated with the recapitulation emerging just at that moment when all is being brought together (measure 284), again at the fff dynamic level. A quick eight-measure synopsis of the primary material (leaving out A^2 and the transitional material) leads to the subordinate theme and the closing section, the latter missing its second part. An insertion of the motto theme at measure 355 signals the beginning of the coda. A new lyric tune is added which has some traits of a chorale tune or a solemn march theme. The coda then is accelerated to *Molto piu mosso* (measure 381), the new tune put in diminution, and the motto theme superimposed above it. Another climax occurs quickly using the A^1 theme (measure 403) and is followed by a still faster section which concludes the movement. This final section (measures 412–22) stresses the original D-flat of the symphony in measures 412–13 as an accented upper neighbor tone, the same contour it had in measures 23–26, when it was introduced as an appoggiatura.

ff (Motto Theme) (Hrn.,Basn.)

II: Andantino in modo di canzona. A folklike melody of a plaintive nature accompanied by the strings (pizzicato) opens the work. A contrasting second portion of the theme (measure 41) becomes involved in a typical Tchaikovsky sequence passage (measures 55–62), which is essential in building another climax (measure 62). A series of sequencelike scale passages then gradually reduces the excitement so that the first section of the theme can reappear at measure 77. This restatement is handled in the style of a variation with various sixteenth-note countermelodies superimposed above the tune. A marchlike middle section has added its own countermelody by its ninth bar; the added line is simply an ascending scale line whose long notes stress melodic dissonance (measures 134–41). After the march reaches another torrid climax (measure 166), it gradually subsides for the return of the first section. This final section features extended solo passages for woodwinds and cello and could be considered developmental or in the nature of an extended coda. The movement very softly (ppp) closes with a pizzicato tonic chord in the lower register of the contrabass, cello, and viola, each on a different chord member.

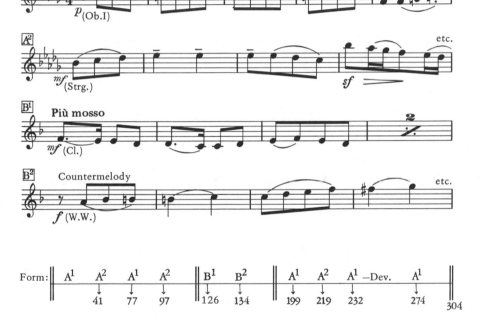

III: Scherzo (Pizzicato ostinato), Allegro. By setting a pizzicato movement in a four- to six-voice string texture, Tchaikovsky created a unique scherzo movement. The eighth-note motion is constant in almost the entire first section of the movement. The middle section consisting of two sections of contrasting materials (the first, for solo woodwinds; the second, for brass) contains brilliant scoring for solo woodwinds. At measure 185 segments of the B¹ tune are introduced above the B² theme. Segments of the A¹ tune are added in a similar fashion at measure 198, showing a close relationship between the A¹ and B² themes. The pizzicato section returns, followed by a coda which touches upon parts of all themes of the movement. The opening bars of the coda contain an antiphonal passage between winds and strings (using the pizzicato theme) in which the winds play the motive in F major and are answered by the strings in D-flat major. The same woodwind passage in A major is repeated in the strings in F major (see measures 349–60). Both passages in this instance stress a tonal freedom (i.e., third relation) typical of the late nineteenth century.

IV: Allegro con fuoco. The first section (Part I) consists of an exposition and a development of three themes. The primary thematic group is ternary in design, the middle tune (A^2) being a version of the Russian folk tune, "A Birch Stood in the Meadow." A marchlike B theme completes the exposition section of Part I. After a convincing cadence in the tonic key, the folk theme returns for an extended development in a series of strophic variations. A double statement of the tune's two phrases generally comprises a single variation. The second section (Part II) begins (measure 119) as an abbreviated repetition of Part I and parallels many of the materials and treatments used in the exposition (Part I), but with greater freedom in the variation section. The movement's final section (Part III) begins with a quotation of the first movement's motto theme in the tonic and then moves into a coda that regroups the second section's thematic material in the tonic key. The finale is one of the most original developmental movements written by Tchaikovsky. In some ways its resembles the sonatina in its subdivision into two main sections. Each of these sections, however, has both exposition and development subsections. A final coda that in some ways resembles a recapitulation further complicates the scheme.

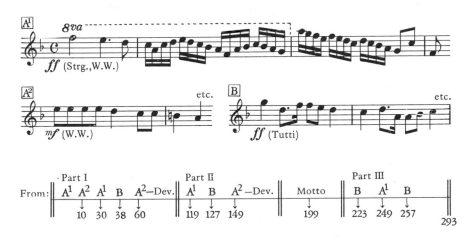

The orchestral style exhibits the composer's excellent skills and careful separation of orchestral choirs. One passage in the first movement uses woodwinds on a descending chromatic countermelody (single octave doubling), with the A^1 theme in the violins and cellos (double octave doubling) and simple chordal accompaniment sustained on the first two beats of the measure in the horns, timpani, and lower strings (measures 70–76). It is an excellent example of choir separation. The sections of a work which tend to show the greatest sensitivity to color are the simpler sections, those with slow-moving lyric tunes carried by reduced orchestral forces, as in the subordinate section of the first movement, the first and third parts of the second movement, and the middle section of the third movement. The use of separate successive orchestral groupings to play phrases of a work also allows the composer to create some orchestral contrast in developing or repeating themes. This concertato scoring often becomes one of the primary devices in sustaining interest in the repetition or sequencing of material. In this way Tchaikovsky used orchestration as a primary tool in his development or extension of materials. Without the benefit of these orchestral skills, the last three symphonies would probably not have had such general appeal.

SUMMARY

The Symphony No. 4 exemplifies both the strengths and the weaknesses of Tchaikovsky as a composer of symphonies. The orchestral craft is superb, and in many instances allows the composer to create the effect of development through the use of contrasting tone colors in long, repetitive passages. The craft is at its best when used to set off each line in a passage where clarity of texture is important. Sensitive orchestration thus works to preserve the basic lyric style of the work by this enhancement of line. Many of the style devices are present in abundance (tunes, scales, repetition, sequence, color, clarity of phrase structure, countermelodies, fanfares, waltzlike sections, marchlike sections, folk tunes, variation, unending expressive climaxes, etc.). Development sections are weak, except for the section in movement IV that is a set of strophic variations. Here, as noted before, the orchestral technique is essential to the variation style used by the composer. The work cannot be considered one of the nineteenth century's noblest creations, but it contains a wealth of first-rate tunes that make listening to it an exciting and pleasurable experience. It carries forward the lyric concept of the symphony and emphasizes the basic orchestral nature of symphonic music. Tchaikovsky's symphonies have endured as some of the most appealing works written in the nineteenth century and still popular today. His last three symphonies, in many ways, have helped to bridge the gap between the public that attends most symphony concerts and the vast and complex literature that is available for these concerts.

Anton Bruckner (1824–1896)

Bruckner is known as the most important church music composer of the late nineteenth century. His simple, solitary, and religious approach to life resulted in a series of works that seemed to reflect both this personal dedication and a unique manner for handling some of his musical projects. His skill as a contrapuntalist, his background as a church organist, and his ability to react both to strong musical influences and to criticism by his peers created a most unusual style mixture that frequently surfaced in his symphonies.

    Writing eleven symphonies over a period of about thirty years, Bruckner attempted to restore a balance between the classic and romantic traditions of the symphony. Brahms, trying to accomplish the same thing, had developed a style that became more concise, more integrated, and more involved intellectually, yet was designed to stress the lyric and continuous nature of late-nineteenth-century music. Bruckner, on the other hand, sought a solution influenced by the more expansive composers of his time, in particular Wagner. Early in his symphonic output he settled upon a style that remained fairly constant in all of his symphonies, a fact which caused a variety of comments.

> A good starting-point for our investigation of Bruckner's special quality is the famous bon mot that he composed, not nine symphonies, but one symphony nine times.*

There is a striking sameness in all of the symphonies. A typical Bruckner symphony begins with a tremolo of a vague quality in the strings. Above this, or from this, emerges a primary or unifying theme, with the tremolo building up in a crescendo. These first themes are usually quite elemental, often based on notes of a principal triad. They are called *Urthema* by the Germans, meaning "primordial theme." The theme is very firmly placed in the tonic triad and thus establishes the home key from the outset. Finales also tend to start in the same manner. Other mannerisms worth noting:

1 There is the use of the rhythmic figure of a duplet followed by a triplet:

2 A repetition of a short rhythmic phrase in progressive diminution is employed to achieve a climax:

3 Unison themes are stated fortissimo, with pauses between phrases, and are often scored for full orchestra.

4 Bruckner uses a secondary theme called *Gesangsperiode* (song period).† This theme usually has at least two melodies, generally superimposed upon each other in polyphonic fashion. This effect sometimes is vague since both tunes usually lose a certain degree of independence and melodic integrity in the process.

5 A third theme in sonata-allegro movements is often a chorale or chorale-like section. Sometimes it is preceded by a marchlike tune.

6 Most slow movements are in five-part form (ABABA) with repetitions of both A and B being developmental.

---

* Deryck Cooke, "Anton Bruckner," in *The Symphony,* ed. Robert Simpson (Baltimore: Penguin Books, 1966), 1:287. Used by permission of Penguin Books.

† H. F. Redlich, *Bruckner and Mahler* (London: J. M. Dent & Sons, Ltd., 1955), p. 56. Used by permission of J. M. Dent & Sons, Ltd.

7 Third movements (or scherzo movements) all follow the song form with trio outline, with much greater emphasis on development in the contrasting middle section of both scherzo and trio. The form of many scherzo sections closely approximates the sonata-allegro outline:

Scherzo

A	B (V)	A—Dev. B—Dev.	A	B (I)	Trio	Scherzo Da Capo

Trios tend to sound like Ländler. Some change meter from triple to duple.

8 The form of finales is somewhat freer than that of the first movements. Sonata-allegro is used in the finales of seven of the eleven symphonies; the remaining finales have the same general outline, with some other formal elements, such as fugue and rondo, being equally important.

9 Bruckner often closes a symphony with a long coda in which there is a presentation of the Urthema in a variety of versions, broad and loud, with an orchestral ostinato supporting both the theme and the tonic chord, which is invariably the only harmony for the final part of the coda. This tends to balance the long introductory passage, which has the same tonal stability.

Bruckner's general style seems to have sprung from both classic and romantic sources. Wagner influenced his harmonic, tonal, and melodic style, the great length of his works, and the size and sound of his large orchestra. Beethoven was probably responsible for Bruckner's grandiose conception of the symphony and for his use of cyclic themes. The expressive melodic style is created by stressing dissonance, an emphasis related to the nineteenth century.

The harmonic style is a strange mixture of the two periods. His studies with Simon Sechter created a very disciplined approach to classical harmony as systemized in the writings of Rameau, this resulting in an emphasis on traditional root relationships and a strong tonal gravitation toward the cadence. On the other hand, his use of almost free dissonance, disjunct melodic writing, and abrupt chromatic chord progressions places him in advance of many of his peers. The latter aspect of the style suffers primarily from lack of consistency. Bruckner's use of the harmonic sequence may have resulted from Wagnerian influence. Somewhat akin to the same influence were his principal themes, which freely modulated before returning to a strong cadence in the tonic key. He also used pedal points to stabilize the tonality of a passage.

Bruckner's contrapuntal style, while often free in appearance, had a solid harmonic basis. The metric and rhythmic freedom noted in some of the imitative passages shows a strong sixteenth-century influence.

The composer's orchestral technique is not colorful or unique. The size of the orchestra grows from the typical nineteenth-century ensemble of woodwinds in pairs, four horns, two trumpets, three trombones, timpani, and strings to an enlarged group of piccolo, triple woodwinds, eight horns (four alternating on Wagner tubas), triple brass (F trumpets usually included), bass tuba, timpani, harp, and strings in the last two symphonies. Choirs are generally kept separate but not to the extent seen in the works of Tchaikovsky. Several orchestral effects predominate including the use of string tremolo, an emphasis on brass instruments (especially with F trumpets on the top voice), and octave doublings in the strings. The codas are generally huge brass vistas with strings in an accompanying role and woodwinds doubling the brass lines. The Wagnerian tubas are emphasized in the final two works. His attempts at color are somewhat limited. He used the harp only in the eighth symphony and then required three players. Some use of divisi strings is seen in slow movements. Unison scoring is frequent in tutti passages. Themes are often initially stated by brass instruments. While his orchestra is not the largest of the period, the effect of massive orchestral sonority is achieved through brass emphasis, frequent tutti passages, and broad scoring for the twenty-seven wind instruments.

Information on Individual Symphonies

No.	Key	Date	Intro.	I	II	III	IV
?	f	1863 *	no	SA	ABA	Scherzo	SA
0	d	1864	no	SA	ABABA	Scherzo	SA
1	c	1866	no	SA	ABA	Scherzo	SA
2	c	1872	no	SA	ABABA	Scherzo	Sonata-rondo
3	d	1873	no	SA	ABA	Scherzo	SA
4	E-flat	1874	no	SA	SA	Scherzo	SA
5	B-flat	1876	yes	SA	ABABA	Scherzo	Sectional (fugal)
6	A	1881	no	SA	SA	Scherzo	SA
7	E	1883	no	SA	ABABA	Scherzo	SA
8	c	1887	no	SA	Scherzo	ABABA (slow)	SA
9	d	1894	no	SA	Scherzo	ABABA (slow)	none

* Date indicates date of completion by composer of first version of symphony.

One major problem remains to be explained: Bruckner's constant revision of his works. While the dates above do apply to the first version of each symphony, as far as it can be determined only one of his symphonies exists today in its original version, Symphony No. 7. All others had at least one revision. Three were revised after his death (Nos. 5, 6, and 9). When studying a Bruckner symphony score, it is important to discover exactly what (or whose) version of the symphony is being examined. A scholarly edition of Bruckner's symphonies in their original settings was begun by the International Bruckner Society in the early 1950s and has produced a complete set of the symphonies plus editions of several of the later versions of each symphony. The puzzle, however, still continues as to which version is the best for performance; Redlich even suggests that it might be better to make additional revisions.

It is quite possible that in a more distant future conductors will try to coalesce versions II/III and IV [of the fourth symphony] in an ultimate "practical version," embodying the best solutions, taken from all existing variants of the symphony.*

To compound matters even further, Bruckner wrote and discarded two additional symphonies, one in f minor (1863) and another in d minor (1864). He numbered the d minor work as his Symphony No. 0.

SYMPHONY IN F MINOR

Although a student symphony, the work shows a maturing symphonic mastery and an expressive gift typical of the nineteenth century. Wagnerian sonorities and suspended melodic dissonances (first movement, measures 12, 23, 25–26, 60, 85–100, 119) provide some evidence of Wagner's influence. This linear dissonance style emphasis increases in the second movement. The scherzo third movement is more closely associated with the Schubert style in its folk-tune trio, which is scored in parallel thirds in the woodwinds. The finale, a more straightforward marchlike movement, returns to the earlier expressive melodic style (secondary theme, measures 60–91), again borrowing sonorities and melodic devices from the Wagnerian style.

SYMPHONY NO. 0 IN D MINOR

Although initially completed in 1864, the symphony was revised by the composer in 1869. The vague tremolo opening mentioned above starts the first movement. In this work, and in many of the subsequent symphonies, Bruckner equates expansiveness of symphonic style with length obtained through repetition of materials, a formal weakness associated with late Schubert symphonies. This can be seen in the symphony's first movement: a long transition from development to recapitulation, measures 160–213, or an extended coda, measures 285–353. The second movement uses the more Wagnerian and mid-nineteenth-century melodic and harmonic style (especially measures 28–44). The level of chromaticism is intensified in the unison theme of the scherzo, in this case a developmental movement. The finale contrasts a martial first theme with a scherzolike second theme (measure 69).

SYMPHONY NO. 1 IN C MINOR

The opening is as above. A secondary theme is the first example in the symphonies of Bruckner's *Gesangsperiode*. In the long coda, brass instruments

---

* Anton Bruckner, *Symphony No. 4*, rev. Hans F. Redlich (London: Ernst Eulenberg, Ltd., 1954), preface by Redlich, p. vii.Reprinted by permission of C. F. Peters Corporation, sole selling agents for the Western Hemisphere.

are emphasized to such an extent that the orchestral mass seems larger than it is. The Adagio drifts indecisively through its opening themes, finally arriving at a more lyric tune (measure 18). Both melodic and harmonic styles are based on Wagnerian devices. Orchestration is also reminiscent of Wagner scores (measures 103–40). A virtuosic string passage opens the scherzo. The trio theme is more in the style of a *Gesangsperiode*. In the finale the prominence of brass instruments lends a martial mood. Strings doubled at the unison and octave play demanding accompaniment figures. Another Bruckner mannerism is seen in a series of inverted triads harmonizing a line (trombones, measures 264–68, or strings, measures 64–65 or 249–63). The orchestral style is brilliant in the work while the harmonic and tonal materials are characterized both by a Wagnerian touch and an original approach to chromaticism by Bruckner.

SYMPHONY NO. 2 IN C MINOR

The expansive nature of this work is seen in its longer codas, longer thematic groups, and longer development sections. The work's greater length allowed the composer a longer time-span for tonal changes, this encouraging a somewhat freer tonal scheme. The composer's special rhythmic figure (see above) makes its first appearance in this symphony (first movement, measure 20). The length of the second movement is exaggerated by long transitions between themes measures (16–33 or measures 56–69). The expressive nature of the movement depends more on unusual chord progressions than on stressed dissonance in a melodic line. The scherzo proper is monothematic, developing this theme through tonal contrast. The finale's introductory passage (measure 132) relates to the first movement's initial theme. The exposition ends with a statement of a portion of the Kyrie theme from the composer's f minor mass (see measure 200). The same quotation prefaces the coda (measure 547).

SYMPHONY NO. 3 IN D MINOR

This work causes problems in determining the composer's original, final, or authentic intent. Surviving three editions by the composer, the symphony is usually performed either from second or third version sources. The original score contained direct quotes from Wagner's *Tristan und Isolde, Die Walküre,* and *Die Meistersinger* which were removed by the composer in subsequent editions. The first movement fits the Bruckner mold in almost every respect. The only trace of Wagner, other than the brass emphasis, is a brief ninth chord derivation (measure 127). The remaining movements adhere to the composer's established pattern fairly closely.

SYMPHONY NO. 4 IN E-FLAT MAJOR, ROMANTIC

This work will be discussed fully beginning on page 186.

SYMPHONY NO. 5 IN B-FLAT MAJOR

The first movement has a more articulated structure in which *Urthemen* help to integrate the formal dimension much more effectively than in earlier symphonies. The first movement illustrates many Bruckner devices: frequent unison and octave string doublings, parallel sixth chords, and an increased prominence of brass instruments (including Bruckner's first use of the tuba in his symphonies). The composer restricts his expansive tendency in the *Adagio* second movement by inserting fewer and shorter transitions between themes (see measures 51–54). Less daring harmonic and tonal treatment also stabilizes the movement. By seeking a balance between the tonal integrity of the phrase and his venturesome harmonic and tonal style, Bruckner achieves a tonal style easier to grasp in this particular movement. The scherzo proper is in sonata-allegro form with a second theme in the style of a Ländler. An introduction which recalls first themes from the first and second movements leads to a finale in a massive four-sectioned form. Both sections one and three are fugal. Section two is a non-imitative *Gesangsperiode*. A double fugue closes both third and fourth sections, the latter having started originally as a restatement of the *Gesangsperiode*.

SYMPHONY NO. 6 IN A MAJOR

The composer's shortest mature symphony opens in the expected fashion. One of its unique features is the polymetric design (6/4 meter against 4/4 meter) of the first movement. The melodic style of the scherzo's themes is almost amelodic in the themes' dependence on chord outlines for their primary motivic structure. The finale has this same melodic indeterminacy with much of the first theme reverting to sectional design.

SYMPHONY NO. 7 IN E MAJOR

Although a longer and more expansive work than the sixth symphony, the seventh moderates both tonal and harmonic styles by re-emphasizing Wagnerian harmonic and melodic devices. The first movement depends upon a principal theme of considerable length and lyricism, a contrast to the *Urthema* concept. This theme uses accented dissonance for expression and undergoes frequent sequential settings similar to those by Wagner. The closing theme (measures 131–34, 148–64) shows a Schubert influence. The *Adagio* includes Wagnerian tubas in the Bruckner orchestra for the first time, calling for two tenor and two bass plus the normal contrabass tuba. With a sound that resembles that of the baritone horn, these new horns are used in quartet most of the time with some doubling by tenor strings. The scherzo and trio are both developmental. The finale is similar to previous finales but does employ a chorale tune as its secondary theme. The tune modulates in mid-phrase as did some earlier Bruckner themes. Development and recapitulation are combined, a coda also restating the first theme. In spite of the availability of sixteen brass instruments in the finale, Bruckner rarely exceeds thirteen separate lines or parts for these wind players. In final tutti passages, brass are piled one on another in the doubling of lines, much the same as Strauss did in his later scores. One learns to expect this kind of rousing brass ending, usually with a lot of thrashing around by all within a single final tonic chord, in most Bruckner symphonies.

SYMPHONY NO. 8 IN C MINOR

While the work exists in at least two versions attributable to the composer, the second version (1890) is the subject of this analysis. The first movement includes Bruckner's enlarged brass and woodwind sections, a total of twenty-seven wind instruments. All are used in the climax of the first theme (measures 26–40). The second movement is a monothematic scherzo. Its trio adds a harp part, the first such appearance in the symphonies, with three players required. The *Adagio* is one of Bruckner's most expressive movements and one of his most impressive orchestral settings, especially the six-part divisi scoring in middle and lower strings of the opening D-flat major pedal chord. A tuba quintet plays the opening phrase of the second theme (measures 67–70). Relying on both tonal shifts and melodic dissonance, Bruckner writes with impressive eloquence. One passage for ten-part strings and harp is notable (measures 43–46). The finale's themes are mostly introduced by the expanded brass section and supported by the six timpani the composer prescribes. The flow of the work tends to be episodic, especially in development and recapitulation sections. The principal themes of the symphony's four movements are assembled together in the final thirteen measures of the finale.

SYMPHONY NO. 9 IN D MINOR

Bruckner was unable to complete his final symphony prior to his death, leaving only brief sketches of the fourth movement. Each theme of the first movement is extended and developed at great length when first presented. Although properly regrouped in the recapitulation, these themes are subjected to continuing development. A bombastic coda ends the movement. The scherzo and trio are both in ternary form with clearly defined secondary themes. The harmonic style of the *Adagio* third movement's first theme (measures 1–7) is unusual, both pandiatonic (measures 2–4) and Wagnerian (measures 5–7). The harmonic style remains expansive as in many earlier works.

EXAMPLES FOR STUDY

Bruckner: *Symphony No. 4 in E-flat major (Romantic), 1873; final revision, 1889*

The current Eulenberg score (#462) contains a fifth revision by Hans Redlich made in 1954. The finale of the 1954 version contains a major revision wherein the recapitulation omits the principal theme and the coda is shortened from the form it took in the fourth Bruckner revision.* Revisions of the symphonies have significantly diminished their musical credibility and historical importance.

I: **Ruhig bewegt.** The first movement starts (as do most Bruckner first movements) with a tremolo in the strings and a typical Urthema principal theme in the first horn. Bruckner extended this part of the movement for forty-two measures and then built a gradual transition to the second part (A²) of the main theme, which he designed to work in crab style (going up or down). In fact, in the first forthright statement, both upward and downward versions appear simultaneously (measure 51 and A² below). The second theme uses the Bruckner polyrhythm ♩ ♩ ♩♩♩ . By measure 75, after having exhausted the polyrhythmic theme, he begins the subordinate theme B¹, a typical *Gesangsperiode* tune. Measure 87 starts a mini-development of a new tune (B²), which lasts until measure 119. Here Bruckner returns to the A² polyrhythmic theme for his closing material. In measure 169 he takes up the subordinate tunes for the final portion of this closing section.

The development section (172 measures in length) deals with most of the motives of the exposition. The development technique is motivic and obviously related to the classical style of Beethoven. Contrary motion and one-measure imitation are frequently employed. Harmonic progression and effect seems to be a primary thrust in the development, a feature which might have been influenced by Mozart. Wagner's influence can be noted in the deceptive cadence that propels the music out of the exposition in measures 340–41. The recapitulation of the Bruckner fourth version is normal, all tunes present. The coda, also abbreviated, is based on the rhythm of the Urthema. An effective crescendo using an ostinato can be observed starting in measure 545.

---

* This 1880 version is used for the above analysis.

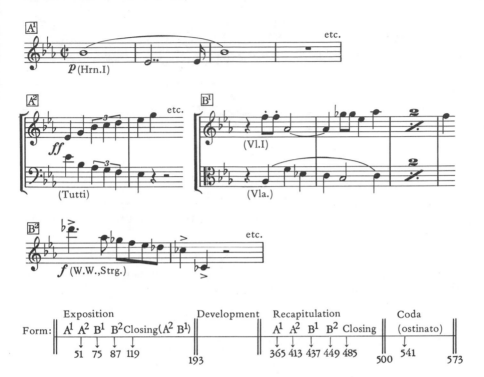

	Exposition				Development	Recapitulation					Coda
Form:	A¹ A² B¹ B² Closing(A² B¹)					A¹ A² B¹ B² Closing					(ostinato)
	51 75 87 119				193	365 413 437 449 485				500 541	573

II: Andante. Of the second movements (or, more correctly, inner slow movements) five are primarily part forms with the remaining two in sonata-allegro. The five part form movements, however, employ a hybrid form which combines five-part form with sonata-allegro, this showing the composer's tendency to convert traditionally nondevelopmental movements into developmental forms. This particular movement is one of the two slow movements cast originally in sonata-allegro form. The movement starts with a two-bar vamp which leads to the tune in the cellos. It appears to have a model origin. At measure 25, a choralelike tune is inserted. The secondary tune enters in measure 51, again in the cellos. Its rhythmic flow relates somewhat to sixteenth-century style. After this new tune has been developed for thirty-two bars, the development of the principal theme begins (measure 83). The recapitulation resembles the exposition fairly closely and covers the requisite material. The coda (measure 187) relates only to the first tune. The movement ends in the tonic major.

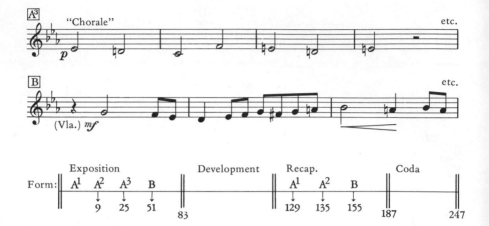

III: Bewegt (Scherzo).   The scherzos of the Bruckner symphonies, along with the second movements, show the composer's attempt to infuse these basically nondevelopmental movements with a strong developmental character. Bruckner thus tends to follow the pattern established by Beethoven in making all of the symphony's four movements developmental. It has been previously noted that both Haydn and Mozart manifested certain developmental tendencies in many of their minuets. Bruckner's attempt, apparently successful since he used it so much, was to expand the scherzo proper (*not* including the trio) to approximate the shape of a sonata-allegro movement:

A   B   A   ‖   Development   ‖   A   B   A

It should be noted that the third section of the scherzo form as used by Bruckner does not involve exact repetition of the material of the first section as the form outline implies. The material after the development is varied to such an extent that the form sounds continuous. The tune of the ensuing trio has roots in the folk tradition and resembles the dance tunes often used by Schubert in similar movements. After a da capo of the scherzo, Bruckner indicates a short coda for the final measures.

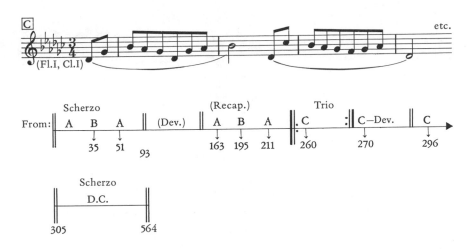

IV: **Bewegt, doch nicht zu schnell.** The introduction of this finale is almost a carbon copy of the opening bars of the symphony's first movement: tremolo in the strings and a slow-moving *Urthema* in the woodwinds. An ostinato (another Bruckner favorite) supports the entire introduction. At measure 43, the tutti version of the primary theme finally enters. It has the same duality of the rhythmic style noted in the polyrhythmic theme (A²) of the first movement. Bruckner injects the main tune of the first movement into the exposition (measure 79), a cyclic technique characteristic of his symphonies. The same tune reappears in the development section (measure 163). This particular development section divides itself into several subsections, each of which employs a particular portion of the movement's thematic material. By measure 383 (fourth version, not Redlich's), the recapitulation has started. An extended coda completes the movement.

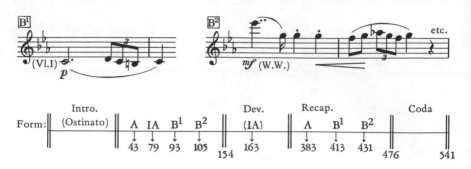

SUMMARY

Bruckner's position in symphonic literature is not as secure as one would desire. The works are long and tend to become too involved in establishing some kind of logic within thematic groups. Symphony No. 4 is very typical of most of the Bruckner symphonies. It is of an extended length. All four movements are developmental in nature, underlining Bruckner's tendency to "developmentalize" the inner movements. Other style mannerisms of the symphonies are present in abundance. In all, the work exemplifies Bruckner's lyricism and formal preoccupation. It also fits into the line of development of the more expansive nineteenth-century symphony composers. The conversion of the inner movements to developmental movements best shows Bruckner's expansion of symphonic form.

Antonin Dvořák (1841–1904)

Dvořák lived in a time when the two main streams in orchestral music—the programmatic and the absolute—ebbed and flowed according to the most recent influence on a composer's individual style. His own style shows this dichotomy, since his output is indeed a mixture of both trends. There are nine symphonies (generally absolute in nature) and five symphonic poems.* Only the symphonies remain in current repertoire in most countries.

Several composers exerted considerable stylistic influence on Dvořák: Beethoven, Schubert, Wagner, and, above all, Brahms. A fifth influence was to the surge of nationalism which swept Europe during Dvořák's life. These various influences continued throughout his creative life, but with varying degrees of relative emphasis depending on the style period and specific work in question. For instance, the early works favored the Wagnerian style. Nationalism was more dominant in the composer's middle period. The Brahms influence was felt more during the third and final creative period. Dvořák's mature sym-

---

* A detailed discussion of the programs and music of the symphonic poems can be found in John Chapham, *Antonin Dvořák* (New York: St. Martin's Press, 1966), pp. 117–26.

phonies (5–9, 1875–1893) were written at about the same time as those by Brahms (1876–1885). Brahms by that time had become a close friend and strong supporter of Dvořák. Schubert's influence can be seen in the emphasis on lyricism in all of the symphonies and in some of the tonal manipulations. Beethoven's formal and motivic values are in evidence in all nine symphonies. How these forces ebb and flow in the style makes fascinating study.

In the first symphony the influence of Beethoven is evident in extended passages on a single chord and in the use of unifying motives. The first movement's secondary theme recalls the simple lyricism of Schubert. Wagner's presence is felt in the second movement. The long and repetitious finale reeks of Schubert. The second symphony follows the Schubert-Beethoven style and uses Wagnerian devices in the finale. The third symphony is the most Wagnerian of all the symphonies, but the Brahms style surfaces in the second movement. The composer's individual style becomes more evident in the finale. In Symphony No. 4 some traces of Wagnerian harmony and melody survive. The folk element shows in the scherzo. Wagnerian lyricism returns in the finale's subordinate tune. Bohemian color is more evident in the fifth symphony. Some of

On April 11, 1888, the Concertgebouw Hall was opened with a concert using an orchestra especially organized for that event. The Board of Governors of the hall subsequently decided to establish an official orchestra for the hall with that orchestra giving its first concert on November 3, 1888. The picture below is from a concert presented in December, 1975, and shows conductor Bernard Haitink on the podium. Information and picture courtesy Dr. H. J. van Royen, artistic director, the Concertgebouw Orchestra. Photograph by Phonogram International B. V.

the more expressive passages retain the Wagner taint. The mature Dvořák style emerges more forcefully in this work. Symphony No. 6 at times sounds as if Brahms wrote it, especially the first movement. The second movement reverts to the long and sustained melodic style of Beethoven. Even the "Furiant" dance third movement has Beethoven influences. Brahms seems to have strongly influenced the finale. It is Dvořák's most German symphony. In Symphony No. 7 the Brahms style remains in evidence. Dvořák's own personal folk style is dominant in the third movement and in parts of the finale. The eighth symphony is one of Dvořák's most original works, with traces of older influences still in evidence. Schubert's lyricism is still a guiding force in the slow movement. The waltzlike third movement has passages reminiscent of Brahms. The ninth symphony is almost devoid of obvious style influences. The folk factor is probably the only residue of the style pasticcio noted in the earlier works and remains a major element of the Dvořák style.

The general style has other constant elements. Though the folk style tends to predominate in the middle symphonies, the modal and rhythmic writing of many of the other works is also in the folk tradition. The use of counterpoint is limited. Imitation is rarely used. Countermelodies seem to be the only contrapuntal preference. The harmonic idiom is fairly conservative, with functional root relationships and triadic harmony predominant. There are, however, certain passages which can be attributed to Wagner's influence. The entire first theme of the fourth symphony's second movement involves some third relation in consecutive chords and a few deceptive progressions (V–VI, etc.). A passage in the fifth symphony's second movement (measures 90–111) shows an augmented tonic chord going to a subdominant, as well as further examples of third relation. Other harmonic devices, quite original in design, occur infrequently but in places within a movement which are quite noticeable (Symphony No. 9, second movement, measures 1–4). Most of the striking harmonic progressions involve a shift of key at the break in the phrase. One of Dvořák's favored such modulations is from the major tonic to the major mediant. There is some interchange of major and minor on the same tonic center. Modal movements often use the lowered seventh scale degree; in one instance this is harmonized with the mediant triad (Symphony No. 4, third movement, measure 24).

Dvořák's melodic style is directly related to the style of whichever composer is influencing a particular work or movement. Thus, in the "Schubert" works, lyric lines are quite simple in construction and not overly expressive. Those movements or sections which show Beethoven's influence can contain short, motivic themes or long, spun-out slow tunes (as used in Beethoven's slow movements). The Wagner tunes often contain the characteristic "turn" found in the Rienzi tune. The folk style used in Dvořák symphonies is similar to that of his other works. The phrase structure is simple; the tunes are not elaborate rhythmically; the tonality often tends to be modal. Folk tunes usually have a strong motivic basis.

The orchestral technique is quite skillful from the very beginning. There is a certain degree of choir separation, with colorful doubling to emphasize melodic lines. Winds, especially the brass, are used ᵗo great advantage. Trombones and trumpets frequently are used thematically. Symphonies 1 through 4 contain a certain amount of expressive or colorful orchestration, which tends to diminish as Dvořák works more in the German style. The folk nature of some of the final two movements of the later symphonies tends to create an emphasis on woodwinds. In the Brahms-style works, there is usage of some of the Brahms orchestral devices (arpeggiation, pizzicato, etc.). Evidence of the Beethoven style sometimes surfaces in the earlier symphonies in woodwind voicings.

Rather than describe early works as "immature," and middle-period works as "transitional," it might be wise to consider the entire evolutionary aspect of the style, with each work having a place of importance in a line of style development. The basic conflict (or variable?) in the style is the alternation between strong German influence and strong folk influence. In the end Dvořák abandoned both his emphasis on learned skills and his fondness for Wagner and Brahms.

Information on Individual Symphonies *

No.	Date	Key	Intro.	I	II	III	IV
1	1865	e	yes	SA	Sonatina	Scherzo w/trio	SA
2	1865	B-flat	no	SA	ABA	Scherzo w/trio	SA
3	1873	E-flat	no	SA	ABA	Sonata rondo	—
4	1874	d	no	SA	Variation	Scherzo w/trio	ABABAB
5	1875	F	no	SA	ABA	Scherzo w/trio	SA
6	1880	D	no	SA	ABA	Scherzo w/trio	SA
7	1885	d	no	SA	ABA	Scherzo w/trio	SA
8	1889	G	no	SA	SA	Scherzo w/trio	Variation
9	1893	e	yes	SA	ABA	Scherzo w/trio	SA

* An earlier source readers may wish to check is Otakar Sourek, *The Orchestral Works of Antonin Dvořák*, trans. Roberta F. Samsour (Czechoslovakia: Artia, n.d.). Sourek's four-volume biography of Dvořák dates from 1916 to 1933. The book on orchestral works gives concise formal analysis with printed themes while dealing some of the time at the affective level. It also includes all of the programs for the symphonic poems.

SYMPHONY NO. 1

This symphony was called *The Bells of Zlonice* after Dvořák's death, since the work ostensibly was reminiscent of the composer's youthful days in that town. The first movement, in 3/4 meter, adheres quite closely to the Beethoven style, as previously noted. The level of melodic expression is greater than in the Beethoven works; thus the work is more aligned with the Schubert lyric concept of the symphony. The second movement uses a good Wagner-style tune, complete with the melodic turn and upward leap. A fugal section in the slow movement is seemingly patterned after similar passages in Beethoven works. The finale is extremely long.

SYMPHONY NO. 2

The second movement is quite expressive; the secondary theme (measure 25) is actually a section that stresses sonority and harmonic effect. A brief fugato occurs at measure 73. The style of the scherzo is more lyric than before.

SYMPHONY NO. 3

Called the *Eroica* because of its strong German influence, the work is in only three movements. The Wagner influence is quite pronounced. The melodic turn becomes one of the unifying motives in the first movement. Violins doubled at the octave are used in expressive playing of some of the lyric lines. The second movement ("Funeral March") uses tonalities of c-sharp minor and D-flat major. The finale is marchlike in style, with the march tune having a typical "expressive" appoggiatura at the top of its phrase.

SYMPHONY NO. 4

"The theme of the Andante starts with the same harmony and tonality as the second portion of the Pilgrims' March in Tannhauser. . . ." *

Variation 3 (second movement) features the cello on the tune in a very expressive scoring. The end of variation 5 (measures 99–105) has a Brahmsian sound because of the nature of the scoring (tune doubled at the octave in the violins, syncopated chordal accompaniment in the horns and violas, plus an arpeggiated pizzicato accompaniment in the cellos). The scherzo (3/4) has a 2/4 trio. The first appearance of the A tune is in a minor, returning in A major. The composer adds the harp to the trio resources.

SYMPHONY NO. 5

This work represents a return to a more folklike style. The tunes of the first movement are very simple in structure. The middle section of the slow movement dwells on very slow-moving sonorities, similar to Wagner's usage. The finale starts in a minor.

---

* Chapham, *Antonin Dvořák*, p. 65.

SYMPHONY NO. 6

This is the most Brahmsian of the symphonies, especially the first and final movements. The first movement uses imitative writing (measures 23–34), metric contraction (measures 43–45), pedal with contrapuntal materials above it (measures 78–86), contrary motion above a pedal (measures 90–93), parallel thirds in contrary motion to another line above a pedal (measures 120–30), and other familiar style devices of Brahms. The second and third movements hew more closely to the Beethoven style.

SYMPHONY NO. 7

Another of the "German" symphonies, this work begins to show more of the Dvořák folk style than Symphony No. 6. The work is analyzed in detail below.

SYMPHONY NO. 8

The first movement begins with in introductory passage in the *Allegro* tempo, with the entrance of the principal theme delayed until measure 18. The introductory passage is omitted in the recapitulation. The second movement, quite dramatic, features woodwinds and solo violin. The third movement is more waltz than scherzo, and, like many third movements which reflect folk characteristics, is modal. The rhythmic phrasing of the accompaniment in the trio is duple against a triple metrical scheme in the tune. The finale is a variation movement based on a tune related to the first tune of the first movement.

SYMPHONY NO. 9

The *New World* is probably Dvořák's best-known symphony; it enjoys tremendous popularity in the United States. The introduction of the first movement is thematically linked to the following *Allegro*. The subordinate theme is modal. The second movement is one of the most familiar in symphonic literature. The English horn solo is one of the few such solos in the history of the symphony. In measures 54–63, one of the secondary tunes is accompanied by muted string basses, pizzicato, a most effective passage orchestrally. Theme IA returns in the third movement briefly. The scherzo movement accompanies the first tune with a tonic seventh chord (egbd). Cellos are voiced lower than basses in this chord. Theme IA also appears in this movement (measure 154). Themes from all movements reappear in the finale but not as primary themes.

The typical Dvořák orchestra contains flutes, oboes, clarinets, bassoons, four horns, trumpets, three trombones (plus tuba in Symphonies 6 and 8), timpani, and strings.

It is difficult to characterize the Dvořák symphonic style because of the shifting influences noted in the nine symphonies. It evolved from a Beethoven-Schubert beginning, routed itself through a "German Period" (two types: Wagner, Brahms), began including basic folk elements (melody, rhythm, and modality) in the middle symphonies, and ended up with an individual style in the eighth and ninth symphonies which was primarily a Dvořák style. The symphonies which seem to have the strongest folk influence are 4, 5, 8, and 9. Those with emphasis on the German style are 1 and 2 (Beethoven, Schubert), 3 (Wagner), and 6 and 7 (Brahms). The one conclusion to be drawn is that Dvořák experienced a gradual change in musical style which affected his basic musical language. His overall handling of the symphony did remain fairly constant through his twenty years of symphonic composition. While Tchaikovsky tended to avoid developmental forms, Dvořák showed a decided preference for forms which allowed him to work out his themes. Thus sixteen (46 percent) of the thirty-five symphonic movements are in a developmental form. Those slow movements in ternary design also encompass some development in their middle sections. Each of the eight scherzos, in addition, depends on developmental techniques for its extended span. Motivic development is the primary device used in these developments, with repetition and sequence being essential developmental tools. Whereas the tendency of most major composers had been to develop material as soon as it was presented, Dvořák in some cases preferred to generate more melodic material in spinning out the line in the exposition of his tunes. Thus his first movements may have more than one or two basic thematic groups. Many of the slow movements are very expressive; none are insignificant in either the nature of their materials or the treatment of these materials. The second movement of the fourth symphony is particularly interesting because of its variation form, especially since the theme is quite chromatic (Wagnerian) in tonal organization.

Third movements (in four-movement symphonies) are generally designed as scherzo movements. Several are more restrained in style: symphonies 2, 7, and 8. The more dancelike and agitated are in symphonies 1, 4, 5, 6, and 9. All are in triple meter except 1, 4, and 7. The form of the scherzo is generally three-part rondo rather than a true song form with trio. Repetition marks are generally not used in either the scherzo or the trio. Finales are generally (six out of eight) sonata-allegro and dancelike in nature. They tend to approximate the style focus of their respective first movements. Some are folklike in melodic style (symphonies 4, 7, 8, and 9). The finale of the eighth symphony is a set of variations on a lyric tune which is interrupted by a more vigorous dance tune from time to time.

The Dvořák symphonies are basically lyric works with some of the motivic traits of the German learned (Beethoven) style in evidence and with a preponderance of folk traits in many of the symphonies. They provide an interesting contrast to the intellectually involved works of Brahms and the

hyperexpressive works of Tchaikovsky. Dvořák may have had limited contrapuntal skills, since he apparently avoided polyphonic textures in most of the
symphonies. The Brahms-style works (6, 7), however, use imitation and contrary motion extensively. Other works do not. Musical interest is sustained
through lyricism, development, style mannerisms of other composers (Schubert,
Beethoven, Wagner, and Brahms) and folk traits. His orchestral style is attractive if not striking. Dvořák was not interested in color as an expressive device
as much as a device for clarity of line. The symphonies are well constructed
and project a rational sequence of musical ideas. The tunes are appealing; some
of the settings are exciting. The works remain in modern symphonic repertory
because of excellent craftsmanship shown in their design and their overall
tunefulness.

EXAMPLES FOR STUDY

Dvořák: Symphony No. 7 in d minor, Op. 70 (1885)

I: Allegro maestoso. The opening theme of the movement stresses the
modal style Dvořák frequently used in relating his tunes to the folk tradition.
Extracting the short motive ① which concludes the theme, Dvořák completes
the first sixteen bars of the movement with a climax on this short motive under
a slight variation of its rhythm and pitch (motive ②). Much of the passage
is harmonized with a diminished seventh chord on the raised mediant (F-
sharp–A–C–E–flat), the important pitch of which appears to be the E-flat as
the passage leads to the A^2 tune (measure 16). This new melody has a rhythmic
structure familiar to most students of Brahms with its shifted accents and contracted metrical implication. After exactly eight bars Dvořák starts the third
part of the first tune (A^3, measure 25), more of a section than a theme, since
its components consist of not only the A^3 theme but also a continuation of the
first motive from A^1 (motive ①) as an accompanying figure. This passage also
begins with the previously mentioned diminished seventh chord; the high note
of the A^3 theme is treated as an appoggiatura, adding considerably to the expressive quality of the passage. Each time this theme appears (A^3), the same
dissonant treatment of the topmost pitch is repeated. After four bars Dvořák
extracts the descending scale motive for a continued contrapuntal development
(motivic) for an additional four bars (measures 29–32). The passage concludes with a contrary motion section equally typical of the Brahms idiom. A
fourth section (A^4) starts at measure 33 and proves to be the most complex
of the principal sections because of its contrapuntal texture. This is drawn from
the same Brahms tradition, i.e., imitative, contrapuntal lines in contrary motion
to a line in parallel thirds, with all of this set over a pedal bass. The principal
section closes with a tune (A^5) less involved in format and featuring the horn
and oboe in an imitative relationship. Dvořák then constructs a transition to
the secondary tune from the motive ② and the A^1 theme.

The second theme (B¹) enters at measure 73 as a much simpler and more lyric entity. Its continuous nature is enhanced by the delaying of the resolution of the dominant harmonies until the passage begins again at measure 83. The texture is quite Brahmsian, with much of the accompaniment placed on the weak beats and played pizzicato in the lower strings. Part motion in parallel thirds also enhances the German connection in the style. The subordinate section closes with a theme (B²) which is used sequentially on a descending pattern of major triads (G, F, E-flat). The mode changes to e minor in the measure (96) previous to the entry of the closing theme (C¹), which then enters in the dominant key, B major. The stress on the pitch E-flat can then be understood as an emphasis on the plagal effect (lowered supertonic in d minor or diatonic subdominant in B-flat major), a usage not rare in Brahms's works. The final section of the closing theme (C²) adds an expressive climax to the exposition, which then subsides to lead quietly into the development section. This working-out part of the movement continues both the lyric and motivic quality of the basic materials of the movement and can be divided into six loosely defined sections:

Measures

114–22   The A¹ motive dominates this section with an occasional use of its motive ①.

123–28   A counterpoint from B¹ (clarinets, bassoons, trombones) is used over the A³ theme.

129–31   A tutti passage is based on the modified B¹ theme.

132–43   This section contains an extensive contrapuntal treatment of the motive from the fourth measure of the B¹ theme (♪♪♪♩. | ♩. ♪♪♪♩. | etc.). A section from measure 129 to measure 136 is placed above a pedal B-flat with some parts in parallel thirds and is imitated by another line in the bass and tenor instruments.

149–56   The secondary theme is emphasized. A sixteenth-note motive from B is in the background.

157–95   The A¹ theme is manipulated through various keys until a climax is reached on the return of the tonic key (and the recapitulation) at measure 196.

The recapitulation is shortened considerably, with a number of the segments of the principal section being omitted. The first portion of the coda (measures 248–86) is developmental; several motives from the principal section are manipulated simultaneously. A quieter section at measure 287 restates the A¹ theme in its original version. In measure 293 the raised seventh scale degree

(C-sharp) appears as a melodic cadence figure for the first time, a contrast to the lowered seventh in the principal theme (C-natural). The C-sharp leading tone is never used as a part of a harmonic cadence and thus does not diminish the natural minor flavor of the main theme. However, Dvořák's avoidance of the lowered seventh scale degree in the final statement of the A^1 tune (measure 304–9) is ingenious. The solution of the problem can be seen in the horn parts in the final statement of the tune.

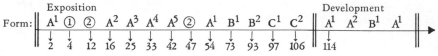

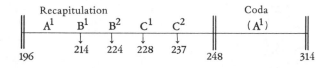

II: Poco Adagio.

II: Poco Adagio. The second movement is one of Dvořák's most exquisite lyric inspirations. The first eight bars expose the basic theme with the opening part played by the woodwinds with string pizzicato doubling the harmonic support. The repetition of the theme actually presents a slightly different version (A²), which begins to involve more of the Brahms textural devices (pizzicato arpeggios in the cellos and contrary motion between soprano and bass line). The subordinate theme features the horn quartet in a more placid section (B¹) which then is followed by a wide-range theme in the solo clarinet (B²). A brief middle section (C¹ and C²) with some motivic imitation follows. A deceptive cadence (measures 69–70) leads to the restatement of the earlier material, somewhat abbreviated. This movement lacks in strong cadences, since the composer apparently preferred melodic to harmonic cadences.

III: **Vivace (Scherzo).** As is often the case, Dvořák's own individual style appears most clearly in the dancelike third movement of this symphony. The first section has a dancelike tune with a strong rhythmic organization. A lyric countermelody is located in the bassoons and cellos. Measures 6–9 contain a descending sequence based on the vertical sonority of the seventh chord as follows: d mm7th→A Mm7th→B-flat MM7th→A major. A repetition of the first theme starts at measure 19 with a slight variation of the countermelody. After a short contrasting segment, the theme returns again at measure 44 with still another variation of the countermelody. The fourth statement of the theme begins at measure 61, *fortissimo*. An impressive climax ends the scherzo, followed by a much quieter trio (measure 93). A countermelody also accompanies this tune. After a brief contrasting section the B tune returns at measure 128. A short transition precedes the return of the scherzo. A coda concludes this graceful dance movement with a brilliant flourish.

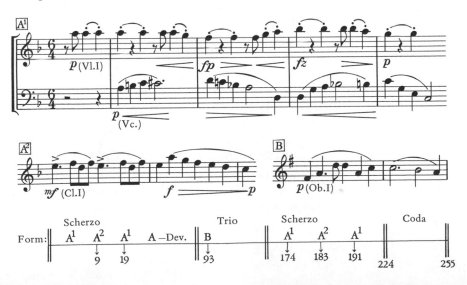

IV: Allegro. The finale's first theme is slow-moving but expressive in its use of inflected fourth (G-sharp) and seventh (C-sharp) scale degrees. After over one hundred measures of development of the first tune, a lilting second theme appears as the subordinate tune with a modified "um-pah" accompaniment, which reveals the folk influence of this section. A restless closing section based on the A major triad closes the exposition. The development section is one of Dvořák's most contrapuntal experiments, with an almost equal emphasis on imitation and the combination of theme and countermelody. It generally follows the same type of scheme as did that of the first movement as far as the sequence of treatments (and themes) is concerned:

Measures	
170–85	This section involves three treatments of the A^1 theme: an eight-bar phrase played in its first half pizzicato by the strings and in its second half legato by the woodwinds and an eight-bar sequence on the theme.
186–90	A short, imitative treatment of A^1 is played pianissimo.
191–204	A four-bar phrase is sequenced up a half step. A new countermelody in the flute is imitated by the oboes as the violins imitate a half-note motive from the theme.
205–8	A transition uses a diminished seventh chord on D-sharp. A motive in the woodwinds relates to the sixteenth-note motive in A^1.
209–16	A fugal development ensues in which the violas imitate the first violins. A countermelody also occurs in the violas (measure 209) which is handed to the first violins, creating an effective double counterpoint.
217–24	The more rhythmic fugue theme is restated without imitation, tutti. The A^2 theme becomes more prominent in the accompaniment.
225–32	This passage starts out somewhat fugally (in violins) but subsides to repeat the second measure of the subject with a constant flow of eighth notes in a countermelody. The melody is set in parallel sixths.
233–40	The same tune is imitated in the strings with a whole-note countermelody. The A^2 motive becomes active again. A new counterpoint in the woodwinds is based on some of the notes of the tune in the strings. The rhythmic style is new.
241–50	The violins, violas, and cellos become involved in another imitative passage with a modified version of the A^2 theme in the woodwinds. The passage subsides to ppp.

251–56   The clarinet states the entire A^1 theme, slightly modified, in an eight-bar passage which is repeated up a half step. An imitative voice in the upper woodwinds intensifies the contrapuntal effect. In the first eight bars the strings arpeggiate the F-sharp minor triad, then G minor in the next eight bars. Sequential treatment remains important as a device of development.

257–80   A transition to the recapitulation serves primarily as a harmonic and tonal link. A canon occurs between the first violins and bass strings. There is a double pedal (A-flat, C-flat) in the other instruments.

The recapitulation begins at measure 281 and follows an abbreviated pattern. A coda, based primarily on the main tune, closes the work in the tonic major key.

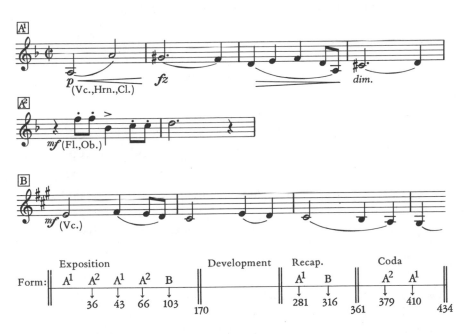

SUMMARY

This work, of all the symphonies, in many ways best sums up Dvořák's symphonic style. It shows the composer as an eclectic craftsman who absorbed the strong influences around him and yet was able to create a logical and exciting work of art. In spite of the dearth of contrapuntal writing in the other symphonies, there is enough counterpoint in Symphony No. 7 to indicate that the composer might have enhanced his overall style considerably if he had used this texture earlier in his musical development. The third movement, perhaps the most appealing to the listener, is undoubtedly Dvořák's original concept of the scherzo style: a special kind of folk-dance movement which has considerable grace and appeal. Dvořák must have seen his task as seeking a way to reflect his cultural heritage and at the same time articulate his efforts with the mainstream of symphonic development carried forward by Beethoven, Schubert, and Brahms. Alas, he could not resist the intoxicating tonal high jinks of Wagner and thus became the one symphonic composer in the nineteenth century whose works mirror most of the crosscurrents of style occurring in that century. His symphonies carried forward primarily the learned German concept of the symphony but imbued it with a lyricism and charm unequaled in the late nineteenth century.

French Orchestral Music of the Nineteenth Century

For reasons cultural, sociological, and national, France, during the nineteenth century, showed an almost total disregard for the nurturing of the concert symphony. Those works, which have been noted after Berlioz's *Fantastic* Symphony (1830), are:

Georges Bizet (1838–1875):	Symphony in C (1855)
Charles Gounod (1818–1893):	Symphony No. 1 (1855)
	Symphony No. 2 (1855)
Camille Saint-Saëns (1835–1921):	Symphony No. 1 (1855)
	Symphony No. 2 (1859)
	Symphony No. 3 (1866)
César Franck (1822–1890):	Symphony in D Minor (1888)

The Bizet work was not discovered until 1935 and since then has enjoyed nominal success. It was written during the composer's seventeenth year. Of the Saint-Saëns symphonies, only the third has achieved any fame. This organ symphony and the Franck symphony are the two most popular French symphonies of the latter part of the nineteenth century. Including the Berlioz *Fantastic Symphony* one can conclude that only three major symphonies have survived from this scant output of French composers. The gap of fifty-eight years between the Berlioz work (1830) and the Franck work (1888) does indicate that as a nation France had little love for the absolute orchestral forms in the nineteenth century.

César Franck

Primarily a composer of sacred music and organ works, Franck wrote relatively few works for instruments other than organ: one symphony, three symphonic poems, a violin sonata, a string quartet, and a quintet. Franck's musical style is fairly conservative, considering the span of his active career as a composer (1846–1890). His musical roots for some reason rejected much of the Liszt-Wagner expansive style and drew sustenance from the more classically oriented composers, especially Bach. The symphonic poems, composed prior to his symphony, are rarely played in this country. They do represent the composer's efforts to create works in the mainstream of musical thought in the nineteenth century.

Franck's style is characterized by a preference for the use of orthodox ways of handling form and shape in music. His developmental techniques show this same traditional treatment of themes. This enabled him to avoid the excesses of some of his peers, who used orchestral expression and melodic and harmonic dissonance *only* to serve expressive purposes. While he did carry forward some of the cyclic and transformational concepts of Liszt, he did not share Liszt's or Wagner's ultraexpressive credo.

Franck's melody is based on the short phrase as the primary formal unit. Phrase structure is extremely regular (square), with one device occurring quite frequently: Franck often designs a phrase around a single pitch, using this pitch as a pivot from which very narrow excursions are taken and to which frequent returns are seen. One of the tunes from the symphony shows this:

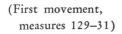 

(First movement, measures 129–31)

Tunes are compact with frequent half-step motion. In addition to the half step, Franck seemed to be fond of the diminished fourth and the diminished third. Like other nineteenth-century composers, he made frequent use of the appoggiatura in his tunes. Motivic structure in melody is the rule rather than the exception. A fondness for motivic organization may have led to another Franck mannerism: the phrase motive, a short (usually two-measure) subject from which many of his tunes are built. Chromaticism in his tunes tends to produce the half-step motion noted above.

Rhythm is quite regular with one exception: Franck's affection for weak-beat accents, or syncopation, in his tunes. Long notes often start on the second or fourth beat in a four-beat meter in some of his tunes. Other than this mannerism, the treatment of rhythm and meter is quite traditional (and conservative).

Franck's harmonic style is more progressive than his rhythmic style. His emphasis on chromaticism in his harmonies may have resulted from his interest in linear matters rather than harmonic effect. One can find progressions which contain parallel seventh and ninth chords. The melodic emphasis on the half step produces chromatic harmonic support which can defy sometimes traditional analysis. His sense of tonality is very strong, with his "planned" excursions often leading away from and back to the primary key of a work.

His treatment of form is conservative except for the cyclic elements in the symphony. His other instrumental works show a strong formal organization. His preferences tend toward the part forms and sonata-allegro. The cyclic element in the symphony may have sprung from the thematic manipulations of Berlioz and Liszt.

As a church composer his exposure to basic contrapuntal devices must have been extreme. His reverence for Bach is well known.[*] His use of counterpoint includes some canonic passages and a contrapuntal figuring of the inner parts of his music. His textures are primarily homophonic with polyphonic devices serving to enrich textures and to develop ideas.

EXAMPLES FOR STUDY

Franck: *Symphony in d minor*

I: Lento, Allegro. The form of the first movement is an expansive version of sonata-allegro with some minor variations of the basic pattern. The work is distinguished by two tempos for the principal theme (*Lento* and *Allegro*). The slow presentation of the first set of tunes is characterized by uneven phrase lengths, quite an exception to the regularity of phrase structure noted in the remaining thematic construction of the work. The *Allegro* opens with a statement of the four two- or three-measure phrases from A. Most of the tunes are constructed in this manner, i.e., a theme made up of several individual phrase-motives of two measures each. Two of the phrase-motives (A^3, A^5) have an accented offbeat rhythmic structure, a characteristic of the Franck style. The B theme also is constructed of phrase-motives of two measures each. Using the second phrase-motive (B^2), Franck built a climactic passage which leads to the closing theme (C^1), a theme structured around a single pitch (another Franck mannerism). Measures 145–58 primarily serve a harmonic function by using melodic materials based on a series of arpeggiated chords which can be related to the opening measure of the A^2 theme.

The music subsides as the development section starts with a treatment of the C^1 theme. By measure 199 Franck has taken up the principal material, in some instances combining as many as three of the phrase motives simultaneously (measures 210–12). At measure 213 a new theme occurs which does not reappear subsequently. Another unrelated and new tune enters at measure 221 in

---

[*] Einstein, *Music in the Romantic Era*, p. 78.

canon between upper and lower string and woodwinds. After continued development of the A² and the A⁵ tunes, a third new passage is inserted (measures 249–50). A climax is reached on the A² tune around measure 280, with a quieter transition on the C tune leading to another major expressive point at measure 331, at which time the recapitulation begins. The length of the restatement is decreased by some fifty measures with the omission of much of the principal material and its repetitions. A coda which continues some development concludes with a brief canon on the principal theme.

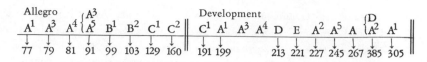

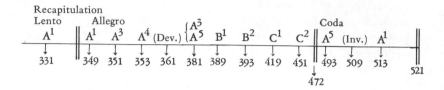

II: Allegretto. The orchestral setting of the second movement is more colorful than that of other movements. It also helps to delineate sections within the form by retaining much of the individual color of each section as that section reappears in the form. The opening scoring always seems to be associated subsequently with the first tune: pizzicato strings doubling the harp. Franck's orchestration of the movement may have had a thematic significance, since two of the orchestral treatments (at measures 16 and 109) are combined in the final return of A at measure 200. The overall form of the movement combines elements of a developmental form with rondo principles and may need this clarification by color. The first theme is conceived in two parts: a rhythmic "accompaniment" theme followed by a lyric countermelody which is actually the primary lyric element of the movement. Franck uses the English horn for the principal lyric theme, thereby predating by some five years Dvořák's usage of the horn in his slow movement of the *New World* Symphony (No. 9). As the music increases in dynamics, the French horn and clarinet replace the English horn (measure 32), both scored at the unison.

The second tune (B) is one of Franck's narrow-range melodies which hovers around a single pitch. A sixteenth-note harmonic figure in the second violins and violas moves forward throughout the whole theme. The section noted as "A-Dev." in the graph below has a triplet countermelody played tremolo in the strings which is embossed over the pizzicato tune. A similar figure is used in the third group (C) starting at measure 135. The final statement of the A theme (measure 200) uses the same device. The final harmonic cadence (measures 258–59) is plagal (e-flat minor seventh chord to tonic B-flat). The melodic cadence is authentic (A-B-flat, i.e., leading tone to tonic). The form of the movement could be considered a modified rondo form.

III **Allegro non troppo.** Franck's cyclic leanings produced a somewhat original version of sonata-allegro form (see below). Themes from both first and second movements reappear throughout the movement. The English horn tune from the second movement is used in all three sections of the finale. Two themes from the opening movement (IA, IC) tend to dominate the recapitulation. The exposition contains the expected three groups of themes (two phrase-motives for each of the principal and subordinate themes, with phrase lengths more extended than in the first movement). Franck, as before, states each group of themes and then immediately repeats that section. The repetition of the principal section involves some amount of development and extension. The subordinate section, shorter in length, is not subject to as much thematic manipulation. The closing theme (C) is undergirded with a ground-bass-like tune which creates a more contrapuntal effect than noted in other parts of the movement. An extended development of the A^1 tune starts the middle section, leading to an impressive climax on the subordinate tune (measure 187). The development of the first theme is primarily tonal. At measure 212 of the development parts of the IIA^2 theme intermingle with portions of the C theme of the finale. It is not a contrapuntal manipulation. The recapitulation restates the principal section as before but omits the entire subordinate section in favor of the return of themes from other movements. Most of this section alternates brief versions of these recycled tunes. A plagal cadence (measures 425–26) closes the movement.

Franck's orchestra contains a large complement of instruments. These

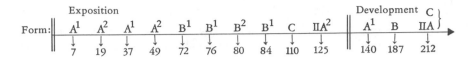

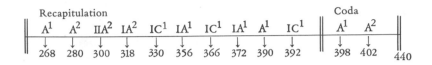

have been added to the typical orchestra of Brahms and Tchaikovsky: English horn, bass clarinet, two cornets (in addition to two trumpets), and harp. Franck's orchestration is often faulted because of its emphasis on the bass line and on a rather stylized and rigid use of wind instruments. In the d minor symphony he follows the same principles used by other nineteenth-century composers to achieve a more expressive orchestral setting: for example, doubling string parts at the octave as in measures 213–26 of the first movement, using string tremolo to build climaxes as in measures 21–28 of the first movement, and having the full string section plus harp play a pizzicato accompaniment to wind solo as in measures 24–32 of the second movement. At times the scoring appears awkward (as noted in measures 130–44 and 269–82) in the first movement because unison scoring is used with violins, flute, oboe, and clarinet with trumpets scored an octave lower. In the latter passage, the doubling varies with the range of the instruments, so that the color changes rather abruptly in measure 273 when oboes and clarinets cannot reach the upper octave being played in the flutes and violins. In the very next measure Franck resumes the unison scoring, since the tune has returned to a manageable range for the oboes and clarinets.

A passage which shows much greater sensitivity to color occurs in measures 200–7, second movement. The melody is doubled at the octave in the English horn and bass clarinet, quite an interesting mixture of basic instrumental colors. The harp strums an accompaniment similar to that heard at the beginning of the movement in the full string section (pizzicato). The most interesting color arises from the violins, where Franck has designed a harmonic countermelody in eighth notes to be played in measured tremolo with mutes. Later clarinets and bassoons are added to double the harp support, with the remainder of the string section (pizzicato) being added as the passage concludes. Some of the other doublings in this second movement are not quite as well designed. All, however, show Franck attempting to write both colorfully and sensitively for his orchestra. His failing often comes when intruments are doubled at the unison: often he selects two instruments of unequal balance (e.g., horn doubling clarinet, measures 207–15, second movement) to place on a single line and thereby assures that the weaker instrumental sound will never penetrate the sound of the stronger instrument. Authorities who considered

Franck primarily "organistic" in his orchestral technique may have a point, since the doubling shows the same additive technique available to the organist within a group of stops. Franck is consistent in this principle so must have liked the effect.

SUMMARY

The Franck d minor symphony is in three movements. It is cyclical. Its form is concise and well within the more conservative approach to the symphony. Franck's use of what has been termed "phrase-motives" was not altogether original, since it probably sprang from the antecedent-consequent phrase structure used by many classical composers. What was individual about his approach to the developmental forms was his rejection of the motive concept used by Brahms and Beethoven to unify movements of a symphony. It is true that the first and third movements are tied together by the primary theme of the first movement. Franck, however, did not articulate or integrate a single movement through the use of two or three unifying motives. His tendency was to let the symphony become a more lyric specimen through the repetition of longer phrase-motives and melodies, allowing these more expressive lines to provide whatever unity is implied. Conclusions based on the study of only two development sections are hardly more than tentative but do show that Franck followed Schubert's methods of development rather than Beethoven's. His tendency to repeat passages did allow him to move these sections around into rather striking and surprising tonal areas. Counterpoint is almost nonexistent in the symphony. Short canon is used a number of times. The first movement shows a few examples of combining tunes into a contrapuntal fabric. Texture has nowhere the complexity of the texture of Brahms or Wagner. Tchaikovsky and other lyric composers of the nineteenth century showed greater skills in setting melody against countermelody.

As a symphony composer of the late nineteenth century, Franck undoubtedly reflected France's disinterest in symphonic music. The Symphony in D Minor attaches itself to the mainstream of symphonic development more as an appendage than as an essential unit in that development. The work probably owes its popularity in this country to its concise tunes and the uncomplicated treatment of those tunes. Its expressive tonal manipulations may also appeal to the fans of nineteenth-century music.

Richard Strauss (1864–1949)

Strauss's position in music history is often described as that of the post-romanticist. Most of his major instrumental works, however, were written prior to 1900. His operas, with one exception, were composed in the twentieth century. His musical style development reached a point of relative stability around 1890 and did not change markedly during his major creative periods. His orchestral works, together with those of Mahler, can be viewed in some respects as the last major orchestral compositions of the romantic era. It might be more appropriate, then, to label Strauss as a late romanticist who sustained his style well into the twentieth century.

Strauss wrote five symphonies or works of multimovement symphonic proportions:

> Symphony in D Minor, Op. 4 (1880): The work was withdrawn by the composer.
>
> Symphony in F Major, Op. 12 (1884): Strauss's second traditional symphony is in four movements (SA, scherzo, SA, SA). It enjoyed some popularity during his life.
>
> *Aus Italien* (1886): This programmatic work of four movements depicts Strauss's impressions of a trip to Italy. All movements are in sonata-allegro form.
>
> *Domestic Symphony* (1903): In four large sections, this work tried to describe Strauss's own family, using elements of sonata-allegro to unify the work; the last section is fugal.
>
> *Alpine Symphony* (1915): The symphony is in twenty-four sections (for twenty-four hours of the day). It describes a day in the life of a mountain and its climbers; each section was subtitled by the composer.

His greatest impact on the history of orchestral music was, however, through the medium of the symphonic poem (called "tone poem" by Strauss). Because of this impact and because of the failure of any of the symphonies to attract a supportive audience through the years, the symphonic poems will be discussed in this text as the best examples of the Strauss style. This inconsistency with the basic thrust of the text can be justified by the significant impact of the Strauss symphonic poems on the history of orchestral music and their unique mirroring of the style of late-nineteenth-century music for the orchestra. The works are generally in traditional forms. *Macbeth* (1888, rev. 1890), *Don Juan* (1888), *Death and Transfiguration* (1899) and *A Hero's Life* (1898) are in sonata-allegro form; *Till Eulenspiegel's Merry Pranks* (1895) combines variation and rondo form; *Thus Spake Zarathustra* (1896) is sectional; *Don Quixote* is in variation form. Strauss's treatment of the symphonic poem followed the basic traditions of both Berlioz and Liszt, either descriptive to the point of almost endless detail or only suggestive of a more philosophical meaning to the music. *Till Eulenspiegel* and *Don Quixote* are excellent examples of Strauss's descriptive powers, while *Death and Transfiguration* and *Zarathustra* serve as more philosophically oriented works.

Strauss's musical style underwent changes in his earlier works. Strongly influenced by nineteenth-century German music (Schumann, Brahms, etc.), Strauss developed considerable skill in developmental and variation forms in his early works, a skill that remained an important aspect of his style throughout his life. By the time he wrote his first tone poem in 1888, he was a mature composer from the standpoint of his classical craftsmanship. Liszt and Wagner became his next strong influences. Much of his melodic style and especially his harmonic style sprang from the style of Wagner. His concept of transforming a theme to reflect changes in a program came from both Liszt and Wagner. It was this unique mixture of the classical (thematic development) and the romantic (chromatic harmony and an endless spinning-out of the music) which in part elevated Strauss to a position of importance in the history of symphonic music. In many ways both Brahms and Strauss combined the best of both classic and romantic traditions in their music. Brahms, however, chose to emphasize the intellectual tradition of the art form, while Strauss opted for the expressive above all else.

The overall musical style shows a texture of great complexity. Strauss used a large orchestra and involved this orchestra in the enhancement of polyphonic writing. Counterpoint exists in almost every section of one of Strauss's works, be it motivic or thematic imitation, fugal passages, or the simple part-writing of a passage to achieve a polyphonic effect. Melody, as in many nineteenth-century styles, is the keystone to Strauss's style. An extremely gifted melodist, Strauss often introduced a long and complex tune from which he would later extract several motives for development. Some of his tunes at the outset very rapidly ascend an arpeggio outline to reach a level one or two octaves above the starting point. Long and spun-out lines are typical of the style. The use of unifying motives, or leitmotivs, exists in every symphonic poem. Melodies are frequently constructed in part from syncopated materials. Melodic dissonance, in addition to chromatic writing, helps Strauss achieve a high degree of expression. Rhythm is also of a complex nature. There are frequent changes of meter and tempo as the music seeks to portray a particular effect required by the program. Syncopation occurs frequently. Rhythmic motives are also typical. A rhapsodic style is achieved not only by melodic and harmonic devices but also by a deemphasis of the obvious: periodicity of meter and exaggerated cadential pauses. Harmonic materials spring from both Liszt and Wagner. There is some use of the augmented triad. Static chords which seem not to require or imply eventual resolution tend to negate certain fixed biases regarding harmonic progression and parallel to some extent the harmonic innovations of Debussy. Dominant-type harmonies often fail to resolve as such. In some of the more expressive passages, especially in the operas, dissonant sonorities stand by themselves, unresolved. Rapid modulation is typical in some works, with choice of key completely open.

Strauss achieved fame also because of his virtuosic orchestral skills. Techcal demands on all instruments are among the most severe in orchestral history. String parts appear to ask for skills beyond the capacity of many orchestras. The enhanced angularity of some rapid passages for strings (see *Don Juan*, measures 30–36; *Death and Transfiguration*, measures 96–100) increases these demands frequently. Similar demands are made on wind players. Strauss's virtuosic writing for orchestra indeed requires virtuosic playing.

The size of the orchestra varies (upward) from work to work. His usual orchestral core is:

piccolo	four horns	strings (subdivided)	three timpani
three flutes	three trumpets	harp	cymbals
two oboes	three trombones		bass drum
English horn	tuba		snare drum
two clarinets			
two bassoons			
contrabassoon			

An accompanying chart, which lists the orchestral resources for eight of the Strauss orchestral works, shows how the orchestra became somewhat flexible according to the needs of the moment.

Strauss required effects from his orchestra which, at the time, were considered at least exceptional: *sul ponticello;* rapidly played four-note arpeggios in the strings in accompaniment passages somewhat akin to the measured tremolo of the classical period; frequent solo string parts; muted brass instruments; fortissimo passages for stopped horns; the striking of various percussion instruments (timpani, drums, cymbals, tamtam, etc.) with wooden-headed sticks; harp tremolo; glockenspiel tremolo; and other unusual usages. The doubling of important melodic parts by similar instruments at the single or double octave continued and became more frequent until in the later scores dissimilar instruments were added to promote the intensity of a particular line. Solo passages for brass instruments which include some of the wide-range tunes previously mentioned not only placed technical demands on the players but also required a type of tonal intensity almost forced in quality. The need for a greater volume of sound eventually required that the composer score for larger and larger orchestras. Subdivision of strings in some instances seemed without restriction: six viola parts playing tremolo harmonics (*Zarathustra,* Eulenberg score #3506, p. 109), twelve separate parts for tremolo or trills in the violas (*Don Quixote,* Kalmus score #132, rehearsal #23, p. 33), four-part pizzicato chords for contrabass (same score, rehearsal #13, p. 23; there are frequent examples of four-part bass chords in this score), and similar examples in practically every score. Woodwinds were exploited through many new effects: measured tremolo on single tones (*Don Quixote,* Kalmus score #132, rehearsal #19, p. 29), rapid tremolo on two notes (same work, pp. 46–47), and flute flutter-tonguing on rapid chromatic scale passages (same work, rehearsal #57, p. 65). Brass single-note tremolo can also be noted in *Don Quixote* (same score, pp. 32–33), an effect similar to flute flutter-tonguing.

The orchestral scoring of the "figured" harmonic background of his mature works heightened the contrapuntal nature of this Wagnerian type of part-writing. As the style became more complex, conflicting lines made it

Instrumentation Chart

	Don Juan	Death and Transfig.	Till Eulenspiegel	Thus Spake Zarathustra
Picc.	1		1	2
Fl.	3	3	3	3
Ob. d'Amore				
Ob.	2	2	3	3
E. Hn.	1	1	1	1
Cl.	2	2	3 (1 D)	3 (1 E-flat)
B. Cl.		1	1	1
Heckelphone				
Bsn.	2	2	3	3
Dbl. Bsn.	1	1	1	1
Saxophone				
Hn.	4	4	8 (5,6,7,8 ad lib)	6
Trpt.	3	3	6 (4,5,6 ad lib)	4
Trb.	3	3	3	3
Ten. Tuba				
Tuba	1	1	1	2
Bells				1
Thunder Mach.				
Wind Mach.				
Timp.	3	3	3	X
Cel.				
Triangle	1		1	1
Herdengelaute (cow bells)				
B.D.			1	1
S.D.			1	
Cym.	1		1	1
Tambourine				
Rattle			1	
Gong		1		
Glock.	1			1
Lg. Field Drum				
Hp.	1	2		2
Organ				1
Str.	X	X	X	X

Instrumentation Chart

	Alpine Symphony	A Hero's Life	Don Quixote	Domestica Symphonia
Picc.	2	1	1	1
Fl.	4	3	2	3
Ob. d'Amore				1
Ob.	3	4	2	2
E. Hn.	1	1	1	1
Cl.	4	3	3	4
	(1 E-flat)	(1 E-flat)	(1 E-flat)	(1 E-flat)
B. Cl.	1	1	1	1
Heckelphone	1			
Bsn.	4	3	3	4
Dbl. Bsn.	1	1	1	1
Saxophone				4
Hn.	20	8	6	8
	(12 behind sc.)			
Trpt.	6	5	3	4
	(2 behind sc.)			
Trb.	6	3	3	3
	(2 behind sc.)			
Ten. Tuba	4	1	1	
	(with Hns.5,6,7,8)			
Tuba	2	1	1	1
Bells				
Thunder Mach.	1			
Wind Mach.	1		1	
Timp.	2 players	X	X	X
Cel.	1			
Triangle	1	1	1	1
Herdengelaute	1			
B.D.	1	1	1	1
S.D.	1	1	1	
Cym.	1	1	1	1
Tambourine			1	1
Rattle				
Gong	1	1		
	3 players			
Glock.	1		1	1
Lg. Field Drum		1		
Hp.	2	2	1	2
Organ	1			
Str.	X	X	X	X
			(includes solo cello)	

difficult to distinguish primary line from supportive material (see *Zarathustra,* pp. 80–82; also *Don Quixote,* pp. 72–73). Since orchestral effect is prerequisite to tone painting, the expanded scope and treatment of the orchestra can be understood in part as Strauss's effort to depict or describe. Few composers in history have exhibited such powers of orchestral characterization and brilliance of scoring.

EXAMPLES FOR STUDY

Strauss: *Till Eulenspiegel's Merry Pranks*

Strauss's fourth tone poem is somewhat less expansive in both musical and orchestral style than many of his other works from the same period. Selecting a folk tale for his program, Strauss employs a hybrid form which is primarily rondo in structure but also contains elements of variation and sonata-allegro. The various sections supposedly correspond with the adventures of Till and have been described by Strauss as follows (numbers refer to numbers in the form graph on p. 222):

Prologue:	An introduction of the Till character
I:	"Up to new pranks"
II:	In the marketplace where Till rides his horse to upset the various vendors
III:	"Dressed as a priest he oozes unction and morality." As he masquerades "he is seized with a horrid premonition as to the outcome of his mockery. . . ."
IV:	"Till the cavalier, exchanging sweet courtesies with beautiful girls." He is jilted. He vows to take revenge.
V:	Till among the learned professors. "After he has posed a few atrocious theses to the philistines, he leaves them to their fate dumbfounded."
VI:	An interlude which begins with Till innocently leaving the pedagogues in a light and frivolous mood. Strauss has marked this transition with the words "fleeting and ghostly."
Recapitulation:	Most of the tunes reappear in a section which continues to develop the two primary motives.
VII:	Till's execution: "Up the ladder with him! There he dangles, the breath leaves his body, the last convulsion and Till's mortal self is finished." *

---

* Norman Del Mar, *Richard Strauss: a Critical Commentary of His Life and Work,* 2 vols. (London: Barrie and Jenkins, 1962–69), I,125–30. Quoted with permission of publisher.

Geburtstags-Konzert

Sonntag, den 11. Juni 1944, 11 Uhr 30
im Großen Musikvereins-Saal

Dirigent:

Dr. Richard Strauß*

Programm:

Richard Strauß ... ... Till Eulenspiegels lustige Streiche, nach alter Schelmenweise (in Rondoform), für großes Orchester, op. 28

Richard Strauß ... ... Sinfonia domestica für großes Orchester, op. 53

* Ehrenmitglied der Wiener Philharmoniker

A 1944 concert by the Vienna Philharmonic shows Strauss still an active conductor, conducting both *Till Eulenspiegel* and the *Domestic Symphony*. Courtesy Vienna Philharmonic.

The procedure in the various sections of the form is quite similar for the most part. Each section (or adventure) begins either with a new tune or a version of one of the unifying motives (motives 1 or 2). Then follows a new theme which is always a transformation of one of the two motives. Odd-numbered sections begin with new themes; even-numbered sections begin with transformations of one of the two motives, thereby achieving the rondo effect Strauss wanted. More important is the use of a transformed version of one of the unifying motives to help describe the mood or nature of each particular adventure. This gives each section an overall variation style once the unifying motive enters. Strauss's skill as a developer is supportive of this seemingly difficult task of transforming a motive and developing it in the mood of the particular adventure. Even without the story, the work has a high level of appeal because of its skillful and musical handling of the development of the two unifying themes. A summary of this treatment follows:

Section	*Measures*	*Treatment*
Prologue	1–45	Both of the work's two themes are presented.
I	46–112	The Till theme (A^1) is subjected to a fuller development with a brief appearance of the B theme noted in measures 76–79.
II	113–178	A transformed A theme opens the section with another version (IIA) entering later. The opening motive of A^1 (first three pitches) unifies the section.
III	179–221	A new theme represents Till in priest's clothing in a section more contrapuntal than previous sections. Measure 187 seems a transformation of the A tune added below the new tune. A solo violin connects this section to the next by using a new version of the A theme (measures 202–6).
IV	222–292	Contrapuntal complexity increases as several tunes are superimposed. The horn slips in the B theme at measure 244. Counterpoint continues to pile up with a canon starting at measure 271.
V	293–372	Another new tune appears. It characterizes the learned professors. The subsequent VB theme attempts to describe Till's role in the conversation. Counterpoint again helps to describe the confusing theses of Till (see canonic passages at measures 313–18). Unison tutti statements of the A^1 tune which tend to dominate the closing measures of the section contrast quite clearly with the complexities of the "conversation" section which precedes it.
VI	374–409	After the "departure music" in measures 374–86, a slow-moving section based on parts of the two motives leads to the transition which contains a typical Strauss "soaring" theme built from theme B. Imitation is used throughout the section.

Recap. 429–575   A résumé begins. This section is really a further development of the work's primary tunes: A, B, A¹. Extensive use
of imitation and counterpoint can be noted at measures 463–
71. At measure 485, the B theme is stated in augmentation
by the brass with a florid sixteenth-note countermelody in
strings and woodwinds; at measure 500, the B theme is
heard in the horn and viola with a rhythmic version of the
A theme in the strings and woodwinds; the development
continues until measure 575 with Strauss combining as
many as three motives at one time; a quasi-canonic passage
(measures 558–66) leads to the drum roll which connects
this section with section VII (measures 573–81).

VII   576–631   This section is primarily a series of sustained triads (f
minor predominates) with the A¹ theme shrieking in the
solo clarinet between chordal passages; a leap downward
of a major seventh (f–g-flat) in the bass winds supposedly
signifies the act of hanging (measures 613–14); the g-flat
acts as the Neapolitan scale degree, resolving to the tonic F
in measure 624.

Epilogue   632–657   Starting very much as did the prologue, the section moves
from a rather placid A theme and modified B theme to a
final tutti statement of the A¹ tune, fast tempo.

Strauss served as the conductor of the Berlin Philharmonic for the 1894–95 season, succeeding von Bülow. The orchestra did not premiere any of his works until its performance of the *Alpine Symphony* in 1915. The picture above is from the 1976–77 season and shows the orchestra being conducted by Herbert von Karajan in the orchestra's new hall in Berlin. Courtesy Berlin Philharmonic Orchestra.

SUMMARY

The work in many ways is typical of the Strauss style. The orchestra, while not the largest the composer used, is impressive (see measures 567–73, where Strauss has scored for a total of eight horns and six trumpets in the tutti). Counterpoint, not as frequent as in some of the other works, still does appear (see sections noted as I, IV, and V). Syncopation is particularly characteristic of the B theme. The transition theme is one of the composer's rapidly ascending tunes. Rhythmic motives are used throughout the work. Melodic dissonance in the nineteenth-century expressive style can be found in all sections. Chromatic harmony is not as evident as in other Strauss works. *Till* also shows how adept Strauss was in the classical skills of development and variation. The lyric nature of the music is enhanced considerably in the basic flow of all parts in the Strauss figured contrapuntal texture. The work, because of its two short basic motives, tends to be more motivic than lyric in melodic structure. In spite of the limitations of program and short unifying motives, Strauss was still able to maintain a sustained line of thought in each of the sections.

The work also shows Strauss in proper perspective in the history of symphonic music. He carried forward the Berlioz-Liszt concept of orchestral program music while at the same time maintaining a strong connection with the learned symphonic style of Haydn, Mozart, Beethoven, and Brahms. Strauss selected a goal (program music) which required that he place emphasis on expression and depiction. While he did blend quite well the technique of the classicist with the coloristic and expressive goals of program music, he achieved results which could not be sustained subsequently as mainstreams of symphonic history. Program music as a major idiom died with Strauss's final orchestral works. The works continue to enjoy respect throughout the musical world because of their essentially expressive and lyric qualities, their brilliant sound, and their skillful formal organization.

Gustav Mahler (1860–1911)

Mahler and Strauss represent the final decay of symphonic romanticism. Strauss selected the path of program music; Mahler attempted to expand the scope of the symphony and yet keep within the traditions of the Viennese symphonists represented by Beethoven, Schubert, and Brahms. Mahler's basic style is primarily expansive and yet shows a change in emphasis from large, programmatic, and augmented works to more classical works of more modest dimensions. The overall style is also one of contradictions. The most perplexing of all is the attempt by the composer to create an imaginative and intellectually challenging style base while relying upon almost naive materials (folk songs). The simplicity of the basic materials is then offset by the employment of the most complex and oversized orchestral resources in the history of the symphony. In the midst of the vast and overblown rhetoric is a thin thread of the contemporary practice which was to settle upon the art form some twenty-five years later.

It is possible to divide Mahler's symphonic output into periods of creative activity:

1888–1900   *Folk Period*

Mahler's first period is characterized by the use of sectional forms and programmatic works, although Mahler modified this latter aspect of the style when the programmatic vogue waned. All symphonies except the first in this period use vocal resources in at least one movement. The works include symphonies 1–4.

1900–1905   *Neoclassical Period*

Mahler's folk influence declines; there is an emphasis on more absolute forms. Most of the works remain expansive in overall style although orchestral resources are reduced somewhat. No vocal resources are used. Symphonies in this period are numbers 5–7.

1907–1909   *Eclectic Period*

Works in the final period reflect both previous styles. The eighth symphony was a return to the earlier, more expressive, and possibly programmatic first-period values. This period includes symphonies 8–10.

The roots of Mahler's symphonic style can be traced to the same German folk song tradition that influenced the Schubert style. Mahler, in 1888, discovered a collection of German folk poems dating from 1539 to 1807, published beginning in 1805 as *Des Knaben Wunderhorn*. As a result his symphonies frequently use either folklike tunes or almost literal quotations from the folk tradition. Many of the symphonic scherzos are in the spirit of the Austrian ländler. Further, his interest in song in general led him to expand some of the movements to include vocal or choral resources. One of his late works (*Das Lied von der Erde*) was actually a song cycle expanded to symphonic proportions.

Mahler's roots were also firmly planted in the Austro-German traditions of the symphony. While the first four symphonies do reflect strong programmatic origins and thus take their inspiration from the Berlioz-Liszt-Wagner line of symphonic development, the basic style of the symphonies still shows an emphasis on development, contrapuntal skills, and motivic (often cyclic) unity within specific symphonies.

Mahler also attempted to expand the scope of the symphony by increasing the size of the symphony and of the orchestra. The form was enlarged through the use of additional movements and through the increased length and scope of some of the movements. A quick study of the form chart of the nine complete instrumental symphonies shows that only four were written in four movements; three were constructed in five movements, one in six, and one in two large movements using chorus and other vocal resources (Symphony No. 8).

The performance forces employed by Mahler are considerably larger than those used by other late-nineteenth-century symphony composers (see the chart of instrumentation which follows). His ten symphonies or symphonylike works include large brass sections, with only three of the works being restricted to as few as four horns (symphonies 4, 7, 9, and *Das Lied von der Erde*); the remaining use from six to ten horns. Six of the symphonies use four oboes; nine use either four or five (Symphony No. 3) clarinets. Two harps are required in seven of the works. Two piccolos are required in seven symphonies; Symphony No. 5 uses four piccolos. A large and varied percussion section is called for in all symphonies and includes such exotic instruments as cowbells (symphonies 4, 6, and 8), hammer, birch switch, chimes, and tamtam (*all* works). The mandolin is found in symphonies 7 and 8. Two timpani players are required in most of the symphonies.

Mahler's textural style underwent a gradual change from a simpler, late-nineteenth-century homophony to an increasingly complex contrapuntal involvement. The middle symphonies (5, 6, and 8) are much more linear than the first four. Fugal movements (or sections) exist in the *Adagio* of 4, the finales of 5 and 7, and the rondo of 9. A double fugue is used in the first part of 8. Mahler seemed to develop an affection for two-voice counterpoint (imitative or free) with essential intervals of fourths and fifths. The linear aspect of some of his works seems to deemphasize the vertical relationship, which in the past had produced a semblance of harmonic progression, somewhat anticipating the linear counterpoint of the twentieth century.

Mahler's melodic style adhered to the Viennese classical concept of melody but was tempered by his affection for folk songs. The melodies tend to fit one of four basic styles: Hungarian-Slavonic and German folk songs; Viennese melodies in the style of Brahms, Schubert, etc.; chorale or chant melodies; and nature motives (bird calls, cow bells, etc.). Expressive use of melodic dissonance is more typical of the Viennese style. Military music often finds expression in the marches or marchlike melodies in some of the works. Many of his tunes use the interval of the descending fourth.

His harmonic style is perplexing. The primary vertical unit appears to be the triad or the interval of the fifth. Examples of traditional diatonic harmonic progression or systematic chromatic progression are not as numerous as those noted in the styles of Brahms or Strauss. The emphasis on contrapuntal writing tends to reduce the vertical element to minimal contact points of perfect intervals and triads within a tonal area. The choral movements frequently make use of more traditional harmonic progressions. In other instances in individual symphony movements a return to a more traditional harmonic idiom can be seen. This conflicting swing between two extremes of harmonic practice is no more contradictory than other dichotomous usages noted above. Points of repose are generally characterized by an emphasis on the tonic sonority with some kind of melodic motion leading into the final chord. There are some plagal cadences. Mahler appears to anticipate the decay of traditional root relationships and systematic chromaticism in some of his harmonic writing and in this way becomes a part of the more progressive group of composers in the late nineteenth and early twentieth century. For this reason Mahler's exact position in the style time-line of music history is at times difficult to assess.

The composer's command of the form of the symphony is traditional and yet original. Each symphony was an effort on the composer's part to embrace the largest possible field of inspiration, and therefore he frequently felt compelled to illustrate the earlier works with elaborate programs. As he sought to

PHILHARMONISCHE CONCERTE.

Sonntag, den 18. November 1900

Mittags präcise $\frac{1}{2}$1 Uhr

im grossen Saale der Gesellschaft der Musikfreunde

II. Abonnement-Concert

veranstaltet von den

Mitgliedern des k. k. Hof-Opernorchesters

unter Leitung des Herrn

GUSTAV MAHLER

k. u. k. Hofopern-Director.

PROGRAMM:

L. v. BEETHOVEN .... Ouverture zu »Prometheus«

R. SCHUMANN .... Ouverture zu »Manfred«.

G. MAHLER....... .....Symphonie Nr. 1, D-dur.

                    Einleitung — Allegro commodo.

                    Scherzo.

                    Feierlich und gemessen.

                    Stürmisch bewegt.

               (I. Aufführung in den Philharmonischen Concerten.)

Das III. Abonnement-Concert findet am 2. December 1900 statt.

Bösendorfer Concertflügel

Benützten in diesen Concerten: Eugen d'Albert, Marie Baumayer, Dr. Johannes Brahms, Dr. Hans von Bülow, B. F. Busoni, Teresa Carreno, Fanny Davies, Illona Eibenschütz, Annette Essipoff, Art. Friedheim, Alfred Grünfeld, Josef Hofmann, Sofie Menter, Adele a. d Ohe, Max Pauer, Wladimir de Pachmann, Hugo Reinhold, Anton Rubinstein, Moriz Rosenthal, Camillo Saint-Saënt, Emil Sauer, F. X. Scharwenka, Ed. Schütt, Bernhard Stavenhagen etc

---

Mahler conducts the Vienna premiere of his first symphony. The composer at that time was the director of the Vienna Opera. The first symphony had its initial hearing in Budapest in 1889 where the composer was serving as director of the Royal Opera there. Note Bösendorfer piano "testimonials" at the bottom of the program that lists Brahms, von Bülow, Busoni, Rubinstein, Saint-Saens and others. Courtesy Vienna Philharmonic.

Mahler's final appearances with New York Philharmonic. Two printed programs show Mahler's scheduling of his own fourth symphony on the January 17 and 20 concerts. While he was able to conduct the concert on February 21, his rapidly declining health prevented his working the February 24 date. He returned to Vienna in May of that year. His reputation as a conductor was of the highest order. Courtesy of the New York Philharmonic Symphony Society.

228

The Philharmonic Society
of New York

1910... SIXTY-NINTH SEASON ...1911

Gustav Mahler . . . Conductor

MANAGEMENT LOUDON CHARLTON

Carnegie Hall

TUESDAY NIGHT, JANUARY 17
AT EIGHT-FIFTEEN

FRIDAY AFTERNOON, JANUARY 20
AT TWO-THIRTY

Soloist
MME. BELLA ALTEN
(of the Metropolitan Opera House)

All-Modern Programme

1. OVERTURE "Das Kätchen von Heilbronn" . . . . *Pfitzner*

2. SYMPHONY No. 4, in G major . . . . *Mahler*

    I   Recht gemilchlich
    II In gemilchlicher Bewegung
    III Ruhevoll
    IV Sehr behaglich
          Solo Part: MME. ALTEN

3. "EIN HELDENLEBEN" Opus 40 . . . . *Richard Strauss*

The Steinway Piano is the Official Piano of the Philharmonic Society

229

expand the size and scope of the symphony he often added vocal movements
with texts which reinforced the sources of his inspiration. Those movements
which did not include a choral or vocal section often expanded beyond the
traditional outlines (e.g., two development sections in both the first movement
of Symphony No. 3 and the finale of Symphony No. 6). Many of the works
use cyclic themes.

Information on Individual Symphonies

No.	Key	Date	I	II	III	IV	V	VI
1	D	1888	SA	Scherzo	ABACABA	SA		
2	c	1894	SA	ABABA	Scherzo	Through-com-posed	Hybrid	
3	d	1896	SA	Minuet ABABA	Scherzo	Through-com-posed	March Through-com-posed	Variation
4	G	1900	SA	Scherzo	Variation	Strophic		
5	c-sharp	1902	ABA	SA	Scherzo	ABA	Rondo	
6	a	1904	SA	ABA	Scherzo	SA		
7	e	1905	SA	Rondo	Scherzo	Rondo	Rondo	
8	E-flat	1907	SA	Free variations				
9	D	1909	SA	Scherzo	Rondo	ABA		
10								

10 A reduced score to two movements was written in 1910. Ernst Krenek completed these movements and had them performed in 1924. Mahler originally
planned five movements for the work.

SYMPHONY NO. 1

Called the *Titan* by Mahler, the work had a program which the composer
later retracted. He had organized the work into two large parts with a total
of five movements. In 1893 he wrote a new program for the work. By 1900 he
had abandoned using a program. Mahler used some of his own songs, extracted
from his *Lieder eines fahrenden Gesellen* (1884), as themes in the symphony.
The first movement uses figures and sections from "Ging' heut morgens über
Feld." Mahler's original second movement, *Blumine,* was later withdrawn by
the composer. The movement which remains is a moderate scherzo with trio,
very much in the style of the ländler. It uses several short motives from his
song *Hansel and Gretel* (1880–1883). Only the first strain of the scherzo is
repeated. The third movement was originally called the "Huntsman's Funeral"
and thus became one of the composer's most controversial movements. The
principal tune of the first section is a minor-key version of the "Frère Jacques"
folk tune. The movement is intended as a musical parody, as shown both in the

selection of tunes and in their orchestration. The "village tunes" employed are set in a humorous fashion along with another song from the *Gesellen Lieder*: "Die zwei blauen Augen." The march has been better received in recent years. The finale has a long introduction (fifty-four bars) which presents some of the material of the movement proper. The recapitulation reverses the order of the two main tunes. A coda touches on all tunes. The size of the orchestra is large with seven horns and four each of flutes, oboes, clarinets, and trumpets.

SYMPHONY NO. 2

The first movement was originally written as a funeral march and later became the opening movement of this symphony. An elaborate program, appearing somewhat autobiographical, was provided by the composer. The program was revised several times. The second movement is another slow ländler. The final appearance of the first theme is played by the entire string section pizzicato. The third movement is still another ländlerlike movement with almost incessant sixteenth-note motion throughout. Much of the music is based on Mahler's song "Des Antonius von Padua Fischpredight." The fourth movement ("Urlicht") is scored for alto solo with the text taken from *Des Knaben Wunderhorn*. The finale calls for one of Mahler's largest orchestras (ten horns with four "in the distance" or offstage, quadruple woodwinds, six trumpets, large percussion section, two harps plus organ) and also includes soprano and alto soloists plus choir. The last part of the finale includes a chorale section and a "Redemption" theme (from measure 26), which alternate as the two important themes of the closing section.

SYMPHONY NO. 3

Mahler called this symphony his great "Hymn to Nature." * Mahler's original program provided the following titles to the movements:

I:	Introduction: Pan's Awakening
	Movement proper: Summer Marches in (Procession of Bacchus)
II:	What the Flowers of the Field Tell Me
III:	What the Animals of the Forest Tell Me
IV:	What Man Tells Me
V:	What the Angels Tell Me
VI:	What Love Tells Me
VII:	What the Child Tells Me

---

* Henry-Louis de La Grange, *Mahler* (Garden City, N.Y.: Doubleday and Company, Inc., 1973), I, 175.

No less than eight versions of a program were developed by Mahler.* In the end the seventh movement was deleted and subsequently reappeared as the fourth movement of the fourth symphony. The first movement is the longest orchestral movement written by Mahler. It has a double exposition (measures 369–529). The opening theme is similar to the opening tune of the finale of Brahms' first symphony. A march section occurs at measures 254 and 737. The development uses the march rhythm throughout (measures 530–642). The second movement minuet has a succession of meters which are not typical of the form's original dance: basic 3/4 with 3/8, 2/4, and 9/8. The third movement, a scherzo in 2/4 meter with the implication of a *bourrée*, has an overall form of ABACABCA (C = trio). A solo for posthorn occurs in the trio. Other than this tune, most of the themes were taken from the *lied* "Ablösung im Sommer" (*Wunderhorn Lieder*). The fourth movement uses the poem "O Mensch!" as a text for alto solo and orchestra. The poem is from the Zarathustra epic by Nietzsche. A D-A pedal ostinato in the cellos dominates most of the movement. The fifth movement is a lively march which includes women's choir, children's choir, and alto solo. The text is from the *Des Knaben Wunderhorn*, "Armer Kinder Bettlerlied." No violins are used in the scoring. The children's choir only accompanies the bells in the opening measures and in subsequent sections where the bells are heard again. The finale, an *Adagio*, is often scored for multiple subdivision of the string section.

SYMPHONY NO. 4

Mahler reduced both the size of the orchestra and the lengths of the developmental movements in this work. The first tune of the opening movement uses (in part) a short birdcall motive (measures 2–3). The first part of the theme (open fifths) is used more as a refrain to open each new section of the symphony. The second movement, a scherzo, tunes the solo violin up a whole step. The form is S-T-S-T-S. The influence of the ländler is still present. The theme of the trio is taken from the main theme of the finale. The third movement is a set of variations on two themes. The bass line of the opening section of the movement is treated in the style of a passacaglia. The first set of variations has five variations; the second set has four. The variations reveal a new technique which Mahler followed in variation movements: each subsequent variation is a variation of the preceding variation rather than of the primary theme. A coda which begins with multi-divisi strings on rapidly played four-note arpeggios is based on motives from each theme. The final dynamic marking is "'pppp . . . morendo." The finale is a song for soprano and orchestra based on "Das himmlische Leben" (*Des Knaben Wunderhorn*) and was orig-

---

* LaGrange, *Mahler*, I, 798–99.

inally planned as the seventh movement of the third symphony ("What the Child Tells Me"). The work is in three sections with a coda. The second section (measure 57) quotes one of the themes from the third symphony. The section beginning at measure 40 is identical with the opening bars of the first movement. This theme occurs frequently in the movement.

SYMPHONY NO. 5

Symphonies 5, 6, and 7 represent a change of style for Mahler in which he seems to have returned to the traditions of the Austro-German symphonies of Beethoven, Schubert, and Brahms. Symphony No. 5 is discussed in complete detail beginning on page 238.

SYMPHONY NO. 6

While the formal elements of the symphonies of Mahler's classical period are more in conformity with those of more conservative composers, the orchestral style remains expansive and colorful. Generally the orchestra remains quite large. In addition, Mahler again uses cowbells to depict rustic moods. The first movement has a repetition of its exposition section. The development is primarily motivic and reflects the style of Beethoven. The recapitulation starts briefly in A major but reverts quickly to the tonic a minor. After a short reprise, an extended coda continues the development. The work ends in A major. Mahler tampered with the order of the inner movements, finally settling on a slow second movement. One score, published in 1906, still had the scherzo as the second movement. The *Andante* second movement is more typical of the expressive nineteenth-century style, using fairly stable harmony with some chromaticism, the most characteristic of which is the dual modality Mahler employs in consecutive sonorities. Thus, a tonality might have (in E-flat major) an F or an F-flat, a G or G-flat, or a D or a D-flat. Many of the chromatic inflections occur as nonharmonic tones in either a homophonic or polyphonic texture. The scherzo uses as its principal theme a modification of the opening bars of the first movement. The form, like that of the late Beethoven scherzos, is five parts: S-T-S-T-S-Coda. The trio is multimetric, alternating the following meters: 3/8, 4/8, 3/8, 4/8, with 3/4 inserted at least once in a twelve-measure span. The shifting meter of the trio is anticipated in a five-bar section in the scherzo. The finale uses themes from previous movements (first and scherzo). It begins with a long, slow introduction in which several themes are generated. One of the oddities of the work is Mahler's use of a hammer for expressive purposes: "The hero receives three blows from fate, the third of which fells him like a tree. . . ." [*] The first hammer stroke comes in the first development

* Redlich, *Bruckner and Mahler*, p. 208. Quoted with permission of publisher.

section (measure 336); the second occurs at the climax of the second development section (measure 479); the final stroke (measure 783) is located just prior
to the coda, where Mahler is introducing his "Fate" motive for the final time. The
entire symphony is probably the best example of Mahler's polyphonic style.
Again, in spite of Mahler's efforts to return to the more absolute style of
writing, the most significant movement (the finale) depends on a program
(autobiographical?) for an explanation of its ultraexpressive nature.

SYMPHONY NO. 7

In the seventh symphony, composed during the summer holidays of 1904 and
1905, an alarming thing becomes apparent for the first time in Mahler's
career as a composer: the self-repetition which was destined to mar the last
two symphonies and to weaken their artistic impact. Not only do the outer
movements reveal striking similarities with the parallel movements of Symphony V, but the primeval ruggedness of the introductory tenor-horn solo
re-echoes the solo trombone in the first movement of Symphony III. The first
principal theme of the movement is rhythmically all but identical with its
opposite number in Symphony VI. The first "Nachtmusik" works almost
throughout with thematic matter already used in the last *Wunderhorn*
songs. . . .*

The seventh symphony does exhibit one of Mahler's favorite tonal devices:
progressive tonality, a device by which a movement starts in one key and moves
to another for its close. The first movement opens in b minor and closes in E
major. The finale is placed in C major. Mahler also returns to his more progressive harmonic style, which emphasizes open fifths and linearly derived triads.
Those few essentially vertical passages tend to revert to the experimental procedures of Wagner. The first movement (rehearsal number 66–67, pp. 78–79)
has a progression as follows: E major, C major, A major-minor seventh, F major,
C major, all in third relation. The second "Nachtmusik" movement (movement
four in the symphony) uses a mandolin and guitar in subdued chamber style.
The third movement scherzo has an interesting use of timpani, bass, and brass
in its opening bars (repeated almost as a refrain throughout the movement).

SYMPHONY NO. 8

Mahler had hoped to write a four-movement eighth symphony. Returning
to the more philosophical and programmatic sources of his style, he created a

---

* Redlich, *Bruckner and Mahler,* pp. 202–3. Quoted with permission of publisher.

vast two-movement work which uses a huge orchestra, boys' choir, mixed choir, and vocal soloists. The text for the first movement is a Latin hymn, "Veni Creator." The text for the final movement is from the closing scene of Goethe's *Faust*. The first movement fits into a sonata-allegro pattern, while the second is more sectional in design. His expansion of the symphony to this scope and direction represents a culmination of a thrust which began with the Beethoven Symphony No. 9. It continues the polyphonic emphasis seen in many of the symphonies, a style which fittingly accommodates the choral resources required.

SYMPHONY NO. 9

Mahler wrote three final orchestral works which he supposedly never heard in orchestral performance: *Das Lied von der Erde*, Symphony No. 9, and the first two movements of Symphony No. 10. Alban Berg felt at the time of his hearing the ninth symphony for the first time (as he played it at the piano) that the work was autobiographical.

> . . . Once again I have played through the score of Mahler's ninth Symphony: the first movement is the most heavenly thing Mahler ever wrote. It is the expression of an exceptional fondness for this earth, the longing to live in peace on it, to enjoy nature to its depths—before death comes.
> For he comes irresistibly. The whole movement is permeated by premonitions of death. . . .*

The work adjusts the tempo scheme of the symphony so that the order is as follows: andante, tempo of a ländler, allegro assai, adagio. Themes in the symphony are occasionally taken from previous works. The opening theme of the rondo is identical with the opening theme of the second movement of Symphony No. 5. From time to time, Mahler reverts to older style mannerisms which tend to underline the reflective nature of the work. Note the use of melodic embellishments (Wagner "turns") in the first movement starting with the eighth bar before rehearsal number 14. A fugue occurs in the rondo starting between rehearsal numbers 35 and 36. The preceding ländler movement has two trios, one in the style of a waltz and the other similar to a minuet. The symphony begins in D major and ends in D-flat major. The orchestra is one of the smallest used by Mahler (only four horns, three trumpets, limited percussion, but two harps). The size of the woodwind section remains fairly equal to that of other symphonies.

---

* Redlich, *Bruckner and Mahler*, p. 220. Quoted with permission of publisher.

Symphonies

	I	*II*	*III*	*IV*	*V*
Picc.	2	2	2	2	4
Fl.	4	4	4	4	4
Ob.	4	4	4	3	3
E. Hn.	1	2	1	1	1
Cl.	4	4	5	4	3
	(1 E-flat)	(1 E-flat)	(2 E-flat)	(1 E-flat)	(1 D)
B. Cl.	1	1	1	1	1
Bsn.	3	4	4	3	3
Dbl. Bsn.		1	1	1	1
Ten. Hn.					
Hn.	7	10 [1]	8	4	6
Post Hn.			1		
Hn. Obbligato					1
Trpt.	4	6 [1]	4	3	4
Trb.	3	4	4		3
Tuba	1	1	1		1
Wd. Clapper					
Xyl.					
Timp.	2 plyrs.	3 [2] plyrs.	2 plys.	X	X
Herdengelauten (cow bells)				1	
Sonagli (cluster of little bells)				1	
Rute (birch switch)					
Tambourine			1		
Triangle	1	2 [2]	1	1	1
Hammer					
Cel.					
Chimes			1		
B.D.	1	2 [2]	1	1	1
Gong	1	2	1	1	1
Cym.	1	2 [2]	1	1	1
Glock.		1	1	1	1
Pfte.					
Harmonium					
Organ		1			
Mandolin					
S.D.		1	1		1
Guitar					
Hp.	1	2	2	1	1
Str.	X	X	X	X [4]	X
Mixed Chorus		1			
Boy Choir			1 (2 pt.)		
Female Chorus			1 (3 pt.)		
Sop. Solo		1		1	
Alto Solo		1	1		
Ten. Solo			1		
Bass Solo					

[1] 4 Hns. and 4 Trpts. "in the distance." [2] 1 Timp., 1 B.D., 1 Cym. and 1 Triangle "in the distance." [3] 4 Trpts. and 3 Trbs. "in another place." [4] Solo Vn. tuned up step.

Symphonies

	VI	VII	VIII	IX
Picc.	2	2	1	1
Fl.	4	4	4	4
Ob.	4	3	4	4
E. Hn.	1	1	1	1
Cl.	4	5	4	4
	(1 D)	(1 E-flat)	(1 E-flat)	(1 E-flat)
B. Cl.	1	1	1	1
Bsn.	4	3	4	4
Dbl. Bsn.	1	1	1	1
Ten. Hn.		1		
Hn.	8	4	8	4
Post Hn.				
Hn. Obbligato				
Trpt.	6	3	8 [3]	3
Trb.	4	3	7 [3]	3
Tuba	1	1	1	1
Wd. Clapper	1			
Xyl.	1			
Timp.	2 plyrs.	X	3 plyrs.	2 plyrs.
Herdengelauten (cow bells)	1	1		
Sonagli (cluster of little bells)				
Rute (birch switch)	1			
Tambourine	1	1		
Triangle	1	1	1	1
Hammer	1			
Cel.	1		1	
Chimes		1	1	
B.D.	1	1	1	1
Gong	1	1	1	1
Cym.	1	1	1	1
Glock.	1	1	1	1
Pfte.			1	
Harmonium			1	
Organ			1	
Mandolin		1	1	
S.D.	1			1
Guitar		1		
Hp.	2	2	2	2
Str.	X	X	X	X
Mixed Chorus			2	
Boy Choir			1	
Female Chorus			3	
Sop. Solo			2	
Alto Solo			1	
Ten. Solo			2	
Bass Solo			(1 bar.; 1 bass)	

EXAMPLES FOR STUDY

Mahler: *Symphony No. 5 in c-sharp minor*

As mentioned above, symphonies 5–7 represented a style change for Mahler in that program descriptions were omitted in the score, choral and vocal resources were deemphasized, and an attempt to return to the absolute or abstract style of the classical symphony was made. Two of the three works have five movements. It is also possible to think of the symphony as being in three movements: I—*Trauermarch*, followed by *Sturmisch bewegt* (In Stormy Motion); II—*Scherzo*; III—*Adagietto*, followed by the rondo. The 1904 edition of the score (Peters) suggests the latter subdivision of the movements. Mahler's intentions are not too clear in the matter. What is clear, however, is that the expansiveness of the overall symphonic style continues in this group (5–7) as in the other symphonies. Some of the movements are long and complex. The cyclic use of themes continues. The orchestra in each of the three "classic" works is only slightly smaller than the orchestras used in previous works. Symphony No. 6, of the three, has the largest orchestra.

I: Trauermarch. The movement is in a large ternary design with an extended coda (see form graph below). The themes presented in the funeral march are basically the same themes treated in the second movement. This creates a possible introductory relationship with the second movement. For the present each of the five movements will be treated as an independent movement regardless of its connection to a previous or subsequent movement in the symphony. In the funeral march three themes can be noted as part of an opening (or introductory) section of the principal section. The primary melody of the A section is a long-lined lyric theme starting at measure 34. The introductory motives return in the same style of the opening measures, thus giving the opening section of the movement an ABAB shape (A^1 A^4 A^1 A^4 actually). The large middle section of the funeral march starts with a long, spun-out trumpet theme accompanied by a counterpoint in the first violins (B^1, B^1-cpt.). This large middle section appears to present four basic subthemes. A new counterpoint for the A^4 melody starts at measure 278 (see theme A^4 cpt. below). The rhythmic motive of A^1 closes this section. A possible coda which includes much of the previous material starts at measure 323. The harmonic materials of the march imply certain basic chord functions (tonic, dominant, etc.) that might be expected in a marchstyle work. This is done with some degree of freedom. Note that the first six bars (measures 155–60) of the B^1 theme are supported primarily by the tonic triad (B-flat minor). The counterpoint in the violins reflects the same freedom, since both it and the trumpet tune tend to stress both diatonic and chromatic nonharmonic tones, not atypical of nineteenth-century melodic style.

II: In Stormy Motion. With Utmost Vehemence. The "second" movement is based on both new themes and themes from the funeral march (as per
the form chart below). The form is an expanded sonata-allegro with a basic
style tending toward Mahler's complex contrapuntal texture. The form chart
and thematic summary below contain much of the thematic material and the
combinations of thematic material in polyphonic sections. This polyphonic style
was primarily developed by applying layer upon layer of contrasting thematic
materials with as many as four themes (sometimes motives) being used simultaneously. The countermelody type of counterpoint is typical of many nineteenth-century styles. It lacks the learnedness of imitative counterpoint, fugue,
or canon. Mahler decidedly preferred the countermelody (or additive) style in
polyphony. The movement finally climaxes (according to Mahler's own indication) during a section where he has introduced a choralelike theme. The particu-

lar section is not as complex texturally as other sections but soon leads to a coda which contains many of the main themes of the movement set in a more contrapuntal fashion.

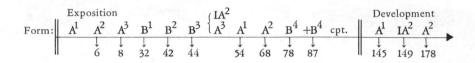

III: Scherzo. This is one of the longest such movements in symphonic literature. The form of the movement is traditional in overall outline (song form with trio and coda). Mahler has adjusted the internal dimensions of the form to allow for extensive development of some of the motives and has designed countermelodies for many of the primary themes, which make the movement more complex than a typical nineteenth-century scherzo. Mahler also reduces the orchestration considerably for the trio. The internal workings of the form are also expanded by the composer's constructing transitions which anticipate subsequent sections, as noted in that section prior to the start of the trio. The movement closes with a lively coda based on materials of the scherzo.

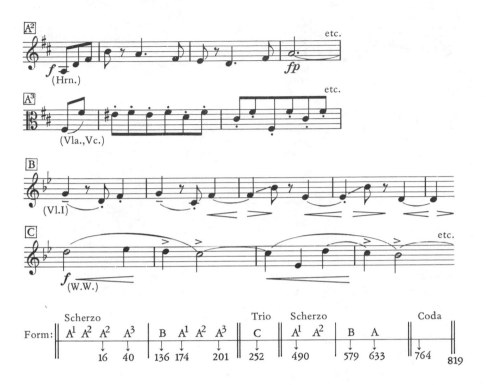

IV: Adagietto. While it has been suggested that the fourth and fifth movements might be considered as two large sections within a long third movement, with the *Adagietto* serving as an introduction to the rondo-finale, it should be noted that the two movements are not thematically linked. There is an indication in the score that the movement proceeds without undue pause ("attaca") to the finale. The movement is brief and is scored for strings and harp only. Subdivision of the strings creates as many as seven string parts, not nearly as lush a texture as would be available with multisubdivision. The overall style is a reversion to the simpler expressive style of the late nineteenth century, in which expressiveness is equated with stressed dissonance in the melody, shifting harmonic resources that elide and retrogress to avoid points of obvious repose, etc. The middle section moves through a series of unrelated keys (c minor, G-flat major, E major, D major) before returning to the first theme at measure 72. Some of the material in the middle section appears to be related to the first theme. The final restatement is not exact. Mahler omitted the harp in most of the middle section and brought it back with the return of the first section.

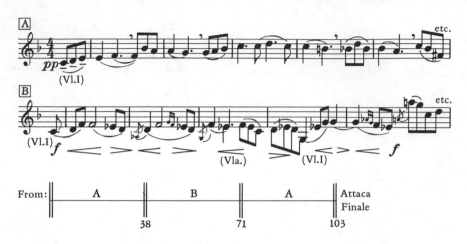

V: Rondo-Finale. In the twenty-two-measure introduction various solo instruments present seven short passages which later become identified as components of much of the thematic materials of the movement. The form of the subsequent main section is an elaborate rondo which applies the rondo principle with great abandon as the form graph below notes. The basic texture is again polyphonic, with theme after theme being layered into many sections of the work. The chorale theme (noted in the analysis of the second movement) appears to be the main unifying melody of the finale. The compositional principle which seemingly permeates this movement is similar to that found in other movements: restatement is never exact in that themes are always added to themes to achieve some degree of contrast even in the return of a principal theme in the rondo movement. Note should be made of this combining of themes in some sections on the form graph. Counterpoints written for the B theme are generally based on motives from the chorale melody; the B counterpoint no. 1 is a complete statement of the chorale. The B theme originally is the subject of a fugato (measures 55–87) in which these several "counterpoints" (as noted) occur. The C theme could be considered a derivative of the second phrase of the chorale. Mahler's fondness for the melodic interval of the fourth is evident in this finale. The climax of the work apparently occurs in the final statement of the chorale melody starting at measure 732, an expressive decision similar to that noted in the second movement where a climax is related to an appearance of the same chorale tune.

SUMMARY

Mahler's Symphony No. 5, although it rejects the choral-programmatic aspects of his style, is still a work which in many ways supports the composer's place at the high point of nineteenth-century expansive style. Its style, in some instances, is also an anticipation of at least one aspect of the style of the twentieth century (linear counterpoint). The symphony is cyclic, uses expanded forms, and yet adheres to the general movement outlines of the traditional symphony. Mahler's ability to infuse these accepted forms with an almost unlimited amount of flexibility and individuality is not unique to his own particular style and does represent the general approach taken by several composers in the late nineteenth century (Strauss, Brahms, etc.). Mahler may have taken the element of formal flexibility to an extreme which few other composers have approached. The folk element can be noted in passages in the scherzo, although this particular symphony does depart considerably from dependence on the *Wunderhorn* tradition. Certainly the entire work can be considered representative of the Austro-German symphonic tradition's use of development, counterpoint, and motivic unity as cornerstones of the symphonic art. This compositional foundation is tempered considerably, however, by Mahler's ultraexpressive and expansive treatment of the symphony.

VI

The Symphony in the Twentieth Century

Introduction to Twentieth-Century Music

As the nineteenth century was in many ways a refutation of the values of the eighteenth century, so was the twentieth century a refutation of much that was held dear in the nineteenth. Unfortunately, since the pendulum of musical style does not swing with a clean arc in each century, generalizations and style simplifications are even more difficult when referring to twentieth-century music than they are with nineteenth-century music. What was rejected by modern composers was generally the excesses of the romantic period: the ultraexpressiveness, the use of effect in place of logic, the nonperiodic and rambling quality of the music, and, above all, the intoxication with the sound of music. Even this last factor is refuted by one of the major trends of the early modern period: impressionism. Orchestral music written under an impressionistic influence places considerable emphasis on orchestral sonority, color (although generally subdued and restrained) and nondevelopmental forms. Like all periods previous, however, much of what had gone on in the romantic period finds continued acceptance in modern times. What one begins to sense is the basic contradictory quality of much of what has been composed in the twentieth century. Some things were refuted by some and accepted by others. Some were accepted and rejected by the same composer as he went through several style periods. From all of this one can see several trends, or style categories, in modern music.

Neoromanticism endured far beyond the wildest dreams of those who regularly chanted its requiem. Degrees of a composer's involvement with the style vary from discrete to unabashed. Several traits of neoromanticism are holdovers from the romantic period: a fondness for lyric melody, a tendency to

247

write for large and opulent orchestral forces, the complete avoidance of small groups (chamber music, etc.), the continued use of melodic dissonance as an expressive device, a general adherence to triadic harmony while dabbling in some of the newer trends, a retention of strong centers of tonality in most works, and an attempt to relate music to the experiences of the audience. Not all composers showed all of these traits. Most alternated between a romantic art and the next style discussed, neoclassicism.

The neoclassical composer revered form as much as the neoromanticist loved lyricism. Contrapuntal textures and small chamber works were favorite mannerisms. Rhythmic style lacked the rambling and free-spinning quality of the neoromantic beat. Much of the rhythmic style takes one back to the baroque or *style galant*. Harmonic materials varied; and there was some preference for nontertian chords. Tonal systems were not as clearly defined and often resulted from emphasis rather than from any systematic procedures. The reborn classicist was an overt creature, since his art represented a return to what he considered the true values of the calling. Some neoclassicists wrote books, proposed new theories of music, and gathered their cohorts around them with the zeal of camp meeting leaders. Many composers of the modern period drank from the regenerative waters of neoclassicism. It appears as a common thread through much of the twentieth century.

Atonalists were the revolutionaries of the modern period. From this group came an entirely new way of relating pitch sounds (serialism); so intriguing was this new procedure that it soon overran its cup and began to reshape rhythmic values also. Serialists, using a twelve-tone system advocated by Arnold Schoenberg and his followers, became the single most influential group of composers in the twentieth century. Some serialists were almost romantic in the excessive nature of their style. There are few common traits shared by this group. Counterpoint was exceedingly important as was the use of strong metrical and rhythm design. Many used traditional forms. Serialists generally wrote works for modest sources.

Experimentation produced even more challenging procedures: electronic music, aleatoric music, synthesized music, and even environmental music. Each of these has enjoyed wide application. One can compose an entire work using the results disgorged from a large synthesizer programmed by the composer or employ a single part (as an instrument) drawn up by the synthesizer. Synthesizers vary in description and capability. Some can be "played" like a keyboard instrument. The common denominator in all electronic or synthesized music is the tape recorder, the only way of capturing much of what has been created from nontraditional sound sources. Again, a single part can be supplied by the tape for a large orchestral work or the whole composition can exist solely on tape. Aleatoric music shifts more of the responsibility for the composition to the performer of the moment. Score directions are often quite vague—for example, "Play for fifteen seconds using any pattern of pitches on the A string (violin), increasing the speed of what you play by 100 percent." New notational systems abound for describing the composer's intent.

Few composers fit one of these style categories precisely. Many tend to use a more eclectic style by employing treatments and devices from a variety of style sources. Many composers, including some of the true leaders of the art, have gone through as many as four different style periods. These are not the "imitative" style re-creations like those noted in the works of Dvořák but major changes (e.g., from neoclassicism to serialism).

Impressionism anticipates the modern period to some extent, starting in the works of Claude Debussy (1862–1918) in the late nineteenth century. Basically an offshoot of romanticism in its affection for sound and, especially, its sonority, impressionism was at its best in orchestral works. Debussy's orchestral nocturnes and Maurice Ravel's ballet scores exerted major influences on the writing of many symphony composers who followed them. Some of the unique features of the Debussy style include a nontraditional harmonic system in which the meaning of a chord did not have to be related to how the chord resolved and a somewhat fragmented formal style in which a rondo principle generally applied. Developmental forms, counterpoint, and thin textures seem to have been avoided. Impressionistic orchestral scores use huge resources generally, while the sound often is lacking in brilliance (except for extended passages or movements by Ravel) because of the use of mutes and multiple subdivision in the strings. Woodwind sounds, muted strings, harp, and mellowed brass registers characterize many scores in the style. Much of Debussy's music is programmatic, thereby illustrating that modern music has its backward-looking as well as forward-looking aspects.

The Symphony

The first twenty to thirty years of the twentieth century were marked by a general upheaval in the creative direction of the art form. The lush results of orchestral impressionism existed side by side with the lyricism of neoromanticism. The thin line of late-nineteenth-century romanticism can be seen preserved in the continuing works of Strauss, by then writing operas almost exclusively. Mahler made attempts to respond to the new textural concepts by becoming a more linear composer in some of his works. Sibelius was to continue much of the post-romantic practice, which was tempered by his own individuality. Germany and France were the scenes of the greatest foment. Arnold Schoenberg, Anton Webern, and Alban Berg became focal points of experimentation with the basic pitch structure of music by their advocacy of serialism. The symphony as a form was preserved through all of this upheaval primarily in the works of composers who reflected more the values of the post-romantic style. Other kinds of orchestral works, however, were being written in addition to traditional symphonies. The following listing of some of these works may serve to illustrate much better the nature of the unsettled period.

1899	Debussy	*Nocturnes for Orchestra*
1900	Mahler	*Symphony No. 4*
1901	Rachmaninoff	*Second Piano Concerto*
1902	Sibelius	*Symphony No. 2*
	Mahler	*Symphony No. 5*
1903	Strauss	*Sinfonia Domestica* (conducted by composer with New York Philharmonic in New York the next year)
	Schoenberg	*Pelleas et Melisande* (symphonic poem)
1904	Ives	*Symphony No. 3* (not performed until 1947)
	Mahler	*Symphony No. 6*
	D'Indy	*Symphony No. 2*
1905	Debussy	*La Mer*
	Mahler	*Symphony No. 7*
1906	Schoenberg	*Chamber Symphony*
1907	Delius	*Brigg Fair*
	Stravinsky	*Symphony in E-flat Major*
	Bartók	*Two Portraits for Orchestra*
	Mahler	*Symphony No. 8*
	Ravel	*Rhapsodie Espagnole*
1908	Scriabin	*Poem of Ecstasy*
	Sibelius	*Symphony No. 3*
	Rachmaninoff	*Symphony No. 2*
	Elgar	*Symphony No. 1*
	Miaskovsky	*Symphony No. 1*
1909	Schoenberg	*Five Pieces for Orchestra, Op. 16*
	Mahler	*Symphony No. 9*
1910	Scriabin	*Prometheus*
	Stravinsky	*The Firebird*
	Vaughan Williams	*A Sea Symphony* (No. 1)
1911	Stravinsky	*Petrushka*
	Ravel	*Daphnis and Chloe*
	Sibelius	*Symphony No. 4*
	Elgar	*Symphony No. 2*
1912	Debussy	*Images*
	Bartók	*Four Pieces for Orchestra*
	Stravinsky	*Sacre du Printemps*

1913	Webern	*Six Orchestral Pieces*
1914	Vaughan Williams	*London Symphony* (No. 2)
1915	Sibelius	*Symphony No. 5*
1916	Holst	*The Planets*
	Respighi	*Fountains of Rome*
	Ives	*Symphony No. 4* (second movement performed in 1927)
1917	Prokofiev	*Classical Symphony* (No. 1)
	Griffes	*The White Peacock* (orchestral version)
1918	D'Indy	*Symphony No. 3*
1919	Ravel	*La Valse*
1920	Stravinsky	*Symphonies of Wind Instruments*

One can note from the above several lines of musical development moving forward. The dearth of symphonies, however, is particularly revealing: between 1909 and 1920 only nine orchestral symphonies were written. Of these nine, the Prokofiev *Classical* Symphony was possibly the most avant garde work to gain a public performance. The two Ives symphonies, revolutionary in many respects, did not get a complete hearing for over forty years. The lines of development reveal Elgar, Sibelius, and Vaughan Williams picking up the thread of the traditional symphony after the death of Mahler; Debussy, Ravel, Delius, Respighi, and Griffes sustaining the impressionistic style; a pitifully small output by Schoenberg, Berg, and Webern in orchestral music; Stravinsky's three ballets, which later became popular orchestral suites and showed his change of style from that of a Russian impressionist to that of almost a primitive expressionist in *Sacre;* Bartók's very meager orchestral efforts; and the continuation of program music in isolated scores (Scriabin, the impressionists, Vaughan Williams, and Holst).

Since 1920 composers have shown a reawakening of interest in the symphony, enough to categorize it as one of the twentieth century's major forms. Some composers, notably the Russians, have concentrated on the genre. Nicolai Miaskovsky's (1881–1950) twenty-seven symphonies are undoubtedly unequalled in quantity since the time of Haydn and Mozart. Almost all countries have been participants in this activity with the possible exception of Italy.

Composers selected in this and subsequent chapters in general represent major contributors to current symphonic programming. Space would not allow inclusion of many (Nielsen, Piston, Honneger, Walton, Ligeti, Sessions, and others) whose works exhibit important trends. Many able symphonists will possibly not be mentioned. This chapter will continue with a discussion of the symphonies of six European composers: Sibelius, Vaughan Williams, Prokofiev, Shostakovich, Stravinsky, and Hindemith.

Jean Sibelius (1865–1957)

Sibelius' music can be divided into four stylistic periods*

1892–1900   *Finnish Period*

The primary influences on the composer were Russian music, Finnish folk legends (especially the *Kalevala*), and Robert Kajanus's symphonic poem *Aino*. The works of this period are quite intense, brilliantly scored, and expressive. Since mood and expression were so important, the works border on the programmatic. The major works of the period include *En Saga* (symphonic poem) and the first and second symphonies.

1903–1909   *Classical Period*

Sibelius's travels in Europe and his study of the Beethoven works were dominant influences in this second period. It was at this time that the young composer strove to perfect his handling of form. He also further refined the emotional impact of his music so that increased lyricism became a more productive expression of that emotionalism. The concept of organic growth began during this period. An emphasis on proportion, restraint, and continuity can be noted in the music.

1911–1915   *Period of Complexity*

The composer's serious concerns over his health (a possibility of cancer), World War I, and the subjugation of the Finns by the Russians led to a more subjective and personal feeling in his music. The works become more intense and concentrated in form. Organic growth becomes greatly refined. There is a more abstract and sometimes vague sense of tonality, rhythm, harmony, and form. Only the growth concept gives the music continuity at times. It was the composer's most advanced style period and includes his fourth and fifth symphonies.

1924–1957   *Period of Maturity*

There is some indication that the composer's study of the music of Palestrina exerted some influence on him at this time. Other outside influences are difficult to isolate. The period exhibits more of a synthesis in the compositional style. Very concen-

---

* David Cherniavsky, "Special Characteristics of Sibelius' Style," in *The Music of Sibelius*, ed. Gerald Abraham (New York: W. W. Norton & Company, Inc., 1947), pp. 147–52.

trated thematic groups serve to emphasize concepts of organic growth. Very few works were written after 1929. This period includes works such as the six and seventh symphonies, *Tapiola* (symphonic poem), and the incidental music to the *Tempest*.

The evolution of Sibelius's symphonies can be viewed primarily as a manifestation of the above style development. The first symphony, written in Sibelius's thirty-fourth year, is a mature work and can be considered an admirable contribution to orchestral literature. While the expressive and musical influences of the Russian composers are evident in the work, it nevertheless allowed the composer to establish a firm style with which he could gradually create a much more personal approach to the symphony. His devotion to the Finnish traditions never disappeared from his music. Rather than abandon the developmental-tonal focal point of the symphonic style of Beethoven, Sibelius refined this focus into a much tighter and more unified approach, seeking to evolve themes from short motives, having his forms grow as natural organisms, and restricting his materials to the simplest of sources (melodic intervals of thirds, harmonic entities of simple triads, etc.). It was an approach which avoided the excessive chromatic thrust of post-romanticists as well as the rejection of traditional concepts such as tonality and development, a practice of many early-twentieth-century musical pioneers. Thus Sibelius continued the Austro-German line of development in the history of the symphony in both an original and a quite personal way. The music generally shares overall style features appropriate to Sibelius's historical placement: it is expressive; some is programmatic; it is nationalistic; it borders on the neoclassical in its emphasis on organic growth; orchestrally it adheres, at times, to the expressive writing of the late-nineteenth-century composers, especially Tchaikovsky. Specific exceptions are noted below.

Sibelius's symphonic style is unique. From the second symphony onward the organic concept dominates the style and must be considered the most individual feature. The effect of his love for Finland and the folk traditions also results in specific traits: the use of modes in some of the melodies; an emphasis on minor tonalities; a subjective mood which is aided by long, sustained "static" chords, particularly in the lower and middle registers of the brass instruments; a melancholy which seems to cause some expressive melodic writing. The melodic style is essentially motivic in almost all movements of a symphony. The organic growth feature of the style places several short motives at the beginning of a development section (having introduced each in the exposition) and then gradually synthesizes most into a more understandable relationship. By defining a link between these seemingly nonrelated short motives, the gradual working out of this relationship in the development section creates the impression of the growth of these ideas into a unified whole. Mention should be made of Sibelius's fondness for the melodic interval of the falling fifth with the accent on the upper pitch. Rising thirds are also frequent, accented on the lower pitch. Many slowly moving tunes begin with a long note on a weak beat. Some of Sibelius's melodies are long, spun-out examples, almost ametric. A favorite melodic device involves starting a tune with slow note values and injecting faster notes near the end of a phrase. Many examples exist:

(*Symphony No. 2,* first mvt., measures 9–13)

(*Symphony No. 1,* first mvt., measures 70–72)

Used by permission of VEB Breitkopf & Härtel Musikverlag, Leipzig.

(*Symphony No. 7,* measures 60–64)

Used by permission of Edition Wilhelm Hansen.

One particular rhythmic figure abounds in themes:

(*Symphony No. 6,* page 43, measures 7–8)

Used by permission of Kalmus Orchestral Scores, Inc.

The triplet in the figure tends to fall on the strong beat.

Harmony favors simple triads with very little use made of seventh or ninth chords. Static harmony often occurs for extended sections of a work. Where progression is not functional in the eighteenth- or nineteenth-century sense of the word, Sibelius has allowed the flow of his parts to determine the vertical element. There are a few examples of parallel vertical structures; it is not a significant tendency. Some sequential harmonic passages also exist.

Counterpoint is also important in the style but not to the extent noted in the Mahler style. Sibelius's use of counterpoint does involve imitation and an occasional fugato. His primary contrapuntal devices are contrary motion, free counterpoint, pedal or ostinato techniques, and the use of two melodies simultaneously (infrequently).

Orchestration does not involve large resources. Other than the use of harp in the first and sixth symphonies Sibelius employs woodwinds in pairs (bass clarinet added in the sixth symphony), four horns, three trumpets, three trombones, timpani, and strings. The tuba is used in the first and second symphonies. Triangle, bass drum, cymbal, and a third timpani are found in the first symphony also. Strings are frequently subdivided, especially violins and violas. Some orchestral devices are typical: long, quiet, and sustained chords in the brass (lower or middle register) as accompanying forces frequently in development sections; lower register of the oboe in melodic passages; dotted figures in brass choir accompaniment passages; muted tremolo ostinato figures (often long and continuous passages) in the strings which create a rushing or swirling effect; doubling of important melodic lines at the octave in all instruments (especially strings and woodwinds), and brass instruments playing short passages of sustained chords (usually two chords) for either emphasis or the punctuation of phrases. Sometimes thematic material played by the brass fits into this latter concept. Sibelius generally kept the basic choirs of the orchestra separated. His use of a single pair of woodwinds on a passage of parallel thirds or sixths is an orchestral trademark. The writing for the orchestra is not virtuosic.

Information on Individual Symphonies

No.	Key	Date	I	II	III	IV
1	e	1899	SA	ABA	Scherzo	"Fantasia" (ABAB)
2	D	1902	SA	SA	Scherzo	SA
3	C	1908	SA	ABA	AB	
4	a	1911	SA	Scherzo	SA	SA
5	E-flat	1915 (rev. 1919)	SA	Variation	SA	
6	d	1924	SA	ABA	Scherzo	SA
7	C	1925	The symphony is one movement but has clearly defined sections (see below).			

SYMPHONY NO. 1

The first movement has a long *Andante* introduction for solo clarinet which touches briefly upon motives found in the subsequent *Allegro*. Sibelius appears to have been influenced by both Borodin and Tchaikovsky in the symphony. Borodin's influence can be observed in the opening theme of the *Allegro* (similar to the same theme in Borodin's second symphony) and in the emphasis on brass instruments.* The development and recapitulation sections overlap in the first movement with the recapitulation omitting the second theme. Tchaikovsky's influence is heard in the opening theme of the *Andante*. Sibelius made effective use of harp in the slow movement's middle section (accompanying horn solo, etc.). He restricted his use of the harp to the first and sixth symphonies. A fugato for woodwinds occurs near the end of the first statement of the scherzo. This scherzo is shortened after the trio. The finale opens with the initial clarinet theme of the first movement, this time played unison by the strings. It does not reappear in the *Allegro* which follows. The second section (*Andante*) is a broad theme played unison on the G string by all violins. The harp joins the accompaniment in the second phrase. The return of the first section is imitative in part. The return of the B theme is typical Sibelius in texture: ostinatolike figures on almost stationary pitches in the strings with the tune in the woodwinds.

SYMPHONY NO. 2

The first movement establishes a formal principle which, according to Abraham, Sibelius picked up from Borodin's second symphony. The principle allows seemingly unrelated fragments to be presented in the exposition and then gradually to be synthesized into a more meaningful relationship in the development section. The procedure becomes the composer's organic growth principal. The second movement opens essentially with a two-voice section: the theme in the bassoons, doubled at the octave; a "walking" bass line, pizzicato in the contrabassi; intermittent tonic pedal rolls in the timpani. A modality in some themes reflects the folk tradition affecting the style. The trio of the scherzo features a solo oboe on a plaintive repeated-note tune in e-flat minor. The trio returns after a second appearance of the scherzo as a transition to the finale; the third and fourth movements are connected with a passage which gradually evolves the first theme of the finale. The first section of the finale is accompanied by a pedal bass for a total of twenty-one measures (some of which is interrupted). The closing theme also has an ostinato for over thirty measures. The development section uses a steady tremolo figure in the strings over which fragments of themes are stated in the winds, a Sibelius development texture.

---

* Gerald Abraham, "The Symphonies," in *The Music of Sibelius*, ed. Gerald Abraham, pp. 15–16. Used by permission of W. W. Norton & Co., Inc.

SYMPHONY NO. 3

This work is a more classically oriented symphony in spite of its three-movement form. Not only is the form of each movement more concise but the orchestration is more classical in its emphasis on strings rather than on the brass as in the first two symphonies. This return to classicism does not, however, diminish many of the composer's individual mannerisms. Note the first movement's development section, in which a most characteristic rush of sixteenth notes supplies an ostinatolike thread of support constructed from a one-measure figure. The pattern in the violas (*spiccato*) is broadened by the addition of the violins in the passage's final fourteen bars. Above this steady stream of sound from the strings motives from the principal tunes are cast about. It is difficult to find a development section in a symphony where this is not done. The third and final movement divides itself into two main sections. The first section, a 6/8 *Moderato*, presents several short, unrelated motives which then are synthesized into a more understandable relationship as the movement progresses with a full development. The second theme of the movement gets particular emphasis. Just as this process begins to achieve some degree of unity it and the first section are terminated. A marchlike final section closes the movement. This section is marked by several passages built upon bass-line ostinatos. In fact, the entire final section of the movement relies quite heavily on these bass grounds for the unification of much of the materials of the movement.

SYMPHONY NO. 4

This work is discussed beginning on page 259.

SYMPHONY NO. 5

Again, this work is in three movements. The first movement divides itself into two sections: *Tempo molto moderato* and *Allegro molto,* the latter *Allegro* serving to some extent as a scherzo. In the overall plan of the first movement, however, the *Moderato* serves as the movement's exposition and opening section of the development. The *Allegro* is the substitute scherzo and, as such, continues the development of the opening materials. A trio precedes a return of the scherzo, the latter serving as a recapitulation. The variation second movement starts with a gradual derivation of the movement's theme. Twice, near the end of the movement, the theme of the finale is implied. The finale's opening theme is somewhat unusual in its use of a texture found most often in the development section of the Sibelius symphonies, a kind of swirling motion in the strings over which the composer often develops his themes in short fragments. In the case of the finale the swirling motion is actually thematically significant. A second subject in half notes later is adapted to an accompanying role for the third subject.

SYMPHONY NO. 6

While no two authorities agree on the identification of the main thematic groups of the first movement, there is a germinal procedure used starting with the imitative opening introduction in the strings. Most of this material emphasizes the melodic intervals of the minor third and the major third. A Dorian tune finally emerges as the antecedent phrase in the oboes with the consequent phrase in the flutes. Subdivision in the strings is used extensively. The first movement frequently has violins in four parts, with middle and lower strings in two voices each. In a few instances each upper (violins, violas) string part is split into three voices (p. 9–11 of Hansen score). The development uses the rushing string ostinato technique with sustained motives above or below in other instruments. The movement is an excellent example of the organic growth of isolated motives into longer and more significant themes. The second movement abbreviates the return of the first section, ending the movement quite abruptly. The scherzo movement has no trio and is also in the Dorian mode. The finale relates its material to the opening bars of the first movement (melodic intervals of a third especially). Opening with an introduction which contains most of the motives for the subsequent exposition, this movement is more complex in its derivation of themes. Again, much of the string passage work in the latter part of the movement involves divisi work, often octave doubling within a part. The ending is quite expressive.

SYMPHONY NO. 7

Gerald Abraham has provided an analysis of the "one-movement" symphony which implies an underlying multi-movement plan:*

A   Exposition. *Adagio* (92 bars; pages 1–12 in minature score)

B   Development. *Un pochettini meno adagio* (41 bars; pages 12–20); Transition (22 bars)

C   Scherzo. *Vivacissimo* (53 bars; pages 23–29) Transition (13 bars)

D   Development, continued *Adagio* (20 bars; pages 30–36) Transition (16 bars)

---

* Gerald Abraham, "The Symphonies," in *The Music of Sibelius,* ed. Gerald Abraham, pp. 35–36. Used by permission of W. W. Norton & Co., Inc.

    E   *Allegro molto moderato* (151 bars; pages 40–59)

    F   Second Scherzo. *Presto* (40 bars; pages 59–64) Transition (27 bars)

    G   Recapitulation. *Adagio* (50 bars; pages 68–76)

"The remarkable aspect of Sibelius' *Seventh Symphony* is that it is an organic symphony in one movement; not merely a long movement in which various sections correspond to slow movement, scherzo and so on, but a single indivisible organism."* Again, the symphony makes uses of extensive divisi writing in the strings. Several germinal motives unite the entire work.

EXAMPLES FOR STUDY

Sibelius: *Symphony No. 4 in a minor*

Although not as well-known by the public as symphonies 1, 2, and 5, Sibelius's fourth symphony is universally respected as his best effort.

> If the third symphony sounds a note of classical understatement, it is the fourth which, by general consent, enshrines the essential Sibelius. In this work he has distilled a language more economical and concentrated than in any other of his works (with the possible exception of *Tapiola*). . . .
> Sibelius spoke of the fourth symphony as a reaction against "modern trends," and there seems little doubt that he had in mind the large canvas and opulent colours of Mahler and Strauss.†

It is a work which contrasts with all of the composer's other symphonies with the possible exception of the seventh. Nowhere are there in evidence the long lyric lines of the first five symphonies. The orchestration is thin and lacking generally in color effects. The form of each movement is concise, concentrated, and, sometimes, obscure. Germinating motives tend to unite the entire work. Organic growth of materials is characteristic of all movements, especially the first, third, and fourth movements. While traditional forms seem to be implied in all movements, far more important is the growth of materials and the inter-relationship of these materials.

    The work is unified primarily by a single musical idea: the interval of the tritone or augmented fourth. Major or minor thirds also provide a secondary melodic unifying element. The interval of the falling fifth continues also to be one of Sibelius's favorite "motto" intervals in the symphony.

---

* Abraham, "The Symphonies," p. 35. Quoted with permission of publisher.

† Robert Layton, *Sibelius* (London: J. M. Dent & Sons, Ltd., 1965), p. 42. Used by permission of J. M. Dent & Sons, Ltd.

I: Tempo molto moderato, quasi adagio. It is possible to place most of the materials of the first movement in sonata-allegro form with a development section typical of Sibelius development sections. Seven basic motives occur, with two of the motives (A, B) being the most important. Motive A presents the unifying interval (tritone as both a melodic and a harmonic interval) in the first three bars. A second short theme built from major and minor thirds appears in measure 6, supplying the other unifying ingredients for the symphony. After a short development of this idea (over a ground in the bass on the upper two pitches of the A theme: E, F-sharp), a group of short themes is presented to complete the basic materials of the movement (themes C, D, E, and F). Theme C is a brass ensemble theme of typical Sibelius structure: quick crescendo with a short chord of resolution in a two-chord progression (see theme sheet below). The development section starts as a single line which spins out the B theme. At measure 66 a brief contrapuntal section starts with the G theme outlining the minor-major seventh chord on B. Finally a tremolo accompaniment evolves, with frequent use of the tritone as a harmonic interval in the accompaniment. Above this, as would be expected, Sibelius restates the A theme in a long initial note followed by two quick pitches that announce the tritone. The G theme evolves into a filled-in chord and replaces the A theme above the ostinato accompaniment. The recapitulation omits the A and B themes except for their appearances in the closing section. Note the use of long sustained chords in the lower brass registers for the opening measures of the closing section. The movement seemingly serves to present the two enigmas of the symphony: the unresolved tritone and the conflict between major and minor thirds on the same pitch. The symphony, in the remaining three movements, should seek ways of relating the tritone to some meaningful base and of dispelling the conflict between the two kinds of thirds.

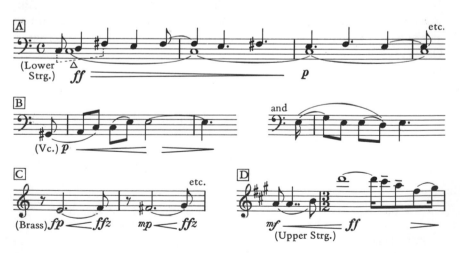

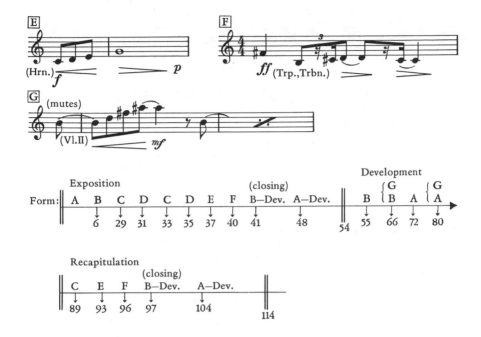

II: **Allegro molto vivace.** This scherzo movement appears to have the traditional form of a scherzo. A studied glance at the form chart shows, however, that the final appearance of the A theme is restricted to a single five-measure statement at the conclusion of the movement. Sibelius has selected a second theme for the scherzo which contrasts with the first themes. It is based on the same generating interval of the tritone but contrasts so much in texture that it might be possible to consider it as the first trio in a two-trio scherzo. The analysis chart below provides a minute fracturing of the first tune into five components. Only the A^5 part lacks one appearance of the tritone. The B theme (or first trio?) is divided into two portions: one quite rhythmic and repetitious, the other consisting of sustained chords in the winds. The C theme, in parallel thirds in the flutes (another Sibelius style mannerism), interrupts the flow of the A section in its return prior to the trio. The melodic material of the trio also stresses both the tritone and the interval of the major seventh, continuing some of the unifying ideas from the first movement. Horns also play elongated tritone motives related to the IA theme.

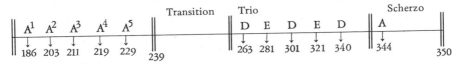

III: Il tempo largo. The third movement is the most concise of the four movements. Its organic handling of unifying intervals is subtle even though the texture is thin and the opportunity to hear even the smallest motive is ample. A tritone motive opens the movement followed by a similar motive using the major seventh. Immediately a long line is spun out by the woodwinds, much of it based on the first five-note motive. A free counterpoint in the bass strings completes a two-part texture for most of the opening section. A second (B) theme based on the interval of a rising fifth leads to a single line in the cellos (theme C); these latter two themes become the raw material for an expressive theme yet to be synthesized or presented. Two other themes (D, E), both quite similar, stress the falling fifth. A closing section based on an elongated A theme (measures 18–21) quietly presents the first thematic synthesis of the B and C themes in measures 23–27 (see B + C in theme sheet).

A linear display of the A theme opens the development section with this theme being transformed and modified to achieve a little more expressive impact, all of this over a sustained chord background in the strings. The chord sustained is an incomplete dominant ninth on D with the fifth, A, omitted; the tunes above supply an A-sharp for the overall sonority, with this A-sharp setting up an augmented-minor-major ninth chord. A brief extended version of the D (or the E?) theme is followed by Sibelius' first fully scored B + C statement with an accompaniment based on intervals from the D theme. The movement returns to a more expressive version of D (measure 47), then to the B + C again, and finally to a broadly spun-out statement of D over a pizzicato bass line (extracted from the B theme). As this subsides, a long pedal passage on G-sharp starts which will support the composer's most frequent development technique: motives repeated over a subdued ostinato or pedal, in this instance the A motive. As the section nears completion, another harmonic *ostinato* starts in the woodwinds, the materials being extracted from the D theme. The full string section, doubled at the single octave, on the B + C theme, is then added.

The recapitulation briefly mentions the A theme, adds the spun-out version from measure 28–35, and then continues short statements of the B + C melody. At measure 82 an extremely expressive statement of this lyric theme occurs, finally accompanied at the tune's high point by the intervals of the augmented fifth and the tritone in the trumpets and trombones, doubled at the single octave. A coda mentions briefly the principal tune of the fourth movement and then lays down a pedal C-sharp in the strings and horns for several quiet statements of A again above and below this pedal. The movement, which was started in a minor, ends on the unison pitch C-sharp, thereby reinforcing the c-sharp minor implication of much of the movement.

IV: Allegro. The movement starts with a sixteen-bar opening section (see A[1] below) which seemingly has little thematic relation to the rest of the movement. A closer perusal of these first measures shows, however, that the opening tune does contain the primary generating intervals of the finale: the tritone and the major-minor third. After this long-lined tune is repeated, four more short motives are presented in an unrelated fashion (A[2], A[3], A[4], and A[5]). The A[2] continues the tritone emphasis in the symphony. A[6] is a much longer tune, again stressing major or minor thirds and tritones. Theme A[7] is based on filled-in versions of the major-third, minor-third intervals. A repetition of A[2–5] completes a quasi "double exposition" of the materials. The development which begins at measure 56 can be placed into short sections as follows:

Part 1—measures 56–88: A measured tremolo in most of the strings is organized into a two-voice basic texture (violin IA, viola, and bass doubling what could be called an ostinato line). The ostinato consists of two pitches, G-sharp and A. Above this string ostinatolike support Sibelius uses two statements in the woodwinds of the minor third interval, the lower pitch elongated to at least three measures. The ostinato is in A major; the intervals are in E-flat major. This combination of tonal areas (A, E-flat) stresses the tritone relationships within the symphony.

Part 2—measures 89–109: This section is another ostinatolike passage in strings above which two of the themes are stated (A^6, A^3). The underlying harmonic support in the ostinato implies the dominant seventh on E (V^7 in the tonic key). In measure 96 the nature of the ostinato changes with the addition of the two violin parts. The group of strings then begins moving up sequentially while the winds sustain a pedal on the tonic center, A. The motion in the ostinato is similar to the harmonic device of planing, or chord streams, used in the works of the impressionistic composers (E Mm7th→ F-sharp Mm7th→ G-sharp Mm7th). Themes A^{2-5} are then quickly restated.

Part 3—measures 110–21: This passage approximates a restatement of measures 26–37 and contains a pedal on the major second, D-E, in the bass strings. The ostinato in the lower strings changes to a scalelike passage at measure 119 which appears to be implying the key of E-flat major.

Part 4—measures 122–37: A continuation of the scalar bass ostinatolike line carries this passage first back to the A major center and then to E-flat (Mixolydian). Fragments of the A^2 and A^3 themes are stated above this syncopated bass line in the winds and soprano strings. There is a noticeable mixture of A major and E major in some of the motivic passages. The flute excerpt, measure 134–35, ascends a scale in E-flat, descends in A.

Part 5—measures 138–41: Starting with a transition passage stressing the dominant seventh chord on E-flat (strings) in a clash with the A major triad in the woodwinds, the movement moves toward a new pair of themes (B^1, B^2).

Statement of B^1, B^2—measures 142–217: An ostinato in the lower strings begins in C major and then moves through passages which seem to emphasize G, G-sharp, B-flat, E-flat, and A-flat. By measure 180, the movement has begun to relate the chordal patterns to dominant-type sonorities and then moves the tonal emphasis up sequentially in whole steps (B, C, and D-sharp). The passage closes with an emphasis on E major. The technique for this long section is similar to other developmentlike sections: an ostinato organization in lower and middle parts which support short statements of the B^1 and B^2 themes in the upper strings.

Part 6—measures 218–37: Very rapid C major scales in the strings (the ostinato) undergird one long statement of the A^2 theme in the E trumpet. The woodwinds have opened the section with an A^2 theme in much shorter rhythmic values. The remainder of the winds play the same C major triad. In measure 230 the bells play a rhythmically augmented version of the A³ theme.

Part 7—measures 238–313: A development of B motives continues over an ostinato in melodic fifths in the lower strings. The passage reverts to the original texture of the first B section at measure 281. The tune over the original ostinato is a more lyric version of a segment of the A¹ tune. The B tune also continues, alternating with this newer theme. Just prior to the end of the development section, a long D-sharp enters in the violin I part, resolving in a contour which is similar to theme A² (see measure 308).

The recapitulation restates most of the main themes in an abbreviated fashion and enters into the same "double exposition" noted in measures 48–52 of the exposition, this time in the key of E-flat. A development of the materials continues starting at measure 349. It would also be reasonable to identify this section as Coda I. The two parts of the new development are complex in structure with both A and B themes being combined in a contrapuntal effect. The final section (measures 441–84) places considerable emphasis on the major- or minor-third unifying motives in an elongated harmonic passage in the strings with minor thirds interjected at phrase endings by the woodwinds. The coda briefly mentions the minor third and the major seventh, and closes with a strong emphasis on the tonic of a minor. The minor third is thus clarified (G-sharp–B) as the seventh and second scale degrees and as a member of the dominant seventh in a minor. The major seventh seems to have meaning as an inversion of the second and third scale degrees (b, c) of the a minor tonality. The tritone, by this time, has filtered out as a significant interval in this movement. The final use of the A² theme (tritone vehicle) occurs in measures 434–40, where the E trumpet, accompanied by tutti orchestra (fff), announces the last three notes of the A² theme (D-sharp–A–E) in the appropriate rhythm. The E pitch is harmonized with an extended A major triad, fff also. The bells also repeat the first three pitches of the A³ theme in the background (A–B–C-sharp). Thus, the tritone is seen in a relationship which embellishes the tonic triad: the D-sharp (or E-flat) serves as a nonharmonic tone which resolves to the E pitch in the tonic triad (A, C-sharp, E). In the opening bars of the symphony it is not clear how this vague interval will be related to a logical flow of musical ideas or how it will articulate with an internal relationship of pitches in the work. As the symphony moves ahead through its four movements, the implied significance of all intervals becomes clearer. Finally, in the closing measures of the finale, the interval is placed into a perspective within the home key which has been hinted at since the opening bars of the first movement.

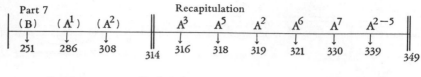

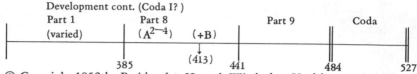

† © Copyright 1952 by Breitkopf & Haertel, Wiesbaden. Used by permission.

SUMMARY

The Sibelius fourth symphony is an experiment in economy of means. The process is enhanced by an interrelationship between all movements established through the use of several unifying themes (or intervals), with one interval, the tritone, assuming a much more significant role than the others. The shape of the symphonic form is not altered externally, though the order of the internal movements is rearranged. The opening movement has a much more moderate flow than would be expected in an opening sonata-allegro movement. What Sibelius appears to have accomplished in the fourth symphony is an anticipation of the structure and style of the seventh symphony, a one-movement work with common thematic materials throughout much of the work. The fourth symphony is even more concise than the seventh in that three or four motives are used throughout the entire four-movement symphony, with each successive movement further expanding upon and qualifying these seemingly unrelated motives. While the organic synthesis process which Sibelius has been attempting to employ has been for the greater part restricted to single movements (and, after the fourth symphony, to single movements also), in this work there is organic growth and synthesis in individual movements *in addition to* the more significant growth throughout the symphony as a whole. One can see, then, a new emphasis (and perhaps a new concept) in the symphony which has its roots in the motivic values expressed by Beethoven and Brahms, in the unifying themes of Liszt and Berlioz, and in the Wagner leitmotiv. This emphasis treats the four-movement form as a single art work in which the four parts or movements become more closely integrated and articulated. The process is continuous in spite of the sectioning of the work into movements and the movements into traditional forms. Sibelius has also anticipated the twentieth century's neoclassical developments by some twenty to thirty years with his emphasis on intellectual, as well as expressive, values in the art form. Rather than abandon tonal organization of Western music (as did the serialists), Sibelius further refined the possibilities within the tonal system both by lifting some of the traditional restrictions (key relationships, harmonic progression, etc.) and by tightening up formal expectations into an extremely concise and unified relationship of musical ideas.

Ralph Vaughan Williams (1872–1958)

Vaughan Williams's life spanned a large portion of the twentieth century. During his sixty years of creativity he viewed the death of post-romanticism, the rise and fall of impressionism and expressionism, the restoration of English composers to the forefront of creative activity, the ascendancy of an American school of composers, and a host of other major musical happenings or historical developments including neoclassicism and aleatoric music. His own creative symphonic efforts extended over a period of forty-eight years, sufficient time for his overall style to experience the effects of many influences. The dedication to and the nurturing of the concert symphony by Vaughan Williams is an indication of the route his art was to follow, the influences he chose to respect, and the values he considered important in his own creative life.

The major influences in his life were numerous: Sir Hubert Parry, Sir Charles Stanford, the English hymnal (for the Church of England), J. S. Bach, the English folk song, Richard Wagner, sixteenth-century English polyphony

In a July 31, 1946 BBC-sponsored concert, as a part of the summer Henry Wood Promenade Concerts at Royal Albert Hall, Vaughan Williams led the London Symphony Orchestra in a performance of his *London Symphony*. One of the world's largest multi-purpose halls, Royal Albert Hall was dedicated in 1871 by Queen Victoria as a memorial to the Prince Consort. Two of its three tiers of box seats can be seen in the background. BBC copyright photograph.

(Tudor church music), Gustav Holst, Max Bruch, and Maurice Ravel.* To say that his style tended to be eclectic is probably an understatement. Of these many influences, however, two were dominant: folk song and Tudor church music.

The Tudor influence in the style is significant; modality, an almost vocal approach to instrumental music, speech rhythms, simple triads, cross-relations, and nonmetric spinning out of his music all can be traced back in part to the vocal polyphonic style of the sixteenth-century English composers.

The melodic style is of two primary types. Some tunes are more influenced by the Tudor style. They are not always modal or pentatonic but tend to use patterns of fourths and fifths. The tunes are generally slow and somewhat contemplative. Their rhythm is complex and not particularly metric. Melodies (and even sections of a work) can be almost nonmetric in their disregard for the bar line or regular accents. The flatted seventh scale degree (modal influence) is quite frequent. The second melodic type is more in the folk tradition. Vaughan Williams' folk tunes tend to be in a major or minor mode; some are modal. Folk tune meter is overt and regular. Pitches in the style are generally organized into a diatonic scheme. The rhythm and phrasing are quite regular. The tritone and the major-minor third inflection are frequent in both melodic styles.

The harmonic style makes use of impressionist style mannerisms. The use of parallel chord structures (chord streams, or "planing") occurs throughout his works. At times Vaughan Williams employed streams of chords in a contrapuntal texture. Those sections which employ regular harmonic progression tend to be modal. The basic vertical unit is still the triad. Vaughan Williams apparently did not use any systematic kind of chord progression in most of the symphonies. The alternation between major and minor on the same root has harmonic as well as tonal significance.

His textures tend to be essentially contrapuntal. His affection for the Tudor style created frequent textures of nonmetric counterpoint of a nonimitative type. Many times the various lines were manipulated within a basic sonority very much in the style of the expanded noncontrapuntal sonorities of the impressionist composers. His usage of counterpoint expanded to embrace fugue and passacaglia as well as imitation, fugato, ground bass, ostinato, countermelodies, and free counterpoint. Since the essential vertical unit in the style is the triad, the contrapuntal style does not create the tension of the linear polyphony of the serial and atonal composers.

Vaughan Williams' use of rhythm reflected both folk and Tudor influences. The free-spinning quality of some passages is enhanced by nonmetric

---

* Elliott S. Schwartz, *The Symphonies of Ralph Vaughan Williams* (Amherst: University of Massachusetts Press, 1964), pp. 13–14.

values he absorbed from the Tudor style. The contrapuntal manipulation of rhythm produces superimposition of conflicting meters and rhythmic values (two versus three, etc.).

The orchestral style places an emphasis on the string section. His style was conservative with not too much effort at orchestral color in spite of his studies with Ravel. He frequently subdivided the string section. The harp is primarily a nineteenth-century instrument in the Vaughan Williams scores. He was one of the early modern composers to dignify the sound of the saxophone by using it in two of his symphonies. Invariably, in spite of the large instrumental component some of the works required, the composer cued copiously in other parts and directed that most of his symphonies could be played satisfactorily with a smaller ensemble. The largeness of the orchestral sound is undoubtedly related to the frequency of tutti passages. Only in the *Sinfonia Antartica* did he resort to orchestral tricks and effects to depict. His primary concerns were musical, not orchestral. Most of Vaughan Williams' symphonies use woodwinds in pairs, four horns, two or three trumpets, three trombones, tuba, harp, timpani, percussion, and strings.

In general his symphonic style follows the Austro-German line of evolution. His works were not experimental as much as they were a reflection of his own personal musical upbringing. The symphonies can be divided into style groups:

Symphonies 1–3	Programmatic in nature
Symphonies 4, 5, 6, 9,	Symphonies of a complex nature
Symphonies 7, 8	A simplification of style

All of the symphonies, however, share in the basic style mannerisms mentioned above. The difference among the three styles above is only a matter of emphasis. Formally, the only unique feature of his symphonies was his use of the epilogue as a final section or movement. His concept of this movement was one of a coda to the entire symphony, not just to the finale. Two of the epilogues are fifth movements which are attached as codalike structures to the fourth movements. Most contain tunes from previous movements. The epilogue of the sixth symphony is a separate and self-sufficient movement which does clarify a thematic complexity that has plagued the whole work. He used sonata-allegro (or sonatina) form in fifteen (38.5 percent) of the thirty-nine movements (counting all epilogues as separate movements). In addition, his scherzo forms are developmental, adding another eight developmental movements to the total of fifteen already noted. Thus, twenty-three (59 percent) out of thirty-nine movements are developmental in nature. Only two of the movements are in variation form. Two of the finales are in a large binary form, in which each part of the finale is in a separate form. Common thematic material generally unites both parts of these finales.

The London Symphony Orchestra, formed in 1904, recently finished a complete recording of the Vaughan Williams' symphonies. This photo shows the orchestra performing the Verdi *Requiem* in St. Paul's cathedral in a 1970 concert conducted by Leonard Bernstein. Permission the London Symphony Orchestra and London Weekend Television.

Information on Individual Symphonies

Number	Key	Date	I	II	III	IV	V
1 Sea	D,e,g, E-flat	1910	SA	ABA	Sonatina	Two Parts: I—SA II—Arch	
2 London	G	1914	SA	ABA	Scherzo	ABA	Epilogue
3 Pastoral	G,f,G,a	1921	SA	ABAB	Scherzo	SA	
4	f	1935	SA	SA	Scherzo	SA	"Epilogue fugato"
5	D	1943	Sonatina	Scherzo	SA	Passacaglia	
6	e	1947	Sonatina	ABA	Scherzo	Epilogue	
7 Sinfonia Antartica	G?	1953	ABC	Scherzo	ABCBA	ABA	March w/Trio
8	d	1956	Variation	Scherzo	Sonatina	Rondo	
9	e	1957	SA	ABAB	Scherzo	Two Parts: I—ABAB II—SA	

SYMPHONY NO. 1

Vaughan Williams's first symphony (*Sea* Symphony) is primarily a choral symphony in which the choral group participates in each of the four movements. The composer selected the poems of the American poet Walt Whitman for the text, which he slightly adapted. Three motives unite all four movements. The Tudor influence is noted in several choral sections in which a sixteenth century polyphonic setting or a simple, declamatory (similar to plainsong) style can be observed. In the latter the effect is of the chorus speaking directly to the audience. Two solo singers, baritone and soprano, are also used. The orchestra is one of the composer's largest because of the addition of two harps and organ.

SYMPHONY NO. 2

A motto theme in the first two measures unifies the entire symphony. In the first movement, the composer included the sounds of the chimes of Big Ben (measure 31). A London street cry was the source for a tune in the second movement (measure 70). The scherzo has two trios. The epilogue is actually a codalike appendage to the fourth movement and quotes from previous movements.

SYMPHONY NO. 3

The first movement of this symphony opens with a theme in parallel triads, an impressionistic device. This pattern is also used in the two-voice setting of themes throughout the symphony. It established a style feature in which the composer used chord streams as a single line supporting another melody. At times each line will have its own set of parallel chords. The scherzo is in five parts: scherzo–trio–scherzo–trio–scherzo. A vocal solo (tenor or soprano offstage), without words, opens the finale and does not reappear until the coda. Much of the thematic material sounds related throughout the movement because of the extensive use of pentatonic themes.

SYMPHONY NO. 4

With the fourth symphony, Vaughan Williams departed from overt programmatic inspirations for his symphonies. The work is extremely dissonant, makes wide use of complex linear textures, and yet includes many of the typical devices of the composer's symphonic style. As in previous works two motto themes are used to unite all of the four movements. The second movement is almost completely contrapuntal. Extensive canon, imitation, and free counterpoint characterize the movement. The trio of the scherzo is also quasi-fugal, with tuba and bassoons first stating the fugue subject. A transition connects the scherzo to the finale. This finale has a marchlike setting associated with the first theme. The fugal epilogue is based on themes of the finale and concludes with a quotation from the opening measures of the symphony. The work ends with an emphasis on the tense dissonances of the symphony, which finally resolve on the tonic (F) chord with the third missing. Previously in all movements Vaughan Williams had alternated major and minor thirds on various tonic centers. The conclusion of the symphony does not clarify his intentions.

SYMPHONY NO. 5

The score was inscribed: "Dedicated without permission to Jean Sibelius." Its style is much simpler from a tonal standpoint, since it is primarily a diatonic work with minimal chromatic intrusion. Thus, it contrasts with the preceding fourth symphony. The structure and materials are not difficult to grasp. The first movement opens with a fifty-nine-measure pedal (or pedallike figure similar to a modified ground) which supports an extended contrapuntal working out of the first tune. The first movement, as well as the rest of the symphony, is characterized by Tudor-like contrapuntal manipulations with essentially diatonic materials. The scherzo second movement has a less imitative style but employs quartal melodic material of a diatonic nature. The movement has two trios, the second being in 2/4 meter (versus the 3/4 in the balance of the movement). Portions of the scherzo theme (in 3/4) are superimposed upon the 2/4 material of the second trio. The romanza again stresses the diatonic contrapuntal style of Vaughan Williams's Tudor works. The finale, designed as a passacaglia, organizes itself into three basic sections plus a coda. Variations are rather free, especially in the second and third sections. The coda restates the material which opened the symphony and then returns to the quiet counter-subject which has accompanied the passacaglia ground. Whereas the first movement has ended on a major second C–D which stressed the conflict between the C pedal and a horn figure in D major in the opening section, the finale ends quietly in D major.

SYMPHONY NO. 6

This work is discussed beginning on page 277.

SYMPHONY NO. 7

The work (*Sinfonia Antartica*) is based on a score to a film entitled "Scott of the Antarctic," a work about the tragic voyage of Captain Robert Falcon Scott, R.N., to the South Pole. He lost his life trying to return to his base camp after a series of errors and mishaps had doomed his race to the pole. He subsequently become one of England's great heroes, since the courage of his undertaking was monumental considering the year of the voyage (1912). Vaughan Williams in the score prefaces each of the five movements with an appropriate quotation from a literary source. Three indicate the depth of the composer's feelings for Scott's sacrifice:*

Prelude:

To suffer woes which hope thinks infinite,
To forgive wrongs darker than death or night,
To defy power which seems omnipotent,
Neither to change, nor falter, nor repent:
This . . . is to be
Good, great and joyous, beautiful and free,
This is alone life, joy, empire and victory.

Shelley: *Prometheus Unbound*

Intermezzo:

Love, all alike, no season knows, nor clime,
Nor hours, days, months, which are the
rags of time.

Donne: *The Sun Rising*

Epilogue:

I do not regret this journey; we took risks,
we knew we took them, things have come
out against us, therefore we have no
cause for complaint.

Captain Scott's last journal

The orchestral resources in the work are larger than usual, with an expanded percussion section (including vibraphone, wind machine, etc.), piano, organ,

---

* All prefaces are reproduced in Hugh Ottaway, *Vaughan Williams Symphonies* (Seattle: University of Washington Press, 1973), pp. 50–53.

soprano solo (wordless), and three-part women's chorus (also wordless). The voices are used only in the first and final movements. While the symphony can be analyzed in five movements with traditional formal outlines, the basic intent of the music is still the expressive support of the film score. Much of the composer's efforts were directed toward orchestral effect. This work is surprisingly devoid of the complex contrapuntal style used in other symphonies. There is some cyclic treatment between the first and last movements wherein the composer brings back the material of the prelude in the final coda. The symphony closes with the soprano and the women's chorus repeating the half-step motive characteristic of much of the melodic material. The addition of the wind machine to the final few bars enhances the stark effect implied.

SYMPHONY NO. 8

The eighth symphony is a lighter relief to the preceding works. It uses few wind instruments (in pairs except for three trombones), avoids developmental forms and minimizes its expressive dimension. Vaughan Williams scored the second movement for winds alone and the third for strings only. The first movement he termed "seven variations in search of a theme," but a theme does exist in the first four pitches of the opening movement. The seven variations can also be placed into sonata-allegro form, according to the composer's suggestion.* The second movement is a scherzo in the style of a march with trio.† The third movement is more contrapuntal than the march and interrupts the return of the first section by inserting a twenty-six-bar interlude. The final toccata is in rondo form. The large percussion section is a striking feature of the finale. The symphony contains references to earlier symphonies and has been thought of as a synthesis of earlier styles.‡

---

* Program notes provided by the composer for the Mercury recording, MG-50115, state, "I understand that some hearers may have their withers wrung by a work being called a symphony whose first movement does not correspond to the usual symphonic form. It may perhaps be suggested that by a little verbal jugglery this movement may be referred to the conventional design. Thus, the first section may be called the first subject; the second (presto) section, can become the "bridge passage," the third section, starting at (d), may be described as the second subject. Sections four and five we will call the development, the allegro will be the reprise of the first subject, though this, I admit, will be skating over rather thin ice: but there will be no difficulty in referring the final section to the recapitulation and coda. Thus all wounds will be healed and honour satisfied."

† American audiences have become well acquainted with the scherzo second movement of the composers's eighth symphony because of its popularity on band programs. The movement is scored for winds alone.

‡ Schwartz, *The Symphonies of Ralph Vaughan Williams*, p. 150.

SYMPHONY NO. 9

Three of Vaughan Williams's symphonies are the most complex of the nine: numbers 4, 6, and 9. They are all in minor keys and are the most contrapuntal by far of all of the symphonies. The ninth symphony, written in the composer's eighty-fifth year, tends to solidify many of the style features and formal concepts seen in the other two complex works. It presents one main concept to unify the symphony, the major-minor third on a common root, a motive which appears in many of the symphonies. Many of the themes in all four movements use this tonal dichotomy, never fully resolving it. The first movement features a trio of saxophones and a flügelhorn for two of the primary themes. The movement is contrapuntal and returns to the ametric style of Tudor counterpoint in some of the sections. The recapitulation brings back the first theme in the solo violin with a countermelody in the flügelhorn, an excellent example of the composer's contrapuntal skills. The expressive second movement stresses the major-minor third motive but surprisingly ends in C major. The third movement, a scherzo, inserts a fugato for the three saxophones in the return of the first section within the scherzo and then begins a lenthy development of the primary theme. The trio alternates 2/4 with 6/8 and superimposes duple and triple meters to enhance the contrapuntal nature of much of the movement. The da capo of the scherzo is abbreviated to a few bars. The finale is actually two movements: one a part form and the second a sonata-allegro. Both forms exhibit the same emphasis on counterpoint as noted in other movements. The opening section of each main part is fugal. A coda which sums up several of the themes from previous movements finally resolves the half-step problem presented by the first movement with a final cadence in E major.

EXAMPLES FOR STUDY

Vaughan Williams: *Symphony No. 6 in e minor*

Mention has been made of the place shared by symphonies 4, 6, and 9 in the overall output of symphonies. Each is quite complex and avoids the relaxed nature of the fifth symphony or the lightness of the eighth symphony. Each lacks any overt programmatic connotation as found in the first three symphonies and in the film-related seventh. The orchestra for the sixth symphony is average in size for Vaughan Williams. The only additions which should be noted are tenor saxophone, bass clarinet, and xylophone. English horn is also required, as well as three to four percussion players.

I: Allegro. The first movement states the motto, or unifying theme, for the entire symphony in the first five pitches of the opening measure: the juxtaposition of major or minor thirds on the same root, a frequent melodic motive in many of the Vaughan Williams's symphonies. The initial minor third (F–A-flat) is modified to become E–A-flat (G-sharp) and E–G, the tonic sonority with dual modality. In a descending passage emphasizing this dual modality motive, a three-beat pattern emerges in a four-beat rhythm, a contraction of rhythm that is rather typical of the composer's Tudor-related rhythmic style. In measure 12, a counterpoint in the brass starts, this particular line being a group of parallel triads which has a bitonal implication when combined with the A^1 ostinato in the upper voices. The two keys most prominent at that instant are g minor and e minor. The composer then combines polyphonically the two primary motives from the A section starting at measure 20. The new A3 theme is related to the opening motive. A working out of this concept lasts until measure 34. The subordinate material is in two parts, the first in a march tempo (12/8 meter) with the theme in 4/4, another two-versus-three super-imposition so typical of Vaughan Williams' rhythmic preferences. A triplet figure in the woodwinds (measure 43) which precedes the tune is an important motive for the B^1 section. As before, this motive is developed to some length before the second part of the subordinate material enters (B^2, measure 72). The third part of the section (B^3, measure 82) is cast in the folk song mold—square, modal, and lyric. It is in 6/4 meter while the accompaniment continues the 12/8 triplet figure from B^1. A lengthy development follows with other parts of the subordinate section appearing.

The recapitulation is shortened in both the principal and subordinate sections (see graph on page 279). A surprising contrast occurs when the folk tune returns in the tonic major with a rich harp accompaniment rather than with the 12/8 triplet figures used previously. The section then continues a lyric development of this tune, also employing both major and minor thirds on the tonic center from time to time. The minor tonic seems to prevail in the folk tune as well as in the brief return of the A^1 motive in the final measures of the movement.

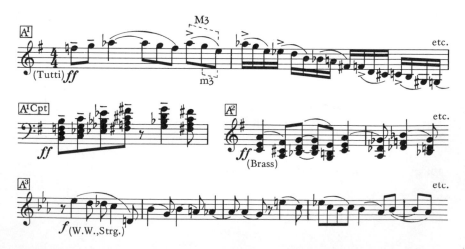

II: Moderato. A large ternary design outlines the slow second movement. The principal motive for the A section (see theme sheet below) retains the major-minor third puzzle. A B-flat pedal (and later an ostinato) undergirds most of the first section. The development of this motive assumes lyric proportions (measure 14) and sequential motivic shaping (measures 20–26) before the middle section begins. Both B themes exhibit a connection with the symphony's motto theme. An extended development of these two motives leads back to the first section. The third part of the movement continues the development of the A themes, with a climax being reached around measure 124. The high point involves a short motive of a descending major third harmonized with a g minor triad on the first member (B-flat) and a G-flat major triad on the lower member (G-flat). The trumpet ostinato continues during this passage. A short coda again fails to resolve the conflict between B and B-flat; the English horn sustains a C-flat over a B-flat–F fifth in the accompanying parts.

III: Allegro vivace. The first theme of the third movement is based on the tritone, which might be related to a passage from the B^3 tune in the opening movement. The second portion of the theme (A^2) also outlines the tritone. The balance of the scherzo section is a lengthy development of both these themes, which usually appear together in a contrapuntal texture. The slower-moving theme undergoes some rhythmic changes in some parts of the development. The trio (B theme below) is constructed with alternating 2/4 and 3/4 meters. An ostinatolike counterpoint in the viola accompanies the first entrance of the trio theme (measure 110). This countermelody is related to the A² theme of the scherzo. The trio also has considerable development, most of which continues the two-voice contrapuntal texture established at the outset. The return of the scherzo is more properly a continued development of the scherzo themes in inversion. The second appearance of the trio lacks the countermelody of the first version but supplies another slower-moving counterpoint as this section goes through more development.

IV: Moderato. Called an "Epilogue" by the composer, the finale is another enigma of symphonic literature. Vaughan Williams constructed the movement in a sectional design which can also be placed in sonata-allegro form if one considers Part III as a development of previous material. The first section is essentially contrapuntal. The theme is based on the major-minor motive from the opening movement. The second section (Part II) is more homophonic. The B^1 theme is especially interesting since it spins out a series of triads which are both major and minor. The third section (Part III) is related to the opening theme of the movement and concludes with a section of two-voice counterpoint. The final section (Part IV) brings back the first theme, tremolo in the strings. The passage is imitative. The remaining themes of the finale reappear briefly as the movement concludes on the e minor triad. The final cadence is taken from previous third-related materials, using an E-flat major triad resolving to the final e minor triad.

SUMMARY

Vaughan Williams's sixth symphony is unified through the basic nature of its materials rather than through simple cyclic juxtaposition of one or two themes. The entire symphony is one large development section of a primary motive with the exception of the scherzo. In the case of this third movement Vaughan Williams offered the tritone as a relief from the unifying motive. The extensive use of counterpoint in all movements (possible exception: the slow movement) makes the symphony an even greater challenge to the listener. Other Vaughan Williams "devices" abound: modal writing, a folk tune, parallel chord structures for almost all harmonized passages in all movements except the finale, chord streams in polyphonic textures, freely phrased rhythm and meter, and free counterpoint in the Tudor style. Like Sibelius, Vaughan Williams did not turn his back on the tradition of the symphony established by Beethoven and Brahms but elected to continue that tradition in his own personal manner, imprinting on it his own affection for the folk song and Tudor contrapuntal traditions. What comes through as the more important contribution was the composer's intellectual involvement with the symphony, which resulted in a highly articulated four-movement work.

Music in Russia

In light of the political orientation of the arts in Soviet Russia, it has been difficult to view contemporary art in that country from the same points of reference as those used in discussing contemporary arts in other parts of the Western world. In the nineteenth century, Russia (St. Petersburg, in particular) established itself as one of the leading centers of the arts, especially music. Berlioz enjoyed considerable success in that country, as did other major performers and composers who either lived or performed there. The fact that a major group of composers ("The Five") developed in Russia during the late nineteenth century indicates a high level of musical accomplishment. More important perhaps is the existence of a Russian as one of the major composers of the twentieth century. Igor Stravinsky remained basically a Russian composer throughout his creative life in spite of a sweeping stylistic evolution after he left Russia in 1911 to take up residence in Paris.

The history of the political supervision of the arts in Russia is well known. In Russia, art must serve *all* of the people. In order to do this, art must be designed so that its structure and purpose are understood by the people. This creates an accountability which Soviet composers must respect: their public must grasp what it is they are doing in a work of art or they chance "falling from favor" in the eyes of the Party. In 1958 there was some relaxation of control of the art forms. Since that time there has not been an observable increase in the level of overt experimentation, be it serialism, aleatoric music, or other style tendencies generally seen in Western music. The basic style which most Russian composers appear to emulate is eclectic with a strong adherence to traditional formal values and an emphasis on nationalistic traits. A number of contemporary mannerisms associated more closely with the 1930s have characterized the music of Sergei Prokofiev and Dmitri Shostakovich, especially ostinato patterns, motor rhythm, extremely angular melody, polytonality, occasionally dissonant harmony, and an emphasis on clarity of form which somewhat parallels the neoclassical developments in the 1920s and 1930s.

Sergei Prokofiev (1891–1953)

Prokofiev was a child of czarist Russia. His early studies were with Russia's leading musicians (Gliere, Liadov, Rimsky-Korsakov, Tcherepnin). By the time of the revolution he had written works of considerable merit: four piano sonatas, a violin concerto, two piano concertos, the piano *Toccata, Sarcasms,* the *Scythian Suite,* and others. In the years 1918–1932, he lived outside Russia, performing as a concert pianist and producing his works in most of the countries of the Western world. In 1933, he settled in Russia. By that time he had added the following major works to his output: three more piano concertos (3–5), three more symphonies (2–4), the fifth piano sonata, and the opera *Love for Three Oranges.* The major orchestral works yet to be written while he lived under the Soviet regime included: symphonies 5–7, the cello concerto, the second violin concerto, *Peter and the Wolf,* and several suites drawn from dramatic and choral works. In 1936 he was denounced by *Pravda* for his musical decadence. His answer, also published in *Pravda,* was a contrite affirmation of the political manifestations of musical style which he was to emphasize. In 1948, he and others were again condemned. In spite of this, he was awarded a Stalin Prize in 1951. Since most of Prokofiev's major orchestral works (four of seven symphonies, all five piano concertos, one of the two violin concertos, and several suites from choral and dramatic works) were written before his return to Russia, it is possible to view some of his total output as more representative of the contemporary symphony's growth.

Prokofiev gave some insight into the derivation of his musical style by writing of four major style elements. A classical influence could be traced back to his early childhood and the Beethoven sonatas he frequently heard his mother play. This influence manifests itself as a neoclassical trend in the instrumental works. The modern thrust in the style he attributes to a severe criticism he received from his teacher Taneyev to update his harmonic syle. A motor or toccata element the composer attributes to the influence of Schumann's *Toccata.* Prokofiev's rhythmic style retains this incessant motor activity much of the time. His lyric gift was slow in developing and really came into full flavor in his later works.

There is another aspect of the style to which the composer does not refer: the Russian element. This affects both harmonic style and melodic design. It is responsible for the emphasis on nationalistic heroes, an emphasis which resulted in frequent operatic and choral works commemorating national figures or events. His use of folk tunes was often accompanied by the use of variation technique in some of his works. Folk influence created a strong diatonicism in his works as well as some instances of modality. Free polyphony might also be attributable to the same style in folk singing. The incidence of overt folklorism became much greater after 1935, as he tried to conform to the official Soviet attitude toward music.

An early publicity picture of Prokofiev probably associated with his visits to this country in 1918, 1921 or 1938. Courtesy Chicago Symphony Orchestra.

The harmonic style is unique in its sudden modulation to unrelated keys within a phrase structure. These abrupt detours are invariably followed by a return to the home key of the phrase. The basic vertical unit is the triad. In works of the pre-Soviet days, the incidence of dissonant sonorities and polychords is much greater. Some harmonic passages appear to result from linear considerations, the latter being rare.

Prokofiev's use of form is drawn from Beethoven and other classicists. The motive is the foundation stone of formal manipulation in the style. Prokofiev possessed skills as a developer and thus did not shy away completely from developmental forms. Of the twenty-five movements in the seven symphonies, only ten are developmental. Eight are in rondo or part forms.

The melodic style is characterized by lyricism and angularity. Melody, reacting to harmonic shifts, frequently moves up or down a half step, a minor third, or an augmented fourth. Folk tunes or folklike tunes appear in the style. In some instances slow-moving lyric themes are diverted by wide leaps.

Rhythmic style is characterized by the motor, or toccata, element discussed by the composer. Dance rhythms, folk rhythms, extended rhythmic repetition, multimetric inserts, and usages which tend to emphasize a kind of rhythmic vitality in style can be noted.

Counterpoint is of two types: free or superimposition of two melodies. Imitation is not frequent. Basso ostinato is a most characteristic feature. Extensive two-voice free counterpoint can be noted in all symphonies.

The symphonic style follows an expected course. The first four symphonies are more responsive to the composer's search for a contemporary idiom. The fifth symphony, written during the harsh days of World War II, still shows the composer's retention of many of the more contemporary devices from the earlier symphonies but with considerable relaxation of dissonant harmonies. The sixth and seventh symphonies recede even further from the rigors of a more linear and abstract style. The final symphony is one of the composer's most lyric works, thus fulfilling his "promise" (in his letter to the Soviet Art Committee in 1948) to continue an emphasis on lyricism rather than on "formalism." *

The orchestral style is a mixture of Rimsky-Korsakov, Ravel, and some rather individual mannerisms cultivated by Prokofiev. The orchestral complement generally remains the same for all seven symphonies with the exception of the *Classical* Symphony, which uses winds in pairs and only timpani in the percussion section. This percussion section gets considerable emphasis in many of the symphonies; five use at least seven different percussive instruments. The types used are not particularly unusual with the exception of the woodblock, castanets, and large gong (tamtam). Five of the works also use piano, an instrument which makes a fairly successful intrusion into modern orchestral scores. Harp is also used in the last five symphonies, an indication of a more romanticized concept of orchestral sound. Some scores also employ solo passages for various string instruments. The addition of the bass clarinet and contra-

---

* Alexander Werth, *Musical Uproar in Moscow* (London: Turnstile Press, 1944), p. 95.

bassoon to bass-line scoring in some of the symphonies adds a distinctive color to that line.

Prokofiev's concern is not always for color but more for clarity of line in his orchestral scoring. A special kind of heterogeneous bass-line doubling (mentioned below) gives the composer's bass parts a high degree of clarity. Strings, as in Tchaikovsky scores, are often doubled at the octave and the double octave for emphasis of lyric lines. There is not much divisi in string parts or expressive closely-voiced harmonic scoring for that section.

The composer's orchestral trademarks include use of the lower register of the trumpet in staccato passages which gravitate around one pitch, doubling of the bass line at the octave by lower strings and woodwinds (bass clarinet, bassoon, contrabassoon, viola, cello and contrabass), and piano and harp doubling of percussive chords or arpeggios. There is also a frequent doubling in instruments from unlike families where the basic texture is primarily two voices in free counterpoint. This device creates the impression of a much larger sound that the extremely lean and linear organization might actually produce.

Information on Individual Symphonies

Number	Key	Date	I	II	III	IV
1 *Classical*	D	1917	SA	ABA	Gavotte (SF w/trio)	Rondo
2	d	1924	SA	Variation		
3	C	1927	SA	ABA	Scherzo	SA
4	C(?)	1930	SA	ABA	Scherzo	SA
5	B-flat	1944	SA	Scherzo	ABA	SA
6	e-flat	1947	SA	SF w/trio	SA	
7	c-sharp (D-flat)	1952	SA	ABABA	ABA	ABA

SYMPHONY NO. 1

Prokofiev's first symphony is a remarkable work in its anticipation of the neoclassical turn of events in the early twentieth century. In spite of its classical transparency (Mozartian?), it anticipates many of the style devices which were to remain with Prokofiev for the balance of his life: ostinato, motor rhythm, angular melody, sudden and unexpected modulation, exploitation of the lower register of the trumpet, and others. It may be Prokofiev's most popular symphonic work other than *Peter and the Wolf*.

SYMPHONY NO. 2

This second symphony is one of the composer's more unusual works. It has only two movements, the second of which is an extended set of variations.

Prokofiev made an attempt in this symphony to appeal to the taste of Parisian audiences with an avant garde work. The first movement is particularly challenging and dissonant with angular themes, motor rhythms, polychords, tritones, minor seconds frequently employed in sonorities and ostinato after ostinato. Harmonic support in the first movement often sounds like indeterminate webs of sound which may have been drawn from the impressionist sonority concept. Brass instruments are emphasized. The six variations vary in tempo and mood. The fourth, fifth, and sixth variations are particularly complex.

SYMPHONY NO. 3

Many of the materials of this symphony may have been drawn from Prokofiev's opera *The Flaming Angel*.* The first theme of the work is associated with the heroine's love for her Angel, Madiel. The subordinate theme is representative of the Knight Ruprecht. The development section is based in part on an entr'acte in Act III. A passage (rehearsal numbers 56–64) which is based on a single sonority is typical of impressionist scores. The third movement, a scherzo, emphasizes orchestral color, unlike any of the other symphonies. One passage (rehearsal numbers 91–95) is a mass of string glissando and multisubdivision inspired by the finale (funeral march) in Chopin's second piano sonata. This passage represents the heroine's conjuring up of the Angel in the opera. The orchestral setting between rehearsal numbers 110 and 115 is strikingly similar to Ravel's orchestral style. The final cadence of the third movement is typically Prokofiev, resolving a sudden leading tone in C major after considerable digression in the final phrases. The finale restates themes from previous movements, ending with another abrupt cadence: an altered leading-tone seventh, B–D (D-sharp)–F–A-flat, resolving to a first inversion tonic chord (no fifth), C–E.

SYMPHONY NO. 4

Some of the materials for the symphony were supposedly drawn from the composer's ballet *The Prodigal Son*.† The first movement has a short introduction which leads to a typical motor rhythm *Allegro* section. This motor rhythm dominates most of the first movement. The music of the homecoming of the son was used for the second movement, quite contemporary in its melodic and harmonic structures (for 1930 Prokofiev). There is some emphasis on diatonic materials with linear relationships between parts. The scherzo is in five parts (S–T–S–T–S). Winds receive considerable attention in the scoring.

---

* Boris Schwarz, *Music and Musical Life in Soviet Russia, 1917–1970* (New York: W. W. Norton & Company, Inc., 1972), p. 196.

† Schwarz, *Music and Musical Life in Soviet Russia*, p. 196.

SYMPHONY NO. 5

See below.

SYMPHONY NO. 6

The style of the sixth symphony is less involved texturally and harmonically but better thought-out tonally than previous works. Each theme of the first movement is followed by a genuine development of the theme. A marchlike interlude opens and closes the development section. The *Largo* second movement has a two-dimensional theme similar to that employed by Beethoven. The first is primarily a slowly moving rhythmic theme built around a single pitch. The second is a more lyric and expressive melody. The final third movement quotes from previous movements in its coda. The main theme is reminiscent of the *Classical* Symphony in its Haydn-like construction and motor rhythm.

SYMPHONY NO. 7

The formal layout of all four movements is extremely clear as the composer seems to revert to a simpler musical style. The simplicity is deceiving since many passages are organized in two-voice counterpoint. The second movement, a waltz, exploits the sonority of the major seventh chord for the first theme. The third (slow) movement is expressive if traditional in its materials. A faint recall of the Brahms style can be noted in the figuring of the inner parts of a traditional harmonic passage associated with the first theme. The finale has a motor first theme, a slow march for the middle section, and a development of the first theme for its third section. In the coda themes B and C from the first movement reappear, followed quickly by a return to the opening tune of the finale which concludes the movement.

EXAMPLES FOR STUDY

Prokofiev: *Symphony No. 5 in B-flat Major*

In September of 1944 Prokofiev completed the piano score for the fifth symphony, playing it for the Central House of the Composers in October.* After his return to Moscow from Europe he set about to orchestrate the score, completing this by the end of the year. It had its premiere in Moscow on January 13, 1945. The work came as the fortunes of war for Russia had taken a turn for the better. Prokofiev's reaction to the end of the long and bitter struggle in the fifth symphony was more philosophical than openly programmatic. "The

---

* Israel V. Nestyev, *Prokofiev* (Stanford, Calif.: Stanford University Press, 1960), p. 350.

Fifth Symphony was intended as a hymn to free and happy Man, to his mighty power, his pure and noble spirit." *

I: Andante. The first movement's form is traditional in almost all respects except possibly tempo. The opening bars offer the principal theme, which is then developed briefly. The A² theme is an example of the bass-line unison doubling mentioned previously. In this instance the instruments involved are supplemented by horn and tuba with violas omitted. This is a very characteristic unison doubling. A more lengthy development of the principal material then ensues. Some of this is contrapuntal (measures 37–44), with both parts of the first tune alternating. The lyric secondary theme (B¹) is accompanied by a contrapuntal manipulation of spiraling chord members (tertian) which imply thirteenth chords (measures 54–61). The B² theme is set against a harmonic figure in the brass and piano which continues a contrapuntal application of harmony in a stream of chords, an effect that can be reduced to a basic two-voice texture (measures 74–81). The development section appears to be in five sections:

> *Section 1 (measures 92–102):* A¹ is restated in the tonic key (B-flat) and then in E-flat.
>
> *Section 2 (measures 103–20):* Themes A², B², and C are developed in that order. Motives from some of these themes are extracted and also moved about above another of these tunes.
>
> *Section 3 (measures 121–36):* Themes A² and C are placed in two-voice counterpoint with chords frequently punctuating phrase or motive endings. The passage emphasizes the C theme.
>
> *Section 4 (measures 137–50):* Theme B¹ is manipulated over fragments of C; A² appears. Much of the passage is in two-voice counterpoint.
>
> *Section 5 (measures 151–62):* This is another two-voice texture with the B¹ theme combined with the inverted and original forms of the A² theme. Some parts fill in harmony intermittently.

The development apparently includes a treatment of all themes of the exposition.

The recapitulation is similar to the exposition, returning all themes in the proper order. A coda which starts with a low pedal B-flat in the tuba and trombones is based on a variation of the A¹ theme.

---

* Schwarz, *Music and Musical Life in Soviet Russia,* p. 196.

Form:

	Exposition						Development		
A¹	A²	(A¹ , A² Dev.)	B¹	B²	C		Part 1	Part 2	Part 3
	29	33	54	73	83	92	103	121

			Recapitulation							
Part 4	Part 5		A¹	A²	(A¹ , A² Dev.)	B¹	B²	C
137	157	165	180	186	204	213	219	227

Coda
(A¹ Var.)
262

II: **Allegro marcato.** The second movement has strong motor characteristics in the ostinatolike pattern of the minor third (d-f) pattern of the accompaniment. The movement is in d minor. The quick modulation to F major in the third measure of the tune (see theme sheet below) shows the chromatic manipulation of pitches which Prokofiev had developed. Half-step motion is crucial to this particular harmonic style. At measure 33 a development of the initial theme begins, with the half-step motion continuing in the harmonic accompaniment. The middle section continues the motor quality of the movement but with a more lyric tune. The initial doubling is between clarinet and viola at the unison. At the conclusion of each initial phrase of B² an extension of some four bars (measures 126–29) follows. This extension has an interesting embellished harmonic pattern which implies an added sixth (measure 126) and a modified parallel harmonic structure, C-sharp major to c minor (measure 127). The passage has a ground bass (D, E, F-sharp, G, F-natural, E-flat) plus a tenor pedal on the dominant A. The pattern in the bass line shows the downward shifting of tonal materials by half step. The marchlike propulsion of the middle section seems characteristic of many similar march movements by Prokofiev. It is an essential mannerism in the style. The return of the first section is developmental, with the A¹ theme never quite stated in its original shape. The lower trumpet register is effective in this section. A coda which heightens the motor quality of the movement without strict thematic accountability closes the movement.

$$B^1$$ (Ob.,Cl.)

$$B^2$$ *p* (Cl.)

$$B^3$$ *mf* (W.W.) *mf*

$$B^4$$ *8va* *p* (Fl.,Piano,Harp)

Form: ‖	A^1	A^2	A^1—Dev.	A^2	A^3	A^1—Var. ^{1}	A^1—Var. ^{2} ‖	B^1	B^2	B^3
		23	33	51	56	69	82	112	120	141

B^4	B^1	B^{2-4} Dev.	B^1	A^1— Dev.	A^2	A^1— Var. ^{1}	A^3	A^1—Dev.
154	170	178	216	225	256	260	269	279

Coda

302   320

III: Adagio. After a three-bar vamp which vacillates between a major and minor tonic chord, a first tune starts, doubled at the double octave in the clarinet and bass clarinet. The third and fourth bars of the tune contain a soaring part which is set against a triplet counterpoint in a most expressive manner. This basic two-voice texture remains constant with the opening portion of the first theme. Gradually both the theme and the triplet counterpoint are doubled at the double octave, creating a depth to the section which disguises its basic two-voice texture. A return of the A^1 theme at measure 43 includes a pianoforte doubling (at the double octave) in the violins, violas, piccolo, and

English horn (measures 43–49). The passage is most expressive. A long middle section which develops three parts of the B theme contains both a lyric (B²) and a rhythmic (B¹) emphasis. There is a shortened return of the A section. A new theme (C) occurs in the coda. The final eight measures of the coda return to the dual-modality section which opened the movement.

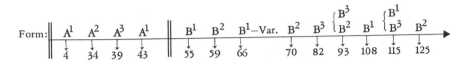

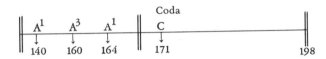

IV: Allegro giocoso. A twenty-two-measure introduction presents two themes, the first of which is to be part of the development section of the movement and the second a restatement of the IA[1] theme (first movement). The exposition proper starts with a motor accompaniment in the strings which will return in the final section of the coda as the primary unifying device. A solo clarinet presents the principal theme in measure 28. The section has been divided into three thematic groups (A[1], A[2], and A[3]). The A[3] theme is followed by a short cadence figure in eighth notes in measure 63, a motive that then appears as a part of the development section. The B section also has tripartite structure. The development starts immediately with a tonic statement of the A themes, creating a rondo effect. Very quickly Prokofiev adds a new theme (C) in measure 122. After a contrapuntal setting of the A[2] and the introductory ① motive, a new theme (D) is injected in a fugal passage (measures 164–89). It is at this point that the cadence figure noted in measure 63 appears in augmentation. The recapitulation is concise and nondevelopmental. The C theme opens the coda at measure 284 and is developed momentarily. The coda then moves into a more contrapuntal style, combining several of the themes from previous sections (see form chart below). The closing twenty-seven measures are built upon the motor accompaniment from the A[1] theme with two new motives placed above it. At measure 360 Prokofiev reduces the string section to a solo setting (one each of two violins, viola, cello, and bass) and then restores the orchestral tutti for the final measure and a half. Another half-step-derived cadence concludes the symphony.

SUMMARY

The fifth symphony of Prokofiev contains many of the primary style features of the composer's symphonies. The form is traditional and concise with at least one cyclic theme. Lyricism is prominent in almost all movements. Motivic extraction and development are also seen in several movements. The setting of two motives in a contrapuntal style occurs in two of the movements. This contrapuntal texture tends to use a two-voice freely contrapuntal style rather than a more complex procedure (imitation, etc.). Imitation is rare, with only one theme being treated in fugal style.

There is nothing particularly unique about Prokofiev's handling of the fifth symphony with these possible exceptions:

The broad, flowing style of the first movement (*Andante* rather than *Allegro*)
A fast dancelike second movement of an unknown folk origin
A finale quite typical of movements of folklike origin, in very rapid tempo with strong motor undercurrents

All of the Prokofiev symphonies share a fairly conservative creative style with the exception of the dissonant third symphony. They do not hold as unique a place in symphonic literature as do the works of Sibelius. Most of the symphonies are in the line of evolution begun by Beethoven and sustained by the conservative composers of the nineteenth century. The works are contemporary in some of the linear treatments of counterpoint and harmony. The orchestral treatment is individual and should be considered a vital part of the symphonic compositional style. Instrumental doubling is employed for coloristic purposes primarily to define individual lines more clearly or expressively. The individuality of the symphonies lies in the individual style of the composer rather than in any special symphonic treatment. The Prokofiev symphonies are important in symphonic history because they represent a continuation of the Beethoven tradition by a talented Russian composer who somehow managed to endure Soviet policies and still continue his individual handling of the symphony.

Dmitri Shostakovich (1906–1975)

Whereas Prokofiev spent his formative years in czarist Russia, the musical career of Shostakovich was dominated by the Soviet era in Russian history. Starting with a first symphony completely in sympathy with contemporary thought in the 1920s, the fifteen symphonies show quite well the effects of the pressures under which Shostakovich operated for most of his creative life.

Dmtri Shostakovich and Eugene Ormandy, conductor of the Philadelphia Orchestra, confer during the composer's visit to the United States in 1959. Ormandy and the Philadelphia Orchestra have issued an impressive number of Shostakovich symphony recordings. Courtesy the Philadelphia Orchestra.

These pressures . . . forced him to become increasingly self-conscious . . . and undermined his musical confidence. More vulnerable than many composers . . . Shostakovich suffered increasingly from a kind of split focus in his output. On the one hand, the symphonies up to No. 4 continued the stylistic trends of the earlier works, though progressively adding to the density and inflation of resources. On the other hand, a group of much smaller works contradicted this tendency by concentrating on linear writing, cool neoclassic forms, and succinct understatement.*

It is possible to categorize his symphonic output on the basis of this duality of style.

Shostakovich's symphonies can thus be divided into two groups: the "progressive" and more contemporary works, which include symphonies 1, 4, 5, 6, 9, 10, 13, 14, and 15, and the more expansive and inflated "Russian" works, which include symphonies 2, 3, 7, 8, 11 and 12.

The progressive works all differ and could not be considered representative of one basic style. They all, however, avoid the expanded rhetoric and the pro-

---

* Norman Kay, *Shostakovich* (London: Oxford University Press, 1971), p. 20. By permission of Oxford University Press.

grammatic connotations often required of the Russian works. If one were to extract the more experimental works from the above listing, symphonies, 1, 10, 13, and 15 would probably be the best examples. The fourth symphony is influenced considerably by Mahler and uses one of the composer's largest orchestras. What is suggested is that each symphony must be related to the political climate at the time of its composition to understand the basic nature of the work's style (its relatively progressive or Russian character). As this political climate moderated or became more hostile the style of the symphonies adjusted to Soviet expectations. The tenth symphony's more progressive style conformed with the relaxation of national tensions after the death of Stalin that same year (1953). The last three symphonies also mirrored the growing independence of the creative artist in Russia, in the 1960s and 1970s.

The chart of individual movement forms shows that the composer liked slow opening movements. He often placed the scherzo movement as the second movement. Only seven of the fifteen works are in four movements. Two have only three movements. Two are in one movement (with a sectional design). There are three five-movement symphonies. The fourteenth symphony has eleven short movements. Two of the early symphonies use choral resources. Two of the last works use choral and/or vocal soloist components. Several of the works connect movements by either a score direction ("attaca"), or an actual music connection (sustained chord, repeated rhythmic figure, or continuing theme). Style mannerisms vary with the work. In the more complex works, linear writing is quite typical. Melodic style is angular and widely spaced by extreme leaps. Motivic writing is also typical. Many of the symphonies open with a slow-moving melody in the bass instruments. Some of the themes of slow movements are long and spun-out. Russian folk tunes or revolutionary songs appear in the Russian works. Many of the finale movements adhere to the festive nature of most of the finales in symphonies by Russian composers. The melodic device of the ostinato is present in almost all symphonies as a primary device for organizing the undergirding of sections. Melodies are generally diatonic with the exception of the thirteenth and fourteenth symphonies, where there is some evidence of serial melodic writing.

The harmonic style varies from conservative and functional to completely linear. The Russian works use a simple harmonic style, mostly functional with diatonic materials. The progressive works tend to use functional harmony as a starting point and then move into more linear and dissonant procedures. The last three works show use of the half step as the harmonic generating interval in some sections. The use of quartal harmony can be noted in the first symphony as well as in the more neoclassically oriented works (symphonies 6, 10, 13, and 14). The basic tonality of most of the works is minor; most symphonies end in the tonic major key.

The texture of the symphonies also bears a relationship to the basic style of the works. Counterpoint is an important ingredient in all symphonies but especially in the more progressive works. Symphonies 9 and 14 both emphasize pure linear writing to a much greater extent than in earlier works. Comments on individual symphonies will emphasize several contrapuntal devices the composer used frequently. Extended imitative writing is not one of those devices. Canon can be seen as vital to the style. Free polyphonic writing is even more important. Ostinato bass lines and ostinato harmonies are typical of the textural style.

Orchestration uses subdivision of strings frequently in slow movements. Choir separation is retained except for coloristic doubling (bass woodwinds plus bass strings, etc.). Several instruments receive more emphasis than in scores by past composers: xylophone, piano, snare drum, harp (especially harmonics), piccolo, and solo trumpet. In final movements the martial effect frequently requires the prominence of brass and percussion instruments. String tremolo in the support voices of a passage is also most typical. The typical orchestra contains woodwinds in pairs (plus E-flat clarinet and contrabassoon), four horns, three trumpets, three trombones, and tuba. The percussion section is usually quite large, employing xylophone (and sometimes vibraphone in later works) and traditional percussion instruments of great variety. Harp is used in most of the scores. Celeste appears in some of them.

Information on Individual Symphonies

No.	Date	Key	I	II	III	IV	V
1	1925	f	SA	Scherzo	ABA	SA	
2	1927	C	One movement with five internal sections; fifth section with chorus				
3	1930	E-flat	One movement with chorus				
4	1936	C	Sectional	ABA	Sectional		
5	1937	d	SA	ABA	SA	SA	
6	1939	b	ABA	Scherzo	Rondo		
7	1941	C	SA	Scherzo	ABA	SA (abridged)	
8	1943	C	SA	March	Scherzo	Passacaglia	Rondo
9	1946	E-flat	SA	ABAB	Scherzo	Recitative	Sonata-rondo
10	1953	e	SA	Scherzo	Hybrid	Rondo	
11 (*1905*)	1957	g	Palace Square	Jan. 9	In Memoriam	Tocsin	
12	1961	d	Revolutionary Petrograd	Razliv	Aurora	Dawn of Humanity	
13 (*Babi Yar*)	1962	b-flat	Babi Yar	Humor	In the Grocery	Fears	Career
14	1969		Eleven short movements with solo bass and soprano on poems of death				
15	1971	A	SA	ABA	Scherzo	ABA	

SYMPHONY NO. 1

Shostakovich's first symphony is one of his most contemporary works. Written when he was only nineteen years old, the work immediately placed him in a position of prominence in Russia.

I: Allegretto. The movement has a long introduction (fifty-seven measures), two of the introductory themes being treated in the development. The recapitulation does not regroup these earlier themes. The work has serial tendencies: the first three bars of the work contain eleven of the twelve tones (only A is missing). The first tune of the *Allegretto* (measure 42) is built from segments of the first nine pitches of another row. The principal theme of the movement (measure 58) contains all twelve pitches. A basic tonality of f minor undergirds this chromatic tune. A meter change (from 4/4 to 3/4) accompanies the introduction of the secondary theme.

II: Allegro. This scherzo movement also dabbles with serial principles: the first tune in the clarinet covers eleven of the twelve pitches of another row. The treatment is also in segments (see measures 3–6). When the true principal theme enters (measure 14), the serial properties all but disappear. The principal tune is related to the themes in the introduction. The repetition of the first tune is in the piano, a relatively new instrument in the symphony. The trio is built over a tremolo E in the violins and reverts to traditional 3/4 meter. A short canon (six measures) concludes the trio. The return of the scherzo is more developmental than before.

III: Lento. Shostakovich's unique melodic style, which is characterized by wide leaps, makes an early appearance in this movement.

IV: Lento, etc. One of the third-movement themes reappears in the introduction. The movement has no recapitulation. An *Adagio* coda uses the fourth movement's subordinate theme and the previously quoted third movement theme.

SYMPHONY NO. 2

This work is in one large movement. The instrument portion of the work divides itself into four separate sections which approximate movements of a symphony. The fifth section is a choral movement based on a poem by Alexander Bezymensky (1898–   ) which glorifies the October (1917) Revolution. The opening section is an extended introduction of dissonant string sonorities, which shows that the composer was still able to experiment with newer sounds. The fifth section is noted for its use of a factory whistle. The choral finale features considerable unison and two-voice singing. The final coda shows an influence of Ravel.

SYMPHONY NO. 3

This is another one-movement symphony scored with chorus which also subdivides into sections. The symphony's subtitle, "First of May," commemorates the May Day national celebration in the Soviet Union. For some reason Shostakovich did not develop his materials to any great extent but rather moved into new themes once a tune had been fully stated. There are about fifteen themes associated with the multiple sections.

SYMPHONY NO. 4

Mahler's influence is the strongest in this work of all of the fifteen symphonies. Movements are quite long; contrasts are somewhat emotional in nature; the ländler is apparent in the second movement; the forms are basically extended rondolike conglomerations. The orchestra is one of the composer's largest. Shostakovich withdrew the work during its first rehearsal and reworked it for its premiere in 1962. It is generally more dissonant than many other works written prior to 1950, especially the fifth symphony. All of its three movements are connected without pause. The first movement starts with a marchlike section, passes through a waltz for strings, a woodwind toccata, a string fugue, and a typical Russian gallop using one of the composer's favorite rhythmic ostinato devices (𝅘𝅥𝅯𝅘𝅥𝅯𝅘𝅥 𝅘𝅥𝅯𝅘𝅥𝅯𝅘𝅥 𝅘𝅥𝅯𝅘𝅥𝅯𝅘𝅥 𝅘𝅥𝅯𝅘𝅥𝅯𝅘𝅥). The second movement appears to be in ABA form. Its second tune also uses a chordal ostinato of a simple nature with another rhythmic pattern (𝅗𝅥 𝅘𝅥𝅮𝅘𝅥𝅮 | 𝅗𝅥 𝅘𝅥𝅮𝅘𝅥𝅮 | 𝅗𝅥 𝅘𝅥𝅮𝅘𝅥𝅮). The finale returns to the sectional design of the opening movement with at least five sections which do not appear to be interrelated. Another waltz section occurs, this time more a scherzo in which the bassoon provides a familiar ostinato pattern: 𝅘𝅥 𝅘𝅥𝅮𝅘𝅥𝅮 | 𝅘𝅥 𝅘𝅥𝅮𝅘𝅥𝅮 . The final section has an extended chorale-like theme for brass with an underlying timpani ostinato. The work closes in c minor with the celeste or glockenspiel adding a sixth and a ninth to the final chord.

SYMPHONY NO. 5

See discussion beginning on page 309.

SYMPHONY NO. 6

This work represents a continuation of the concise formal style of some of the Shostakovich works (symphonies 1 and 5). It is in three separate movements, none of which are in developmental form.

I: Largo. The first movement is basically contrapuntal in style; the opening unison passage contains most of the motives for the rest of the movement. A secondary theme in measure 19 is derived from the first theme. A minor third motive from the opening of the first theme then becomes the nucleus for the middle section. The triplet rhythmic style of the first and final sections contrasts with the duple, more rhapsodic style of the middle section. The major-minor third quandary noted in the works of Sibelius and Vaughan Williams continued to intrigue composers—even Shostakovich, as seen in this symphony.

II: Allegro. The middle movement is another virtuosic scherzo similar in style to other scherzo movements. Incessant rhythmic activity and ostinato lines remain characteristic of Shostakovich scherzos.

III: Presto. The light-hearted and somewhat satirical style of the composer continues in this fast-moving finale. Satire is nowhere better seen than in the final cadence, where Shostakovich reversed the order of the typical scale formula for a cadence from 6–7–8 to 7–6–8 (see the final ten measures of the movement).

SYMPHONY NO. 7

During World War II this work became symbolic of the Russian struggle against the Germans. In fact, Shostakovich replaced the development section of the first movement with an extended passage wherein a new theme, representing the German invader, is repeated over a dozen times. One quote, while not as indicative of the author's musical insight as of his humor, should be noted:

> Of the three wartime symphonies conceived as a trilogy, it is the "Leningrad," his Seventh (1941), that has come in for the most savage mauling. Its seventy minutes inspired Ernest Newman's quip that to find its place on the musical map one should look along the seventieth degree of longitude and the last degree of platitude.[*]

---

[*] Robert Layton, "Dmitri Shostakovich," in *The Symphony*, ed. Robert Simpson, 2 vols. (London: Penguin Books, 1966–67), II:208. Quoted with permission of publisher.

The work was used extensively during World War II and has since fallen from favor. Its style is a return to the gigantic orchestral style of the fourth symphony and thus seeks to address itself to the masses. The orchestra is large, as said before, and requires extra brass: three more trumpets, four more horns, and three more trombones. As in some previous scores, the composer specifies a minimum-maximum string complement (e.g., violin I: 16–20). The composer spoke quite openly of the programmatic content of the work. The first movement represents the peaceful existence of Russia prior to Nazi invasion; the "substitute" development section (a set of eleven variations on a new theme) seeks to describe the Nazi invasion as seen through the eyes of many Soviet authorities. The recapitulation changes the style of the opening themes, becoming more reflective and pathetic than before.

> Ordinary people honor the memory of heroes. At first I wanted words here. . . . I managed without a text. . . . Music expresses everything more strongly.*

Each subsequent movement depicts the siege of Leningrad and its effect on the Russian people. The finale is a typical Russian festive finale with an emphasis on bombastic effect. The style of the work is more simplified than that of most previous symphonies. The theme-and-variation section in the opening movement is placed in E-flat major, contrasting with the tonic C major. The variations are actually little more than simple repetitions of the theme, each in a different instrumental garb. An incessant snare drum ostinato of a military style undergirds the entire section. The theme of the variations appears briefly in the recapitulation. The second movement starts in simple two-voice style, with each repetition of the theme adding another voice until four are available. The contrapuntal texture is erected from essentially diatonic melodies and ostinatolike chordal accompaniments. The finale is more sectional but retains a relationship with sonata-allegro in spite of its combining the exposition with the development. The finale, as other movements, is quite extended in length.

SYMPHONY NO. 8

This work is the middle work of the wartime trilogy. It is in five movements with an opening slow movement, three middle movements all in march style, and a final rondo. The third march (fourth movement) is a passacaglia with twelve repetitions of the ground bass theme. The work also has the same programmatic foundations as did the seventh symphony.

---

* James Bakst, *A History of Russian-Soviet Music* (New York: Dodd, Mead, 1966), p. 322. Quoted with permission of the publisher.

SYMPHONY NO. 9

Shostakovich returns to a more classically oriented style to create a short five-movement work similar in many respects to the Prokofiev *Classical* Symphony. The orchestration is reduced to woodwinds in pairs, four horns, two trumpets, three trombones, tuba, a modest percussion section (including two timpani), and strings. The movements are in concise forms with the exception of the fourth, which appears to be an introductory recitative for bassoon connecting instrumentally with the finale. The final three movements are played without pause. In the first movement, the secondary theme is set as a march tune. The exposition is repeated according to classical traditions. A coda continues the development of both themes. The second movement starts as one of the composer's lean two-voice contrapuntal slow movements with a lyric tune above a sparse bass line (with some ostinato features). As the section progresses an additional line is added to make a two-voice contrapuntal experiment above the bass. Finally a third set of voices is added in parallel fifths. The middle section is completely homophonic but uses parallel triadic structures (all minor triads) in its first phrase in an ascending chromatic pattern, with the second phrase descending in minor triads also. The scherzo is a wildly fast dance with a trio which features a solo trumpet over an ostinatolike string accompaniment. The bassoon recitative of the fourth movement vacillates between major and minor on some of the thirds in the melody. As the finale gathers strength in its opening measures, the bassoon states the first tune and then retires to allow the strings to carry the burden. The coda accelerates to a fast *Allegro,* making the movement similar to other festive finales by the composer. The symphony ranks with the composer's best orchestral works.

SYMPHONY NO. 10

The tenth symphony has become known in some quarters as Shostakovich's best symphony. Its structure retains much of the lyric element of the earlier works and yet shows an internal organization very concise and articulate, much like the mature works of composers like Sibelius and Vaughan Williams. The work was written in 1953, "the year of Stalin's death, and perhaps owes some of its outstanding qualities to the anticipation of a more liberal atmosphere in Russia." * The slow first movement is based on three themes, two of which are announced in the introduction, the second actually the subordinate theme. Each theme is developed as presented. The development section combines portions of these themes quite skillfully. Much of the movement is contrapuntal.

---

* Norman Key, *Shostakovich,* p. 48.

The scherzo falls in the second movement and is one of the composer's most brilliant and difficult scherzos. The trio is constructed in parallel thirds above a drone or ostinato bass, all still quite fast. The third movement is moderately slow (*Allegretto*) and seems to mimic a waltz tempo. Its form is a hybrid of part form and song form with trio. The introduction to the finale contains fragments of themes which follow and contains the recitativelike wind solos which preface many of the Shostakovich movements. The climax of the movement proper is on the pitches D, E-flat, C, and B; the pitch names representing the composer's initials (from the German terminology: D, Ess or S, C, and H) and first three letters of his last name. This motto theme occurs in many of his works. The ensuing coda brings back themes from previous movements and develops the name-motto to some extent. The typical frantic (festive?) closing occurs. This time, however, it is accomplished much more effectively, since thematic material and tonal resources are much better worked out and related than in some earlier works. The symphony is one of his most contemporary efforts.

SYMPHONY NO. 11

Shostakovich returns to the programmatic aspect of his symphonic writing in the eleventh symphony, selecting the abortive 1905 revolution for the commemorative work entitled *The Year 1905*. The scene is the palace square in St. Petersburg, where a small uprising culminated with the imperial troops' firing on the demonstrating crowd. This date, January 9, is also known as "Bloody Sunday" in Soviet history. The second movement seeks to describe this conflict in an elongated fashion which is primarily sectional in form. The main theme of the third movement ("In Memoriam") is extracted from a revolutionary song of the period, "You Fell, Victims." The finale draws upon four revolutionary songs: "Rage, Tyrants," "Varshavyanka," "March Bravely in Step, Comrades," and "Uncover Your Head." The symphony does not have any relevance for non-Soviet audiences and subsequently has not gained many performances outside of Russia proper.

SYMPHONY NO. 12

This follows the same pattern as that in the eleventh symphony. It is dedicated to Lenin. The subtitle of the work is *The Year of 1917*. Each of the movements has significance in relation to the October Revolution. The first movement generally follows the outline of sonata-allegro form. All movements are connected and are performed without pause. The work is not a part of symphony repertory in this country.

SYMPHONY NO. 13

This symphony is a setting of five poems (1961) by Yevgeny Yevtusenko, the first entitled "Babi Yar." Babi Yar was a large ravine near Kiev where the Germans held many Russian prisoners during World War II. In September of 1941, the Germans executed over 34,000 Ukrainian Jews at Babi Yar. Later, in August or September of 1943, when the tide of battle turned, the Germans attempted to conceal their slaughter by destroying the camp, burning all of the corpses in gas ovens, and scattering the ashes near Babi Yar.* Yevtushenko's poem not only speaks about the massacre but points out the lingering anti-Semitism in Russia today. The second poem (and movement) relates how difficult it is to kill humor. "Czars, kings . . . commanded parades . . . but humor they could not." The third poem recalls the Soviet exploitation of women. The fourth poem, "Fears," tells of the power of fear in the past. "Fears, like shadows, slithered about everywhere . . . bit by bit they tamed the people. . . ." While Russia was losing its fears, the fears of the past were hard to forget. The final poem, "Career," asserts that a genius should not compromise his career. The composer's setting is with male chorus and bass solo. The musical resources are the composer's most radical since the tenth symphony, descriptive, colorful, but biting in the support of the satirical poetry. The work could become a masterpiece except for its somewhat limited relevance. It ranks with the composer's very best works.

SYMPHONY NO. 14

Completed in 1969, the work set eleven poems about death in a very modern style, at times reminiscent of the early atonal works of Schoenberg and Webern. The poems are from the works of Frederic García Lorca (1898–1936), Guillaume Apollinaire (1880–1918), Wilhelm Küchelbecker (1797–1846), and Rainer Maria Rilke (1875–1926). The work shows traces of serialism, is quite linear, and, above all, is highly expressive of the concept of death shown in most of the poetry. The scoring is for a chamber ensemble of ten violins (I and II, divisi); four violas, divisi; three cellos, divisi; two basses, divisi; plus an impressive battery of percussion instruments: vibraphone, xylophone, tamtam (three), woodblock, etc. Most of the movements are linear in conception, often employing a lean two- or three-voice contrapuntal texture. One of the greatest surprises in the score is a marvelous *col legno* fugue in four voices in the seventh movement ("At the Sante Jail"). Harmonic entities are reminiscent of Bartók at times, with the half step the frequent generating interval in many of the sonorities. Triads appear in some of the more conservative texts. The

---

* *Great Soviet Encyclopedia,* 3rd ed., English translation (1973), s.v. "Babi Yar."

final chord of the symphony is a d minor triad with an added D-flat and A-flat. The symphony is undoubtedly one of the composer's masterpieces, even though it is not in essence a true symphony but more a song cycle scored for strings and percussion.

SYMPHONY NO. 15

Shostakovich, in this work, returns to the traditional outline of the symphony and to the more concise style of the classically oriented symphonies. The orchestra is reduced to woodwinds in pairs and a reduced brass section (four horns, two trumpets, three trombones, and tuba). The percussion section remains large (woodblock, xylophone, vibraphone, etc.). Shostakovich quotes from a variety of sources in this last work. The *Vivace* theme from Rossini's *William Tell* overture becomes the focal point of the first movement. The *Adagio* quotes from the eleventh symphony. The scherzo uses the D, E-flat, C, B (DSCH) motive. The opening of the finale quotes the "Fate" motive from Wagner's *Ring* cycle. The symphony retreats somewhat from the ultralinear basis of the fourteenth symphony, the half step as the primary harmonic interval, and the ultraexpressive nature of the song cycle on death. The final three symphonies, only one of which is a true orchestral symphony, best illustrate Shostakovich's return to the experimental style of his first symphony.

EXAMPLES FOR STUDY

Shostakovich: *Symphony No. 5 in d minor*

In 1934 Shostakovich produced his new opera, *Lady Macbeth of Mtzensky,* in Leningrad. For reasons never fully explained, in a *Pravda* editorial following its 1936 performance in Moscow, Soviet authorities totally rejected the work as being the product of a composer who was "a disciple of foreign modernists and a propagandist of morbid naturalism." * Having thus fallen from favor, the young composer sought to reestablish his credentials by writing a work which would follow Soviet style guidelines. The fifth symphony seemingly accomplished that. The official decision to "restore" the composer was probably based on the supposed programmatic nature of the work, which Shostakovich described as an attempt to relate the work to the shaping of a man's character with a man's experiences, illustrated by the work's lyricism. The final movement, supposedly in its happier mood, portrays a hopeful ending as compared to the more tragic aspects of the opening movement. The work, however, backs

---

* "Shostakovich," *Baker's Biographical Dictionary of Musicians,* 5th ed., rev. Nicholas Slonimsky (New York: G. Schirmer, Inc., 1958), p. 1510.

away from the huge scoring and expansive style of the fourth symphony and returns to the more neoclassical flavor of the first symphony. In spite of the composer's explanation of the meaning of the symphony, it generally is not considered one of his programmatic works. It also does not match in some respects the progressive quality of the first, tenth, and last three symphonies. In America it is probably the composer's most popular symphony.

I: Moderato. As do many of the composer's symphonies, the fifth starts with a slow movement. The first theme, as is often the case, is placed in the bass instruments. It is also in canon. A motive is extracted from A^1 to become the ostinato rhythm for the underlying accompaniment of A^2. Both the A^2 and A^3 themes have extended lyric lines in addition to a certain motivic integrity. After a brief development of some of the principal themes the subordinate section begins with a complete contrast of texture and melodic style. A harmonic ostinato stressing the tonality of e-flat minor accompanies a slowly moving B^1 theme, a tune with exaggerated and wide skips. As the theme concludes, the composer evolves (measure 74) another motive (B^2 motive below) which becomes part of the B^2 theme. A return to the first portion of the subordinate material closes the exposition. The development section begins with the B^2 motive being announced in the lower strings and piano. This section of the symphony divides itself into ten small segments, none as clearly as those sections noted in works by Sibelius and others.

I (120–39):   The A^2 theme is scored in the lower register of the horns over the B^2 motive in the lower strings and piano.

II (140–47):   The woodwinds play the A^4 tune over the B^2 motive in the strings and piano.

III (148–56): The $A^4 + A^4$ counterpoint is combined into a continuous theme and used in a slightly different imitative texture in the strings and woodwinds.

IV (157–67):   A new ostinato or rhythmic figure in the trumpets enhances the martial quality of the section. These themes appear in order: B^1, A^4 counterpoint, and A^1.

V (168–79):   Another new ostinato is drawn from a motive of A^4 (♩♫ ♫♩ ♩♫ ♫) over which the A^1 and B^1 themes are stated. Again the trumpets play the ostinato. The A^2 theme in canon concludes this section.

VI (180–87):   A spinning-out of the A^4 counterpoint motive (inverted) occurs.

VII (188–201):   The ostinato rhythm from measures 168–79 returns in the snare drum with a march version of A^2 above it. A new second portion of the theme is evolved.

VIII (202–16): A^4 opens this section in the woodwinds and strings, unison, followed by an extended treatment of the A^1 theme above the marchlike ostinato from the previous section. The A^1 theme retains its canonic structure. In measure 208 the A^2 theme appears in augmentation.

IX (217–42):   The woodwinds and strings combine to present a web of support based on the A^1 theme, again retaining the canonic format. The brass then enter with the B^1 theme in canon, all over the accompaniment provided by the woodwinds and strings.

X (243–52):   An extended climactic section is based on the A^3 theme; this passage could be interpreted as the beginning of the recapitulation. In some respects Shostakovich combined both development and recapitulation between measures 217 and 256.

The recapitulation is brief, with only a portion of the principal material appearing. The secondary material is also shortened. The coda reverts to some of the developmental concepts by placing the A^4 theme above an ostinato-like accompaniment drawn from the A^1 motive.

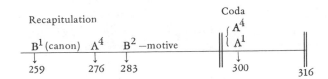

II: **Allegretto.** The scherzo movement is generally the second movement in the Shostakovich four-movement symphonies. The structure of this scherzo is traditional: a large three-part form with a triolike middle section. The texture is basically homophonic. The trio uses reduced orchestral forces and tends to develop material to a greater extent than does the scherzo proper.

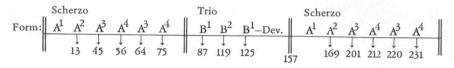

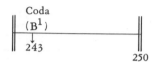

III: Largo. The principal material of the slow movement is set for sub-divided strings in eight parts. A portion of this section assumes contrapuntal dimensions (measures 8–11). A motive is extracted from the second and third measures of the first theme to be used with some degree of effectiveness later in the movement. The A^2 theme shows that the composer's harmonic style employs contrapuntal sonorities in a manner similar to that used by Vaughan Williams: a melody and bass line are enriched by a stream of parallel chords (in this case, major triads) in the inner parts. The A^3 melody is supported by an arpeggiated unison passage in the harp under strict rhythmic organization akin to an ostinato. The subordinate theme (B) also has a similar presentation with only a pedal C (tremolo) supporting it. The development starts with the B theme stated up a half step but with the pedal shifted from C to G-sharp. The use of the harmonic interval of a third (major or minor) for the primary harmonic support of an extended section of the development section (measures 121–46) should be noted. The scoring of the pedal device is striking and shows two procedures. The first (measures 121–29) sustains the third in the clarinets, doubling at the unison in tremolo violas, divisi. This is also doubled at the unison and at the octave higher in piano, again tremolo. The second half of the passage (measures 130–46) doubles the thirds in two strings lines (violas, violins, etc.) at the unison, tremolo. This is then doubled at the unison in the clarinets, legato tremolo (fingered tremolo in winds). As this passage moves to its conclusion, the bassoons are added to the third at the unison (measure 142). Long passages of static harmony are characteristic of this section. In the recapitulation the A^3 theme returns transposed up a half step (both theme and ostinato). The B theme in its final statement has also been transposed from its original pitch level, this time the distance of the augmented fourth. The movement ends in F-sharp major.

IV: Allegro non troppo. The finale is another of Shostakovich's "festive" concluding movements which is short on organic growth and rationality and long on repetition and frenzy. Many of the finales of the composer's symphonies seem to follow this style. The development section treats only the B and C themes, using the first theme as a motive to accompany a new theme (C, measure 165). The recapitulation becomes more of a rush to conclusion rather than a true summing up of previous materials.

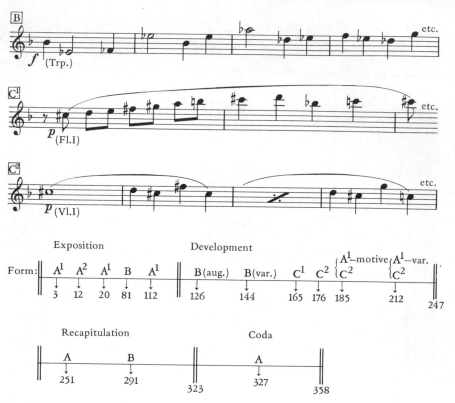

Used by permission of Kalmus Orchestral Scores, Inc.

SUMMARY

The fifth symphony exhibits both progressive and regressive style elements which can be related to the political climate in which Shostakovich worked. The style of the work is simpler than the more involved first symphony; it lacks many of the contrapuntal applications of the last three symphonies. It does, however, have concise forms and the symptoms of an underlying craft which related well to contemporary requirements. In view of the dual style which Shostakovich employed in his symphonies (usually not a duality within individual works), it is easy to see why he was able to survive as a composer of symphonies in Russia. As the political tensions between Russia and the Western world relaxed in the 1960s and 1970s, Shostakovich's symphonic style came close to closing the gap between himself and symphonists in other countries. The fifth symphony, written under the most rigid of political expectations for the art form, demonstrates how, without the overt folkloristic inclusion of traditional tunes, the composer would seek to keep the symphony a viable art form in the subsequent thirty-five years remaining in his creative life: by simplifying the overall style, relating some of the materials to the people of Russia (folk tunes, national subjects, folk rhythms, etc.), retaining melody as the paramount element in the music, and responding to relaxations in the political climate whenever possible in order to bring the musical style more into the musical mainstream of the rest of the modern world.

Stravinsky conducting a recording session with the Chicago Symphony Orchestra in the early 1960s. The principal cellist is Frank Miller, former NBC Symphony principal. Courtesy Chicago Symphony Orchestra.

Igor Stravinsky (1882–1971)

Although one of the three or four major composers of the twentieth century, Stravinsky did not elect to pursue the composition of the symphony with any degree of diligence even though he appended the name "symphony" to a number of his works. These works should be noted as part of his output:

Symphony in E-flat Major, Opus 1 (1908)
Symphonies of Wind Instruments (1920)
Symphony of Psalms (1930)
Symphony in C Major (1940)
Symphony in Three Movements (1946)

Of these works, only three are authentic symphonies. The five works fall within that period of creative activity in which the composer was generally writing in the neoclassical style. With the exception of the student symphony (E-flat Major), no symphonies were written outside of that period (1920–1954). The works in the expressionist period (1912–1919) and in the serial period (1955–1971) seem to avoid the form of the concert symphony. His *Movements for Piano and Orchestra* (1959) is the only work of a purely orchestral nature written during the final creative period.

Many of the neoclassical works by Stravinsky show the composer's constant searching for an older or historical basis for techniques or forms which can be applied in a more contemporary fashion. Some of this searching carries him back to the Renaissance (as in the *Symphony of Psalms*) or to the classical era (*Rake's Progress* and *Symphony in C*). The patterning of the exterior dimensions of the *Symphony in Three Movements* may imply this same reaching back into history for a model. The work's interior dimensions, however, depart from classical traditions by employing the same sectional forms used in the *Symphonies of Wind Instruments*. In spite of the four works' being associated with the neoclassical style, there is really no consistent symphonic style in this small output. Each work must be considered individually.

The tonal resources of the period are fairly diatonic, with functional cadences and harmonic progressions. Polychords are still evident, while the triad remains the most frequent sonority. Only the rhythmic style retains its uniqueness and for this reason maintains a line of continuity through the "classical" period works. Counterpoint is quite frequent, be it imitative or free counterpoint.

Only the first symphony seems to have a consistent orchestral style. The later works tend to keep instrumental choirs separate for most instances. Much of the writing is in the nature of chamber writing, with a limited number of instruments being employed at one time. The use of the piano in the *Symphony in Three Movements* to sustain important thematic (in this case, chords) material is significant. Stravinsky's three earlier ballet scores (*The Firebird*, 1910; *Petrouchka*, 1911; *The Rite of Spring*, 1912) enjoy wide popularity as general fare for symphony concerts. Their orchestral style is situated much more closely to that of the impressionists than is that of the Symphony in C and the *Symphony in Three Movements*. The three ballet scores require a much larger orchestra than does the more conservative scoring of the two symphonies—e.g., quadruple woodwinds and five trumpets in *Petrouchka* or the eight horns and five timpani in *Rites of Spring*. Orchestration in the three works evolves from a style quite similar to Rimsky-Korsakov's in its use of clarity and color, through the lushness and more subdued colors of the Debussy scores, and then to a more individual style in *The Rite of Spring*. Unusual doublings and increased tessitura demands contribute to this uniqueness.

Information on Individual Symphonies

Name	Date	Key	I	II	III	IV
Symphony in E-flat	1907	E-flat	SA	Scherzo	ABA	ABACABA
Symphony in C	1940	C	SA	ABA	Rondo	Sectional
Symphony in Three Movements	1946	C,D, D-flat	Sectional	ABA	Sectional	

SYMPHONY IN E-FLAT

Stravinsky completed this work in 1907 while he was still a private student of Rimsky-Korsakov. At that time Alexander Glazunov was the director of the St. Petersburg Conservatory and one of the leading Russian symphonists. He had completed his own eighth symphony in 1906. Glazunov's style is apparent in Stravinsky's first symphony, as is that of Tchaikovsky and Rimsky-Korsakov. The E-flat symphony is traditional in formal organization and tonal materials and gives little hint of the mature style of the young composer.

The first movement (*Allegro moderato*) has a two-measure principal theme which dominates most of the movement. Only in the accompaniment to the secondary tune can any indication be seen of some of the rhythmic or melodic devices to be used in later works. In this case the narrow range of the ostinatolike accompaniment might be considered related to similar usages in the years ahead. An occasional abrupt modulation occurs at the beginning of a phrase. In the first movement (rehearsal number 11) an F major dominant chord in B-flat major resolves to D-flat major, a deceptive progression which borrows a chord from the parallel minor key. This modulation to the mediant is characteristic of some Russian folk music.

The scherzo (*Allegretto*) is in a part form and resembles ballet music with its emphasis on simple melodic materials and regularity of meter and accent. The transition of the trio uses a harmonic ostinato figure of repeated sixteenth notes in the brass, which shows Stravinsky's early liking for this color in an ostinato figure. The trio tune is a Russian folk tune.

The *Largo* slow movement uses orchestral colors reminiscent of Tchaikovsky. The contrapuntal part-writing of the opening phrases may be indicative of polyphonic skills not yet fully exhibited in the early symphony. A horn countermelody at rehearsal number 2 places a dissonance on the first or accented beat of each measure, also similar to Tchaikovsky's handling of such a passage. Stravinsky placed another expressive horn countermelody between rehearsal numbers 19 and 20 in which every first beat of successive measures is accented by this dissonant effect. The third section (a return of the first section) is varied with the addition of a clarinet countermelody, again in the Tchaikovsky tradition.

The finale (*Allegro molto*) fits well into the Russian festive finale concept. The form is a simple rondo; the orchestration is colorful and includes much triangle ringing in the closing measures of the coda. Stravinsky includes another Russian folk tune between rehearsal numbers 13 and 14, marking its origin in Russian. Some of the cerebral things to come are indicated by the last twenty measures of the work. A figure in the second violins in eighth notes is stated simultaneously in quarter notes in the bass strings and then augmented into triplet half notes to continue the rush toward the final cadence. Though the cadence is plagal, the bass line implies dominant harmonies, one of the few passages where the composer is moving away from a very traditional tonal and harmonic style. The linear quality of the closing measures implies a static (or slow-moving) harmony as one line, with the bass line as the other melodic unit. Other than a few such adventuresome examples, the entire symphony fits well into the traditional confines of works by Glazunov and Tchaikovsky.

SYMPHONY IN C

This work is somewhat a parallel to Prokofiev's *Classical* Symphony in that it adopts the forms and some of the style features of Haydn's approach to the symphony. One particular motive dominates much of the first movement. A rush of eighth notes characteristic of the *style galant* is present in almost every measure of the first movement. The effect of adhering for the greater part to many of the style norms of the classical symphony while employing various individual devices of the composer (a multitude of rhythmic devices, frequent ostinato, parallel seconds in inner parts, etc.) is unique. The scherzo is rhythmically complex with frequent meter changes (2/8, 5/16, etc.). A short fugue concludes the coda of the movement. A finale in a sectional form which approaches rondo concludes the symphony with quotations of the first theme from the opening movement. The Haydn spirit of the opening movement with its rush of eighth notes is again manifest in the finale. The line of development from Haydn to the Symphony in C seems to be through Beethoven (1, 2, 4, and 8), Mendelssohn, and possibly Prokofiev. The work should enjoy more popularity than it does in this country. It is an excellent example of the neoclassical style.

EXAMPLES FOR STUDY

Stravinsky: *Symphony in Three Movements*

After the Symphony in C Stravinsky continued his preoccupation with the classic style by returning to the three-movement form of the early classical symphony. The orchestra is of mid-nineteenth-century dimensions with some exceptions: woodwinds in pairs (plus piccolo, bass clarinet, and contrabassoon), four horns, three trumpets, three trombones, tuba, timpani, bass drum, piano, harp, and strings.

I: ♩ = 160. The form of the opening movement is sectional, perhaps implying a free association of ideas. But the form is far from free: it is strictly organized through a tight control of texture, motive, ostinato, and (in some cases) sonority. This application of a nondevelopmental form in an instrumental milieu which traditionally has required developmental forms for a major portion of its movements represents a contribution by Stravinsky that should be noted. The work opens with an introduction which contains two short motives, both closely related to the other through the germinal motive of a descending minor third (A-flat, F). The main substance of the movement begins at measure 20 (rehearsal number 5) with the introduction of the first section of the multi-sectioned movement. This section (and each subsequent part of the A section) is organized around a single theme with an accompanying ostinato. The movement divides itself into three parts. The first part (A) has four basic sections, as noted below. The middle part has two sections, the first of which (B) stresses sixteenth-note activity. The second portion (C) of the middle section departs from sixteenth-note motion but still relies on several short passages tightly organized within themselves. The major second appears as the unifying interval in most of this section (measures 269–89). After a return to the sixteenth-note motion, the final third part of the movement begins at measure 336. This third section acts as an abbreviated recapitulation of the first two parts. One "theme" from the first part and one "theme" from the second part are included. A twenty-eight-measure coda, based on the material of the introduction, completes the movement. An ostinato figure in the bass instruments (and later, the bass clarinet) is extracted from the ostinato figure (B^1 ostinato) which accompanies the opening measures of the middle section of the movement. The movement ends on a C major triad.

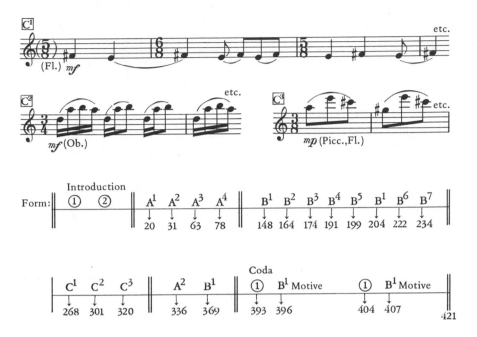

II: Andante. The structure of the middle movement is a simple ternary design (ABA). The materials of the movement are related to those of the first movement. The opening passage presents an accompaniment figure which contains both major and minor thirds on the tonic root (D). The middle section (measure 49) fits its primary thematic material within the interval of the major third. The second portion of the middle section uses the minor third for its melodic generating interval.

Interlude. This passage serves as an introduction to the third and final movement.

III: Con moto. The finale uses sectional form but without the strict interrelation of theme and ostinato noted in the first movement. A ternary organization of the first three primary sections is followed by a fugue on a subject which continues the major-second motive from previous movements. A coda also based on the major second concludes the movement. The movement ends on a D-flat major triad with both added sixth and ninth.

SUMMARY

Sectional, nondevelopmental form is often characteristic of the Stravinsky style. When applied to the symphony, sectional form tends to destroy the concept of musical line which characterized the symphony in the nineteenth and twentieth centuries. The many-sectioned movement forms employed represent a unique way of handling the twentieth-century symphony. Stravinsky's unique melodic style, which stressed rhythmic factors over pitch, at times produced an almost amelodic result characterized by terse rhythmic motives and extremely abbreviated pitch segments. Lyricism did not appear to be a primary goal in many works. A form constructed from short segments of sections, each organized within itself by snippets of rhythmic or pitch units, would appear to be an outgrowth of a melodic style which aspired to musical goals other than line. Thus the style may have fallen very naturally into a nondevelopmental sectional form which did not require extended themes and melodies that could be dissected in a subsequent developmental process. While the Symphony in C is patterned after the practices of classical composers, the *Symphony in Three Movements* returns to this unique concept of sectional form. It is this unusual combination of a symphonic form that implies developmental structures with Stravinsky's nondevelopmental procedures which gives this work its special place in the history of the symphony.

Paul Hindemith (1895–1963)

Most of the musical output of Paul Hindemith falls outside the medium of orchestral music. The majority of his works are either for small ensembles or for solo instruments. He wrote nine operas and a large number of works which he classified as *Gebrauchsmusik*, or music for use. Many orchestral works are concertos. He wrote three "pure" symphonies. Several other of his works he called symphonies, one a "symphonic metamorphosis," another "concert music." All were probably symphonies or symphonylike in his own eyes, since he often found it necessary to expand or adjust the definition of the concert symphony when creating his own works for orchestra.

Hindemith's style was influenced by Bach more than by any other single composer. His treatment of the symphony was conditioned by Brahms. Reger also influenced his general style to some extent. As Hindemith moved toward stylistic maturity, his music showed tendencies toward post-romanticism, impressionism, expressionism, neoclassicism, Gebrauchsmusik, and, finally, a return to neoromanticism. He, along with Stravinsky and Bartók, participated enthusiastically in the neoclassical movement of the 1920s and 1930s. Hindemith's woodwind quintet (Opus 24, No. 2) remains one of the prime examples of the neoclassical style even today.

His orchestral taste, however, ran more to the sensuous. As an orchestral performer and conductor, he could not resist the possibilities of the full ensemble and reacted in most of his orchestral works more as a romanticist, particularly in scoring. None of his works are in the classical tradition.

Hindemith's harmonic idiom was codified in his theoretical writings. Assaying sonority as a chemist would compounds, he established classifications of chords based on intervallic content. In his own works he gravitated in general toward the use of mild dissonances (no tritones, minor seconds, and major sevenths). His useful vocabulary includes quartal and triadic chords and chords of coloration (chords with added notes). Since the basic style is linear, resultant sonorities can vary from open fifths to complex sonorities (according to Hindemith's classification system).

The melodic style is based more on major and minor seconds than on wide skips. Narrow skips are frequent, especially fourths. Skips of successive fourths without a change of direction were the same to him as skipping up a triad outline. While he used the entire chromatic scale for his tunes, he did this in a nonchromatic way. As a result the works sound diatonic or, often, modal.

His sense of tonality was conservatively chromatic. The key feeling within a work is quite strong, created primarily through emphasis and final cadences. He did not employ traditional key signature but wrote tonally in all of his works. Almost every work ends in a tonic triad, usually major.

The primary style feature is textural; he was essentially a contrapuntal composer. His admiration for J. S. Bach and other contrapuntal composers led him into a type of neoclassicism which stressed linear writing. In this way he maintained a polarity between the upper melody and the bass line, very much in the baroque tradition. His fugal writing may encompass three or four imitative lines. Often, however, only two lines will be involved in imitative devices while the other inner parts either supply needed harmonic material or freely move about. At times the inner parts are figured, as in the nineteenth-century tradition of freely implying counterpoint in the "stimulated" inner parts rather than actually writing it. His impressionistic period contributed a share of parallelism, often fifths or thirds but sometimes entire sonorities. Some of these chord streams participate as a single melody in a polyphonic texture. He tended to mix parallelism, polyphony, and homophony in a single passage.

His orchestral style is Germanic. Like Brahms and other German composers, he favored doubling rather than the Russian practice of separation into choirs. Hindemith liked the brass instruments and thus scored heavily for them. Some of his writing for the B-flat trumpet is the most demanding in symphonic literature because of the upper range required. His scoring for the string section was often for a single instrument with extended passages in unison or octave doubling for the entire section (except the contrabass). While he often decried orchestral effect for effect's sake, he used solo winds repeatedly in his symphonies both in presenting and in varying materials. As far as can be determined he consistently avoided only one instrument: the harp.

Hindemith's symphonic style is difficult to categorize. In some respects he wrote only three symphonies: the Symphony in E-Flat, the *Symphonia Serena*, and the *Pittsburgh* Symphony. Of these only the E-flat symphony tends to be an authentic four-movement work. The *Serena*, according to the composer, is more a concerto grosso. The *Pittsburgh* is a three-movement work which employs borrowed tunes in two of its movements. The *Symphonic Metamorphosis on Themes by Carl Maria von Weber* is based almost entirely on borrowed tunes but does have four movements. *Mathis* and *Harmonie*, both in three movements, are based upon materials from operas. The *Concert Music for Strings and Brass*, one of his most popular orchestral scores, has only two movements. Thus one would have to group the output as follows: one concert-symphony in four movements, one symphony-concerto in four movements, one four-movement symphony based on themes by Weber, two three-movement opera-symphonies, one three-movement symphony using Pennsylvania traditional tunes, one two-movement symphonylike work for strings and brass, and one chamber symphony. Hindemith did not number his "symphonies" as "No. 2" or the like. He gave them frank titles which generally mirrored their true nature or derivation. He wrote three of the works on direct commissions, two he evolved from opera scores, and the rest came about for reasons unknown. Rather than following any plan to evolve gradually as a symphonist, Hindemith adjusted, modified, and (sometimes) created legitimate concert symphonies. More important, however, than his unique definition of a symphony was the internal structure of the works he did write. Of the works included in this study relatively few of the movements are in sonata-allegro form. A number are in part forms. Contrapuntal and variation forms are used in four movements. Developmental form, the essential and basic movement form in the symphony, is used in only 18 percent of the movements. One must then conclude that the symphony for Hindemith was not a work which required him to respect symphonic traditions but was one which allowed his individual preference for nonsymphonic forms to prevail.

His hesitancy to write a large number of four-movement concert symphonies may have been aided by his primary interest in linear writing and baroque forms and by his practicality in scoring works for chamber or solo instruments. While he failed to establish a Hindemith symphonic tradition of the same order as that of Vaughan Williams, Shostakovich, or Sibelius, he did leave works of admirable craft and interesting variety which could enrich orchestral programs for many years. One, the Weber work, is probably one of the cleverest and most attractive modern works available today and, by itself, reveals to audiences the true Hindemith, a man of consummate cleverness and musical craft.

Information on Individual Symphonies

Name	Key	Date	I	II	III	IV
Concert Music for Strings and Brass	C-sharp (D-flat)	1930	Sonatina	ABA	—	—
Symphony: Mathis der Maler		1934	SA	ABAB	Hybrid	
Symphony in E flat	E-flat	1940	SA	Rondo-variation	Scherzo	Sonata-rondo-variation
Symphonic Metamorphosis on Themes of Weber		1943	Sectional	Scherzo	ABA	Sonatina
Symphonia Serena	a	1946	SA	Scherzo	ABA	Sonata-allegro
Sinfonietta in E	E	1950	SA	AB	Scherzo	Rondo
Symphony: Die Harmonie der Welt		1951	Sectional	AB	Passacaglia w/interlude	
Pittsburgh Symphony		1958	SA	ABA	Variations	

CONCERT MUSIC FOR STRINGS AND BRASS, OP. 50

See pp. 333–337 for full analysis.

SYMPHONY: MATHIS DER MALER

This work was extracted from Hindemith's opera *Mathis der Maler* in 1934, each of the three movements representing an important panel in an altar piece created by Mathis Grünewald in the early sixteenth century. The altar piece was a series of paintings relating to the life of St. Anthony, for whom the church in Isenheim was named. The first movement, "Angelic Concert," is actually the opera's overture. The second movement, "Entombment," was originally an intermezzo in the opera's final scene. The finale, "The Temptation of St. Anthony," was originally for chorus. It is located in the sixth scene of the opera. The first movement uses a folk tune, "Three Angels Were Singing," as a cantus in its introduction, with the strings providing a faster-moving countermelody. The folk tune reappears at the start of the recapitulation section. The finale starts with a recitativelike theme containing all twelve tones. This melody is developed in unison by most of the orchestra with sparse support in general. The ensuing fast section is constructed along rondo principles. A slower section interrupts this faster section and works with both old and new material. As the work nears conclusion Hindemith adds a sequence, from the feast of Corpus Christi, *Lauda Sion Salvatorem*, slightly modified, above a fugal subject in the violins. The work closes with an *Alleluia*.

SYMPHONY IN E-FLAT

This is one of three four-movement concert symphonies written as symphonies and not as arrangements of other works. The work is organized in general along traditional formal lines. The first movement is in a brief sonata-allegro which presents two main themes that are related in intervallic structure. The development is repetitive, extracting short motives from the first theme for antiphonal orchestral treatment and involving materials from the second theme in a brief contrapuntal exercise. The recapitulation continues the contrapuntal development of the first theme and regroups the secondary material. The coda is more interesting since it restates the second theme seven times in augmentation with florid scale patterns under it in the strings, and then states the first theme three times in augmentation over a similar florid string part. The second movement is a slow rondo which combines with some elements of variation form by developing the first theme in both of its restatements. The contrapuntal activity is greater in this movement than in the opening movement. As in the coda of the first movement, much of the contrapuntal procedure involves rapid scale passages (repetitive) in the strings while themes are being manipulated above these scales. The third movement is a scherzo with trio which relies on rhythmic repetition and ostinato for forward propulsion in the scherzo section. The trio is much more subdued and continues some of the more modest counterpoint of the movement (rapid scale figurations in the strings and short antiphonal motives scattered intermittently among statements of the trio material). The finale combines elements of sonata-allegro, rondo, and variation form. The form could be seen as:

A   B   B-dev   C   A-dev   A-varied   B-dev   A-varied

The variations often involve polyphony, especially free counterpoint. The "development" of B is actually an inversion. The final variation of A is in augmentation, with Hindemith's running counterpoint in the strings. The composer relies considerably on brass instruments not only for important thematic material but also to provide a basic sonority for the symphony that is more characteristic of the nineteenth century than the eighteenth. Some feel that the composer modified his strict neoclassicism in his later works.* This work, considered as an orchestral sound, would support that view.

SYMPHONIC METAMORPHOSIS ON THEMES BY CARL MARIA VON WEBER

Hindemith composed one of his most attractive orchestral works in the *Metamorphosis*. The four movements are treated as traditional symphony movements. The challenge, however, was to breathe life into a collection of Weber's rather uninspiring tunes. The first movement is in sectional form (ABCDA) and uses themes from Weber's fourth work in the *Eight Pieces* for piano duet (Op. 60). The second movement mimics one of the ancient Chinese melodies associated with the Turandot legend. Weber contributed an overture to preface a Schiller play on the story.† The scherzo setting is unique in many respects. First, the opening scherzo is set as eight variations on the old theme. A fugal section for trombones and other instruments (later) serves as a trio. Hindemith adjusted the tune to fit a much jazzier criterion. The opening section returns in a modified version. Percussion solo sections connect all three major divisions of the movement. The slow third movement uses a theme from the second work in Weber's *Six Easy Pieces* for piano duet (Op. 3). The ternary form is varied slightly by the addition of a flute countermelody in the restatement of the first section. The finale is a march in expanded binary form (ABAB). The tunes are from Weber's march in the *Eight Pieces* (Op. 60). The scherzolike B section uses a triplet figure to energize a countermelody in the woodwinds while the horns play the primary melody. The work gave the composer opportunity to contribute a symphony based on borrowed tunes. Hindemith's solution was to adjust the tunes as much as he could, to set them in a straightforward personal style, and to synthesize the effort into one of the cleverest symphonies in modern repertory.

SYMPHONIA SERENA

Hindemith wrote this work on a commission from the Dallas Symphony Orchestra when Antal Dorati began his conducting career in this country with

---

* Ian Kemp, *Hindemith* (London: Oxford University Press, 1970), pp. 40–41.

† Weber found the tune in Rousseau's dictionary under "Chinese Music," See Kemp, *Hindemith*, p. 50.

that orchestra. The basic premise of the work was to combine an orchestral display piece with the formal outline of the concert symphony. Hindemith's gift for variation and his formal skills made the work one of his more challenging scores. The first movement generally allows solo winds to present most of the thematic material (horn, oboe, English horn, piccolo, etc.). The coda also uses the familiar device of rapid scale fragments in the strings under statements of the theme in the winds. The second movement is a march for winds alone and uses a march theme by Beethoven * as its cantus. The theme is inserted very much in the style of a chorale prelude with intervening sections which have their own thematic integrity, although they lack any relationship to the Beethoven materials. Since the Hindemith materials are in short rhythmic values and the Beethoven materials are in longer notes, the contrapuntal effect is similar to that of other works where the composer has embroidered tunes with ornate running parts or countermelodies. As in many other similar examples of this treatment, what appears to be "busy work" in this counterpoint is actually built upon previous thematic material.

The second movement is another unusual work. It is divided into three major sections. The first section is played by strings, bowed. The second section requires strings, pizzicato. The third section simultaneously combines both previous sections, as done in a string octet by the French composer Darius Milhaud.† The two transitions between sections are designed as canonic cadenzas for two violins (or violas in the second cadenza), with one such instrument offstage. The finale is another experiment in compositional dexterity. Five themes are presented in the exposition. Most of these are combined in a contrapuntal fashion in the development section. An orderly recapitulation emerges with almost all themes included. One theme is reserved for the coda to be set as a cantus above a four-voice fugato based on a trill-like subject. The opening chords of the movement reappear as the final chords of the symphony.

SINFONIETTA IN E

Hindemith completed this work in 1950 under a commission from the Louisville Orchestra and conducted that orchestra in the *Sinfonietta*'s premiere on March 1, 1950.†† Its four movements follow a similar overall plan: one developmental movement (the first, a rather free version of sonata-allegro) and three other movements more closely allied with baroque forms. The second movement (*Adagio, Allegretto*) has a slow first section which leads to a faster

---

* A military march composed between 1809 and 1810. See David Ewen, *The Complete Book of the 20th Century Music* (Englewood Cliffs, N.J.: Prentice-Hall, Inc., 1959), p. 178.

† Darius Milhaud (1892–1974) wrote two strings quartets (nos. 14 and 15) which are performed simultaneously as an octet.

†† Geoffrey Skelton, *Paul Hindemith* (London: Victor Gollancz Ltd., 1975), p. 241.

fugato. The third movement is actually a series of free variations above an ostinato which moves with considerable abandon throughout the orchestra. The finale also starts with a slow introduction before concluding with a brisk rondo.

SYMPHONY: DIE HARMONIE DER WELT

This work has an origin similar to that of the *Mathis* symphony. Hindemith reworked portions of the music from his opera *Die Harmonie der Welt* in 1951 for the twenty-fifth anniversary of the Basel chamber orchestra. The story of the opera is based on the life of Johannes Kepler (1571–1630), astronomer and mathematician, whose life was characterized by personal tragedy and considerable scientific and philosophical attainment. The titles of the movements were taken from the work of an earlier philosopher, Boethius. In his *De institutiona musica* Boethius not only transmitted knowledge of the Greek system but also established three divisions of music. *Musica mundana* related musical sounds to the order of the stars and universe. *Musica humana* told of how such harmonious sounds are related to the soul and body of men. *Musica intrumentalis* explained the principles of order in created sounds (instrument or voice), especially intervallic ratios. Hindemith used the three divisions as names of the movements of this symphony. The passacaglia used as the third movement is drawn directly from the opera, where it appears as the final scene.

PITTSBURGH SYMPHONY

One of the composer's last large orchestral works, it was commissioned for the two-hundredth anniversary of the city of Pittsburgh, Pennsylvania, and was conducted by the composer in 1959 in this country. It is scored for an orchestra of moderate proportions but with a large percussion section (including castanets, wood block, tambourine, tamtam, etc.). It was written in three movements and used tunes familiar to the natives of Pennsylvania. Its first movement is a modified sonata-allegro with a main theme of extreme angularity. The development section extracts and works with shorter segments from many themes, leading to an inversion of the principal theme which then dominates this extended section. The recapitulation (rehearsal number 17) contains only the first theme. The brass are used extensively in the recapitulation, with the strings playing an active countermelody above them, as is often done in final sections of Hindemith orchestral works. The second movement is a slow march with an equally angular main tune. A Pennsylvania "Dutch ditty," "Hab lumbedruwwel mit me lumberschatz," is the theme of the movement's trio. The tune is even scored for timpani solo near the end of the trio. The da capo combines the Dutch ditty with the slow-moving tune of the march. The timpani continues to play short segments from the Dutch ditty. The finale is a set of variations on an ostinato. It is possible to see a ternary design in the movement, with a middle section (*Tranquillo*) starting at rehearsal number 5. The final variation is more of a coda with a quasi-folk tune,

"Pittsburgh Is a Great Old Town," superimposed above the ostinato. Needless to say, the brass instruments are held responsible for much of this tune. Quite a bit of the angularity in the writing, the segmental approach to serialism in the finale, and the linear nature of much of the work indicate a leaning toward serial procedures which might even have totally infected Hindemith had he lived longer.

EXAMPLES FOR STUDY

Hindemith: *Concert Music for Strings and Brass*

This work was composed in December, 1930, for the fiftieth anniversary of the Boston Symphony Orchestra and was first performed (by that group) on April 3, 1931. Though the work is not structurally a symphony, it is a concert orchestral work which is symphonylike in some respects while maintaining a relationship to the baroque concerto grosso in other respects. As noted on the form summary, it is in two large sections.

I: Mässig schnell, mit Kraft.   The first movement is in sonatina form with an extended lyric coda based on the first theme (A). The principal theme consists of a long-lined melody in the trumpets over an agitated counterpoint in much quicker note values in the strings. This two-voice contrapuntal texture characterizes the first tune. A secondary tune, more homophonic in nature, is played primarily by the brass. By measure 50, Hindemith began working more imitatively with this secondary theme. The development section returns to the tutti ensemble and its extensive contrapuntal working out of the first theme. During one section of this development it is possible to see three of the primary motives associated with the first theme being used simultaneously in this working out (measures 89–95). The development of the B theme is undertaken by the tutti ensemble also, with A and B being superimposed briefly starting at measure 115. A more declamatory development of the A-counterpoint starts at measure 124, where dissonant chords in the brass punctuate phrase endings. As the work moves ahead, the texture becomes more complex, the chords more dissonant (tritones, minor seconds, etc.). A two-measure transition of parallel sonorities (quite dissonant with streams of fourth chords and thirds on unrelated roots) leads to a coda. In this coda a long spinning-out of the first theme is done in the strings (with horns added slightly later) above a brass chordal accompaniment. The melody stresses C-sharp, as does most of the accompaniment. Two tonal levels are implied: one in the tune, the other in the harmony. Hindemith seems to have moved the melody in and out of "agreement" with the harmony very much as two melodies would be handled in a linear contrapuntal format. A brief contrary-motion passage in the brass (measure 169) leads to the final cadence in C-sharp major.

II: Lebhaft; Langsam; Lebhaft. The second half of the work is designed as an "interrupted" fugue, this interruption contributed by an interlude of a more subdued and expressive nature. The fugue subject is taken from the generating interval of the minor third (C-sharp, E) in the principal theme of the first movement. The subsequent sixteenth notes of the subject also relate generally to this same melodic interval in a somewhat subtle substructure. Three entrances of the subject constitute the fugal exposition. At measure 32 an A² motive enters which is then adjusted metrically in subsequent measures until it takes on considerable prominence as another motto theme based on the minor third. In measures 42–44, the composer has implied a "blues" third in this motive where it touches upon the minor ninth (A-flat) over the G dominant seventh. Suddenly, as development of the fugue thins out, a new theme (A³) appears which in its melodic style and orchestral scoring strongly resembles some of the tunes by Prokofiev. The tune is drawn from the fugue subject but loses much of this identity through its strong rhythmic structure and (later) the rhythmic nature of the accompaniment. The development of the fugal material continues until measure 96 with this new tune dominating most of those measures. The material of the slow middle section, somewhat recitative-like in its melodic style, is also based on the minor third. The B³ theme is the most important of the three segments, with the first two parts being more introductory in nature. The texture is generally homophonic. The third section returns to the fugue with three entrances of the subject, one as the restatement and the other two in the continuing fugal development. The tempo slackens as the coda approaches. During this ritard both A³ and A² reappear briefly, both in longer note values and quite subdued in effect. The coda is a quick restatement of most of the themes of the final movement. First, an accompaniment motive from the A³ theme leads to a statement of the fugue theme, with A² and A³ becoming involved in the closing out of the movement. The blues third in A² is quite obvious in the final measures, where it is harmonized as the lower tonic seventh over the D-flat major triad (tonic sonority). The dominant seventh sonority in a parallel chord passage concludes the movement (A Mm7→ F-sharp Mm7→E-flat Mm7→C Mm7, resolving to D-flat major).

SUMMARY

Concert Music is representative of Hindemith's use of baroque principles in his mature works. It also shows the intellectual involvement of the composer in the relating of most of the thematic materials to the interval of the minor third. His early jazz background even surfaces in the use of a blues third in one of the motives in the final movement. The harmonic and tonal material is also representative of his style. His return to more romantic values in his later works is anticipated in the lyric nature of some of the opening themes. The coda of the first movement emphasizes the expressive possibilities of this theme. The work is a mixture of the classic and romantic versions of the symphony, with more emphasis on formal implications than on melodic expression.

While the bulk of the composer's works were not orchestral works, those works written (or arranged) as symphonies are impressive additions to contemporary literature for the orchestra. In general the works are expressive and have audience appeal. They also fit in many respects into the tradition of the symphony as an intellectual (or developmental) form.

VII

The Twentieth-Century
Symphony in America

The history of the symphony in America includes not only the history of the musical form but also the growth of the symphony orchestra itself in this country. Though most of the composers active in America during the nineneeth century were primarily transplanting a conservative European musical style into concert halls in America, their efforts seemed, in part, to encourage the expansion of this concert tradition. The dates of the founding of American orchestras show better how this expansion fared:*

New York	1842
Boston	1881
Chicago	1891
Cincinnati	1895
Philadelphia	1900
Minneapolis	1903
St. Louis	1907
San Francisco	1911
Detroit	1914
Baltimore	1916
Cleveland	1918
Los Angeles	1919
Rochester	1922

---

* Willi Apel, *Harvard Dictionary of Music,* 2nd ed. (Cambridge, Mass.: Harvard University Press, 1969), p. 606.

Pittsburgh	1926
Indianapolis	1930
Washington, D.C.	1931

The dates of the founding of the great orchestras of Europe roughly parallel that of American orchestras but at a slower pace:*

Gewandhaus Konzerte (Leipzig)	1781
Concerts du Conservatoire (Paris)	1792
Vienna Philharmonic	1842
Berlin Philharmonic	1882
Concertgebouw Orchestra (Amsterdam)	1888
Orchestre National Belge (Brussels)	1895
London Symphony	1904
Bayrisches Staatsorchester (Munich)	1911
Orchestre de la Suisse Romande (Geneva)	1918

American composers in the nineteenth century wrote works primarily in the European tradition, especially showing influences of Brahms, Beethoven, and Schubert. Composers included John Knowles Paine, George Chadwick, Arthur Foote, Horatio Parker, Edward MacDowell, and a few others. In the early twentieth century additional composers appeared: Frederick Converse, John Alden Carpenter, Daniel Gregory Mason, Henry Hadley, Edward Burlingame Hill, Arthur Shepherd, Charles Wakefield Cadman, Charles Griffes and Mrs. H. H. A. Beach. By 1930 another group of young composers was forming and included America's first generation of internationally recognized composers: Aaron Copland, Roy Harris, Walter Piston, Roger Sessions, Douglas Moore, Howard Hanson, and Randall Thompson. Another generation soon followed: Samuel Barber, Leonard Bernstein, David Diamond, William Schuman, Morton Gould, Paul Creston, Vincent Persichetti, Norman Dello Joio, Elliot Carter, Lukas Foss, Ross Lee Finney, and others of at least equal stature. Among these groups were also a few experimental composers whose works drew attention to America's musical frontier: Charles Ives, Charles Ruggles, Henry Cowell, John Cage, Henry Brandt, Vladimir Ussachevsky, and Milton Babbitt. Very few of these composers have concentrated exclusively on the symphony. Those who did specialize in the form to some extent include Harris, Hanson, Cowell, Sessions, Piston, and Schuman.

The composers and works chosen for this study represent a fairly broad spectrum of styles and approaches to the form. The selection also contains works which have some degree of acceptability to the symphony audience in America.

---

* Apel, *Harvard Dictionary of Music*, pp. 606–7.

The Chicago Symphony Orchestra, formed in 1891 and directed in its early days by Theodore Thomas, is known as one of the world's best. Its hall, dedicated in 1904, was designed by Thomas. The above photo, from the 1976–77 season, shows the extreme height of the hall's ceiling, this probably contributing to the hall's modest acoustical reputation. Courtesy Chicago Symphony Orchestra.

Roy Harris (1898–   )

The basic ingredient in the Harris style is melody, especially long-lined melody. Harris's studies of sixteenth-century counterpoint have contributed an interest in a free-flowing and somewhat nonmetric melodic style. Leaps are not wide, with thirds, fourths, and fifths being the most usual. Modal melodic writing is quite typical. At times there is an alternation between major and minor seconds on the same pitch as well as the interchange of major and minor thirds. The melodic style is diatonic with the virtual exclusion of chromatic embellishment. Melodic sequences are avoided.

The emphasis in the style is on counterpoint, a counterpoint which is basically harmonic. The underlying harmony is triadic. Progression and modulation are based on a system of related triads and common-tone progressions. Often two triads are superimposed as polychords. Dual modality is typical. There is some quartal harmony. Pandiatonicism seems to govern harmonic progress in general. Plagal cadences are frequent. Harris avoids dominant sevenths and ninths, diminished sevenths, augmented triads, and whole-tone scales. Key signatures are not used. A strong feeling for tonality, however, is evident.

Contrapuntal passages are generally harmonic counterpoint similar to the sixteenth-century procedures. Some counterpoint resembles the style of organum. Whenever a complicated imitative passage begins (e.g., triple fugue), it usually lapses soon into something considerably less involved.

In the rhythmic style a regular metrical grouping of pulse is avoided. On the contrary, diverse rhythmic patterns and changes of meter typify the style. Ametric effects promote longer melodic lines and less regular phrasing of melody. Rhythmic movements are built on asymmetrical figures of rapid notes and frequently shifting accents. A rhythmic phrase of two notes, crescendo and *sforzando*, is repeatedly used. A strong metrical emphasis rarely coincides with the climax point of a melody.

Harris' *Third Symphony* established his reputation as America's leading symphonist after its premiere by Serge Koussevitzky and the Boston Symphony Orchestra in 1939. Courtesy Chicago Symphony Orchestra.

Form is not one of Harris' outstanding style features. Harris often resorts to fugal forms or contrapuntal devices rather than developmental forms. He avoids motivic development. All forms tend to be lyric, with some movements following contrapuntal forms. Literal recapitulation is avoided.

The orchestral style is functional. Each instrumental choir (string, brass, woodwind) is contrapuntally and harmonically integrated. One group often serves as an element of contrast to another, either in unison or in parts. Part-writing within a section (string, woodwind, brass) as a whole often requires that each member of the section move with others. This simplistic scoring tends to produce quite a bit of doubling within sections and frequent divisi scoring for the strings.

From an overall view, one procedure dominates the style: a way of spinning out melody from one section to another so that the new tune seems to grow out of the old melody. Since most of the forms noted in the symphonies are either part form or hybrid variation forms, one or two themes tend to dominate single movements. Harris' ability to project a continuous line of melodic thought into a single movement is admirable. It is his most unique style feature.*

SYMPHONY—AMERICAN PORTRAIT (1929)

Harris' first symphony, which he withdrew in 1971, was written during his stay in Paris while a student of Nadia Boulanger. Harris was fortunate in having Leopold Stokowski read the work with the Philadelphia Orchestra in 1931. It is in four movements: Initiative, a six-part sectional design primarily contrapuntal; Expectation, a three-part sectional form using a favorite tune of the composer, "When Johnny Comes Marching Home"; Speed, a scherzo with trio; and Collective Force, a two-part form that uses the Johnny tune in its second half.

SYMPHONY NO. 1 (1933)

A three movement symphony favoring sectional and part forms, the work uses a hybrid rondo form in its second movement that places its nine smaller sections into a large ternary outline.

---

* Detailed information on many of the Harris symphonies was based on a recent doctoral dissertation. See Dan Stehman, "The Symphonies of Roy Harris" (unpublished Doctoral dissertation, University of Southern California, 1973).

SYMPHONY NO. 2 (1934)

Another three-movement symphony in which the composer used mood titles for each movement, the work again employs part forms for each movement: Prelude, a five-part shaping of a set of variations on two themes; Contemplative, a three-part movement consisting of five canons; and Feeling of Power, a four-part sectional movement in which the final section regroups the three themes from earlier sections.

SYMPHONY FOR VOICES (1935)

A choral symphony using the poems of Walt Whitman for texts, its three movements again favor part or sectional forms. "Song for All Seas, All Ships" is binary; "Tears" is binary; and "Inscription" has a fugue in each of its four sections, the final fugue using the subjects from fugues 1–3.

SYMPHONY NO. 3 (1937)

Considered by many to be Harris's best symphony, the work is in one movement but subdivides into five sections: Tragic (low string sonorities), Lyric (strings, horns, woodwinds), Pastoral (woodwinds with polytonal string background), Fugue (brass and strings in dramatic setting concluding with lone line in woodwinds) and Dramatic-Tragic (long sustained lines in strings and woodwinds with brass interjections). The naming of a mood for each section indicates a programmatic or expressive conception that Harris projected for many of his symphonies. This type of story-telling is actually more related to the Greek doctrine of *ethos*, which placed meaning on each mode (e.g., Dorian equates with strength), than to a more traditional nineteenth-century style of descriptive music. Harris at one time discussed his theory of emotionalism in music by relating key, melody, and harmony to feelings. He felt, for instance, that the "bright" modes were those that spaced the intervals at the widest intervals as the scale ascended (Lydian), and the "darkest" were those that had the smallest intervals at the lower ends of the scale (Locrian). (His spectrum from dark to bright: Locrian, Phrygian, Aeolian, Dorian, Mixolydian, Ionian, and Lydian.) In sonorities Harris felt brightness was enhanced by the sharing of upper partials in a complex sonority. Darkness was thus created when the upper partials of chord members were not similar or in agreement. Further, the combination of two major sonorities was considered "savage bright" while that of two minor chords was termed "savage dark." Tempo also was related to the heartbeat. Music faster than 72–80 excited; slower paces depressed.*

---

* Peter S. Hansen, *An Introduction to Twentieth Century Music* (Boston: Allyn and Bacon, 1961), pp. 318–19.

The sections of the third symphony also have textural and orchestral characteristics. The introduction is set for strings in an organum style. Parts move in equal note values in a quasi-contrapuntal texture. Section I ("Tragic") gradually adds woodwinds, horns, and trombones, with the woodwinds asserting more and more responsibility for thematic sustenance. Section II ("Lyric") adds trumpets and flutes but retains the woodwind choir as the primary force. A series of overlapping phrases in the woodwinds creates a massive undulating harmonic effect. Section III ("Pastoral") shifts the overlapping phrase accompaniment pattern to the strings (ten parts, divisi) with woodwind and (later) brass solos above. Section IV ("Fugue, Dramatic") adds more brass and percussion to the ensemble. Extended canonic writing (short canon) is used between these brass instruments. The section is not fugal as the title implies. Section V ("Dramatic, Tragic") places the theme in the brass section and sustains a quiet harmonic support in the woodwinds and strings.

SYMPHONY NO. 4 (1940)

Harris' *Folksong Symphony* (its other name) started out as another choral symphony of five movements. He inserted two instrumental movements later to allow more rest for the vocalists. His selection of folk materials was quite diverse, from Civil War to cowboy tunes: the first movement (binary form with coda) uses the Civil War tune "The Gal I Left Behind"; the second (binary form), "The Dying Cowboy," "As I Walked Out in the Streets of Laredo," and "The Old Chisholm Trail"; the third movement, a scherzolike interlude for orchestra, contains three fiddle tunes, "Arkansas Traveler," "The Irish Washerwomen," and "Cod Liver Ile"; the fourth, entitled Mountaineer Love Song, uses "He's Gone Away"; the fifth is a set of orchestra variations on two fiddle tunes, "Blackbird and the Crow" and "Jump Up, My Lady"; the sixth (Negro Fantasy) is a brief series of variations on "De Trumpet Sounds in My Soul" with a short segment of "Little Boy Name David" inserted near the end; and the final movement is a scherzo (Welcome Party) employing Harris' favorite, "When Johnny Comes Marching Home."

SYMPHONY NO. 5 (1942)

Originally dedicated to "the heroic and freedom-loving people of our great ally, the Union of Soviet Socialist Republics,"* this dedication was omitted when the work was revised for recording by the Louisville Symphony in the 1950s. The first of its three movements (Martial in first version, Prelude in revised score) is in a large binary design with a series of free variations on a

---

* Ewen, *The Complete Book of 20th Century Music*, p. 169.

single theme. The second movement (Rhapsodic or Chorale) is a typical Harris slow movement with long melodic lines and a loosely formed ternary design in which each new theme evolves from the preceding section. A final, chorale-like statement closes the movement. The finale (Triple Fugue) is ternary: Fugue I, Fugue II, and Fugue III (the latter being based also on the tunes from fugues I and II). The movement also uses the concept of thematic growth or transformation.

SYMPHONY NO. 6, "GETTYSBURG" (1944)

Commissioned by the Blue Network, the symphony was premiered by the Boston Symphony Orchestra under Koussevitsky on April 4, 1944. Reacting both to the specifics of the commission and to his affinity for Lincoln with whom he shared the same birthdate, Harris based the work on quotations from the Gettysburg address. The first movement, Awakening, is a four-sectioned work in which each successive section grows out of the preceding and which uses the opening passage from the address ("Fourscore and seven years ago . . ."). Conflict, movement two, employs a text that begins, "Now we are engaged in a great civil war," and uses organum-like sonorities and polychords in its two marches (slow, fast). The third movement (Dedication) is based on the words, "We are met on a great battlefield of that war, we have come to dedicate . . .", and scores its somewhat reflective and subdued harmonies primarily for strings in a vague ternary outline. The finale (Affirmation) is another large polyphonic movement of three fugues, the last using its own subject in combination with the two previous subjects. Its text starts with the words, "It is for us the living . . ." A coda on Fugue I closes the symphony.

SYMPHONY NO. 7 (1951)

See pp. 347–353.

SYMPHONY NO. 8, "SAN FRANCISCO SYMPHONY" (1961)

A one-movement work with five major sections (Childhood and Early Manhood, Renunciation of Worldly Goods, Building of His Church, Reflection of Canticle, and Gloria), the symphony is based on the major events in the life of St. Francis of Assisi, the city's patron saint. It is the first symphony in which Harris uses the piano as a prominent solo orchestral instrument. The amplified piano, as added to the fourth movement, makes that section almost into a piano concerto. The first three movements are sectional in design (A–B–C), with the third being a hybrid fugue-variation form. The fourth movement is an adaptation of an earlier work (*Canticle of the Sun,* a cantata for high voice and chamber group based on the writings of St. Francis), and is Harris' best developmental movement although scored in scherzo form. The finale section, Gloria, is in a large tenary design with the first half being a theme with two variations. The work was commissioned for the fiftieth annivnersary of the San Francisco Symphony.

SYMPHONY NO. 9 (1962)

This three-movement work was commissioned by the Philadelphia Orchestra and dedicated to the City of Philadelphia. Each movement is subtitled with an extract from the Preamble of the Constitution: "We, the people," "to form a more perfect Union," and "to promote the general welfare." The latter movement also uses three quotes from Walt Whitman's *Leaves of Grass:* "Of Life immense in passion, pulse, and power," "Cheerful for freest action form'd," and "The Modern Man I sing," for each of its three subsections. The first movement (Prelude) is toccata-like, but more closely approaches the overall form of sonata-allegro than any of Harris' symphony movements (A-Development-A). Most of its tunes are modal, with some sounding like they were extracted from a collection of eighteenth-century American folk tunes (e.g., oboe tune at rehearsal number 10), and others sound more like hymn tunes from the same period (e.g., viola tune at rehearsal number 16). The second movement (Chorale) has a ternary form with some stress on Harris' nonimitative organum-style counterpoint. As the first section of the movement concludes, two themes are superimposed in contrasting orchestral sections. The third movement, called *Contrapuntal Structures* by the composer, follows the three-part textual suggestion. In a fourth section he adds another tune to reinforce the "Modern man" meaning of the movement. The new tune is interpolated above and below the tunes of the first three fugues. The orchestra is one of Harris' largest. Roughly one-third of the scoring for strings is in subdivided parts. In some instances, this produces as many as thirteen separate voices for the five string sections.

SYMPHONY NO. 10, "LINCOLN" (1965)

The work was originally scored for smaller school and university orchestras, but was later reorchestrated for the full symphony ensemble. It uses both chorus and amplified piano and supposedly depicts events or stages in Lincoln's life. Four of its five movements are in part form (AB, ABA, or ABC). The finale tends more toward variation form in its five sections. The second movement erects a series of variants on a single tune. The movements are entitled "Lonesome Boy," "The Young Wrestler," "Abraham Lincoln's Convictions," "Civil War: Brother against Brother," and "Praise and Thanks Given for Peace."

SYMPHONY NO. 11 (1967)

This symphony was commissioned by the New York Philharmonic for its 125th anniversary. Harris conducted the premiere on February 8, 1968. It is in two large sections or movements, the first in a section design (A–B–C), and the second starting with a double fugue that is then followed by two more sections.

SYMPHONY NO. 12, "PERE MARQUETTE" (1969)

This work resulted from a commission from a centennial group commemorating the life and work of Père Marquette. It uses a tenor soloist and narrator in its three sections or movements. Each movement is to honor major portions of Père Marquette's life: "Youth," "Accomplishment," and "Death." The first section is in sectional form (A–B–C–D); the sectional movement is in three sections, the opening for orchestra alone, the second based on a part of the *Symphony No. 8*, and the third a setting of the Nicene Creed for tenor and orchestra; and the final movement is again sectional, the first part called "Wilderness," the second term "Sermon," and the closing section "Sanctus." The finale uses traditional chant tunes.

SYMPHONY NO. 13, "BICENTENNIAL" (1975)

Commissioned by California State University at Los Angeles, the work is in five movements with titles reflective of the Civil War. Its first performance was by the National Symphony on February 12, 1976, the composer's birthday.

SYMPHONY NO. 14, "OLYMPIC" (1978?)

The work was in progress (1978) in anticipation of Los Angeles' hosting of the Olympics.

EXAMPLES FOR STUDY

Harris: *Symphony No. 7*

Completed in 1951 on a commission by the Koussevitzky Foundation, the work was honored with the Walter W. Naumburg Musical Foundation Award in 1955. Its premiere was with the Chicago Symphony on November 20, 1952. The form is in two large sections, the intent of the composer being to make these movements essentially polyphonic. The results were somewhat short of the intended mark. The first section is a passacaglia with a set of five variations. The second section is divided into four smaller parts: a brief set of asymmetrical rhythmic variations, a longer set of symmetrical rhythmic variations, a development that restates the cantus of the passacaglia under further development of the rhythmic elements of both the symmetrical and asymmetrical variations, and, finally a coda which continues some of the rhythmic variation.

I: Passacaglia and Variations.   The theme of the passacaglia is serial only in that it uses all twelve tones in the twenty-seven pitches used in its seven short phrases. The construction of the theme is ternary in design: the first two phrases, as well as the final two, contain only three pitches. The middle three phrases contain six, four, and five pitches. Five of the seven phrases are tunes which descend. The widest leap in any phrase is an interval of a fourth. The range of the phrases is narrow, most within an interval of a fourth. The variations generally follow the same plan which has organized the theme, i.e., segmented statements of the theme (see theme sheet) interspersed with more florid materials (some contrapuntal, others not).

Theme: The passacaglia theme is stated in the tenor and lower woodwinds over a divisi accompaniment in the strings and woodwinds. Most of the phrases of the theme are harmonized in parallel fifths in the piano, lower double reeds, and pizzicato lower strings. The short two to five-measure interludes between theme phrases are "figured" polyphony, with most of this activity located in the violins, where a species approach is in evidence. The basic sound of the theme is strings with woodwinds doubling some of the sustained lower string chords.

Variation I: The strings are subdivided into from twelve to sixteen parts in a motivic harmonic accompaniment which has polytonal implications (see theme sheet). Horns (unison) play the first five phrases of the theme, interspersed over the accompaniment at intervals of four to seven measures. Woodwind passages (unison or octave doubling) are added as the third contrapuntal line, using the same interspersed approach.

Variation II: The theme is in the trumpets in parallel major triads. Trombones are used as the lower half of the passage but do not follow the same parallel stream. Lower woodwinds sustain long chords, usually triads (major or minor). The strings, in double octaves, ornament the sustained chord background. The basic sound is strings with tenor and lower woodwinds but with the added brilliance of the trumpets and trombones on the cantus. Only the first two phrases of the cantus were used by Harris.

Variation III: The cantus is absorbed into the string (violin) line with other related materials inserted in four- to seven-measure lyric passages very much in the same style as that of the theme. A unison passage with selected woodwinds and trumpet is one polyphonic line, fragmented and short-phrased in style and interspersed selectively above the cantus. A chaconnelike and plodding half-note line occupies the tenor and lower strings as the other polyphonic line; it is set in three parts (voices) to imply triadic design also. The basic sound is still strings and woodwinds with a single trumpet or horn being used in some passages with thematic significance.

Variation IV: This section is more heavily scored for brass and percussion with the cantus in the trumpet and trombone, unison and tutti. A figure in the strings involving a superimposed rhythmic background (four where three usually fit) and generally a unison scoring provides the primary rhythmic motive for much of the counterpoint or melodic fragments manipulated by other instruments. The lines become more elongated in the strings, with some phrases stretching to seven measures. The style moderates near the conclusion of the variation. The basic sound now is more representative of the full orchestra but with emphasis still on the strings and woodwinds except for the cantus in the brass.

Variation V: The fifth variation serves more as a transition to the rhythmic variations than as a continuation of the passacaglia. Only short segments of the first two phrases of the cantus are heard, played in parallel triads in the brass. The variation closes with some dissonant sonorities of polychordal origin in the strings. The basic sound for the first half is strings and brass; for the second half, strings alone.

II: Rhythmic Variations

Asymmetrical Variations: This section involves some eighty-five bars of irregular (or asymmetrical) meters (11/8, 5/8, 11/8, 5/8, 11/8). The melodic materials are not particularly significant, since the variations are based more on the rhythmic patterns noted below.

Symmetrical Variations: As in the previous "set" there is no clear demarcation between rhythmic treatments; the composer has written a continuous form which relates to one or two primary figures for much of the section. Smaller divisions of the section rarely exceed eight measures in length. One extended example of parallelism starts in measure 486 with ninth chords and gradually reduces the complexity of the sonorities to unisons in the subsequent thirteen measures.

Restatement and development: The cantus supposedly is restated in augmentation but uses only the first two phrases in this section. The remaining sustained melodic material in the brass does represent an organic growth from the cantus. Some of the sonority of the opening measures of the symphony can be seen in measures 543–69 with the emphasis on tenths in the lower strings. The entire section seems more correctly a continuation of the passacaglia. A long descending thematic line characterizes the counterpoint in the first violin and upper woodwinds; it is the primary melodic feature of the section. A transition to the coda starts at measure 579, with even greater rhythmic impetus to the section starting at measure 585.

Coda: The closing section of the symphony syncopates within a 4/2 metrical scheme. The basic metrical implication is that of 3+3+2, at least in the bass and percussion line. Other lines emphasize 2+3+3 and 2+2+2+2, all three patterns being superimposed. A short jazzy tune is then added with another phrasing: 1+2+3+2 (flute, measure 610). The symphony closes on a tonic ninth chord (no third or seventh).

D **Restatement** (+Passacaglia Theme)

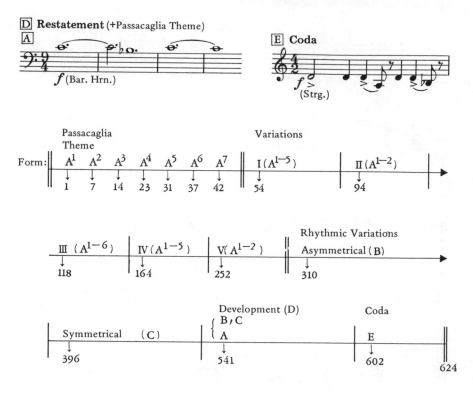

SUMMARY

Harris's seventh symphony exemplifies the composer's original approach to his compositional chores. His works seem to have resisted some of the important style trends of contemporary music. His craft borders deceptively on the primitive at times. His inability to mount an effective developmental movement has characterized much of his symphonic output. The seventh avoids development at all costs. What he seems best at doing is writing lyric movements with some kind of variation or contrapuntal (mild) basis. The passacaglia of this work is probably his best symphonic movement. His interest in sonority keeps him always exploiting harmonic and sonorous effects in the symphony. This work also typifies what it is that Harris calls counterpoint. There is no imitation, only lines which relate harmonically and achieve melodic independence through slight adjustments of contour and major manipulations of rhythm. The complexity of the closing sections of the symphony is caused by the superimposition of polyphrased metrical patterns within 9/4 and 4/2 meters. While some of the earlier symphonies resort to folk tunes and implied programs in their dedications, this work is absolute in its origin.

Harris's originality in handling symphonic form sometimes places him outside the mainstream of twentieth-century symphonic history. He wrote three-movement, one-movement, multimovement, choral, folk-song, nationalistic, and traditional symphonies. As far as can be determined, the seventh represents his most contemporary effort. Its apparent baroque origins have sustained an effort of significant interest.

William Schuman (1910–   )

The primary musical influences in Schuman's music are Orlandus Lassus (1532–1594) and J. S. Bach for contrapuntal skills; Beethoven for form; Berlioz, Ravel, and Debussy for orchestration; Harris for contrapuntal and harmonic matters; Copland for folk and jazz elements; jazz itself for rhythmic style; and Tchaikovsky for prominence of melody. The musical style is thus characterized as basically contrapuntal, melodic, rhythmically diverse (with some jazz influence), and orchestrally attractive. Schuman thinks of himself as a romanticist but writes basically as a neoclassicist with an emphasis on lyricism. Though his melodic striving is for a lyric and singable tune, he often writes tunes of some angularity. Melodies are loosely tonal but rhythmically complex, since the composer's rhythmic style overshadows any unique pitch factors in melody.

Rhythm, then, is one of the composer's important style features. He avoids, however, the repetition of regular rhythmic patterns. He likes to accent the offbeat, a possible influence of his early jazz days. He avoids stressing regularity of meter (accenting bar lines). Many tunes start on offbeats. Many rhythmic patterns are placed across bar lines. Often conflicting patterns are superimposed. Syncopation is his most frequent device. His favorite rhythmic grouping is four: four beats or four subunits, many times grouped in four beats where one might expect three. "Regular" fours can be grouped off the beat or irregularly in this style also. His superimposition of triplets in duple time is frequent.

The tonal implications are fairly stable, with sections, phrases, and movements generally falling within a key scheme. Signatures are not used. At times Schuman shifts keys quite gradually. In certain periods he has used polytonality prominently. Dual modality is frequent. Later works border on the atonal at times. Tonal integrity of melodies preserves a feeling for tonality to a greater extent than vertical matters. The harmonic style results from linear writing. The basic vertical unit in the earlier works is the triad but often with added pitches. As noted above, Schuman at one time used polychords widely. The use of harmonic resources in one key and melodic resources which move in and out of that key is a contrapuntal concept frequently employed. Parallelism in harmony is a characteristic device. Chords of the fourth have decreased in frequency in the later works. The harmonic style after the fifth symphony becomes increasingly complex with vertical sonorities expanding to include considerable emphasis on the half step. Counterpoint is the foundation stone of the overall style. Here he is influenced both by Harris and by the sixteenth-century style. A great many of his works or movements are based on contrapuntal forms or styles.* Schuman's symphonies fit into a variety of overall shapes but show a tendency to evolve into three-movement works with a basic contrapuntal texture.

SYMPHONY NO. 1 (1935)

This symphony was scored for eighteen instruments and was performed once in 1936 only to be withdrawn by the composer. It has not been reissued.

SYMPHONY NO. 2 (1937)

This symphony had a performance by the Boston Symphony in 1939, was hissed as being too radical and was withdrawn for revisions. It has not been seen again.

SYMPHONY NO. 3 (1941)

This was Schuman's first significant orchestral work which enjoyed reasonable success. It is discussed below.

SYMPHONY NO. 4 (1941)

This symphony is more traditionally organized into three movements (fast–slow–fast). It, like most of the other symphonies, is linear in overall style. The slow introduction of the first movement is built on a one-measure ground bass over which Schuman places one, two, or three contrapuntal lines. The form might be considered ternary in that a long contrapuntal section dominates a middle section. Much of the writing of the middle section is fugal. The concluding section primarily develops materials from the opening *Allegro* section. The slow movement ("Tenderly, simply") is ternary in design with a structure similar to that used in the first movement. The texture of the first section is homophonic with evidence of polytonality between harmony and melody at times, with G-flat and C being the points of conflict. The middle sec-

---

* A definitive discussion of Schuman's musical style through the early 1950s is offered by the distinguished American composer, Vincent Persichetti, in Flora Rheta Schreiber and Vincent Persichetti, *William Schuman* (New York: G. Schirmer, Inc., 1954), pp. 49–85.

tion is fugal. The return of the first section is energized with significantly more counterpoint. The work closes in b-flat minor. The finale has the appearance of a sonata-rondo movement but with an emphasis on contrapuntal development in some of the sections. As before, fugal writing occupies much of this polyphonic section.

SYMPHONY NO. 5 (1943)

Schuman called this symphony *Symphony for Strings*. It also is in three movements as the composer once again relates to more traditional forms. The first movement fits into sonata-allegro form fairly well. The secondary theme is fugal. The development section features a harmonic development of a motive from the first theme. The second movement opens with opposing chord streams (one ascending, the other descending) in two keys, followed by a slow-moving tune in one key with its harmony moving at other tonal levels. The movement is an excellent example of polytonal writing. The lyric tune which follows is put into canon at a distance of twelve measures. This tune is then developed with a rapid countermelody in a stream of sixteenth notes around it. The polytonal section returns to complete a basic ternary design. The finale is more homophonic except for two thematic sections which are fugal. Considerable use of ground figures can be noted. Its form is rondo with contrasting textures being a part of this formal delineation.

SYMPHONY NO. 6 (1947)

The sixth symphony was commissioned by the Dallas Symphony and was first performed there in 1949 under Antal Dorati. Though the work is divided into six sections of contrasting tempos and materials, its actual form is determined by a passacaglialike overview which relates most of the materials of the second through sixth sections to the passacaglia opening section, in which four statements of the passacaglia theme occur. The four inner movements create the appearance of the classical symphony with a scherzo second movement, *Adagio* third movement, and *Presto* finale. The symphony is exceedingly complex and departs from some of the more obvious Schuman mannerisms (polychords, parallelism, jazz rhythms, etc.). It is an essentially polyphonic work with Schuman's most complex rhythmic usage to that time. Each of the inner movements has a main theme drawn from themes presented above the opening passacaglia theme. The passacaglia theme appears in each movement, usually in an altered version and often in a repetitive style in the passacaglia tradition. The melodic lines emphasize lyricism as in all Schuman works. Only the rhythm makes performance a problem for less than virtuosic orchestras.

SYMPHONY NO. 7 (1960)

This symphony was commissioned for the seventy-fifth anniversary of the Boston Symphony. It is in four movements but is played without a pause between movements. The overall impression created by the work is of a continued complexity in the style, as noted in the sixth symphony. Schuman employs some of the earlier devices of his style (parallelism, polytonality, rhythmic complexity, etc.) but advances some of these techniques, especially tonal and harmonic devices, to a point of extreme dissonance and tension. All four movements seem to be related through the use of a unifying motive, the ascending major seventh. The first movement, a *Largo assai,* stresses dissonant chords under dotted rhythmic structures similar to those of the French overture. The trumpet sounds the unifying motive at measure 19. In the return of the first section a dialogue between the bass and clarinet contains a simultaneous mirror for a short passage (measures 97–99). The second movement (*Vigoroso*) stresses the unifying motive as its main theme. Much of the imitation and many of the sonorities are based on this interval. A fanfarelike tune from this interval predominates except in a short section (measures 70–91). Schuman even assigned extended solos to the timpani with this theme.

The third movement, *Cantabile* ($\quad$ = ca. 40), is scored for strings alone and relaxes the melodic connection with the major seventh but further intensifies the harmonic interval of the half step. The layout of parts in the extended middle section (measures 16–51) is ingenious. The texture is primarily in three voices but eight string voices are in evidence. The upper two lines are doubled at the unison (later, the octave). What would be the tenor (or third) part in a portion of the second violins and violas is actually a part which runs in parallel major and minor thirds with the bass line. Later this is simplified even further (measure 26) when the lower voices begin to move in parallel triads while the remaining upper five parts are distributed at the unison on only two other real voices. This is again simplified when the upper voices move in parallel thirds (measures 46–48) against the planing triads in the lower parts. It is a refinement of the same technique which Schuman used in earlier works wherein the tune was in one key and the planing harmony was in another. The final scherzo has obvious jazz influences. The dissonance of the sonorities is reduced to make the movement fit into the traditional light mood of the symphony's finale. The use of the major seventh is more subtle. There is also a continuation of the chordal parallelism in much of the movement. The melodic major seventh reappears briefly near the conclusion of the movement (measure 198). The symphony ends on an E-flat major triad. The orchestra for the symphony is large: triple woodwinds, six horns, four trumpets, plus strings and percussion.

SYMPHONY NO. 8 (1963)

This symphony represents a continuation of the more complex style which started with the sixth symphony. It, like many of the multimovement symphonies, is in three movements (slow–slow–fast). The first movement (*Lento sostenuto, Pressante vigoroso, Lento*) was designed as a set of free melodic variations on two themes. The two basic themes are presented in typical Schuman style: long, sustained lines over a simple accompaniment that consists of exceedingly more dissonant sonorities than those used in the *Symphony for Strings*, for instance. Schuman's harmonic idiom has progressed by the time of this work to include basic sonorities with triadic skeletons enriched by tritones, major sevenths, minor seconds, and many of the tense intervals of Hindemith. The additive technique allows him to construct a basic sonority of a variety of intervals in addition to the underlying outline of a triad. The ternary second movement is more contrapuntal than the first movement and continues the basically complex nature of the work. The finale (*Presto, Prestissimo*) is constructed from one germinating interval. The final restatement of a fast-moving tune adds a long, sustained countermelody which emphasizes Schuman's lyricism. The orchestra required is larger than usual (two piccolos, three flutes, English horn, three clarinets, bass clarinet, three bassoons, contrabassoon, six horns, four trumpets, tuba, percussion of various descriptions, two harps, piano, and strings).

SYMPHONY NO. 9 (1968)

This symphony was subtitled *Le Fosse Ardeatine*. It was created in memory of the composer's visit to the Ardeatine Caves in Rome, which contain the bodies of 335 Italians killed in reprisal for the killing of 32 German soldiers by the Italian underground in 1944.

The symphony is in three sections, each connected to the adjacent section. It continues the same basic language and techniques used in the three previous symphonies but perhaps more expressively and successfully. The first movement, entitled "Anteludium," has an almost identical texture to that of the opening section of the third symphony, in which a long and slow fugue is unveiled with each entrance rising a half step. The subject is quite long—eleven bars, to be exact. The movement is not identified as a fugue by the composer so might be thought of as that or as a passacaglia (as the corresponding movement in the third symphony is identified). As the movement progresses, the woodwinds join with the strings (who have alone played the long exposition so far); the brass join as the movement nears its conclusion. The movement flows without break through a transition to the second movement. Unison pitches identify both this transition and the transition which connects the middle movement to the finale.

The second movement ("Offertorium") is basically a fast movement with slower interludes which imply some kind of rondo structure overall. Melodic material is brief, rapid, and angular. The theme of the first movement appears as the middle movement nears its conclusion.

The finale ("Postludium") is in a slow tempo and regroups themes of the first and second movements. The imitative nature of the first movement is not used. Typical parallel harmonies for brass instruments in one instance are used to accompany the former tune. The rhythm of the "Offertorium" in injected by the percussion section as the movement quietly moves toward a climax of great emotional impact. The basic techniques, as mentioned before, are similar to those used in the seventh and eighth symphonies.

The emphasis on lyricism and highly dissonant sonorities gives all of the later Schuman symphonies a consistency in basic sound which may gradually endear them to audiences. The ninth symphony may be one of the best symphonies created by an American composer and may well justify its commission by friends of Alexander Hillsberg, the revered former concertmaster of the Philadelphia Orchestra and later conductor of the New Orleans Symphony.

EXAMPLES FOR STUDY

Schuman: *Symphony No. 3*

Schuman's third symphony is in two large sections, or movements. Each movement is divided into two subsections. Part I Schuman identified as being a passacaglia and fugue. Part II is a chorale and toccata.

Part I: Passacaglia and Fugue. The passacaglia subject is a long, lyric tune which contains all twelve pitches of the chromatic scale and yet has limited chromatic motion. Schuman constructed the passacaglia very much like a fugue with each entry (or repetition) of the theme placed in another instrumental part. The preceding part continues in free counterpoint. Although there are seven entries of the theme, there are never more than five independent parts in evidence. The plan is methodical: the first pitch of each entry is a half step higher than that of the immediately preceding entry. Gradually the entry level moves from the initial E to B-flat, a tritone above this first entrance. The fugue (measures 146–220) starts with an entrance of the fugue subject on B-flat and moves each subsequent entrance up the same half step until the E level has been recovered. Both the passacaglia and the fugue then move into sections which vary or develop pertinent materials:

Passacaglia

Variation I (51–73): The passacaglia theme is varied over a continuous triplet figure in the strings. The transformation of the theme retains several characteristic intervals or motives (major or minor thirds, skips down a quartal chord, and leaps up of an octave). This technique of varying continuously an important unifying theme is one of Schuman's primary formal usages. The effect of the rhythmic accompaniment in the strings is harmonic; a preponderance of leaps within certain sonorities is typical of the melodic motion in those parts. The variation closes with the repetition of triads in the brass instruments.

Variation II (75–86): After erecting a polychordal accompaniment in the strings and lower woodwinds (C major and A major), Schuman varies the cantus again, using the syncopated rhythm of the counterpoint in the previous variation. The accompaniment drops out to leave the theme being treated in parallel minor triads.

Variation III (87–120): The texture of this variation occurs quite often in Schuman orchestral works: a slow cantus supported by a rapidly moving line in the strings. The melodic characteristics of the fast undergirding are scalar, creating the effect of an ostinato of a nondescript nature. In this variation the two-part writing almost merges rhythmically as the note values in the cantus become increasingly shorter. A short passage in parallel fifths closes the variation, leading to a brief transition on the same polychords (A, C, etc.) from Variation II.

Variation IV (121–45): A harmonic texture perhaps inspired by a similar section in the Harris Symphony No. 3 opens the variation. It is basically a harmonic web energized by a polyphonic rhythmic effect (see theme sheet). The cantus appears in parallel $\frac{6}{4}$ chords (major) in the trombones over this harmonic effect. The harmonic voices and cantus often move in and out of tonal agreement, thus creating bitonal effects. The variation closes with parallel triads in contrary motion in the trombones and strings.

Fugue

Exposition: As mentioned above, seven entrances of the fugue subject move the tonal locus of the subject from B-flat back to E, retracing the pattern laid down by the passacaglia. The fugue subject, like the passacaglia theme, has a serial origin but, also like the passacaglia, lacks any significant chromatic motion. The counterpoint in the exposition has several scale patterns which are frequently exploited in subsequent episodes. The third, fifth, and seventh entrances of the subject occur on the third beat of the measure (not first, as in other entrances). A long transition concludes the exposition, beginning a transformation of the fugue theme into a more lyric melody (flute, measure 212–217).

Variation I: Schuman adjusted the fugue in the same way in which he treated the passacaglia by appending a series of variations as the second half of the fugal section. The first variation uses the transformed version of the fugue subject (B) as a long-phrased contrapuntal line over which a variation of the passacaglia theme is set. At measure 248 the style of the variation changes, with the melodic variation of the fugue theme becoming a unison passage for woodwinds. A new version of the passacaglia theme is then placed in the strings in augmentation and parallel minor triads. The melodic writing in the woodwind lines resembles that found in the first variation of the passacaglia.

Variation II: A very rhythmic accompaniment line in the strings is structured from parallel sonorities, primarily polychords of two major triads. Above this, all four horns play another version of the passacaglia theme. At measure 293 the polychordal style of the accompaniment is adjusted to leave only one set of parallel triads in force. A fugal voice in the low woodwinds, trombones, and string bass imitates the passacaglia theme. A third fugal entry occurs at measure 301 in the remaining woodwinds with a change in the style of the accompaniment in the strings. The fourth fugal entry (trumpets, measure 309) also results in another modification of the string accompaniment figures.

Variation III: An antiphonal figure using a modified parallel structure is handed back and forth between woodwinds and strings. The contrapuntal lines from solo brass instruments are sustained bits of motives from the passacaglia theme. An E-flat pedal supports the entire variation. In measure 328, a triplet figure takes over the woodwinds' antiphonal material, with duplets being placed in the string passages. The two antiphonal passages begin to overlap increasingly until a complex contrapuntal texture has been achieved.

Coda: Starting with a passage in triads for winds with a plodding bass line which creates two key levels for the section, the coda retains a parallel feature in this triadic passage as the bass relentlessly repeats a scale figure which emphasizes e-flat minor while the other voices work with a D major sound. The movement closes in B major.

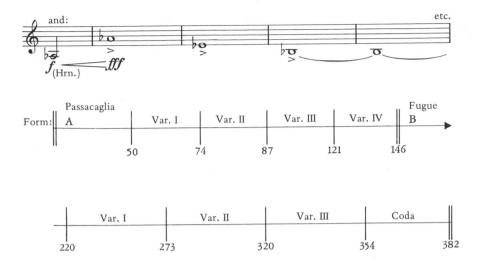

Part II: Chorale and Toccata. Schuman continued in Part II the formal principle used in both the passacaglia and the fugue, in which a basic theme is subjected to a series of variations. The nature of these variations is even freer than before, since Schuman further transformed some of the previous themes until they had almost assumed melodic charactreistics of new material. This organic growth or thematic transformation concept tends to impart a more lyric and rhapsodic style to the Schuman works than one would suspect if only the intellectual requirements of what is being done were considered. Schuman's mixture of the classic and romantic heritages of the symphony through this procedure produced interesting results.

Chorale

An introduction of a subdued but expressive nature opens the chorale. It is scored for violas and cellos divisi. The melodic material is somewhat similar to some of the narrow-ranged lines in the passacaglia variations and thus helps unify the basic sound of this part with the music of Part I. Melodic motion in the introduction is limited to seconds, thirds, and fourths. Most of the writing is in three voices. The tonal organization retains Schuman's implied diatonicism but gradually, as before, moves quite freely (if slowly) through a variety of key centers but with a minimum of chromatic motion. The chorale statement starts at measure 21 in the solo trumpet. The melodic style of this tune is quite angular in its first version. The tune plods in equal note values except for cadence points. The solo flute takes over the theme in a slightly varied version as the accompaniment continues to simplify its style. The use of parallel chord motion in triads and single triads for additional vertical support is typical of the section. The theme section closes with a brief reference to the passacaglia theme.

Variation I: A new version of the chorale is placed in the first violin and cello, two octaves apart. The inner void is filled by a contrapuntal line in eighth notes (violin II and viola, unison). The rhythmic style is similar to that of the passacaglia's first variation.

Variation II: Starting with a fff statement in parallel major triads in most of the orchestra, Schuman places a counterpoint in similar rhythmic values in the lower woodwinds and strings, maintaining this procedure for the balance of the variation.

Coda: This passage involves a return to the introductory materials with a section played by the horn quartet. The coda filters out, with trumpets and strings continuing the introductory materials. The stress in the materials appears to be the interval of the minor third. The chorale, having started on the pitch E, ends on a B-flat major triad; this is basically the same plan used in the passacaglia.

Toccata

The final section of the symphony introduces a rhythmic theme in the snare drum which then becomes the rhythmic skeleton of the toccata theme. The initial statement is over a B-flat pedal. After a complete statement of the rhythm of the theme, the actual theme enters at measure 157 in the bass clarinet. The theme is related to the chorale theme. The snare drum continues with a rhythmic counterpoint. The bass clarinet entrance is on E-flat. The theme is imitated in the oboe and English horn (pitch level D), starting at measure 171. A fourth entrance of the theme (on E-flat) concludes this fugal section of the toccata. The fourth statement also ends on E-flat. Schuman then adds a series of loosely outlined free variations (or developments) on this and other themes of the symphony.

199–229: Rhythmic augmentation of the theme with rhythmic units in the snare provides a connection with the virtuosic spirit of the toccata.

230–43: The toccata theme is stated in parallel fifths with the snare drum doubling the basic rhythm of the theme. A counterpoint using materials related to the theme is in the other instruments.

244–311: An elongated cadenza for cello and then strings stresses the conflict between the major and minor third and closes with a passage in parallel minor triads.

312–29: This section involves a variation of the chorale theme.

330–54: A variation on an augmentation of the toccata theme with an agitated accompaniment in strings involves parallelism in major triads.

355–69: Another treatment of the chorale theme with a similar agitated accompaniment figure in the strings entails more parallelism (fifths).

370–94: A long rhythmic buildup uses a triplet figure and contains a statement of the toccata theme starting at measure 385.

395–407: The rhythmic subject is restated with some rhythmic canon; the triplet figures continue.

408–28: A concluding section which returns the brass chords of the passacaglia (from measure 63–72, that movement), uses the minor third motive, and concludes on an e-flat minor triad.

SUMMARY

Schuman's third symphony, while not as adventuresome or as tonally progressive as some of his later works, shows compositional principles which Schuman retained throughout his style. The emphasis, however, on the gradual transformation of materials throughout an entire work, the use of single-movement (multisectional forms) symphonies, and the linear conception of symphonic texture can be seen clearly in this symphony. The point has been made before and should be restated that Schuman, while thinking of himself as a romantic, has an intellectual conception of the symphony which articulates clearly with the most advanced of contemporary styles except for aleatoric and electronic music. He has absorbed serialism into a rather free tonal style without losing the ability to create a diatonic emphasis and a pattern of lyricism. Tonal procedures have been devised to promote order rather than disorder. While the third symphony emphasizes the vertical unit of the triad (or two triads as a polychord), later works rely on a more complex harmonic idiom which emphasizes tritones, seconds, etc. The third symphony is strongly influenced by baroque principles and Renaissance polyphonic writing.

Copland conducting during his residency at California State University, Fullerton, in the 1976–77 season. Courtesy *Continuum* magazine.

Aaron Copland (1900–   )

Copland's primary output of works is not indicative of a serious commitment to the concert symphony. While the output below lists five symphonies (or symphonylike works), only two of these works are within the tradition of the concert symphony. Two of the works were written in Copland's French-jazz period (1924–1929); two were written in the abstract period (1929–1935); one was written in the folk period (1936–1949). The continuing stylistic period (serial) has seen the composition of at least two works in a more abstract and linear style: *Connotations for Orchestra* (1962) and *Inscape* (1967). Nothing of a multimovement symphonic style has been noted since the composition of the third symphony.

    The composer's own style development is mirrored in the symphonic works. Influenced by his native jazz idiom, which he expanded into a more contemporary idiom during a three-year stay in Paris, he arrived at a style which blended some jazz mannerisms with polytonality, neoclassicism, Ravel's orchestral style, Stravinsky's neoclassical objectivity, and an emphasis on increased dissonance (at the end of the period). Many authorities, however, feel that

Copland's best works were written in the second period, when he reverted to a more abstract and linear style at time bordering on atonality and serialism. Most of the works from that period are instrumental, complex, and somewhat experimental. Typically the textures are thin and linear. Vertical sonorities are quite complex at times. His launching into a more popular "folk" period in 1936 saw the creation of more functional works, often written on direct commissions. Ballet music, radio music, movie music, theater music, and "useful" media seemed to have occupied most of his time. The overall style generally becomes simplified during the folk period with frequent use of folk tunes, diatonic and pandiatonic settings, and a continuation of some jazz influences. Folk elements include cowboy tunes, Quaker hymns, and Latin-American rhythms, among others. Form is quite clear, with a continued emphasis on contrapuntal textures in some of the instrumental works. The works use traditional key signatures and are generally diatonic with an emphasis on the triad. Modes can be noted in some of the folk works. The melodic style in the folk period is fairly simple, with a decided lack of angularity in most of the tunes. Rhythm continues as a key style element: strong pulse, ostinato passages, percussive patterns, frequent changes of meter, syncopation, and other jazz mannerisms. Rhythm is perhaps the only element of the style which remains consistent throughout all periods. In 1950, Copland returned to the more complex style of the abstract period and embraced some serial techniques.

DANCE SYMPHONY

Copland extracted three sections from his ballet *Grohg* (1923) as the three movements of what he called a "dance" symphony to submit in a contest sponsored by the RCA Victor Company for a new symphonic work. The prize was to be $25,000. He originally intended to complete his *Symphonic Ode* in time for this competition. None of the works submitted satisfied the judges, so the award was divided among five works: $5,000 each to Copland, Louis Gruenberg, and Ernest Bloch, and $10,000 to Robert Russell Bennett for his two scores.* The three dances are connected into a continuous work in the *Dance Symphony*. The first movement (originally "Dance of an Adolescent") has a slow introduction and a subsequent *Allegro* in rondolike structure. The second movement ("Dance of a Young Girl Who Moves in a Dream" in the ballet) is an *Andante moderato* which follows a loose part-form outline while retaining a reduced orchestral format for most of the movement. The final measures of this movement contain one of the composer's rare examples of quarter-tone

---

* Arthur Cohn, *The Collector's Twentieth Century Music in the Western Hemisphere* (New York: J. B. Lippincott Company, 1961), p. 54.

usage (viola solo, last three measures). The slow movement has many measures which resemble the sound of some of the music of the impressionists, especially the tendency to remain on one sonority for an extended period of time. The *Allegro vivo* finale is an early example of Copland's diversified rhythmic style and has both jazz and Stravinsky influences. Fluctuating polyrhythms make the closing movement the most attractive. In one passage the composer wrote in a simplified metrical barring of the tune in alternating 5/8 and 3/16 meters. This tune is superimposed upon a steady flow of eighth notes (3/8 meter) in the strings. A *meno mosso* version of the tune is harmonized in a diatonic style but with jazz chords with added sixth (which flats when the third is flatted). The finale, which has been in F major for the greater part, ends on a minor second, A–B-flat.

SYMPHONY FOR ORGAN AND ORCHESTRA (1924, REVISED 1928 AS THE *FIRST SYMPHONY*)

Copland wrote this work for Nadia Boulanger's appearance with the New York Philharmonic in 1925. Later, he revised it as his first symphony. This analysis is based on the organ score. Copland used a motto theme which outlines the three pitches of a minor triad (3–1–5) as the basis for the entire work. While this underlying theme is not too apparent in the opening movement, it becomes increasingly more important as the symphony moves toward conclusion. The first movement (*Andante*) is a prelude based on one theme primarily. The second movement (*Molto allegro*) is a scherzo with the first section in 3/4 meter and with two themes and a second section in 4/4 meter. The scherzo appears to use an ostinato based upon the pitches D–E–A, this undergirding both of the scherzo themes. The first theme stresses the major second as its primary interval, thus gaining some unity with the ostinato figure. The middle section has two jazz influences: a syncopated fox-trot rhythmic pattern and a blues effect enhanced in the restoring for orchestra alone by alto saxophone. The return of the scherzo is brief and emphasizes the major second. The finale (*Lento, Allegro moderato*) is in a fairly free sonata-allegro form. The first tune (solo violas without accompaniment) starts with the three pitches of the motto. The faster B theme uses the motto theme as an ostinato very much in the style of some of the Stravinsky works of the period. In the development section, while weaving a counterpoint above the organ, the violin evolves a new tune based on the motto. The recapitulation is quite brief and merely combines the first tune, the evolved motto tune, the motto ostinato, and the second theme in a unique restatement of all primary themes. The work is a good example of Copland's combining of jazz elements with his unique rhythmic gift, all this still under the influence of such significant European composers as Ravel and Stravinsky.

SHORT SYMPHONY (1933)

This work is probably Copland's best orchestral work to date. Because of its complexity (primarily rhythmic problems) it had few orchestral performances; the premiere in this country did not occur until 1944 (NBC Symphony, January 9). Because of conductors' reluctance to schedule performances of the complex work, Copland arranged the score in 1937 for sextet (string quartet, clarinet, and piano), rebarred many of the difficult metric passages and gained additional recognition from frequent performances of the work. The *Sextet* became known (like the *Short Symphony*) as the best work of his second period. The work is in three movements, played without pause. Both the opening and final movements can accommodate a sonata-allegro outline, while the middle movement is in a song form (ABBA). Copland's primary thrust in the symphony seems to be that of rhythmic complexity set in very clear textures. The harmonic materials have been somewhat simplified in anticipation of the subsequent folk period, with the triad and open fifth the most favored sonorities. Many of the tunes are quite angular, with frequent skips of an octave. The themes of the middle movement are more scalar and diatonic. Ostinato, repeated rhythmic patterns, shifted accents, polyrhythms, frequent changes of meter, irregular meters, and displacement of rhythmic units make the work a performance challenge for most orchestras. The only constant rhythmic feature in the first and third movements is the pulsation of the eighth note. Some orchestral oddities occur: use of the heckelphone, flute in G, and a passage of col legno scoring for strings. The symphony is an important contribution to serious literature and should be attempted by more orchestras.

EXAMPLES FOR STUDY

Copland: *Third Symphony*

Copland's major symphonic contribution in a four-movement form is his Third Symphony, commissioned by the Koussevitsky Music Foundation and performed for the first time by the Boston Symphony Orchestra on October 18, 1946, in Boston's Symphony Hall. The work has a number of interesting implied influences. First, it was a symphony conceived and almost completed during the closing days of World War II. Second, the composer was nearing the end of his folk period, a creative phase which saw not only folk and nationalistic works but also more abstract works like the Third Symphony. Third, the work seems to be influenced to some extent by the style of the then popular Russian symphonists, especially Shostakovich.

I: Molto moderato. The opening movement is in a rondo form (ABABA) and stresses a more contemplative style, especially in the first section. Its angular principal theme is scored originally as an unaccompanied line. The

The Boston Symphony Orchestra, under Koussevitzky, premiered Copland's *Third Symphony* in 1946. The above view shows the orchestra in Symphony Hall being rehearsed by its musical director, Seiji Ozawa, during the 1976–77 season. The hall, completed in 1900, is known as this country's best symphony concert hall and one of the three best in the world. Photo courtesy Boston Symphony Orchestra.

counterpoint which then follows is similar in style to that found in Harris's Third Symphony. A second version (A^2) of the theme starts at measure 36, leading with greater rhythmic activity to the second section. It is this more martial theme (B), as provided by the trombones, which recalls similar sections by Shostakovich. The ostinatolike organization of the accompaniment in equal eighth notes also enhances this connection. After several repetitions of the new tune with increasing rhythmic energy in the accompaniment, the work climaxes on a statement of the first theme. This second appearance of the first theme (A) is followed by a brief return of B and then a more prolonged restatement of A. The slower tempo of the opening accompanies this final return. Copland chose to use key signatures in the symphony with a strong emphasis on E major in the opening movement.

Form: A¹ A² | B | A | B | A¹ A²
         ↓   ↓   ↓   ↓   ↓   ↓   ↓
         36 54   89   109   129   160
                                                   179

II: Allegro molto. Copland has the second movement as the symphony's scherzo, complete with contrasting trio and coda. The introduction presents two basic motives from which most of the materials of the scherzo will be drawn. Much of the spirit of the scherzo, however, is caused more by the incessant flow of repeated eighth notes in the chordal accompaniment. The reappearance of the scherzo tune (in the rounded binary form) at measure 112 is in augmentation. A short codetta (134–56) returns to the texture of the introduction. The trio is in 3/4 meter (scherzo, 4/4) and has the expected two themes), the second of which has all the traits of one of Copland's "western" waltzes. The return of the scherzo is more developmental than is its first statement. A coda contains both major themes with a canonic treatment of the trio theme. The A coda section is again in a slower, more introductory style but rises to a climactic final cadence.

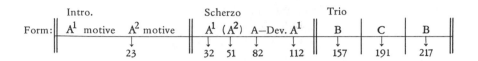

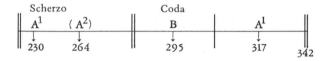

III: Andantino quasi allegretto.

III: **Andantino quasi allegretto.** The third movement is a combination arch form and theme with variations. The movement begins with a long, slow introduction which is based on the first movement's B theme. Its texture is polyphonic with more emphasis on free counterpoint than on imitation. The theme for the variation is an extremely simple contour of descending scale segments—B, A, G-sharp, E—somewhat ornamented. The variations which follow are sometimes contrapuntal but primarily experiment with the rhythmic possiblities of the tune, a fact which brings this section of the symphony in line with some of the rhythmic mannerisms of the earlier abstract period. A coda which returns the material of the introduction closes the movement. The work flows without pause into the finale.

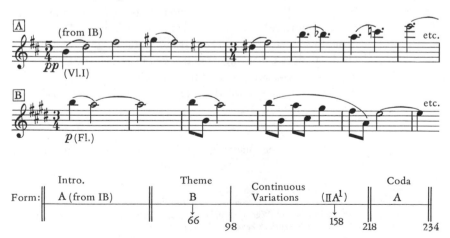

IV: Molto deliberato. Copland grafted an earlier work (*Fanfare for the Common Man*)* into the introductory measures of the finale, possibly for patriotic reasons. After a broad and stirring statement of the fanfare, the movement moves to the exposition of the primary theme (A) in the tonic key, D major. Most of the materials of the first theme are presented in fugal style, with a second fugue subject introduced at measure 53. The fugal style continues during the balance of the exposition with the exception of an extended cadence section (measures 85–98). The development section seems to be organized into sectional developments.

99–122:	Theme A is the subject of fugal and contrapuntal development.
123–26:	This is a modified repetition of a previous cadence passage (measures 85–90).
127–48:	Four string lines, doubled at the octave, evolve a virtuosic statement of a spun-out A theme with a syncopated accompaniment by the brass.
149–73:	A development of the fanfare tune uses augmentation and diminution while the A theme continues as a counterpoint above all of this.
174–213:	The B theme, a new tune, is taken up by the trumpets and horns while the A theme's sixteenth notes continue as a counterpoint.
214–44:	A more extended development of the B theme ensues with elements of the A theme used above it. Contrasts by woodwind and string sections involve parallel motion in the upper three voices of a four-voice setting. The sonority is the simple triad, which gives the music a somewhat archaic or primitive effect.
254–301:	A fugal development of the previous fugue subject from the A section (measure 53) is extended and thorough. The section climaxes with a terrific orchestral din (measure 294) in a passage which involves a shocking (for this work) chord (A, C-sharp, D, D-sharp, E, G-sharp) and flutter-tonguing on flutes, horns and trumpets. Copland added the ratchet to the chord for good measure.

The recapitulation returns to the quiet fugal style of the exposition but quickly

---

* The fanfare was one of several commissioned by Eugene Goosens, conductor of the Cincinnati Symphony during World War II. Copland's was written in the fall of 1942. See Arthur Cohn, *The Collector's Twentieth-century Music in the Western Hemisphere,* p. 62.

departs from the simplicity of the opening section by regrouping many of the symphony's major themes simultaneously (see form chart below). At measure 352 all of this complexity leads to a final statement of the descending scale line from the *Fanfare*. The B theme then returns, accompanied by a completely static harmony (tonic chord, fff dynamic level). A dramatic and exciting coda using the principal theme of the first movement, the fanfare theme, and the principal theme of the finale (all simultaneously in a polyphonic mix) concludes the symphony.

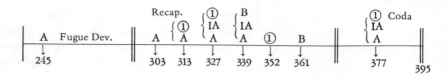

SUMMARY

Copland's symphonic output is characterized by a certain kind of consistency: avoidance of the traditional Austro-German concept of the symphony which seems to have been continued in the works of the more conservative modern composers (some of the Russian scores, some of the Vaughan Williams scores, some of the Sibelius scores, for example). Many of Copland's orchestral works verge on the programmatic (ballet arrangements, folk derivations, etc.). Three of his scores (*Appalachian Spring, El Salon Mexico,* and *Rodeo*) have maintained strong positions in American symphony orchestra's repertories. One of his more complex works, which shows the real depth and nature of his talent— *Short Symphony*—has not attracted widespread audience support. The Third Symphony occupies a position somewhere between these two groups of works. It actually is his only four-movement concert symphony. It shows well how he, as a composer of absolute music, avoided an emphasis on abstract development in favor of polyphonic textures and variation techniques. Above all, the Third Symphony incapsulates the real essence of the Copland style: rhythm. Copland's handling of the orchestra is possibly influenced by his more jazz-oriented and commercial scores which may have shown him the value of scoring heavily for brass and percussion in passages requiring expressive orchestral support. Percussion is essential in the Third Symphony. The finale contains quite an assemblage: three timpani, bass drum, tamtam, tenor drum, snare drum (rim shot used also), suspended cymbal, ratchet, wood block, regular cymbals, anvil, and claves. The score of the finale also requires two harps, celeste, piano, xylophone, tubular bells (chimes), and orchestral bells (glocken). Triangle and slapstick, used in earlier movements, are omitted in the finale. The orchestra for the entire work is large: triple woodwinds (mostly), quadruple brass plus bass clarinet, English horn, and E-flat clarinet. Two piccolos can be noted at times.

The Third Symphony, an exception to some extent to Copland's general orchestral output, may be an indication of how the contemporary American composer might approach the concert symphony: write as few traditional symphonies as possible; concentrate, on the other hand, on works which relate more to the taste and expertise of the American symphony public. In Copland's case this has produced multimovement works (some with single movements of short duration based on one idea or effect), less complex forms, more emphasis on line and combinations of lines, and an avoidance of increasing the complexity of a work without decreasing the challenge to the audience's attention span. The Third Symphony, in its unique position with relation to the composer's overall orchestral output, may show some of these concepts. Like the Harris symphonies, the work continues a lyric thrust in the concert symphony which seems to be a distinct need for American audiences.

Wallingford Riegger (1885–1961): Serialism and the Symphony

While most composers of the traditional four-movement concert symphony have avoided the use of serial techniques for underlying tonal organization of a symphony, a few have made this attempt. Although the results have not become generally popular with the public, those works which have had some degree of acceptance are those that retain some more conservative tonal elements or organizations to balance the basic atonal pitch relationships. Further, in recent years the concert symphony has been replaced by some composers with a type of work which borders on the programmatic or mood-suggesting and which uses even more adventuresome tonal manipulations than serialism would provide. In many of these works the orchestral resources appear to be used as a tone palette in the creation of new sonorities based not only on new or unusually constructed sonorities but, more importantly, on the unique extractions of tone color from the orchestra itself. The mixing of electronic media with orchestral sound sources has expanded the expressive or sensate capabilities of the symphony orchestra even more. Serialism, however, has been the most difficult technique to absorb into orchestral music, particularly the concert symphony.

Wallingford Riegger provides an example of a composer who survived through his own musical wits and yet was able to maintain a career as one of this country's most progressive composers. Born in Georgia, reared in Indianapolis and later in New York, Riegger studied at the very best of schools and with truly outstanding teachers. He was in the first graduating class of the Institute of Musical Art in New York City. Going to Germany for further training, he soon launched a career as a successful conductor. Returning to this country during World War I, he guest-conducted the San Francisco Symphony in 1918. After a ten-year career as a college teacher, he settled in New York, becoming an editor for various music houses and primarily supporting himself writing potboilers for church choirs under assumed names (William Richards, Walter Scottson, Gerald Wilfring Gore, among others). By the time of his death in 1961 he had, as a serious composer, evolved through four different style periods: an academic period (1919–1923); an atonal period (1926–1933), which culminated with his adoption of serial techniques; a dance period (1933–1941), in which he reverted to a simpler style, primarily writing ballet works; and a final absolute period (1942–1961) wherein he returned to serial and more abstract style. It was in this final period that he wrote two of his four symphonies.

Riegger's application of serial principles was quite flexible. Often, in the process of moving a work forward, he would revert to tonal writing if it seemed to serve the needs of the work. The rules of serialism never held any attraction for him. His style is also characterized by a technique of alternating between pure unaccompanied line and masses of sounds, many times quite complex. His developmental style stressed variation and imitation. Frequently his tunes were saturated with repeated notes. Fugato and stretto were favored contrapuntal devices. Most of the rhythmic style seems to have been derived from his dance experiences. Using serial resources he was able to derive an entire vocabulary of sonorities which can be best described as masses of sound. His formal manipulations were traditional in many respects, with motives being extracted from his rows and subsequently developed. He also was able to create certain harmonic focal points which function as substitutes for traditional harmonic polarities (tonic, dominant chords, etc.).

His four symphonies were written during a thirteen-year period:

SYMPHONY NO. 1, OP. 37 (1944)

Unpublished; possibly never performed.

SYMPHONY NO. 2, OP. 41 (1945)

Unpublished; written for high school orchestra.

SYMPHONY NO. 3, OP. 42 (1947)

Published; recorded; revised in 1957 and published in that version.* This work is analyzed in full on pages 379–84.

SYMPHONY NO. 4, OP. 63 (1956)

Published. The fourth symphony is a four-movement work of a more conservative style than the third. The work, while dated by the composer as completed in 1956, may date from the 1930s, since it has a much stronger

---

* Joseph Machlis, *Introduction to Contemporary Music* (New York: W. W. Norton & Company, Inc., 1961), p. 611.

dance organization than many works of the abstract periods. Its assumed serial structure is difficult (if not impossible) to perceive in all movements except the third. The second movement existed previously as a dance work written for Martha Graham in 1936. The work depicts suffering experienced in the Spanish Civil War and thereby mirrors dance rhythms of that country.*

The *Allegro* first movement is in sonata-allegro form and presents a series of rhythmically concise themes or motives around which the movement will be structured. The tonal and harmonic format is conservative. In the opening sections there is an emphasis on diatonic materials and two-voice scoring. A second theme is more complex (rehearsal letter I) because of its fugal structure and shifting tonal environment. It continues the basic rhythmic thrust of the movement. The development (letter K) shows some of the more typical vertical usages associated with Riegger's advanced style, especially the part motion in parallel tritones (letter K). Whole-tone scale resources are also used (letters M–N). Parallelism (intervals, chords, etc.) is most typical of the movement. The second movement is a slow ternary effort. Serial roots are hard to perceive. The middle section (a trio?) starts with a polytonal device, the melody in the bass describing an ostinato in d minor while the harmony in the brass seems to favor G-flat major. The third movement (*Sostenuto*) is closer to the serial style in its angular theme and its linear texture. Most of the melodic material is related to the pitches in the first theme. A more complex type of parallelism infects this movement. The movement is connected to the finale with only a slight pause between them. Chords built on major seconds seem to constitute much of the vertical material of the movement. Its triple meter and rapid tempo create the effect of a scherzo. The work is in sonata-allegro form. It represents a return to the basic style of the first movement but with more emphasis on complex sonorities and on linear writing.

EXAMPLES FOR STUDY

Riegger: *Symphony No. 3* (1947, 1957)

This work was commissioned in 1947 by the Alice M. Ditson Fund of Columbia University and was first performed by the CBS Symphony on May 16, 1948. It subsequently was awarded the New York Music Critic's Circle Award and the Naumburg Award.

I: Allegro. After a three-bar introduction the principal theme is presented in the oboe (A¹). The theme is synonymous with the row. This row can

---

* Arthur Cohn, *The Collector's Twentieth-century Music in the Western Hemisphere*, p. 182.

be divided into two segments, each of which contains a tritone, a fifth, and two minor seconds, plus either a major third (first segment) or another minor second (second segment). The rhythm of the A¹ theme also has certain distinguishing rhythmic characteristics in which no two subdivisions of the beat are similar. A second version of the first tune (A²), in sixteenth notes, starts in measure 11. Chords derived from segments of the row accompany it. This version of the theme then is developed until another version of the theme (A³) starts around measure 55. Riegger's flexible use of row principles can be seen in measure 48, where a sonority based on a segment of the row (f–c–b) is moved in a parallel structure up the chromatic scale, a curious mixing of impressionistic planing and serial construction. The short passage does establish a new motive of ascending semitones which will occur later. A unison statement of the final version of A starts at measure 64.

The secondary theme (B) is constructed from fourth chords (two, on different tonal levels, each a half step removed from the other). This type of dissonant sonority is characteristic of the serial style of the composer. In measure 85, the chromatic semitone motive is placed into the rhythmic style of the A² theme for a portion of the closing section. Just previous to the beginning of the development, pointillistic treatment of the original row begins (measure 99, etc.). Riegger reduced orchestral forces almost to the chamber medium for much of the closing section and the early part of the development. At measure 123, a long series of short climaxes on the semitone motive begins. It ends with a massive orchestral trilling in parallel sonorities extracted from the row. Half- and whole-step sounds predominate. The recapitulation begins with the original introductory flourish. The restatement is shortened by the exclusion of the subordinate material. The coda is a short fugato which rearranges some of the original row to encompass a minor third interval, available only by major tonal surgery in the row's first version. The trilling treatment repeats at measure 238, with the fortissimo statement of the row added at measure 241 with tritone sonorities in the brass.

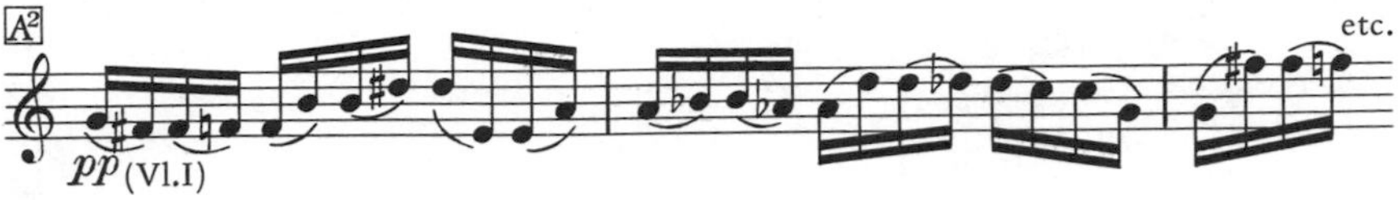

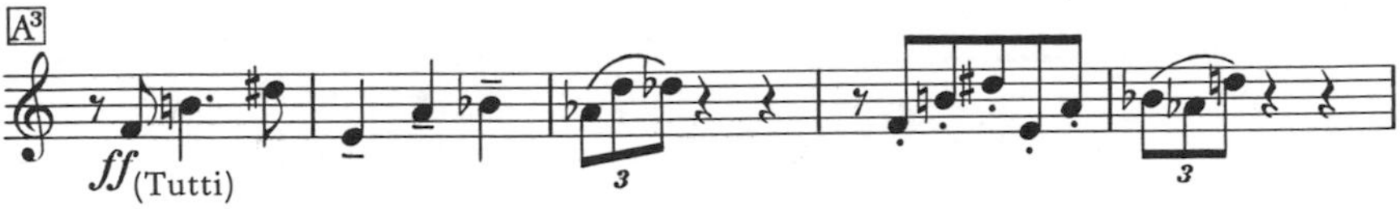

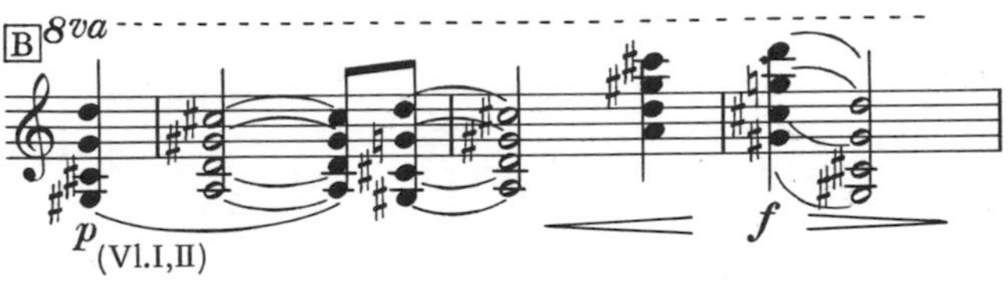

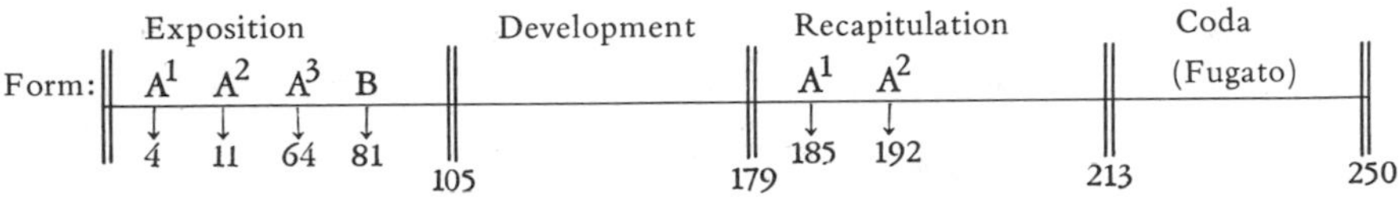

II: Andante affettuoso. The opening theme of the second movement was extracted from a dance written by Riegger in 1936 called "With My Red Fire." * It is not serial although based primarily on melodic half steps and harmonic whole steps. The opening phrase illustrates Riegger's contrapuntal handling of the two-voice texture. The woodwind chamber effect expands somewhat when the second portion of A enters at measure 30. A repetition of A¹ (measure 36) becomes more involved contrapuntally, with a canonic passage in the strings providing one group of two voices and a pedal C the primary harmonic support. The actual second theme (B) is serial, starting with another two-voice contrapuntal setting. The A material returns with the original melodic version followed by a fugato on a new arrangement of the pitches (see fugato theme on theme sheet). The movement closes with the string setting of the original A¹ theme. The final cadence chord is an open fifth (F–C) embellished with a B and a C-sharp.

* Joseph Machlis, *Introduction to Contemporary Music,* p. 612.

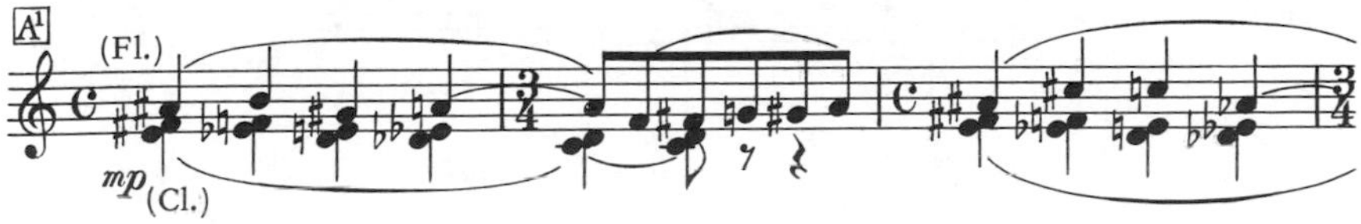

III: **Poco Allegro.** Riegger's scherzo movement does not follow the traditional form. The *Allegro molto* (measure 13) actually starts the scherzo proper, the style of the section being similar to the previous fugal sections. Riegger extracted a new tune (B) from the original row and, again, presented it in fugal style (measure 80). The particular theme is subjected to an extended development, often with reduced orchestral forces. After a return to the introductory material to complete the arch form outline possibly intended, an extended coda concludes the movement. The material of the coda is generally reminiscent of the A theme.

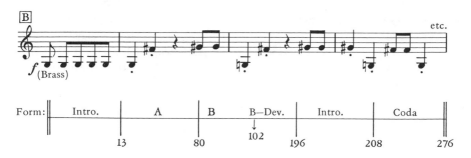

IV: **Beginning rather slowly (Passacaglia and Fugue).** The finale is divided into two large sections, the first being an extended passacaglia based on a seven-pitch bass figure. Most of the passacaglia's variations involve short fragments of the row being placed above the ground bass, with some sections being more harmonically conceived than others. The second section, fugue, uses a subject organized in half steps with a repeated tritone. This half-step motion soon begins to dominate the remainder of the movement with imitative textures receding. The passacaglia returns at measure 280, with the predominantly half-step motion returning for the balance of the movement.

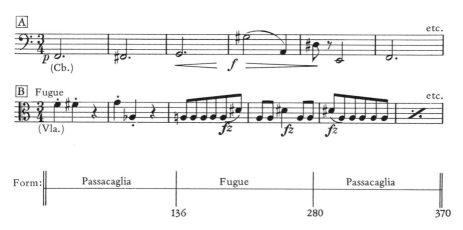

© copyright 1957 by Associated Music Publishers, Inc. Used by permission.

SUMMARY

The Riegger third symphony provides some insight into serialism as a primary compositional organization for the symphony. Riegger felt compelled to use frequent baroque forms and devices for maintaining the musical logic of the

serial movements; this imitative and contrapuntal writing was seemingly pref-
erable to more extended forms normally associated with the symphony. Only
the first movement is in a developmental form. Riegger also relaxed his serial
requirements to include at least one movement which is free of that atonal
organization. The expressive nature of the symphony can be attributed to the
lyric interpretation Riegger often placed on his serial writing. The spinning out
of some of the tunes has a nineteenth-century rhapsodic effect and tends to
ally Riegger with that century. The rhythmic vitality (from the dance period?)
of the work, plus the chromatic nature of much of the writing, makes the symphony one of the composer's most attractive serial works.

VIII

Other Twentieth-Century Symphonists

In addition to those previously mentioned, a large group of symphonists were and are active in the United States. A number of them settled in America either just before or just after World War II. While most did not write more than four or five symphonies, some were responsible for a prodigious output. A fairly representative listing includes:

George Antheil, 1900–1959	6 symphonies
Samuel Barber, b. 1910	2 symphonies
Leonard Bernstein, b. 1918	3 symphonies
Ernest Bloch, 1880–1959	5 symphonies
John Alden Carpenter, 1876–1951	2 symphonies
Henry Cowell, 1897–1965	20 symphonies
Paul Creston, b. 1906	5 symphonies
David Diamond, b. 1915	9 (including a choral symphony, the ninth)
Ross Lee Finney, b. 1906	4 symphonies
Vittorio Giannini, 1903–1966	5 (third is for band)
Don Gillis, 1912–1978	10 symphonies
Morton Gould, b. 1913	3 (plus four "symphonettes")
Alexei Haieff, b. 1914	3 symphonies
Howard Hanson, b. 1896	6 symphonies
Alan Hovaness, b. 1911	28 symphonies
Andrew Imbrie, b. 1921	3 symphonies
Charles Ives, 1874–1954	4 symphonies
Gail Kubik, b. 1914	3 symphonies
Benjamin Lees, b. 1921	3 symphonies

Nikolai Lopatnikoff, b. 1903	4 symphonies
Bohuslav Martinu, 1890–1959	6 symphonies
Peter Mennin, b. 1923	8 symphonies
Vincent Persichetti, b. 1915	9 (sixth for band)
Walter Piston, 1894–1976	8 symphonies
Sergey Rachmaninoff, 1873–1943	3 symphonies
George Rochberg, b. 1918	4 symphonies
Bernard Rogers, 1893–1968	5 symphonies
Ned Rorem, b. 1923	3 symphonies
Arnold Schoenberg, 1874–1951	2 (chamber symphonies)
Roger Sessions, b. 1896	8 symphonies
Elie Siegmeister, b. 1909	5 symphonies
Leo Sowerby, 1895–1968	5 symphonies
William Grant Still, b. 1895	5 symphonies
Alexander Tcherepnin, b. 1899	5 symphonies
Ernest Toch, 1887–1964	7 symphonies
David Van Vactor, b. 1906	5 symphonies
Bernard Wagenaar, b. 1894	4 symphonies

Most of the composers listed above write in somewhat conservative styles, be it neoclassic (Piston, Siegmeister, Persichetti), neoromantic (Hanson, Barber, Sowerby, Giannini), or eclectic (Ives, Antheil, Rorem). Some favor serialism (Finney, Imbrie, Rochberg, Sessions). Many were influenced by national traits such as jazz, folk music, and music associated with the composer's own culture (Ives, Gillis, Cowell, Sowerby, Still, Hovaness, Gould, Bernstein, Antheil, Bloch, Carpenter). Some were quite innovative in their use of experimental harmonies (clusters), simultaneous events, or polytonality (Ives, Cowell).

British composers have written symphonies with the same degree of frequency as have American composers. In an artistic environment that was dominated by the works of Vaughan Williams between both world wars, a strong neoromantic tradition continued in many styles (Bax, Walton, Rubbra), while others embraced more eclectic or neoclassical values (Britten, Rawsthorne, Tippett). As in other countries, few symphonists (Bennett, Searle) have used a basically serial style.

Malcolm Arnold, b. 1921	6 symphonies
Arnold Bax, 1883–1953	7 symphonies
Richard Rodney Bennett, b. 1936	2 symphonies
Benjamin Britten, 1913–1976	5 (of varying types)
Edward Elgar, 1857–1934	2 symphonies
Alan Rawsthorne, 1905–1971	3 symphonies

Edmund Rubbra, b. 1901	8 symphonies
Humphrey Searle, b. 1915	5 symphonies
Michael Tippett, b. 1905	3 symphonies
William Walton, b. 1902	2 symphonies
Malcolm Williamson, b. 1931	2 symphonies

Two Polish composers are serving at the frontier of musical style but have not yet contributed more than minimally. The Penderecki work is based on shifting patterns of contrasting sonorities and textures created by the composer's nonthematic but carefully controlled pitch procedures. It is in four movements.

Witold Lutoslawski, b. 1913	2 symphonies
Krzysztof Penderecki, b. 1933	1 symphony

In Russia, symphonic output has been dominated by Shostakovich and Miaskovsky.

Alexander Glazounov, 1866–1936	8 symphonies
Reinhold Gliere, 1875–1956	3 symphonies
Dmitri Kabalevsky, b. 1904	4 symphonies
Aram Khatchaturian, 1903–1978	3 symphonies
Nicolai Miaskovsky, 1881–1950	27 symphonies
Arvo Pärt, b. 1935	2 symphonies
Rodion Shchedrin, b. 1932	2 symphonies
Valentin Silvestrov, b. 1937	2 (second for chamber orchestra)

Most Russian composers write in an eclecteic style that shifts with the political climate. Some react favorably to the more *avant garde* developments in Poland (Silvestrov, Pärt). As in other countries, many composers who work in more advanced styles seem to avoid the four-movement symphony form.

Austrian and German composers are more involved with serial style; many adapt it with some degree of flexibility to meet their own needs.

Bernd Alois, 1918–1970	1 symphony
Alban Berg, 1885–1935	1 (arranged from opera *Lulu*)
Wolfgang Fortner, b. 1907	1 symphony
Roman Haubenstock-Ramati, b. 1919	2 (native of Poland)
Hans Werner Henze, b. 1926	6 (sixth for chamber orchestra)
Kurt Schwerstik, b. 1935	2 (first is *Draculas Haus und Hofmusik* or *Transylvania Symphony* for strings)

Anton Webern, 1883–1945   3 (includes opus 6 and 10)
Egon Wellesz, b. 1885   8 (settled in England)

Probably because of the strong Sibelius tradition, composers in Scandinavia are more productive as symphony composers. Finnish composers are numerous if not well-known outside Finland. Many write in a style that has derived from neoromantic roots. Englund, a neoclassicist who emigrated from Sweden, is a notable exception to the more numerous neoromantics.

Einmar Sven Englund, b. 1916   3 symphonies
Paavo Heininen, b. 1938   3 symphonies
Joonas Kokkonen, b. 1912   3 symphonies
Tauno Marttinen, b. 1912   4 symphonies
Aarre Merikanto, 1893–1958   3 symphonies
Usko Meriläinen, b. 1930   2 symphonies
Tauno Pylkkänen, b. 1918   1 symphony
Einojuhani Rautavaara, b. 1928   4 symphonies

Symphony composers in Sweden are less numerous if more productive than the Finnish. Alfven and Fernstrom are neoromantic in orientation, in spite of the former's use of serialism in his fourth and fifth symphonies. Atterberg and Rosenberg are neoclassicists, while Nystroem's shifting values make him more eclectic.

Hugo Alfvén, 1872–1960   5 symphonies
Kurt Atterberg, b. 1887   9 symphonies
John Fernstrom, b. 1897   12 symphonies
Gösta Nystroem, 1890–1966   6 symphonies
Hilding Rosenberg, b. 1892   5 (plus two chamber symphonies)

In Denmark symphony composers show the same proclivity either for the neoclassical (Holmboe, Riisager) or neoromantic (Langgaard, Nielsen) styles. Bentzon's style is a more advanced and chromatic neoclassic outgrowth. The symphony is an extremely popular genre in Denmark.

Niels Viggo Bentzon, b. 1919   13 symphonies
Vagn Holmboe, b. 1919   12 (plus four sinfonia and three
                                       chamber symphonies)
Rued Langgaard, 1893–1952   16 symphonies
Carl Nielsen, 1865–1931   6 symphonies
Knudåge Riisager, b. 1897   5 (fifth for strings and timpani)

Two composers are prominent in Norway after the death of the more progressive and almost-serial composer, Valen. Of the two, Egge uses a more extreme approach.

Klaus Egge, b. 1906	5 symphonies
Harald Saeverud, b. 1897	9 symphonies
Fartein Valen, 1887–1952	5 symphonies

Some activity can be noted in Italy. Berio uses the most advanced in style (primarily serialism), and lives outside Italy, as many others have since his time. Casella's style shifted from neoromantic to neoclassic around 1920, while Malipiero remained basically a romantic in spite of an increasing use of dissonance later in his career.

Luciano Berio, b. 1925	1 symphony
Alfredo Casella, 1883–1947	3 symphonies
Gian Francesco Malipiero, b. 1882	11 symphonies

By using a direct, simple, classical approach, composers in France whose careers began during the impressionistic period of Debussy and Ravel show a common tendency to offset the vague style of that period. This classical approach is often enriched by various contemporary devices (e.g., Milhaud's bitonality). Roussel, Dutilleux, and Schmitt were primarily post-impressionists; Roussel absorbed other developments around him and became one of France's leading neoclassicists. Of the remaining composers, Leibowitz and Nigg were serialists. Martinet applied some serial devices in his neoclassical works. Ropartz was a postromantic.

Henri Dutilleux, b. 1916	2 symphonies
Arthur Honneger, 1892–1955	5 symphonies
Jacques Ibert, 1890–1962	2 symphonies
André Jolivet, b. 1905	3 symphonies
René Leibowitz, 1913–1972	4 (plus a chamber symphony)
Jean-Louis Martinet, b. 1912	1 symphony
Darius Milhaud, 1892–1975	12 symphonies
Serge Nigg, b. 1924	1 symphony
Jean Rivier, b. 1896	7 symphonies
Guy Ropartz, 1864–1955	5 symphonies
Albert Roussel, 1869–1937	4 symphonies
Henri Sauget, b. 1901	3 symphonies
Florent Schmitt, 1870–1958	3 symphonies

Symphonists from Mexico often share a strong nationalistic or folk element in their works. Most write in a modern style mix of classic, romantic and folk elements. Carlos Chavez has been Mexico's primary symphonist writing in this style. Mata, Kuri-Aldana and Enriquez are serialists with varying degrees of duodecuple commitment.

Carlos Chavez, b. 1899	6 symphonies
Manuel Enríquez, b. 1926	2 symphonies
Blas Galindo, b. 1910	2 symphonies
Maria Kuri-Aldana, b. 1931	2 (second for strings)
Eduardo Mata, b. 1942	3 (third for winds)
José Moncayo, 1912–1958	1 symphony
Hector Quintanar, b. 1936	3 (second in style of Brahms)

Heitor Villa-Lobos (1896–1959) was Brazil's most productive symphonist, writing twelve symphonies. Claudio Santoro (b. 1919), a serialist after 1960, had two of his eight symphonies performed by the St. Louis Symphony in the 1963 and 1964 seasons.

From Chile, Juan Orrego-Salas, (b. 1919) has gradually become a more complex eclectic composer through his four symphonies. He lives in the United States at this time. Carlos Isamitt (b. 1887) has been writing in serial style since 1939, and he completed his first symphony in 1960.

In Argentina, Alberto Ginastera (b. 1916) has written in an increasingly more complex eclectic style that injects aleatory, serial, and linear counterpoint into a basic mixture of neoclassicism and neoromanticism. He has produced three works that resemble the symphonic form: *Sinfonia Portena, Pampeana No. 3* ("Pastoral Symphony"), and *Sinfonia "Don Rodrigo"* (from opera), which uses a soprano soloist. In addition there is *Estudios sinfonicos*, Op. 35, completed in 1968. Ginastera is known as South America's leading composer.

Spain's leading symphonists left that country to live abroad. Roberto Gerhard (1896–1970) settled in England while contributing four symphonies in serial or more advanced styles (tape recorder, athematic procedures and contrasts of basic textures and sonorities). José Ardevol (b. 1911) moved to Cuba, wrote three symphonies, and subsequently shifted to a serial approach. Gerhard's first symphony (1952) is known as one of the finest symphonies of the postwar period. It was performed by the New York Philharmonic in 1962.

Postlude

During its 250-year history the symphony evolved from a transplanted opera overture to a complex four-movement concert work. As a creative experience the symphony attracted during that period some of the best artistic talents available. The roles which these many composers played sometimes differed. Some invented or created new forms or ways of organizing the symphony. Others sought to inject more stability into the form. Some used the symphony to point to new ways of organizing a musical language. A few were visionary enough to present options for later composers to test in charting the symphony's future course. Finally, there were always a few who passed on to the next generation an enriched and vital form.

In the eighteenth century literally hundreds of composers participated in the evolution of a symphonic form that became an almost rigid overall pattern for the next 200 years. In the latter part of the century, however, composers began to relax this rigidity, which they had either inherited or created. In this manner, Haydn, whose mature works represented the full flowering of the classical symphony, was still able to show what could be done to make each of his later symphonies a work of art without being seriously hampered by the stylistic conventions of his time.

Beethoven, working with feet planted firmly in both classical and romantic periods, created another model, both more expressive and more formally unified. His symphonic legacy thus presented the two options which nineteenth-century composers would explore. Brahms took up the challenge of continuing the highly articulated intellectual approach, while Strauss and Mahler, each in his own way, pushed the expressive dimension to the limits of their inspiration and ability.

Finally, in the twentieth century, a general artistic upheaval in the century's first twenty-five years seriously challenged the value structures of all symphony composers. Through the quiet efforts of composers like Sibelius the integrity of the form, however, was preserved. Soon afterwards the rise of neo-classicism restored formal concepts that in many ways provided a common thread with which the life line of the symphony could be extended.

Each century tended to repeat a process which a previous century had experienced in the development of the symphony. One can see experimentation having an effect on the symphony within a given historical period but not changing the work's basic course in that period. It was as if the process of experimentation in itself resulted in a general enrichment of the form rather than in any major changes such as advocated by those actively involved in the experimentation. Thus, while program music helped to expand the expressive base of the symphony, it failed to establish itself as a viable and lasting concept for the form.

In spite of the experimentation and the multitude of individual styles to which the symphony was subjected, it still moved forward in history with some sense of integrity and self-esteem. In the process not only was a rich body of incomparable literature created but also a hardy and enduring form developed. Through all the works studied one finds a thin line of continuity which is characterized by an inherent creative vitality. This, then, is the true tradition of the symphony, a tradition which has enhanced and will continue to enhance most eloquently its history.

Glossary of Terms

ACCENT   Stress or emphasis on a single sound.

ACCOMPANIMENT   The musical background for a melody.

ADAGIETTO   Slow, slightly faster than *adagio*.

ADAGIO   Slow, between *andante* and *largo*.

AGITATO   Agitated.

ALEATORIC MUSIC   Chance music either in composition or performance. Musical sounds are selected at random either by composer or performer or both.

ALLEGRETTO   Slightly slower than *allegro*.

ALLEGRO   Fast; faster than *allegretto* but slower than *vivace*.

AMOROSO   Loving, lovingly.

ANDANTE   At a slow tempo which approximates a walking tempo; slower than *allegro*, faster than *adagio*.

ANDANTINO   Slightly faster than *andante*.

ANIMA   Spirit (*con anima*, with spirit).

ANIMATO   Spirited, lively.

ANTECEDENT   The first of two phrases which seem to be in a question-answer relationship; can also mean subject-answer relationship in a fugue.

ANTIPHONAL   Pertaining to the process by which two groups alternate or echo in performance.

APPASSIONATO   Passionate.

APPOGGIATURA   A nonharmonic tone, accented, which resolves by step, usually downward. Many are derived by a leap upward.

393

ARCH FORM   Form which is structured as A–B–C–B–A.

ARCO   Bow (*coll' arco*, with bow).

ARPEGGIO   A melodic figure which results from playing a chord's pitches in succession. ARPEGGIATED and ARPEGGIATION are terms related to the process.

ASSAI   Very, much.

ATONAL   Without a key center. Atonality is a system which produces atonal results.

ATTACCA   Attached; indicates that a section or movement is to be connected to the next section or movement without undue pause in performance.

AUGMENTATION   Expanding or stretching the temporal value of musical sounds, normally by doubling rhythmic values.

AUGMENTED   Expanded by a small increment, usually a half step; said of chords or intervals. An AUGMENTED TRIAD is a major triad (e.g., C–E–G) with an expanded fifth (e.g., C–E–G-sharp). An AUGMENTED SIXTH CHORD is an inverted minor triad which has its resulting major sixth expanded by a half step. C–E-flat–G inverts to E-flat–G–C. The C is raised to a C-sharp, creating the augmented sixth.

AUTHENTIC CADENCE   A cadence which involves V–I or vii–I.

BAR   A vertical line used to denote the end of a measure; can also mean a single measure. "Bar line" is also used.

BARBERSHOP HARMONIES   Very traditional harmonies which stress seventh chords with resolutions to other seventh chords in an irregular fashion (e.g., C-sharp d7–D d7).

BASS   The lowest-sounding voice or part in a composition; also the lowest-sounding male voice; also means the CONTRABASS VIOL, the lowest-sounding stringed instrument.

BASS CLARINET   One of the lower-ranged members of the clarinet family; plays an octave below the soprano clarinet in B-flat. CONTRABASS CLARINET plays an octave below the bass clarinet.

BASSO CONTINUO   Bass part in baroque music which is performed on a keyboard instrument (or lute) with harmony added above it according to figures supplied with the bass part. Part is normally doubled on another bass instrument, usually cello.

BASSO OSTINATO   A bass part with a short, repeated melodic pattern. A boogie-woogie bass is a type of *basso ostinato*.

BASSOON   A bass woodwind instrument which uses a double reed to generate the tone.

BELLS   An orchestral instrument which is a set of vertically suspended tubular chimes.

BINARY   Simple part form with two parts, A and B.

BITONALITY   Sound that results from using two keys simultaneously.

BLUES THIRD   Flatting of the third or seventh scale degrees, the latter in the dominant chord especially. In jazz the flatting is only partial so that the resulting pitch lies somewhere between the major and minor third.

BOURRÉE   A seventeenth-century French dance in fast duple meter, usually with a single upbeat.

BRASS   Collective noun used to denote a species of wind instrument constructed of brass such as trumpet, French horn, trombone, tuba, etc.

BRIO   Liveliness; *con brio*, with spirit and vigor.

CADENCE   Stopping place in music, usually a harmonic pattern which promotes a feeling of rest; can be a melodic pattern also.

CADENZA   A passage which is improvised in a brilliant style, normally near the conclusion of a movement in a concerto. Cadenzas have been written into music since the time of Beethoven.

CANON   An imitative contrapuntal form in which a late-entering voice repeats exactly what the first voice has played or sung. "Three Blind Mice" is a canon.

CANTABILE   In a singing style; refers to a lyric style either in performance or in a melody.

CANTATA   Usually a baroque vocal form employing more than one movement with arias, recitatives, and possibly choruses; usually has a small instrumental accompaniment; can be sacred or secular and normally is topical in nature, as contrasted with the more narrative oratorio or opera.

CANTUS   The fixed or "given" voice in a contrapuntal composition above which a voice or counterpoint is added.

CANZONA   An early baroque instrumental form which developed out of the *chanson;* was a multisectioned form with changes of meter, tempo, key, and musical materials. Ensemble canzonas tended to be homophonic with sections which resembled movements.

CELLO   The next-to-lowest-sounding member of the string section of the orchestra; has four strings tuned to C–G–D–A (lowest to highest); played seated, between legs, with bow or may be plucked.

CHACONNE   A variation form which uses a fixed harmonic progression as its theme. The progression is usually short, four to eight measures in length.

CHEST OF VIOLS   A Renaissance ensemble used in England, usually six viols playing in three parts (treble, tenor, bass).

CHORALE   A hymn tune associated with the German Protestant Church.

CHORD   Three or more different pitches sounded simultaneously.

CHROMATIC   Progressing by half steps; a tone modified by an accidental (sharp, flat, or natural). Chromaticism is the use of these raised or lowered notes. A CHROMATIC CHORD PROGRESSION involves the consecutive alteration of a pitch which is common to both chords (e.g., C–E–G going to A–C-sharp–E).

CIRCLE OF FIFTHS   An imaginary theoretical circle which shows how the addition or subtraction of a single sharp (or flat) raises or lowers the key of a musical passage by an interval of a fifth. A circle-of-fifth modulation would be one which progresses in a pattern of ascending or descending fifths (e.g., C–G–D–A–E or C–F–B-flat–E-flat–A-flat, etc.).

CLARINET   A woodwind instrument whose tone is created by a single reed in a mouthpiece; in an orchestra it is one of the lower soprano woodwinds.

CLAVICHORD   A baroque keyboard instrument which creates its sound by striking its strings with a tangent or striker as distinguished from the plucking action of the plectrum of the harpsichord. The tangent, unlike the plectrum, determines the vibrating length of its string.

CLOSE HARMONY   Voicing of a harmonic passage with the parts as close as possible, the upper three in four-voice writing within a range of an octave.

CLOSING SECTION   The final section in a sonata-allegro movement's exposition. A CLOSING THEME is located in the closing section.

CODA   A final segment of a movement or composition which has been added after a point at which the work could have been concluded.

COL   With.

COLOR   In orchestration a term which means an emphasis on effect through combinations of instrumental sounds; the effect obtained by playing the same pitch on different instruments. Tone quality also means tone color.

COLORATION   Ornamentation of a melodic line. Chords of coloration have the same embellishing format in a harmonic sense, having within their structure certain added pitches which embellish the sonority. A chord with an added sixth could be considered a chord with coloration.

COMMON–CHORD MODULATION.   A modulation which involves using a chord as a pivot (or point of modulation between two keys), this chord actually existing in both keys. For instance, in moving from C major to G major, the C major chord would exist in the new key as the IV chord while also serving as the I in C.

COMMON PRACTICE PERIOD   Primarily refers to the harmonic style of composers in the period from 1700 to 1825.

COMMON–TONE PROGRESSION   A two-chord progression in which the chords share at least one pitch (e.g., E–G–B to A–C–E, the E being the common tone). A common-tone modulation would involve the same relationship.

CON   With.

CONCERTATO   The baroque principle of contrast of materials through tone color which led to the cencerto.

CONCERTINO   In the concerto, the name used for the solo group.

CONCERTO   A multimovement (three and four) form based on the contrast of solo player or group with a larger orchestral group.

CONCERTO DA CAMERA   A baroque four-movement concerto of dance-like style with a tempo scheme of fast–slow–fast–slow.

CONCERTO DA CHIESA   A four-movement baroque concerto type whose movements were contrapuntal in style and whose tempo scheme was slow–fast–slow–fast.

CONCERTO GROSSO   A concerto which has a solo group of more than one instrument.

CONJUNCT   Using stepwise movement to create melody (e.g., A–B–C is conjunct motion).

CONSEQUENT PHRASE   The second of two phrases which seem to have a question-answer relationship.

CONTOUR   The shape of a melody expressed in visual terms.

CONTRABASS   The largest string instrument.

CONTRAPUNTAL   Pertaining to counterpoint. A round is contrapuntal.

CONTRAPUNTAL ASSOCIATE   In a fugue a characteristic melodic figure which is used in another voice above or below the fugue theme or subject. The associate is so identified if it retains its individuality throughout the fugue.

CONTRARY MOTION   Relationship between two voices or parts when one part ascends while the other descends.

CORNET   A brass instrument similar to a trumpet but with a large bore at the flared end of the tubing. The section of flared or conical shape is longer than the similar section on a trumpet.

COUNTERMELODY   Tune which is set above another tune.

COUNTERPOINT   Two or more melodies sounding simultaneously, as opposed to a single tune with accompaniment.

COUNTERMELODY   A melody which is sct above or below another melody.

The device is generally used to enrich a melody with accompaniment as distinguished from the more contrapuntal combining of two tunes without harmonic accompaniment.

COUNTERSUBJECT   A special kind of counterpoint used in a fugue over the fugal subject. A countersubject always retains its identity and appears almost as another fugue subject.

COUP D'ARCHET   A broad bow stroke used frequently in the opening measures of works performed in the early classic period in Paris. Effect was similar to that obtained by a brilliant fanfare in the brass.

CRAB STYLE   Backward motion, i.e., performing a melody starting with its last pitch and going backward; frequently used in canonic passages.

CRAFT   The skill of composition.

CRESCENDO   Gradually increasing the volume or loudness level of a composition.

CROSS RELATION   A chromatic alteration of a pitch which occurs in a different voice from that occupied by the original pitch; must be a consecutive alteration.

CYCLIC   Pertaining to the use of the same theme or themes in more than one movement of a multimovement work.

DA CAPO   A score direction which requires that the work be played again from the beginning; used in the minuet or scherzo to ensure that the first section (minuet or scherzo proper) is repeated after the performance of the trio.

DANCE FORMS   Instrumental forms associated with the baroque period primarily. Dance form from that period was generally a binary (A–B) form. Examples included the sarabande, courante, gigue, allemande, and minuet.

DEVELOPMENT   The process of extracting motives or themes from one section of a musical work and, through modulation, repetition, sequence, or other procedures, extending these materials in a later section beyond their original length. Development began in the early eighteenth century as a simple restatement of previous material at another pitch or key level. Development can be contrapuntal and can include imitative or fugal sections. Development also means the middle section of a sonata-allegro movement, where most development occurs.

DEVICE   A concise usage in music intended to produce a particular effect. Tchaikovsky's frequent use of brass fanfares is an idiomatic compositional device in that composer's style. A cadence is a device used to create the effect of a pause in music.

DIATONIC   Descriptive of music which conforms to the pitch spectrum of a major or minor scale or key system without use of extra chromatic pitches.

DIMINISHED INTERVAL   A minor or perfect interval which has been decreased by a half step. A DIMINISHED TRIAD contains a diminished fifth as its outer interval and a minor third as its lower. A DIMINISHED SEVENTH CHORD adds a diminished seventh to a diminished triad.

DIMINUTION   A rhythmic treatment which generally reduces the rhythmic value of a series of notes by one-half.

DISSONANCE   Definition varies with historical period, but the term generally means a disagreeable effect obtained from the sounding together of two or more pitches, which seems to require resolution to some other chord. In the pre-twentieth-century style format, the term was applied to any whole- or half-step relationship which existed in a chord made up of intervals of thirds and fifths; these dissonant pitches were created by adding pitches which did not match the roots, thirds, or fifths of the chords in question. Adding the pitch F to a G–B–D chord created a dissonant effect.

DIVERTIMENTO   An instrumental form of the eighteenth century which combines features of the sonata with those of the suite. It had as many as eight movements, some of which were dances and some of which could be sonata-allegro or rondo.

DIVISI   Divided; a single part (e.g., first violins) splits into two subparts to play two different notes or lines. Simultaneous intervals are sometimes played *divisi* by a single string section.

DOLCE   Sweet; sometimes, soft.

DOMINANT   The fifth scale degree (e.g., G in key of C); term also applied to key and sonority. DOMINANT SEVENTH is the diatonic seventh chord found on the fifth scale degree in a major key (e.g., G–B–D–F in key of C major); the chord is made up of a major triad and a minor seventh. The DOMINANT KEY is the key located on the fifth scale degree (G major is the dominant key of C major).

DORIAN   A mode that starts on D and ascends for an octave on successive pitches without accidentals.

DOTTED RHYTHM   Use of dotted note patterns which produces a long-short rhythmic effect. The dotted note usually is considerably longer than its following short note, especially in the style of the French overture.

DOUBLE BAR   Two vertical lines inserted in a score to denote the end of a section or movement of a work.

DOUBLE FUGUE   Fugue with two subjects.

DOUBLE REED   Family of woodwinds (oboes, bassoons) whose tone is produced by blowing through two reeds, both of which move when blown; distinct from single reeds (clarinet, sax) where a single reed vibrates against a mouthpiece device. Double reeds vibrate rather freely just inside the lips of the player. The reed itself looks like a partially flattened tube.

DOUBLE VARIATIONS   Variation type in which a variation is repeated with enough changes to give it an appearance of a second variation. Basic treatment remains the same in the initial variation and its double. The double merely continues the treatment or expands upon it. Variations on two themes also called double variations.

DOVETAILING   Form term which refers to starting a phrase before a preceding phrase has ended. Many times the final note of one phrase becomes the first note of the next phrase when dovetailing is used.

DRESDEN AMEN   In liturgical usage, a four-voice setting of an Amen that embellishes an important Amen in the liturgy (the final prayer, for example). Richard Wagner used it as a leitmotiv to represent the Holy Grail (cup used at the Last Supper) in his opera *Parsifal*.

DUALISM   Concept of two themes in a single movement, especially sonata-allegro.

DUAL MODALITY   Two modes existing at the same time; generally refers to the practice in the late nineteenth and twentieth centuries of using both major and minor modalities on the same key center. The use of a tonic major chord and a tonic minor chord in close proximity is an example of dual modality.

DUPLE   Generally refers to a meter with two beats per measure.

DUPLETS   Rhythmic effect of subdividing a beat in music into two equal pulses, each exactly half the temporal length of the beat.

DYNAMICS   Markings in a musical score which control the element of loudness in a performance. Accent and emphasis are also suggested by dynamic markings.

EIGHTH NOTES   The symbol which represents an equally subdivided quarter note. Eighth notes also represent a pulsation which occurs in rococo or style galant music in which a constant stream of subdivided beats occurs.

ELISION   A musical sequence or progression which omits what one has anticipated. For instance, the conclusion of one phrase just as another phrase begins is an example of a formal elision. A harmonic progression which, in an eighteenth-century style format, moves a VI chord to a V chord elides, or omits, the II or IV chord which would normally be involved (i.e., VI–II–V).

ENGLISH HORN   An alto double reed instrument similar in appearance to an oboe except for a slight bulge in the barrel of the instrument near its open end, or bell. The reed is connected to the instrument by a short curved metal pipe similar to a bassoon bocal.

ENHARMONIC PITCH   A pitch that sounds the same as another but has a different notation (e.g., B-sharp is the same as C-natural).

EXPOSITION   The first section of a sonata-allegro movement in which all of the themes ostensibly are stated. In a fugue the exposition is the section that states the fugue subject.

EXPRESSIONISM   An artistic movement of the early twentieth century characterized in music by a rejection of the colorful (if subdued) style of the impressionist movement. Expressionism sought to express inner feelings and more introspective matters. Musically the result was a highly original style characterized by angular melody, an avoidance of the lush orchestral and tonal effects of impressionism, highly dissonant harmonies, atonality, rhythmic complexity, and disjointed line. Schoenberg and Berg are generally known as the main representatives of the movement.

EXTENSION   In music, stretching a section either by repetition or by some other means for formal elongation. A musical phrase can be extended by repeating a short fragment, section, or motive of the phrase before reaching a cadence.

FALSE START   The impression of the beginning of the recapitulation created by a restatement of the principal theme near the end of the development section; it is generally in a nontonic key.

FERMATA   A notation symbol which requires sustaining a single sound (chord or pitch) for a greater length than the sound's original rhythm would imply; also called a "hold" or "bird's-eye" (the latter because of its resemblance to an eye).

FIFTH   An interval which embraces five consecutive diatonic scale degrees. The interval of A–E is a fifth. FIFTH RELATIONSHIP is a condition which exists beween two consecutive chord roots or key centers a fifth apart.

FIGURE   A very short melodic fragment; can also be considered a synonym for motive.

FIGURED HARMONY   A procedure in which the separate melodic lines in music (which is essentially harmonic in style) are written so as to create more melodic interest in each separate part and thus result in a more contrapuntal effect.

FINALE   Final movement of a work or final work on a concert program.

FIVE, THE   A group of nineteenth-century Russian composers who banded together to promote a more "Russian" style in their music, as opposed to the more general style of Tchaikovsky. Members included Mily Balakirev (1837–1910), Alexander Borodin (1833–1887), Cesar Cui (1835–1918), Modest Mussorgsky (1839–1881), and Nicolai Rimsky-Korsakov (1844–1908).

FLÜGELHORN   A brass instrument similar in appearance to a cornet but with a wider bore. The tone is mellower than that of the cornet.

FLUTTER–TONGUING   Rapidly moving the tongue when playing brass and some woodwind instruments (flute) to interrupt the stream of air as it enters the lips of the player. It does not affect the pitch of the sound, which is produced by the rapid vibration of the lips in the brass mouthpiece or by the velocity of the airstream into the flute. The effect is that of a fluttering sound similar to the tremolo in strings.

FORM   The shaping of music into recognizable motives, tunes, parts, sections, and larger forms such as variation, sonata-allegro.

FORTE   Loud; score abbreviation: f.

FORTISSIMO   Very loud; score abbreviation: ff.

FOUR–PART HARMONY   The setting of a harmonic passage in four voices or parts (soprano, alto, tenor, and bass).

FOX TROT   An American ballroom dance style or form based on music with duple meter. All such dance music since about 1910 is an outgrowth of the fox trot.

FREE COUNTERPOINT   Non-imitative contrapuntal writing which often de-emphasizes delineation of themes and subjects. Opposite of STRICT COUNTERPOINT which is imitative.

FREE TONE   A nonharmonic tone which is approached and left by skip.

FRENCH HORN   A brass instrument with a narrow conical bore which flares quite widely at its open end with a large bell structure. It is the alto brass instrument in the orchestral brass section.

FUGUE   A contrapuntal form based on the principle of imitative counterpoint. The composition starts with only one voice stating the theme or subject; subsequent voices enter successively with an imitation of the subject while earlier voices continue in more freely contrapuntal lines. FUGAL is an adjective describing the application of the principles of fugue in a composition. FUGHETTA (FUGHETTO) is a short fugue. FUGATO is a short passage in fugal style in a nonfugal composition.

FUOCO   Fire. *Con fuoco,* with fire.

GALLANT STYLE   The musical style of the rococo (1725–1775).

GALOP, GALLOP   A quick dance of the mid-nineteenth century with quick changes of steps and some hopping motions. Music written for the dance was called by the same name. It was in duple meter.

GAVOTTE   French dance of the seventeenth and eighteenth centuries in 4/4 meter, usually starting on the third beat. The tempo is moderate.

GEBRAUCHSMUSIK   "Music for use" primarily written for home consumption. Hindemith supposedly created the genre.

GENERAL PAUSE   A pause that occurs in orchestral scores after a climax; involves a rest for the entire ensemble and is usually quite unexpected; score abbreviation: G. P.

GERMAN ROMANTIC OPERA   German opera of the nineteenth century as seen in the works of Weber, Marschner, and Wagner. Style stresses subjects derived from legend or folklore, nature or natural phenomena as a dramatic force, the supernatural, nationalism.

GERMAN SIXTH CHORD   An augmented sixth chord on the raised fourth scale degree with a lowered third and a diminished seventh (e.g., F-sharp, A-flat, C, E-flat, in the key of C). The chord sounds like a dominant seventh on A-flat.

GIOCOSO   Humorous.

GLISSANDO   A fast scale passage created by very rapidly sliding the finger over the string(s) or keys. Lip glissando is also possible on brass instruments. Slowly sliding is called *portamento*.

GLOCKENSPIEL   A percussion instrument with steel bars which have an appearance of a piano keyboard; played with hammers or mallets. A portable glockenspiel is used in marching bands and is called the bell lyre because of its appearance.

GRAVE   Slow, solemn; the slowest tempo indication.

GRAZIOSO   Graceful.

GROUND BASS   A melody in the bass of four to eight measures length which is repeated constantly while the upper parts change or vary.

GROUND MOTIVE   A shorter ground which could also be called an *ostinato*.

HALF CADENCE   A cadence which ends on the dominant chord (or, more rarely, the subdominant).

HALF NOTE   A notational symbol employing a white (or hollow) note head with a stem.

HALF STEP   The smallest diatonic or chromatic interval available in a pitch system which uses the twelve chromatic pitches of Western music. C to C-sharp is a chromatic half step. E to F is a diatonic half step.

HARMONY   The simultaneous sounding of different musical pitches. A harmonic system categorizes these sounds as chords of varying types (triads, etc.) and the connection of these chords as some kind of progression. Harmony implies both sonority (chord) and motion (progression). HARMONIC is an adjective relating to harmony. HARMONIC RICHNESS results from an emphasis on a certain amount of controlled dissonance and modulation in the nineteenth-century style. Chromaticism can also create the condition.

HARPSICHORD   A stringed keyboard instrument in use from about 1500 to

1800, when it was replaced by instruments of the piano family. The tone is created by a plectrum attached to the keyboard mechanism (called an "action") which plucks the string as the key is depressed.

HECKELPHONE   A larger oboe (bass or baritone) with a range an octave below a regular oboe; resembles a large English horn because of the bulge near its open end. Heckel invented it in 1904.

HOMOPHONIC   Pertaining to a type of musical texture or layout of parts or voices which has a single melody with a more or less chordal accompaniment.

HORN   Shorter name for French horn.

IMITATION   Immediate restatement of a musical entity in another voice, part, or section. A round is based on the principle of imitation. IMITATIVE is descriptive of the condition.

IMPETUOSO   Impetuous.

IMPRESSIONISM   An artistic movement of the late nineteenth and early twentieth centuries which manifested itself in the music of Debussy, Ravel, Delius, and Griffes (among others); favorite musical devices of the impressionists: parallel chord structures, avoidance of developmental forms, sonorities with added sixths and ninths, muted sounds and subdued orchestral colors, use of harp and woodwinds, whole-tone scales or chords, and harmonic schemes which avoided any sense of traditional progression.

INFLECTION   The successive chromatic change of a pitch in the same voice or part (e.g., C, C-sharp).

INSTRUMENTATION   The process of scoring for instruments other than keyboard. The term is usually used when scoring for more than one instrument, especially a large ensemble such as band or orchestra.

INTERVAL   The distance between two pitches. An interval that encompasses five diatonic scale degrees is called a fifth (e.g., C–G). The two pitches of an interval may be sounded individually or simultaneously. INTERVALLIC is an adjective relating to the interval concept.

INVERSION   In harmony, the appearance of chord members other than the chord root in the bass or lowest-sounding voice. In intervals, inversion means placing the lower pitch up an octave, thereby creating another interval (e.g., a third inverts to become a sixth). In melody, inversion means reversing melodic direction (e.g., if tune ascends a fifth in the original version, it will descend a fifth in the inverted version).

IRONICO   Ironical.

LÄNDLER   An Austrian dance which dates from about 1800, in triple meter, resembling the waltz. Its tempo is generally slower than that of the waltz.

LARGO   Very slow; slower than *lento*. LARGHISSIMO is slower than *largo*. LARGHETTO is slightly faster than *largo*.

LEADING TONE   The seventh scale degree which is a half step below the first or tonic pitch of that scale.

LEARNED STYLE   The more contrapuntal or developmental style of the German composers as distinguished from the lyric and less involved style of the Italian composers of the eighteenth century.

LEGNO   Wood. *Col legno* means playing with the stick of the bow on a stringed instrument, usually with a tapping motion.

LENTO   Slower than *adagio* and faster than *largo*.

LIED   Generic name for nineteenth-century German song. LIEDER is the plural form. Can also be used in earlier historical context (songs of Minnesingers, sixteenth-century polyphonic lied, baroque lied, for example).

LINEAR COUNTERPOINT   A twentieth-century style of polyphony which tends to disregard vertical (or harmonic) relationships among the various voices.

MAESTOSO   Majestic.

MAJOR   A description of mode in music since 1650. Major mode (or major scale) has a major third (two whole steps) above its tonic pitch; also describes a triad or chord with a major third as its lowest-sounding third; also describes intervals of thirds and sixths. A major interval is a half step larger than a minor interval.

MARCATO   Marked.

MEASURE   A temporal unit in music denoted by a vertical line at its beginning and end in a musical staff.

MEDIANT   Third scale degree.

MEDIANT MINOR KEY   In a major key, the minor key located on the original key's third scale degree (e.g., e minor is the mediant minor key in C major).

MELODIC VARIATION   A variation procedure in which a new melody is created above the original tune's harmonic pattern. The procedure contrasts with ORNAMENTAL VARIATION, in which the original tune is ornamented with additional pitches and rhythmic patterns.

MELODY   A musical effect created by the successive sounding of individual pitches under some kind of rhythmic organization.

MINOR   A description of mode which locates a minor third above the tonic or first scale degree in a tonality; also describes chords and intervals as in MAJOR (above). A minor interval is a half step smaller than a major interval.

MINOR SEVENTH CHORD   A chord with a minor triad and a minor seventh above its root (e.g., d–f–a–c is a minor seventh chord).

MINUET   A dance in triple meter which dates from seventeenth-century France. Later, in the eighteenth century, the dance became a stylized musical form and appeared as a movement in the suite, symphony, string quartet, etc.

MIXOLYDIAN   A mode dating from the beginning of Western music. Played on the white keys of the piano, the mode starts on the pitch G and encompasses those pitches which are found in successive order up the keyboard to the next G.

MODE   The major or minor quality of a key scheme. In a historical sense the term refers to church modes, which were the primary tonal format in Western music until around 1650. Folk music is often MODAL.

MODERATO   Moderately; a tempo indication faster than *andante* but slower than *allegretto*.

MODULATION   Process of changing tonal focus from one key center to another within a given musical section.

MOLTO   Very (i.e., *molto allegro,* very fast)

MONOTHEMATIC   Having only one theme.

MOTET   A polyphonic vocal composition of either the thirteenth or sixteenth century which uses more than a single text, especially during the earlier period.

MOTIVE   A short melodic fragment which tends to reappear frequently in a composition; can also apply to a rhythmic motive in the same sense.

MOTIVIC DEVELOPMENT   The process of extracting motives from earlier themes in a movement and extending, repeating, imitating, or in other ways developing the motives.

MOTTO THEME   A fanfarelike theme frequently used by Tchaikovsky in his symphonies; can also refer to a theme which appears at the beginning of a composition and subsequently reappears at important junctures of the form. It may have programmatic connotations.

MOVEMENT   A division of a larger work that is complete in itself. It can usually stand alone, since it has its own internal formal structure.

MOVIMENTO   Movement.

MUTE   A device used on certain instruments to dampen or quiet the tone. A mute for a stringed instrument generally clips on its bridge. A mute for a brass instrument is inserted in its bell.

NATIONALISM   A nineteenth-century movement in the arts which sought to dignify and emphasize the national aspect of music through use of native folk tunes, rhythms, programmatic subjects, etc. Dvořák's use of Czech folk materials in his symphonies is a nationalistic trait.

NEAPOLITAN OPERA   An opera style of the late seventeenth and early eighteenth centuries which dominated most of western Europe and England. It was characterized by stringent musical and formal requirements which stressed vocal display above all else.

NEAPOLITAN SCALE DEGREE   The lowered second scale degree.

NEAPOLITAN SIXTH CHORD   The major triad on the lowered second scale degree, usually in first inversion (e.g., in C major, chord spelled D-flat, F, A-flat, with F in the bass voice).

NON   Not.

NONCHORD TONE   A nonharmonic tone foreign to the chord in which it appears.

NONHARMONIC TONE   A melodic pitch which does not coincide with the pitches of the chord supporting it. Same as nonchord tone.

NON TROPPO   Not too much (e.g., *allegro non troppo:* fast but not too fast)

OBOE   A small double reed instrument with a conical bore, similar in appearance to a clarinet.

OCTAVE   An interval which includes eight diatonic scale degrees in its span (e.g., C up to the next highest C).

OFFBEAT   A type of accompaniment in which the notes of each chord are placed on the weaker beat or half-beat while the bass line occupies the strong or downbeats; sometimes referred to as "um-pah" accompaniment.

OPERA BUFFA   Italian comic opera of the eighteenth century.

OPERA SERIA   A type of eighteenth-century Italian opera with a more serious dramatic thrust.

OPUS   Work. The designation is useful in cataloging a composer's works, e.g., Opus 1, No. 1 would generally imply the first work of an early group of similar works by a composer.

ORATORIO   A sacred or contemplative work which uses chorus, vocal soloists, and orchestra. While the work has a plot or a dramatic sequence, it is not staged.

ORCHESTRATION   The procedure used in setting a work for orchestra.

ORGANUM   An early type of counterpoint (A.D. 900–1300) which was set generally for two voices and varied in complexity from simple parallel writing (fifths) to an ornate and freer style which had a strong rhythmic organization.

OSTINATO   A repeated melodic or rhythmic pattern which supports other parts that change somewhat freely in relation to the ostinato. A boogie-woogie bass is an ostinato.

OUVERTURE   French for overture.

PANDIATONICISM   A twentieth-century tonal and harmonic style which reverts to a simpler diatonic style (similar in many respects to that of the eighteenth century) but with considerable flexibility with regard to chord structure and progression.

PARALLEL   Pertaining to a type of part-motion in which each voice or part moves in the same direction for approximately the same distance (varying with the scale patterns or overall tonal style of the music). PARALLEL CHORDS OF THE SIXTH are first-inversion triads which move in this fashion.

PARTIALS   Vibrating segments of a whole vibrating body creating a musical sound; same as OVERTONES or HARMONICS. The presence of partials determines the so-called tone color of a single sound.

PARTITA   An instrumental form which originated in the early baroque and was based on the principal of variation. Later, the term was used by Bach to mean the same as suite.

PART–WRITING   The process of arranging a composition's musical resources into a certain number of voices or parts.

PASSAGE   A section, usually small, of a composition.

PEDAL   Usually a bass note which is sustained for some length while the upper parts, especially the harmonies, change freely. PEDAL TONE has the same meaning.

PENTATONIC   A type of scale with only five different pitches in it (as contrasted with the seven-note scale of differing pitches in a major-minor key system).

PERCUSSION   Family of instruments (drums, gongs, xylophone, cymbal, chimes, etc.) that produce a tone primarily by being struck; in the symphony often means only the timpani (kettledrums).

PHRASE   A unit or section of a melody which compares to a clause or a sentence in grammar.

PHRYGIAN   A mode which in its nontransposed version starts on the pitch E and proceeds upward on the white keys of the piano to the next E.

PIANISSIMO   Very soft; score abbreviation: pp.

PIANO   Soft; score abbreviation: p.

PIANOFORTE   Complete name for the piano.

PICCOLO   A very small instrument of the flute family whose range is an octave higher than the flute's.

PITCH   The musical phenomenon created by a periodic (regular) vibrating body. In music, pitch means also the highness or lowness of a sound: the faster the body vibrates, the higher the pitch; the more slowly it vibrates, the lower the pitch. The rate of vibration is a sound's frequency; frequency is heard in music as pitch.

PIU   More; *piu adagio,* slower than *adagio.*

PIZZICATO   Plucking the strings with the finger; applies to the string section of an orchestra.

PLAGAL CADENCE   Subdominant to tonic harmonies; may also be supertonic to tonic.

POCHETTINO   Comparative of *poco;* littler.

POCO   Little

POLYCHORDS   A chord consisting of triads from two keys (e.g., C major and A major triads combined as a single chord).

POLYPHONIC   Pertaining to texture created by the combining of two or more melodic lines. The use of counterpoint creates a polyphonic texture.

POST HORN   A valveless brass instrument similar in appearance to the trumpet or bugle although much smaller in size. It was once used by postilions to announce arrivals and departures of coaches.

PRESSANTE   Pressing.

PRESTISSIMO   Extremely fast.

PRESTO   Very fast; faster than *vivace.*

PRINCIPAL THEME   The first theme found in the exposition of a sonata-allegro form; also PRINCIPAL MATERIAL.

QUARTAL   Pertaining to a harmonic style which uses chords constructed from the interval of a fourth (e.g., E–A–D–G–C) or fifth (sometimes called QUINTAL harmony).

QUARTER NOTE   A black note with a stem only; often used to represent a beat in a moderate tempo.

RECAPITULATION   The final section of sonata-allegro form in which all themes are restated.

REPEAT SIGNS   Two vertical dots (exactly like a colon) which precede or follow a section which is to be repeated; used in conjunction with vertical lines (||: or :||).

RESOLUTION   The process of moving from a dissonant chord or tone to a consonant chord or tone.

RETROGRESSION   A melodic or harmonic passage which is the reverse of its original statement; also refers to a type of harmonic progression in the Common Practice Period where the normal harmonic flow is reversed (e.g., V going to IV).

RHYTHM   The pulsating quality of music.

RIM SHOT   A stroke on the snare drum in which one stick is placed with its head on the drum head and its stick on the drum rim, and the other stick strikes that portion of the first stick between its head and the drum rim.

RING CYCLE   Wagner's four operas based on a single plot called the *Ring of the Nibelungs.*

ROLL   A continuous drum effect created by rapidly striking a drum head with both sticks in an alternate fashion; also called a trill.

ROOT   The pitch on which a chord is constructed. C is the root of a C major triad, C–E–G.

ROUNDED BINARY   A binary form which has a return to the first theme in its second section; usual form ‖: A :‖: B A :‖.

SALTARELLO   Sixteenth-century Italian dance in triple meter; later, in the nineteenth century, referred to fast dances of a more violent nature.

SCALAR   Scalelike.

SCHERZANDO   Playfully.

SCHERZO   A fast movement usually in triple meter normally found as the third movement of a four-movement sonata, symphony, string quartet, etc.

SECONDARY DOMINANT   A theoretical concept which explains the presence, for instance, of a D major triad in the key of C major as a dominant of the dominant (V of V). A secondary dominant can also be considered an altered chord (e.g., the D major triad in the key of C major as an altered supertonic triad).

SECTION   A more or less self-sufficient part of a larger form. Can also mean a smaller part of a segment of a form (e.g., the opening section of the first theme). Section also means a particular group of instruments in the orchestra (woodwind section, etc.).

SEQUENCE   The repetition of a melodic fragment in the same voice at a higher pitch level. Harmonic sequences are also possible in which a harmonic pattern is repeated at a different pitch level. In early liturgical music another kind of sequence was created by adding a poetic text to the long melismas of some *Alleluias.*

SERIAL   Pertaining to a type of atonality created by systematically arranging all twelve tones of the chromatic scale in an order of the composer's choice and then employing rigid principles which prevent an undue emphasis on any single pitch of the twelve.

SEVENTH CHORD   In tertian harmony, a chord with four members: root, third, fifth, and seventh; can be described by sound or by function (e.g., C–E–G–B-flat is a major-minor seventh chord or a dominant seventh chord).

SFORZANDO   Forced; means placing a very strong accent in the music.

SHORT CANON   Type of canon in which first voice states a short portion of theme and then sustains last pitch while second voice enters and imitates first portion; second voice then sustains last pitch while first voice again takes up a second segment of tune; process continues with each voice alternately sustaining a single pitch while other moves.

SIXTEENTH NOTE   A black note with two flags on its stem. In a fast tempo where a quarter note is the beat unit, sixteenth notes generally are the smallest measured subdivisions employed.

SIXTH   An interval which covers six diatonic scale degrees (or pitch letter names) (e.g., A–F).

SLUR   An indication (arched line) over notes to indicate legato, or smooth, playing; refers also to playing several notes on the same bow.

SOAVE   Gentle.

SONATA   An instrumental form with three or more movements. Most sonatas have four movements.

SONATA–ALLEGRO   A complex form used in almost all multimovement instrumental works since around 1750. The form divides itself into three sections: exposition (where primary themes are introduced), development (where thematic materials are extended and treated), and recapitulation (where themes are restated). Tonal considerations are somewhat stylized in the form. The secondary themes are usually in contrasting keys in the exposition. The development also avoids the tonic key. All themes ostensibly are restated in the tonic key in the recapitulation.

SONATA DA CAMERA   A baroque sonata with a tempo scheme of fast–slow–fast–slow and with movements of a dancelike character.

SONATA DA CHIESA   A baroque sonata with a slow–fast–slow–fast tempo plan and a more contrapuntal texture in its movements.

SONATA–RONDO   A hybrid form used by Haydn and some later composers in which the first theme reappears in the tonic key at what would be the beginning of the development section.

SONATINA   A sonata-allegro form which generally lacks a development section.

SONG FORM WITH TRIO   Overall form used in the minuet third movement of the eighteenth-century symphony. The song form is usually a rounded binary (||:A : ||: B A :||) with the trio often in the same form (||:C : ||: D C :||).

SOPRANO   Generic name for the highest voice or melodic line in a work.

SOPRANO WOODWINDS   Piccolo, flute, oboe, clarinet (as an orchestral section).

SOSTENUTO   Sustained.

SPECIES   In counterpoint a particular kind of treatment defined by the rhythmic relationship between the cantus firmus (given or fixed voice) and the counterpoint (added voice). If one note of the cantus is matched with a single note in the counterpoint, first species exists, etc.

SPIRITOSO   Spirited.

STAVE   Staff.

STIMMTAUSCH   Different instruments playing successive pitches of a melody in an alternative fashion.

STRAIN   A section of a melody (e.g., the second strain of a march).

STRETTO   In fugal writing a procedure in which a second voice imitating another enters before the first voice has completely stated the subject of the imitation.

STRINGS   Those sections of the orchestra made up of the violins, violas, cellos, and contrabasses.

STROPHIC VARIATIONS   A strict variation style in which the length of the theme is retained intact in each variation.

STURM UND DRANG   A literary movement in eighteenth-century Germany whose title became associated with the almost forced expressiveness of the music of C. P. E. Bach and others of the period.

STYLE GALANT   French for gallant style, a style associated with the rococo period in music history; characterized by a simplicity of texture (simple melody with accompaniment), fast tempos, incessant rhythmic activity which propels the music very energetically, and a delicate melodic style sometimes employing grace notes and other elements of melodic embellishment.

SUBDOMINANT   Fourth scale degree or chord on that scale step.

SUBORDINATE   Secondary; name given to the second theme in sonata-allegro movements.

SUBSCRIPTION CONCERTS   A series of concerts for which a subscriber buys a complete set of tickets.

SUITE   A baroque instrumental form with four movements of a dance style (allemande, courante, sarabande, and gigue).

SUL   On; SUL G: on the G string; SUL PONTICELLO: bow near the bridge.

SUPERTONIC   Second scale degree or chord on that scale degree.

SUSPENSION   A nonharmonic tone created by delaying the stepwise resolution of a single voice in a two-chord progression.

SYMPHONIC POEM   A single-movement form for orchestra which has a programmatic origin.

SYNCOPATION   A rhythmic treatment which places stress on the weak beats or offbeats.

TAMTAM   Large suspended gong.

TEMPO   Time; rate of speed at which a composition is played.

TENOR   A high male voice or a middle register of an instrument similar in range to that of the human tenor voice.

TERTIAN   Pertaining to a chord system in which chords are built by the successive adding of intervals of thirds. C–E–G–B-flat is a tertian chord.

TEXTURE   The manner in which a composition is constructed with relation to various emphases which can be placed in melody or harmony. A texture which emphasizes harmony with a single melody is homophonic. A texture which emphasizes several simultaneous melodies is polyphonic.

THEMATIC   Relating to qualities of a theme.

THEMATIC DEVELOPMENT   A procedure by which a theme is extended, fragmented, sequenced, imitated, and repeated to provide contrast with the original statement of the theme.

THEME   A melody which is the primary material of a section or movement.

THEME TRANSFORMATION   The changing of a theme to imply a transformation of the subject represented by the theme (emotion, object, person). Changes usually involve tempo, rhythm, meter, dynamics or harmony; pitch is usually constant. Associated with nineteenth-century program music.

THIRD   An interval which encompasses three diatonic scale degrees or successive letters names of the musical alphabet. C–E is a third.

THIRD RELATION   A concept in tonality or harmony which compares either two successive chords or two adjacent key centers whose roots or tonics are a third apart. Further, the third shared by both keys or chords *always* involves a chromatic change. The key of A major is a third-related key to the key of C major. The third which both tonic chords share (C-sharp–E and C–E) creates the condition. A progression from a C major chord to an A major chord would be a third-related progression.

THROUGH–COMPOSED   Pertaining to a type of song which uses new music for each line of text.

TIMPANI   Large kettledrums of the orchestra; sometimes referred to as percussion.

TOCCATA   A sixteenth-century virtuoso display piece for keyboard, usually organ.

TONAL AREA   A synonym for key; the result of a system of tonality.

TONAL INFLECTIONS   Chromatic changes which *imply* new tonal emphasis.

TONALITY   A system by which all of the pitches in a given work are interrelated so as to produce an emphasis on one of these pitches as the center or place of rest for the work.

TONE COLOR   The unique quality of a sound created by an instrument or a grouping of instruments. Two instruments playing the same pitch will each create a different or unique sound of that pitch because of the element of tone color.

TONIC   The first scale degree; also refers to the chord built on the first scale degree.

TRANSITION   A short section in a musical form which connects two important or primary sections or themes. Transitions often involve a change of key or modulation.

TREMOLO   Effect created by very rapidly applying short bow strokes to a sound being created by a string instrument. The stroke is uncontrolled, with the length of the stroke being very short and the velocity as fast as the player can manage. Finger tremolo is a similar effect but uses the fingers of the left hand for a trill-like sound with two pitches at least a third apart. The bow in finger tremolo is bowed normally with a single long stroke.

TRIAD   A chord with three pitches (usually root, third, and fifth, in tertian systems).

TRIADIC   Relating to triad.

TRIO   Usually a middle section of a dance form such as the minuet or the scherzo. The trio is a relatively self-sufficient section of the larger form and primarily starts and ends in a single key.

TRIO SONATA   A baroque instrumental form played by two soprano instruments (violin, flute, oboe, or combinations thereof) and a bass instrument (cello, bassoon, etc.), with a chord-producing instrument (harpsichord, organ, lute, etc.) filling in the harmonies. See SONATA DA CAMERA and SONATA DA CHIESA.

TRIPARTITE   Pertaining to a form which breaks down into three main sections.

TRIPLE METER   An organization of the rhythmic structure of a work which places three pulsations into a single measure. A waltz is in triple meter.

TRIPLETS   A rhythmic subdivision of a rhythmic pulsation into three subunits. The "Mexican Hat Dance" tune has this triplet subdivision of its rhythm.

TRUMPET   A soprano brass instrument with three valves.

TURN   An embellishing melodic figure played quite rapidly just before the note it embellishes ends. The figure involves four notes: the note being embellished, the note above it, the note below it, and the original note, in this order: upper, note, lower, and note.

TUTTI   The entire ensemble; in the baroque concerto grosso, the full group as contrasted with the solo group.

UNISON   Condition created by two or more different instruments or voices performing identical pitches.

UPPER NEIGHBOR TONE   A nonharmonic tone which is approached by step and resolved by step with a change of direction; two types: upper and lower; sometimes called AUXILIARY TONE.

VALVE   A diverting mechanism which adds additional lengths of tubing to a brass instrument. The valve diverts the vibrating air column through an additional small length of tubing which increases the length of the air column and thereby lowers the pitch. Valves are either rotary or cylindrical in design and function.

VAMP   An introductory passage consisting primarily of simple chords in an accompaniment pattern.

VARIATION   A compositional principle in which a given theme or harmonic pattern is subjected to certain changes. Changes are not so marked as to eliminate any resemblance to the original version. VARIATION FORM is a large form which uses either a melodic pattern or a harmonic pattern as the subject of a series of variations.

VARIATION–RONDO   A hybrid form which combines rondo principles with those of variation. One version varies the first theme in each recurrence of that theme.

VELOCITY PASSAGES   Rapid passages of technically demanding music for wind instruments. The term is used especially in soprano brass literature.

VENETIAN SCHOOL   A sixteenth-century "school" of Italian and Flemish composers working in Venice, particularly at St. Mark's cathedral. They produced primarily choral works, which were noted for innovation and experimentation that led to some aspects of baroque music; emphasis on contrast of choral groups and instrumental groups (*concertato* principle) established a compositional procedure which gave birth to the concerto. The school is sometimes called the VENETIAN POLYCHORAL SCHOOL.

VIBRAPHONE   A percussion instrument similar in appearance to a xylophone or marimba. It has metal tone bars with resonating tubes under each bar.

A rotating disc in each tube creates a steady fluctuation in the pitch, called *vibrato*.

VIOL   Family of bowed string instruments which immediately preceded the violin family in music history. Viols lack the rounded upper and lower curves of the violin and have instead pointed (pear-shaped) upper and lower curves. The tone is much softer and less brilliant than that of the violin. The instrument was used in the sixteenth and seventeenth centuries.

VIOLA   The alto member of the violin family. Its range is exactly an octave higher than that of the cello and a fifth lower than that of the violin.

VIOLONE   In the baroque period, a large viol about the size of today's contrabass.

VIVACE   Quick; faster than *allegro* but slower than *presto*.

VIVACISSIMO   Very quick.

WALKING BASS   A steady and continuous bass line primarily in eighth notes, especially characteristic of baroque music. The aural effect is that of an unending stream of bass notes whose rhythmic values are usually one-half that of the beat.

WHOLE NOTE   A notational symbol employing a white or hollow note head without a stem.

WOODWINDS   A family of wind instruments constructed primarily from wood and including piccolo, flute, oboe, English horn, saxophone, clarinet, and bassoon. The family is also called the reed family or, more simply, reeds, because of the use of either a single or double reed to make the tone.

Index

Abel, C. F., 18, 44
Acronym, Shostakovich use (D. S. C. H.), 307
Added dance to suite, 5
Age of Reason, 17
Aleatoric music, 248
Alfven, H., 388
Alois, B., 387
American composers, list, 339
American symphony in twentieth century, 338–84, 385–86
American symphony orchestras' dates of founding, 338–39
Anna Amalia, 19fn
Antecedent musical forms of symphony, 3–16
  concerto, 6
  French overture, 6
  sinfonia, 7
  suite, 5
  trio sonata, 5
Antheil, G., 385
Apollinaire, G., 308
Ardentine caves (see William Schuman)
Ardevol, J., 390
Arne, T. A., 18, 21fn
Arnold, Malcolm, 386
Aspelmayr, F., 20
Atonal music, 248
Atterberg, K., 388
Aurora, 301

Babbitt, M., 339

Babi Yar, 301, 308
Bach, C. P. E., 17, 20
Bach, J. C., 18, 20
  influence on Mozart, 37, 44
Bach, J. S., 6, 269
  influence on Hindemith, 326
  influence on W. Schuman, 353
  works analyzed:
    Suite No. 3 in D Major, gavotte, 10–11
Bach, W. F., 17
Baltimore Symphony Orchestra, 338
Barber, S., 339, 385
Baroque period, 3–16
  concerts, 4
  concerts, public, 5
  ensemble music, performance practice, 4
  forms, 3
  homophony, 3
  instrumental ensemble music, 3–5
  instrumental forms, 4
  instrumental idiom, 3
  instrumental style, 4
  musical style, 3
  orchestral concept, 3
  orchestral style and texture, 4
  period of contradictions, 3
  small ensemble emphasis, 4
Bartok, B., 250
Basso continuo, 3
Bayrisches Staatsorchester, 339
Bax, A., 386
Beach, Mrs. H. H. A., 339

Beck, F., 20
Beethoven, L. v.
  contribution to growth of symphony, 62
  duality of symphonic styles, 64
    expansive element, 78
    classical element, 85–86, 90–91
  historical position as symphonist, 62
  influence on Bruckner, 180
    on Prokofiev, 284, 286, 289
  march theme in Hindemith work, 331
  ninth symphony's position in music history,
    78
  Ode to Joy, 77
  style, 64–65
    counterpoint
      contrapuntal style, 165
      contrapuntal usages, 69, 79, 85
      fugal development, 89
      fugue in coda, 89
      melodic style, two-dimensional, 69, 79,
        81
    duality of symphonic styles, 64
    form
      architectural-expressive line, 64–65
      cadences, extended final, 73, 86, 89
      coda, 62, 65, 66, 67, 68, 69, 70, 73,
        74, 76, 77, 79, 81, 83, 86, 89
        with fugue, 89
        with new theme, 89
      development, fugal, 89
      development, motivic, 72
      development, new theme, 76
      finale's dance character, 82–83
      introduction, mature style, 78
      minuet, mature style, 88
      motive, generating, 78
      motive, unifying, 71, 73, 75, 78, 87
      scherzo
        developmental emphasis, 71
        final treatment, 76
        five-part, 70, 72, 81
        monothematic (Eroica), 69
        treatment of scherzo, 68
      sonata-allegro usage, 148
      sonata-rondo, 88
      tables, symphonies 1–9, 65
      thematic groupings, multisectional, 71
      themes, multiple, 76
      variation, 72, 77
      variation-song form blend, 80–81
    mature style
      established in Eroica, 68–69
      in seventh symphony, 85
    melody
      cantabile melodic style, 71
      dissonant melodic style, 77

      two-dimensional melodic style, 69, 79,
        81
    orchestration, 66, 87, 90
      bassoon usage, 71, 88
      brass section standardization, 75
      cello in melodic doubling, 67
        solo usage, 74
      clarinet usage, 66, 70, 74, 88
      contrabassoon usage, 73, 75
      echo device, 67, 86
      expanding resources, 69, 73
      four horns, scoring, 65
      horns, extra, 75
      piccolo usage, 73
      timpani usage, 72, 85
      triangle usage, 75
      trombone usage, 73
      trumpet usage, 84–85
      two-choir concept, 84
      vocal resources, 74, 78
      woodwind usage, 71, 74, 75, 76–77
    program symphony, 73–74
      Battle Symphony, 73
    symphonic style contrasted with Haydn's
      and Mozart's, 62–63
    tonality
      key relations, 73–74
      modulatory style, 65, 67, 70
    works analyzed:
      Symphony No. 1, 65–66
      Symphony No. 2, 66–68
      Symphony No. 3, 68–70
      Symphony No. 4, 70–71
      Symphony No. 5, 71–73
      Symphony No. 6, 73–74
      Symphony No. 7, 78–85
      Symphony No. 8, 85–91
      Symphony No. 9, 75–78
Belgium National Orchestra, 339
Benda, G., 17
Bennett, Richard Rodney, 386
Bennett, Robert Russell, 368
Bennett, William Sterndale, 95
Bentzon, N. V., 389
Berg, A., 235, 249, 251, 387
Berio, L., 390
Berlin Philharmonic, 223, 389
Berlioz, H., 92, 95, 123–35, 204, 283
  caricature, 124
  Dies Irae, 133
  form charts, 126–27
  idée fixe, 124, 128, 130, 132, 135
  influence on Liszt, 135
  influence on William Schuman, 353
  orchestral style, 125
    bassoons, four in unison, 132

bells, two, 133, 134fn
col legno, 133
harps, 129
instrumentation for Fantastic Symphony, 127
oboe, offstage, 131
pizzicato contrabass chords, 132
timpani chords, 131, 132
trombone pedal tones, 132
voicing in waltz, 129
parallel chords of sixth, 128
parallel diminished seventh chords, 133
works discussed:
  Damnation of Faust, 125
  Harold in Italy, 124
  Roman Carnival Overture, 125
  Romeo and Juliet, 124–25
  Symphonie Fantastique, 123–24, 125
works analyzed:
  Symphonie Fantastique, 127–35
Bernstein, L., 339, 385
Berwald, F., 95
Bezymensky, A., 302
Binary form, suite form, 5
  monothematic, 9
Bizet, G., 95, 204
Bloch, E., 368, 385
Blue Network, 345
Blues third, 335, 336
Boethius, 332
Borodin, A., 95
Bösendorfer, 227
Boston Symphony Orchestra, 333, 338, 345, 354, 356, 370, 371
Boulanger, N., 342, 369
Brahms, J., 95, 143–65
  Brahms-Wagner, 147
  contribution to symphony, 164–65
  conducting Vienna Philharmonic, 144
  influence on Prokofiev, 289
  place in symphonic history, 147
  premiers:
    Symphony No. 2, 145
    Haydn Variations, 144
  style, 147–53, 164–65
    characteristic style devices:
      arpeggiation, 150
      continuity, 160
      contrapuntal texture, 155
      indefinite tonality, 151
      parallel thirds, 150
      pedal with:
        pizzicato and parallel sixths, 156
        two voices in canon, 150–51
        two voices in parallel thirds and countermelody, 158

pizzicato, 150
plagal tendencies, 153, 163
shifting meter, 155
two versus three (hemiola), 156
counterpoint, 149, 165
dual modality, 153
form, 148–49, 165
  chaconne, 157
  continuity, 151–52
  form tables, 150
  germinal motive, 152, 153, 158, 162
  meter as formal device, 150
  motivic integration, 159
  motto theme, 153, 154
  sonata-allegro usage, 148–49
harmony, 148
learnedness in style, 165
line and lyricism via nonmelodic means, 151
lyricism, 150
melody, 147
melody, chromatic, 153–54
orchestration, 149, 164
  brass emphasis, 152–53
  triangle, 157
  woodwind emphasis, 161
polymodality, 152, 156
rhythm, 147–48, 151, 165
tonality, 148
works analyzed:
  Symphony No. 1, 158–65
  Symphony No. 2, 151–53
  Symphony No. 3, 153–54
  Symphony No. 4, 154–58
Brandt, H., 339
Breitkopf, J. G. I., 19fn
Britten, B., 386
Bruch, Max, influence on Vaughan Williams, 270
Bruckner, A., 95, 178–90
  conducts Vienna Philharmonic, 146
  International Bruckner Society, 181
  position in symphonic history, 190
  quotes from own works, 183
  quotes from Wagner works, 183
  revision of symphonies, 181–82, 186
  style, 178–81
    form:
      form tables, 181
      Gesangsperiode, 179, 182, 183, 184, 186
      Ländler, 180, 184
      sonata-allegro in scherzos, 188
      Urthema, 179, 184, 186
    influences, 180
      Beethoven, 186, 188

Bruckner, A. (*cont.*)
    Mozart, 186
    Schubert, 182, 184
    Wagner, 182, 183, 184, 186
    orchestration, 180–81
        brass emphasis, 181, 184
        timpani, six, 185
        tuba quintet, 185
        Wagner tuba, 180, 184–85
    polymeter, 184
    polyrhythm figure, 176–77, 186
    typical devices, 176
    works analyzed:
        Symphony in f minor, 182
        Symphony No. 0, 182
        Symphony No. 1, 182–83
        Symphony No. 2, 183
        Symphony No. 3, 183
        Symphony No. 4, 186–90
        Symphony No. 5, 183
        Symphony No. 6, 183
        Symphony No. 7, 183–84
        Symphony No. 8, 184
        Symphony No. 9, 185–86

Cadman, C. W., 339
Cage, John, 339
Cannabich, C., 20
Carpenter, J. A., 339, 385
Carter, E., 339
Casella, A., 390
CBS Symphony, 379
Central House of Composers, 289
Chadwick, G., 339
Chausson, E., 95
Chavez, C., 390
Chicago Symphony Orchestra:
    founding, 338
    Orchestra Hall, 340
    premiere of Harris seventh, 347
    Stravinsky conducts, 317
Cincinnati Symphony Orchestra, 330
Clarinet in preclassical symphony, 26
Classical instrumental style, 25–26
Classical style, 17–18
Clementi, M., 44
Cleveland Symphony Orchestra, 338
Concertato principle, 6
    in early Haydn symphonies, 36
Concertgebouw Orchestra, 191, 339
Concertino solo group, 6
Concerto grosso, 11
    contribution to symphonic history, 12–13
Concerts du Conservatoire, 339
Converse, F., 339
Copland, A., 339, 367
    influence on William Schuman, 353

place in symphonic history, 376–77
style, 367–78, 376
    influences, 367–78
    style elements:
        jazz, 369
        motto theme, 369
        percussion use, 376
        rare quarter-tone use, 368–69
        Ravel influence, 369
        rhythmic complexity, 370
        Stravinsky influence, 369
        "western" waltz style, 372
    works analyzed:
        Dance Symphony, 368–69
        Organ Symphony (Symphony No. 1), 369
        Short Symphony, 370
        Third Symphony, 370–77
    works, other:
        Appalachian Spring, 376
        Connotations, 367
        El Salon Mexico, 376
        Fanfare for Common Man, 374
        Grohg, 368
        Inscape, 367
        Rodeo, 376
        Sextet, 370
        Symphonic Ode, 368
Corelli, A., 8
    work analyzed:
        Trio Sonata in f minor, Op. 3, No. 9, 8–9
Counterpoint as developmental device:
    Beethoven's use, 79
    eighteenth century usage, 46
Cowell, H., 339, 385
Creston, P., 339, 385

Dallas Symphony Orchestra, 330, 355
Dances, added to suite, 5
Das Knaben Wunderhorn (see Mahler)
Debussy, C., 249, 250, 251
    influence on Schuman, 353
Delius, F., 250, 251
Dello Joio, N., 339
Detroit Symphony Orchestra, 338
Deutsch, O. E., 100
Diamond, D., 339, 385
Dies irae (see Berlioz)
D'Indy, V., 95, 250, 251
Dittersdorf, K. v., 22
Divertimento's influence on Haydn's symphonies, 33
Donne, J., 275
Duality of forces in concerto, 9
Dukas, P., 95
Dutilleux, H., 388

Dvorak, A., 95, 190–204
  style, 190–93, 196–97, 203–4
    form table, 193
    influences, 190–94, 196–97
      Beethoven, 190–91, 193, 194
      Brahms, 190–91, 193, 194, 195, 197,
        198
      German-Czech conflict, 193
      nationalism (folk), 190–91, 202
      Schubert, 190–91, 194
      Wagner, 190–91, 193, 194
    orchestration, 195
  symphonic poems, 190
  symphonies' place in history, 196–97, 203–4
  works analyzed:
    Symphony No. 1, 193–94
    Symphony No. 2, 194
    Symphony No. 3, 194
    Symphony No. 5, 194
    Symphony No. 6, 195
    Symphony No. 7, 197–204
    Symphony No. 8, 195
    Symphony No. 9, 195

Egge, K., 389
Electronic music, 248
Elgar, E., 95, 250, 251, 386
Empfindsamer Stil, 17, 20
English folk song, 269
Enrique, M., 390
Englund, E. S., 388
Environmental music, 248
Esterhazy, 33, 55
European symphony orchestras, dates of
    founding, 338
Experimental music, 248–49

Factory whistle (see Shostakovich)
Farinelli, 44
Fernstrom, J., 388
Filtz, A., 20
Finney, R. L., 339, 385
Five, the, 283
Foote, A., 339
Form charts, 10fn
Fortner, W., 387
Foss, L., 339
Four and Twenty Fiddlers, 4
Franck, C., 95, 205–12
  place in symphonic history, 212
  style, 205–6, 212
    Bach influence, 206
    form:
      cyclic elements, 209
      phrase motive, 205, 207
  orchestration, 210–11
    English horn, 208, 209, 211
    problems, 211–12
  work analyzed:
    Symphony in d minor, 206–12
Frederick the Great, 19fn
French orchestral music in nineteenth century,
    204–12
French overture, 6–7
  in early Haydn symphonies, 34

Gade, N., 95
Galindo, B., 390
Gebrauchsmusik, 325, 326
Gerhard, R., 390
Gesangsperiode (see Bruckner)
Gewendhaus concerts, 25, 339
Giannini, V., 385
Gillis, Don, 385
Ginastera, A., 390
Glazunov, A., 95, 319, 387
Gliere, R., 284, 387
Gluck, C. W., 45
Goethe, J. W. v., 123, 136, 235
Gossec, F. J., 44
Gould, M., 339, 385
Gounod, C., 204
Graham, Martha, 379
Graun, J. G., 20
Graun, K. H., 19fn, 20
Griffes, C., 251, 339
Gruenberg, L., 368
Grünewald, Mathis, 328

Hadley, H., 339
Haieff, A., 385
Handel, G. F., 6
  Mammoth presentations, 4
  work analyzed:
    Overture to Messiah, 13
Hanson, H., 339, 385
Harpsichord in preclassical symphony, 26
Harris, Roy, 339, 341–53
  influence on Schuman, 353
  place in symphonic history, 352–53
  style, 340–42, 352–53
    borrowing from own works, 347
    chant tunes, 347
    choral symphony, 343, 346
    emotionalism, theory, 343
    folk tune usage, 342, 344, 346
    jazz influence, 350
    modes, ethical meanings, 343
    mood titles for movements, 343, 344–45,
      345
    organum-style counterpoint, 346
    passacaglia, 347

Harris, Roy (*cont.*)
  piano in symphony, 345
  piano, amplified, 346
  serial usage, 348
  sonority theory, 343
  tempo theory, 343
  thematic growth concept, 345
  variations, rhythmic, 348–49
  vocal solo, narrator, 347
  works analyzed:
    Symphony—American Portrait, 342
    Symphony No. 1, 342
    Symphony No. 2, 343
    Symphony for Voices, 343
    Symphony No. 3, 343–44
    Symphony No. 4 (Folksong), 344
    Symphony No. 5, 344–45
    Symphony No. 6 (Gettysburg), 345
    Symphony No. 7, 347–53
    Symphony No. 8 (San Francisco), 345–46
    Symphony No. 9, 346
    Symphony No. 10 (Lincoln), 346
    Symphony No. 11, 347
    Symphony No. 12 (Pere Marquette), 347
    Symphony No. 13 (Bicentennial), 347
    Symphony No. 14 (Olympic), 347
Hasse, J. A., 19fn, 20, 45
Haubenstock-Ramati, R., 387
Haydn, F. J., 17, 19, 24, 26, 45, 165
  chronology of symphonies, 32
  critical edition, 32
  early symphonies:
    divertimento influence, 33
    Fürnberg manuscript symphonies' style, 33
    preclassical features, 32–33
    three-part scoring for strings, 10
  London symphonies, 55–61
    importance, 61
    style, 55–56, 60–61
      form table, 57
      minuet treatment, 59
      orchestration, 56, 60
        clarinet usage, 61
        woodwind concertino, 58, 59
      sonata-allegro, frequency of usage
  middle period style, 40
  monothematic sonata-allegro usage, 41, 43
  names of symphonies, 41fn
  works analyzed:
    Symphony No. 6 (Le Matin), 34–36
    Symphony No. 44 (Trauer), 41–42
    Symphony No. 104 (London), 56–61
Heininen, P., 388
Henze, H. W., 387
Hill, E. B., 339

Hiller, J. A., 25
Hillsberg, Alexander, 358
Hindemith, P., 251, 325–37
  place in symphonic history, 328, 337
  style, 325–28, 337
    Baroque influence, 331
    blues third, 335
    borrowed tunes, 330, 331
    folk tunes, 329, 332
    Gebrauchsmusik, 325, 326
    influences, 326
    neoclassical elements, 326, 330
    orchestration, 326, 327
      brass emphasis, 330
    serialism, 333
  symphonic output, 325–26, 327
  theoretical writings, 326
  works analyzed:
    Concert Music for Strings and Brass, 333–37
    Pittsburg Symphony, 332–33
    Sinfonietta, 331–32
    Symphonia Serena, 331
    Symphonic Metamorphosis on Themes of Weber, 330
    Symphony: Die Harmonie der Welt, 332
    Symphony: Mathis der Maler, 328–29
    Symphony in E-flat, 329–30
Hoffman, L., 22
Holmboe, V., 389
Holst, G., 251
  influence on Vaughan Williams, 270
Holzbauer, I., 20
Honneger, A., 251, 388
Hovaness, A., 385
Hymnal, English, 269

Ibert, J., 389
Idée fixe (see Berlioz, Tchaikovsky)
Imbrie, A., 385
Impressionism, 247, 249
Institute of Musical Art, 377
Irregular sonata-allegro form, 23
Indianapolis Symphony Orchestra, 330
Isamitt, C., 390
Ives, C., 250, 251, 339, 385

Jolivet, A., 389
Jommelli, N., 44

Kabalevsky, D., 387
Kepler, J., 332
Khatchaturian, A., 387
Kokkonen, J., 388
Kubik, G., 385
Küchelbecker, W., 308

Kuri-Aldana, Maria, 390

Lamartine, A. M., 123
Langaard, R., 389
Lassus influence on Schuman, 353
Learned style, 48, 54
Lees, B., 385
Le Fosse Ardeatine (see Schuman)
Leibowitz, R., 389
Leningrad siege, 305
Les Petits Violons, 4
Liadov, A., 284
Ligeti, G., 251
Liszt, F., 95, 123, 135–43
  Liszt-Wagner relationship, 143
  style, 135–36, 142–43
    harmony, 135–36
    orchestration, 136
      Faust Symphony instrumentation, 137,
        138, 141
      addition of chorus, 141–42
    program music conception, 135
      program symphony and symphonic
        poem, 135
    tempo changes, 136
    theme transformation, 135, 139, 142
  work analyzed:
    Faust Symphony, 136–43
London Symphony Orchestra, 269, 272, 339
Lopatnikoff, N., 386
Lorca, F. G., 308
Los Angeles Philharmonic, 338
Louisville Orchestra, 331, 344
Lutoslawski, W., 387

MacDowell, E., 339
Maezel, Johannes, 73
Mahler, G., 95, 224–46, 250, 251
  Berg's impression of ninth symphony, 235
  conducting, 227, 228
  Das Knaben Wunderhorn, 225, 231, 232
  Lieder eines fahrenden Gesellen, 230
  place in symphonic history, 246
  style, 224–30, 246
    contemporary elements, 249
    contradictory aspects, 224
    contrapuntal textures, 240
    cyclic form, 246
    excessive movement length, 242
    folk song, 224, 225, 226, 232
    form table, 230
    harmonic style, dichotomous usage, 226
    influence on Shostakovich, 300, 303
    linear aspect, 249
    melody
      fondness for fourth, 244
      nineteenth-century expression, 243

    orchestration, 225–26, 231
      chart, 236–37
    periods, style, 224–25, 226
    programs in symphonies, 231–32
    quotations from own works, 230–31
    restatement, avoidance of exact, 244
    scherzo in Ländler style, 225, 231, 232,
      235
    self-repetition, 234
    tonality, progressive, 234
    Wagner influence, 234, 235
  works analyzed:
    Symphony No. 1, 230–31
    Symphony No. 2, 231
    Symphony No. 3, 231–32
    Symphony No. 4, 232–33
    Symphony No. 5, 238–46
    Symphony No. 6, 233–34
    Symphony No. 7, 234
    Symphony No. 8, 234–35
    Symphony No. 9, 235
Malipiero, G. F., 390
Mannheim mannerisms, 20
Mannheim roll, 20, 29
Mannheim School, 20
Martinet, J.-L., 389
Martini, Padre, 44
Martinu, Bohuslav, 386
Marttinen, T., 388
Mason, D. G., 339
Mata, E., 390
May Day, 303
Mendelssohn, F., 25, 95
  style, 105–7, 113–14
    Baroque bass line, 110
    counterpoint, 109, 165
    form table, 107
    orchestration, 107
      wind requirement for symphonies,
        107
      woodwinds, 111
        scherzo scoring, 107, 109, 112
    parallel chords, 110
    sonata-allegro usage, 148
  works analyzed:
    Symphony No. 1, 108
    Symphony No. 2, 108
    Symphony No. 3, 108
    Symphony No. 4, 109–14
    Symphony No. 5, 109
Mennin, P., 386
Merikanto, A., 388
Meriläinen, U., 388
Miaskovsky, N., 250, 251, 387
Milhaud, D., 331, 389
Minneapolis Symphony Orchestra (Minnesota
  Orchestra), 338

Minuet:
  form, 15fn
  Haydn's treatment in London symphonies,
    59
  Stamitz's handling, 30
Moncayo, J., 390
Monn, G. M., 8, 22
Monteverdi's large opera orchestra, 4
Moore, D., 339
Mozart, W. A., 17, 24, 165
  style:
    chromaticism, 49, 51
    form:
      minuet treatment, 52
      thematic construction, sectional con-
        cept, 37
      unifying motive, 54
    influences on Mozart's style, 44–45
    orchestration, 51
    style periods in symphonies:
      late, 48
      middle, 44–45
      preclassical, 37–39
        J. C. Bach's influence, 37, 39
  symphonic chronology, 37
  works analyzed:
    Symphony No. 1, K. 16, 37–39
    Symphony No. 29, K. 201, 45–48
    Symphony No. 40, K. 550, 49–54
Mussorgsky, M., 166

Nardini, P., 44
NBC Symphony, 370
National Symphony, 339, 347
Neoclassical style, 248
Neoromantic style, 247–48
New York Philharmonic, 228, 338, 347, 390
Nielsen, C., 251, 389
Nietzsche, F., 123, 232
Nigg, S., 389
Nineteenth-century instrumental music, ex-
    pressive power, 93–94
Nineteenth-century French orchestral music,
    204–12
Nineteenth-century symphonists, 95
Nineteenth-century symphony, 92–246
  orchestration, expressive nature, 95
  style summary, 123
  two divergent courses, 93
North German School, 20
Nystroem, G., 388

October (1917) Revolution, 302
Olimpiade (see Pergolesi)
Orchestre de la Suisse Romande, 339

Orrego-Salas, J., 390

Paganini, N., 124
Paine, J. K., 339
Panharmonicon, 73, 73fn
Parker, H., 339
Parry, H., 95, 269
Pärt, Arvo, 387
Penderecki, K., 387
Pergolesi, G. B., 7
  S. Gugliemo Duca D'Aquitania, 13fn
  work analyzed:
    Sinfonia to L'Olimpiade, 13–14
Periodical overtures, 7, 18
Persichetti, V., 339, 386
Philadelphia Orchestra, 338, 342, 346
Piccini, N., 44
Piston, W., 251, 339, 386
Pittsburg Symphony Orchestra, 339
Pravda, 284, 309
Preclassical symphony, 17–39
  arranged for harpsichord, 19fn
  growth, 18–26
  schools, 18
  style, 22, 24
    form, 22
      fourth movement, early appearance,
        22–23
      French overture first movements, 23
      minuet as finale, 22–23
      minuet, early use, 22–23
      movement form evolution, 23
      second movement form evolution, 23
      sinfonia first movements, 23
        change from binary to sonata-allegro,
          23
      third movement form evolution, 23, 28
    orchestration evolution, 24–26
Premier coup d'archet, 20
Printing of symphonic music, eighteenth cen-
    tury, 18, 19, 21
Program music, 123–43, 224
Prokofiev, S., 251, 284–98
  early training, 284
  place in symphonic history, 298
  publicity photo, c. 1930, 285
  style, 284–87, 298
    advanced style of second symphony, 287–
      88
    borrowing from own works, 288
    cadence, half-step, 295
    chromaticism, 292
    evolution of symphonic style, 286
    form table, 287
    influences, 284–85
    melody, two-dimensional theme, 289
    orchestration, 286–87

distinct bass line, 287
piano usage, 293
Ravel influence, 288
typical devices, 287
Symphony No. 1, 287
works analyzed:
Symphony No. 1 (Classical), 287
Symphony No. 2, 287–88
Symphony No. 3, 288
Symphony No. 4, 288
Symphony No. 5, 289–98
Symphony No. 6, 289
Symphony No. 7, 289
Publication of symphonies, c. 1740, 7, 18
Purcell, H., 6
Pylkkänen, T., 388

Quintanar, H., 390

Rachmaninoff, S., 250, 386
Raff, J., 95
Rameau, J. P., 180
Rautavaare, E., 388
Ravel, M., 249, 250, 251, 270
influence on:
Prokofiev's orchestral style, 286, 288
Shostakovich, 303
Schuman, 353
Rawsthorne, A., 386
Redlich, H., 186
Respighi, O., 251
Richter, F. X., 20
Riegger, W., 377–84
life, 377
assumed names, 377
style, 377–78, 383–84
dance influence, 378
fugue, 383
passacaglia, 383
periods, 377–78
pseudo-styles, 377
serialism, 377–78, 379–80
flexibility, 380
lyricism, 384
works analyzed:
Symphony No. 3, 379–84
Symphony No. 4, 378–79
Riisager, K., 389
Rilke, R. M., 308
Rimsky-Korsakov, N., 95, 166, 284
influence on Prokofiev, 286
Ritter, A., 123
Rivier, J., 389
Robbins Landon, H. C., 32
Rochberg, G., 386
Rochester Philharmonic, 338
Rocket theme, 20

Mozart use, 53
Rococo, 17
Rogers, B., 386
Romantic period, style, 92–93
Ropartz, Guy, 389
Rorem, N., 386
Rosenberg, H., 388
Roussel, A., 389
Royal Albert Hall, 269
Rubbra, E., 387
Ruggles, C., 339
Russian arts in twentieth century, political
influence, 283–84
Russian festive finale:
Shostakovich, 305, 306, 307, 315
Stravinsky, 320
Russian music in twentieth century, 283–84
style, 284

Saeverud, H., 389
Saint Francis of Assisi, 345
St. Louis Symphony, 338
Saint-Saëns, C., 95, 204
Salomon, J. P., 55
Sammartini, G. B., 18, 44
work analyzed:
Symphony No. 1 (J. C. 7), 26–28
San Francisco Symphony Orchestra, 338, 346,
377
Santoro, C., 390
San Petronio Basilica's orchestra, 4
Sauget, H., 389
Scarlatti (A.) sinfonias, 7
Schiller, F. v., 75
Schmitt, F., 389
Schoenberg, A., 248, 249, 250, 251, 386
Schubert, F., 17, 95, 148
style, 96–97, 105
form:
lyric conception of sonata-allegro, 103
form table, 97
French overture influence, 97, 98, 100
Haydn-Mozart influence, 96, 99
key choice, 98, 99, 101–2
melody:
lyricism, 96
Viennese folk tunes, 96, 97, 98, 99
orchestration, 96
Symphony No. 8, 104–5
Symphony No. 9, 101
woodwind emphasis, 97
Rossini influence, 100
works analyzed:
Symphony No. 1, 97
Symphony No. 2, 97–98
Symphony No. 3, 98
Symphony No. 4, 99

Schubert, F. (*cont.*)
   Symphony No. 5, 99–100
   Symphony No. 6, 100
   Symphony No. 8, 102–5
   Symphony No. 9, 100–02
Schuman, William, 339, 353–66
  style, 353–54
   half-step harmonic interval, 356
   harmonic style, 357, 358
   influences, 353
   lyricism, 355, 358
   orchestration, 356, 357
   parallelism, 356
   passacaglia, 355, 358
   polyphonic emphasis, 354–55
   polytonal writing, 355
   serial devices, 359
   stylistic complexity, 355, 356, 357
   unifying motive, 356, 357
  works analyzed:
   Symphony No. 1, 354
   Symphony No. 2, 354
   Symphony No. 3, 358–66
   Symphony No. 4, 354–55
   Symphony No. 5, 355
   Symphony No. 6, 355
   Symphony No. 7, 356
   Symphony No. 8, 357
   Symphony No. 9 (Le Fosse Ardeatine),
     357–58
Schumann, R., 95, 114–22
  style, 114–15, 122
   expressive melody, 119
   form:
     motto theme, 117
     sonata-allegro usage, 148
     table, 115
   influence on Prokofiev, 284
   orchestration:
     wind requirement, 114, 115
      Symphony No. 8, 121–22
   transitional nature, 122
  works analyzed:
   Symphony No. 1, 117–22
   Symphony No. 2, 115–16
   Symphony No. 3, 116
   Symphony No. 4, 116
Schwerstik, K., 387
Scott, Robert Falcon, 275
Scriabin, A., 250
Searle, H., 387
Sechter, S., 180
Sequence, Mozart's chromatic usage, 24
Sequence in preclassical development, 24
Serialism, 248
Sessions, R., 251, 339, 386
Shakespeare, W., 123

Shelley, P. B., 275
Shepherd, A., 339
Shostakovich, D., 251, 298–301
  place in symphonic history, 317–18
  style, 298–301
   atonality, 308
   col legno fugue, 308
   duality of style, 299
   form table, 301
   harmony, 315
   Mahler influence, 300, 303
   major-minor third, 304
   melody, 302, 310
   orchestration, 301
     choral addition, 303, 308
     factory whistle, 303
     snare drum ostinato, 305
     specific string requirement, 305
   passacaglia, 305
   quotations from Rossini, Wagner, 309
   revolutionary songs, 307
   Russian festive finale, 305, 306, 307, 315
   Russian gallop rhythm, 303
   serialism, 302, 308
   thematic acronym (DSCH), 307, 309
  works analyzed:
   Symphony No. 1, 302
   Symphony No. 2, 302–3
   Symphony No. 3, 303
   Symphony No. 4, 303
   Symphony No. 5, 309–17
   Symphony No. 6, 304
   Symphony No. 7, 304–5
   Symphony No. 8, 305
   Symphony No. 9, 306
   Symphony No. 10, 306–7
   Symphony No. 11, 307
   Symphony No. 12, 307
   Symphony No. 13, 308
   Symphony No. 14, 308–9
   Symphony No. 15, 309
Sibelius, J., 249, 250, 251, 252–68, 274
  place in symphonic history, 253, 268
  style, 252–55, 268
   Borodin and Tchaikovsky influence,
     255–56
   evolution, stylistic, 253
   form:
     development texture, 256, 257, 260
     germinating motives, 259
     motto theme, 259
     organic growth, 253, 256, 259
     tables, form, 255
   influences, 252–53
   orchestration, 255
     brass emphasis, 256
     ostinato usage, 256

periods, stylistic, 252–53
specific traits, 253–54
uniqueness, 253
works analyzed:
Symphony No. 1, 255–56
Symphony No. 2, 256
Symphony No. 3, 257
Symphony No. 4, 259–68
Symphony No. 5, 257–58
Symphony No. 6, 258
Symphony No. 7, 258–59
Siegmeister, E., 386
Sigh (Mannheim), 20
Sinfonia, 7–8
advanced style, 15
contributions to symphony, 8, 16
Sixteenth century English polyphony, 269
Sonata-allegro form, declining use in nine-
teenth century, 148
Sonata concept, 18
Sowerby, L., 386
Spohr, L., 95
Stalin Prize, 284
Stamitz, A., 20
Stamitz, J., 8, 20, 45
orchestral style, 31
symphony pioneer, 32
work analyzed:
Sinfonia a 8 (La Melodica Germanica No.
1), 29–32
Stamitz, K., 20
Stanford, C. V., 95, 269
Starzer, J., 22
Still, W. G., 386
Stimmtausch (see Tchaikovsky orchestration)
Strauss, R., 95, 123, 185, 250
conducts Vienna Philharmonic, 219
place in symphonic history, 212, 224
style, 213–18, 223
Brahms-Strauss contrast, 214
changes, 213–14
influences, 214
orchestration, 214–18
chart, 216–17
unusual effects, 215
twentieth century works, 249
tone poems, output, 213
works analyzed:
Alpine Symphony, 213
Aus Italien, 213
Domestic Symphony, 213
Symphony in d minor, 213
Symphony in F Major, 213
Til Eulenspiegel, 218–24
Stravinsky, I., 250, 251, 283, 317–25
ballet scores, 318
conducting, 317

place in symphonic history, 325
style, 317–18, 325
classical style, 320, 321
form table, 319
early influences, 319
major-minor third, 323
orchestral style, 318
ostinato usage, 321
periods, 318
Russian festive finale, 320
Russian folk tune usage, 319, 320
sectional form, 318, 321, 325
style galant elements, 320
symphonic output, 317–18
works analyzed:
Symphony in C, 320
Symphony in E-flat, 319–20
Symphony in Three Movements, 320–25
String section scoring, 37fn
Sturm und Drang, 17, 20, 40, 44
Style galant, 14, 17, 29, 44, 45, 46, 48, 54, 66,
67, 71, 96, 98, 99, 128, 320
Subscription concerts, 18
Suite, added dances, 5
Suite, dance form, 5
Suite, instrumental, 5
Symbols for chart tonality, 38fn
Symphony publication, c. 1740, 7
Synthesized music, 248

Tchaikovsky, P., 92, 95, 166–78
influence on Schuman, 353
place in symphonic history, 166
style, 166–68, 171–72, 178
counterpoint, 167
form, 166–67
Russian festive finale, 169
scherzo style, 168–69
table, 168
waltz, 169, 170, 171, 173
harmony and tonality, 167–68
lyric concept of symphony, 178
melody:
folk songs, 168, 169, 174, 176
idée fixe, 171
motto theme, 170, 172
sequence, 174
types, 166
orchestration, 167
choir separation, 177
concertato, 177
contrabass divisi, 171
developmental device, 177–78
pizzicato, 175
stimmtausch scoring, 171
woodwind usages, 169–70, 173, 177
works analyzed:

Tchaikovsky, P. (*cont.*)
  Manfred Symphony, 171
  Symphony No. 1, 168–69
  Symphony No. 2, 169
  Symphony No. 3, 169–70
  Symphony No. 4, 172–78
  Symphony No. 5, 170
  Symphony No. 6, 170–71
  Symphony in E-flat Major (No. 8?), 171
Tcherepnin, A., 284, 386
Tempo markings, double, 56fn
Theme transformation (see Liszt)
Thompson, Randall, 339
Tippett, M., 387
Toch, Ernest, 386
Tocsin, 301
Trio sonata, 5
Twentieth century music, 247–49
  contradictory nature some styles, 247
  Russian music, 283–84
Twentieth-century symphony, 247–392
  line of development, 251
  list of works, 1899–1920, 250–51
Twentieth-century symphony composers, list-
    ing:
  American, 385–86
  Austrian, German, 387–88
  British, 386–87
  Danish, 389
  Finnish, 388
  French, 388–89
  Italian, 389–90
  Mexican, 390
  Norwegian, 389
  Polish, 387
  Russian, 387
  South American, 390
  Spanish, 390
Twentieth-century symphony in America,
    338–84
Twenty-four Violins of the King, 4

Urthema (see Bruckner)
Ussachevsky, V., 339
U.S.S.R., 344

Valen, F., 389
Vanhall, J. B., 22
Van Vactor, D., 386
Vaughan Williams, R., 250, 251, 269–84
  conducting, 269
  place in music and symphony history, 269,
      271, 283
  Sibelius dedication, 274
  Whitman text use, 273
  style, 269–72, 283
    form, 271

  composer's analysis of Symphony No.
      8, 276fn
  epilogue, 271, 274
  passacaglia, 274
  sonata-allegro usage, 271
  table, 273
  theme, motto, 273, 274, 277, 279
  theme, unifying, 277, 277–78
  harmony, melody, rhythm, texture,
      271–72
  influences, 269–70
    folk song, 278
    impressionism, 273
    Tudor church music, 273, 277, 279
  orchestration, 271–72
    choral and vocal resources, 273, 276
    strings only, 276
    vibraphone, 275
    wind machine, 275, 276
    winds, 276, 277
    xylophone, 277
  works analyzed:
    Symphony No. 1, 273
    Symphony No. 2, 273
    Symphony No. 3, 273–74
    Symphony No. 4, 274
    Symphony No. 5, 274–75
    Symphony No. 6, 277–83
    Symphony No. 7, 275–76
    Symphony No. 8, 276
    Symphony No. 9, 277
Vienna Philharmonic
  picture, 1976–77 season, 143
  programs:
    1842 season, 94
    1860 season, 106
    1873 season:
      Brahms conducting, 144
      Bruckner conducting, 146
    1877 premiere Brahms' second symphony,
        145
    1892 season (Mahler conducting), 227
    1944 season (Strauss conducting), 219
Vienna School (preclassical symphony), 20–21
Villa-Lobos, H., 390
Violone, 35
Vivaldi, A., 24

Wagenaar, B., 386
Wagensiel, G. C., 20, 22
Wagner, R., 92, 143, 165
  Bruckner's quotations from Wagner themes,
      183
  influence on Bruckner, 180
  influence on Mahler, 234, 235
  influence on Vaughan Williams, 269
Wagnerian style, 147

Walsh, I., 21fn
Walton, W., 251, 387
Weber, C. M. v., 95
  Eight Pieces, Op. 60, 330
  Six Easy Pieces, Op. 3, 330
Webern, A., 249, 251, 388
Wellesz, E., 388

Whitman, Walt, 273, 343, 346
Williamson, M., 387
Woodwind concertino in Haydn symphonies, 58–59

Yevtushenko, Y., 308